Cu... ...gy and Politics

History Workshop Series

General Editor
Raphael Samuel, *Ruskin College, Oxford*

Already published
Village Life and Labour
Miners, Quarrymen and Saltworkers
People's History and Socialist Theory
Rothschild Buildings
East End Underworld

ROUTLEDGE & KEGAN PAUL
London, Boston, Melbourne and Henley

by

Raphael Samuel

Tutor in Social History and Sociology
Ruskin College, Oxford

and

Gareth Stedman Jones

Fellow, Kings College, Cambridge

Culture, Ideology and Politics

Essays for Eric Hobsbawm

*First published in 1982
by Routledge & Kegan Paul Ltd.,
39 Store Street, London WC1E 7DD,
9 Park Street, Boston, Mass. 02108, USA,
296 Beaconsfield Parade, Middle Park,
Melbourne, 3206, Australia, and
Broadway House, Newtown Road,
Henley-on-Thames, Oxon RG9 1EN
Printed in Great Britain by
St. Edmundsbury Press, Suffolk*

Library of Congress Cataloging in Publication Data

*Culture, ideology, and politics.
(History workshop series)
Bibliography: p.
1. Communism and society - Addresses, essays,
lectures. 2. Europe - Social conditions -
Addresses, essays, lectures. 3. Hobsbawm, E.J.
(Eric J.), 1917- - Addresses, essays,
lectures. I. Hobsbawm, E.J. (Eric J.),
1917- . II. Samuel, Raphael. III. Jones,
Gareth Stedman. IV. Series.
HX542.C84 1982 306'.345 82-13222*

ISBN 0-7100-9433-7

Contents

Plates

Acknowledgments

The editors and publishers would like to thank the following for permission to reproduce the illustrations: the British Museum, London, for plates 1 and 2; The Early Christian and Byzantine Collection, Staatliche Museen zu Berlin, East Germany, for plates 3 and 7; plates 4 and 9 courtesy of the Dumbarton Oaks Collection, Washington D.C.; the Courtauld Institute, for plate 5; plate 6 reproduced through the courtesy of the Michigan-Princeton-Alexandria Expedition to Mount Sinai; the Mansell Collection, for plates 10 and 11.

Preface

Raphael Samuel
Gareth Stedman Jones

This book originated as an international tribute to the work of Eric Hobsbawm, but it has taken shape around a unifying preoccupation with the symbolic order and its relationship to political and religious belief. The book explores some of the oldest questions in Marxist historiography e.g. the relationship of 'base' and 'superstructure', art and social life; and also some of the newest and most problematic, e.g. the relationship of dreams and fantasy to political action; or of past and present - historical consciousness - to the making of ideology. The essays are intended to break new ground, and to take on difficult questions; at the same time they are accessibly written, and can be read with pleasure as independent studies in their own right.

These essays testify to the influence of Hobsbawm's work far outside the periods with which he has been particularly concerned, and they also help to point up the difficulties and the excitement which his writing has consistently generated. For perhaps one of Hobsbawm's most outstanding and least commented upon achievements has been his ability to bring together the propositions of classical Marxism and the empirical preoccupations of social and economic historians into a virtually seamless web. Moreover, he has done so in such a way that central topics of English and European history from the eighteenth to twentieth centuries and the prevalent approaches to such fundamental themes as industrialisation, popular rebellion, 'pre-industrial' protest, unionisation, urbanisation and revolutionary parties have been populated with questions and research approaches which he more than any other individual historian first tried to map out. In the course of this work, certain ideas or areas of questioning recognisably Marxist in inspiration have lost their sectarian qualities and have become almost the 'common sense' of these subjects. Such a way of working, however, has not so much been an application of Marxism, as a new form of it, the creation of a type of marxist history, which simply did not exist before. The marriage between Marxism and Hobsbawm's sustained and imaginative historical curiosity about the particular cannot be attributed to the product of any one pre-existent historiographical tradition. Nor, except with strong reservations can it be seen as the shared property of an English 'school'. It is true that some abroad have seen in Hobsbawm's peculiar and not very characteristically English combination of detailed but economical primary research, wealth of comparative reference and broad yet immediately testable historical generalisation encased in concise and elegantly written essay form, the distinctive hallmarks of an anglo-Marxist school of historical interpretation. If this interpretation has a moment of truth, it is only with the important caveat that like many of that gifted generation of Central Europeans driven, fortunately, to our shores by Nazism, Hobsbawm was better able to discern and develop the best in native traditions in ways that had never occurred to the native born. Perhaps it was only because of his linguistic fluency, his ease with non-English theoretical idioms and his confrontation with English culture as a whole for the first time as a teenager, that he was able to take so much from the different qualities of Dobb, Postan or Clapham whom he encountered as a history undergraduate in pre-war Cambridge, that he was able so powerfully to use the wealth of scholarship and theorising accumulated by the Webbs in the course of his first essays into historical research and that he was able to discern so sharply the most distinctive and uncommented upon features of the history of the English labour movement in the collection eventually published as *Labouring Men*.

It has been Hobsbawm's quite unusual combination of theoretical clarity, large generalising capacity and an uncanny eye for suggestive detail, pulling in seemingly unusable faits divers and bric-à-brac to produce imaginatively compelling and wholly unexpected syntheses that has made his approach, particularly to social history, so influential, if, of course, not at all easy to reproduce. And it is with some of the issues which arise out of this approach that these essays are concerned. For one thing which arguably remains most distinctively Marxist about his approach is a brilliantly illuminating but ultimately quite orthodox Marxist approach to the old problem of the relationship between 'base' and 'superstructure'. Hobsbawm's work, because of the freshness and unexpectedness of the components it includes in notions of 'culture', 'ideology' and 'politics' is perhaps the best testimony to the strengths of a classical Marxist solution to the relationship between 'social being' and 'social consciousness'. But such an approach has not only strengths, but less visible limitations; and the problems of such a relationship have increasingly engaged the attention of historians and social theorists in recent years. If there is one connecting thread in these essays, it is the problem of how and indeed whether such connections can be established. The solutions are as various as the contributions. But that historians can now intelligently explore this problem in their own work in such diverse directions is perhaps one of the best tributes to a great historian who made these themes so accessible to us in the first place.

Theory

1 IDEOLOGIES AND MENTALITIES

Michel Vovelle*

This enquiry may seem naive; and in fact it accepts openly and unashamedly the charge of naivety. Here I am, a historian formed by Marxist methodologies who is far from denying them, and yet I have come to be widely considered as a historian of mentalities, no doubt rightly so to judge from the works for which I am known - investigations of collective attitudes towards death, essays on fêtes and on aspects of religious history such as the de-christianisation movement of the year II, viewed as a lightning transformation within the revolutionary process.

And yet I do not consider myself to have been unfaithful to my initial objectives: even if my approach may have seemed paradoxical to historians who do not or no longer claim inspiration from Marxism, Emmanuel Le Roy Ladurie, in his review of my work on *Baroque piety and De-christianisation: attitudes to death in Provence in the 18th century*, expressed amazement at finding a Marxist historian adept at describing 'how' but reluctant to ask 'why', a remark which is perhaps just as naive as any of mine since it appears to invest the Marxist historian with the enormous responsibility of providing the answers... which is not a small tribute.

On the other hand, I have had occasion to surprise more than one Marxist historian with an evident liking for improbable themes: and I remember the friendly questioning of Pierre Vilar who wanted to know if, instead of the themes which obviously attracted me - death, even fêtes - it would not have been better to trace the routes by which the masses gained consciousness: a much less dubious calling for a Marxist historian. In their different ways the two anecdotes reflect at least a misunderstanding and perhaps rather more than a misunderstanding. Beyond my own personal experiences I detect a wider and more profound question. The need for Marxist historiography both in response to its own developing problematic and to external promptings to clarify its own concepts. The need also for a new generation of historians of mentalities to define simply yet rigorously the concept of mentality which has gained wide usage without shedding an almost impressionistic haziness.

To do this one has to take due account of the co-existence within the same field of two rival concepts derived from two different traditions which are consequently difficult to square

---

*Michel Vovelle is director of the Centre Meridional d'Histoire Social at the University of Aix-en-Provence.

although undeniably they display a real area of overlap. But quite clearly ideology and mentality are not the same.

1 IDEOLOGY

I am not going to fall into the trap of beginning with a new definition of the Marxist concept of ideology: others have done that, from the founding fathers to commentators such as Louis Althusser who, in 'Ideology and State Ideological Apparatuses' (*La Pensée*, June 1970), defined ideology as 'the imaginary relationship of individuals to their real conditions of existence'. A collection of representations but also of practices and behaviour, conscious and unconscious. The very general character of the definition might seem capable of bringing together Marxists and even non-Marxists around a common working hypothesis: and if it is open to criticism on the grounds of an undeniable vagueness, this may be said to have been encouraged by Marx himself.

Engels in his well-known letter to Bloch in 1890, wrote:

> According to a materialist conception of history the determining factor is, in the last instance, the production and reproduction of real life. Neither Marx nor myself have ever stated anything else. If subsequently someone distorts this proposition to make it say that the economic factor is alone determinant he transforms it into an empty, abstract and ridiculous phrase.

In this way Engels, following Marx, replied in advance to a whole critical approach which persists despite being so simplistic that there should be no need to dwell on it: namely 'vulgar Marxism' i.e. a mechanical economistic explanation envisioning a universe in which ideological superstructures are at the beck and call of the infrastructure. Of course, this is an academic debate which is best left to the 'vulgar' critics of 'vulgar' Marxism. But it must be recognized that such caricatures tend to endure and have real effect. It is not unlikely that this has contributed at least within French historiography to a kind of reticence and even a certain feeling of guilt among Marxist historians, in addressing topics which could lay them open to this kind of reproach. Until recently one had the impression of a sort of unspoken agreement, which judging from their silence involved a number of Marxist historians, confining them to the sphere of the economy, and of social structure but within strict limits...leaving to others more qualified than themselves the more complex territories of religious history, mentalities and sensibilities. So the Goldman of *The Hidden God* remained for a long time the exception proving the rule of a general failure of Marxist researchers to intervene in matters which did not concern them.

Confined below stairs while others enjoyed the grand appartments, Marxist historians were not even well recompensed for their caution, finding themselves surrounded or confronted by objections which research in the new areas was continually throwing up in the way of a Marxist reading.

And they are powerful objections. Take for example, to stay in my own field of research of eighteenth-century studies, the major reappraisal occasioned recently by the study of the disparity between the bourgeois ideology of the Enlightenment and the group which gave it expression in the provincial academies, literary circles and masonic lodges. In the irrefutable statistics of Daniel Roche the bourgeois is nowhere to be seen, leaving the front of the stage to aristocrats or representatives of an 'elite' of talents. How is it then, one might ask, that an ideology is not carried by its 'rightful' bearers, and is even put forward by those whose destruction it carries in embryo? Hence the success, at least for a time, of the theory of the Elites, in suitably Gallicised form, as an attempt to break the 'mechanical' connection between social position and ideological options or consciousness.

When dealing with more complex representations, it becomes increasingly difficult to give proper explanation of, or even engage with, a number of phenomena. A very recent thesis in social history sets out on Marxist lines to reconstruct, in its full complexity, the *parlementaire* aristocracy of Aix in the eighteenth century. But despite gathering together with great flair all the pieces in the case, it comes unstuck over obstacles which it can neither dismiss or take on board: namely the persistence in the eighteenth century of Jansenism among these magistrates. Can it simply be a survival, a form without substance?

These are again 'noble' forms of ideological expression, but a history which is continually enlarging its field of enquiry to encompass all aspects of behaviour through which the whole man defines himself - family, morals, dreams, language, fashion and who knows what else - comes up against the apparently inexplicable, which is not to say that it is without meaning.

But what meaning should we give it? Even more, is there in human behaviour - and this proposition would seem preposterous on the basis of the definition we started out with - a part which escapes ideology - existing beneath or beside it? Current usage of the term in everyday speech may be misleading here: 'now that's a matter of ideology' we often hear: the expression derives from the 'common sense' representation of ideology as a polarised, worked-out system in contrast to native good sense, reflecting the climate of the time perhaps ... Mentality maybe?

2 MENTALITIES

The notion of mentality, as it is understood today forms part of a different and in fact much more recent inheritance, having been in existence some 20 to 30 years to go by the common acceptance of the term. Even then it must be recognised that the concept is far from being universally accepted: one has only to look at the difficulty which historians outside France have had in applying the notion and even translating the term: the Germans have tried to find an equivalent word while the English and Italians have resigned themselves quite simply to a direct borrowing from the French.

On the other hand, I am well aware that one could quite rightly point to the existence of an entire pre-history of the historiography of mentalities, and clearly, just as Monsieur Jourdain wrote prose without knowing it so people have written the history of mentalities before the letter. What else is Georges Lefebvre's *Great Fear of 1789* if not a study, still surprising in its modernity, of one of the last great panics of the old type in French society? Then certain historical classics come to mind, like Huizinga's *Waning of the Middle Ages*, indisputably one of the pioneer works in this new historical approach. But if we can already begin to speak of history of mentalities proper with Lucien Febvre and the *Annales* school - for example in *The Religion of Rabelais and the Problem of the Decline in Religious Belief* - it is only with Robert Mandrou and Georges Duby in the 1960s that despite considerable continuing oppositon, it was officially recognised as a new territory of history. It may be said that it has made up for early difficulties with an irresistable offensive: from its success in the best-sellers' lists the history of mentalities may be seen within current French historiography as the continuation or replacement of yesterday's all-conquering social history. The amount of interest shown by other historical schools and their attempts at emulation make it quite clear that we are dealing here with much more than a passing fashion.

But it is also at this point that we come to the first paradox, namely, that the victorious concept still retains, to say the least, a very vague character. Not that there has been any lack of soul-searching during the last twenty years over the proper definition which should be given to the concept of 'mentality': but I do not know of any better definition than that which Robert Mandrou proposed when interrogated on this point: a history of 'visions of the world'. This definition is neat and satisfying in my view, but undeniably vague.

It would hardly be fair to hold this against Robert Mandrou considering the way the actual content of this history has altered over the last twenty or thirty years. Accepting all the inadequacy, even distortion, involved in such a generalisation, it seems to me that we have passed from a history of mentalities which in its early years remained very much on the level of culture or conscious thought (as in Febvre's *The Religion of Rabelais*, but also in Mandrou's *Popular Culture in the 18th century*) to a history of attitudes, behaviour and unconscious collective representations: for this is what is massively inscribed in the popularity of new centres of interest, the child, the mother, the family, love and sexuality ... death.

To understand this development it is necessary only to follow one or two of a number of themes which appear as constants in historical production on mentalities. In the case of witchcraft, from Robert Mandrou's historical study, *Magistrats et Sorciers*, whose merit cannot be overstated, to the more recent approaches of Carlo Ginzberg and R. Muchembled, the historian's vision has altered significantly. Mandrou revealed to us the historical shift in perceptions occurring within the elites and the authorities when the *parlements* decided, somewhere around 1660, to stop burning witches. Today historians endeavour to pass over to the other side of the fence and try to analyse from the inside the mental universe of outcasts and deviants. Similarly, it would be perhaps too easy to show the change which has taken place between the now somewhat dated *Rabelais* of Lucien Febvre, the product of a history still limited to the elites, half-way between the history of ideas and the history of mentalities, and Mikhail Baktine's *Rabelais*, considered as expression and sign of an appropriated popular culture. The history of mentalities has changed in a very short time and with it the very concept of mentality. It is as if today one is dealing with an omnivorous discipline which instinctively swallows up whole chunks of history: religious, literary, intellectual, but equally folklore and a whole dimension of ethnography. Such an insatiable appetite may prove dangerous: who will eat whom?

It is time to take stock of the situation and redirect our thoughts on the problem at hand of the relationship of mentality and ideology. Between an elaborated concept such as ideology, gradually matured over time, clearly much remains to be said, and a notion like mentality, representing the conceptualisation of a developing if recent practice or discovery which is still undeniably fluid and bears successive layers of meaning, it is understandable that accommodation is difficult: they spring from different inherited traditions and distinct modes of thought, one more systematic, the other avowedly empiricist, with all the risks which that entails.

Yet, between the two there is an undeniable and large area of overlap. To judge by the way both terms are currently used, it would seem - in what may well become a dialogue of the deaf - that for some mentalities are inscribed quite naturally within the ideological field while to others ideology in the narrow sense of the term is nothing but an aspect or level of the field of mentalities: specifically that which concerns consciousness, reasoning and abstract thought. The extent of the basic disagreements within these two formulae may easily be imagined. Those who would like to free the notion of ideology of what amounts to many as the unbearable stigma of being a Marxist concept will talk about the third level ... without ever referring explicitly to the hierarchical arrangement of economic infrastructures, social structures, and ideological superstructures. A bourgeois compromise if you like, but one which at least has the merit - as, for example, it appears in the work of Pierre Chaunu - of drawing attention to the eminent place which history 'on the third level' has acquired over the last decades within the research concerns of the discipline.

Amid this general awakening of interest, within the historiography of liberal countries, and particularly in France, it seems that the more congenial notion of mentality, freed of all ideological connotation, is clearly winning out as more operational and better suited by the very haziness surrounding it to meet the requirements of open-ended research.

3 MENTALITIES VERSUS IDEOLOGIES

Is the history of mentalities then anti-Marxist? Let us make ourselves clear. The problem can only be dealt with in a historical perspective. That for a long time Marxist historians felt a real uneasiness about an approach suspected of leading, consciously or unconsciously, to mystification there can be no doubt. Was the attitude warranted? Most certainly not in the case of certain prominent members of the French school: Mandrou and Duby have been especially concerned to hold on to both ends of the chain, the social and the mental, and, moreover, have been open to all arguments. Perhaps the same cannot be said of the earlier generation, of Lucien Febvre and a part of the original *Annales*. If the founding fathers of the review were careful to keep the accent on the trilogy Economy-Society-Civilisation (with the last term as a reminder of an earlier nomenclature opening the gates of the superstructural) and if Braudel has continued to emphasise the importance of social mediation ('material civilisation *and* capitalism'), it is none the less possible to discern within the ethos of *Annales* a desire to dissociate itself from a Marxist approach to history regarded as dated and imprisoned in the dogmatic schemas of a socio-economic reductionism. On the contrary, the emphasis on mental processes and on the specificity of the 'prison of the long-term' reflects Braudel's concern to affirm, if not the autonomy of the mental, at least the originality of the rhythms which it obeys.

In pursuit of this end, itself historically conditioned, if it is true, as we shall see in a minute, that a good number of current French historians of mentalities have come from social history and have not repudiated it, far from it, one is also witnessing the progressive installation on both sides of the Atlantic of a new generation of specialists who have not come by the earlier prescribed route, preferring to make token gestures in this direction. This new generation of historians of mentalities, predisposed to all the blandishments of psycho-history, will without doubt - and without success - accentuate some already discernible traits and insist on the autonomy of mental processes.

On one level the concept of mentality is already considered, as we have seen, as larger than that of ideology: it embraces what is not formulated, what remains apparently 'insignificant' as well as what remains deeply buried at the level of unconscious motivations. Hence the advantage, perhaps, of this more flexible tool for total history.

In keeping with this first distinction, mentalities are distinguishable from other registers of history by what Robert Mandrou defined as 'a longer time scale', referring to Braudel's conception of the long term acting as historical 'prison'. By their nature, then, mentalities direct us towards recollections, memories and forms which endure: in short, towards what it has become commonplace to define as 'the force of inertia of mental structures' even if the explanation is more verbal than real. In particular, in the perspective which concerns us, this recognition, at first sight irrefutable, of the inertia of mentalities leads on to several types of interpretation or working hypotheses.

The first - which is perhaps a way to reconcile 'ideology' and 'mentality' - would see in a whole range of features of mentalities the translation of a deeper level of ideology, the traces, as it were, of fragmented ideologies. That is what remains of ideological expressions, once embedded in a specific historical context, when they become at variance or lose contact with reality to become free-floating, almost hollow structures, purely formal in character. This first explanatory approach, whilst not entirely satisfying, in my view, has at least the advantage of properly attempting to build into a coherent picture things which the mentalities approach treats as unrelated. But that is also what may be held against it.

But there is another way of accounting for the specific relationship of the time-scale of mentalities to historical time, and the 'force of inertia of mental structures'. Whereas in the previous hypothesis they are made to carry the remnants of dead ideologies, some people today would be inclined to see in these enduring recollections, on the contrary, the treasured possessions of a living identity, inviolable and deeply imbedded structures which give authentic expression to collective character or, in other words, everything of value. During a recent gathering on the theme 'History of mentalities', history of survivals or the 'prisons of the long-term' held at Aix in 1980 this particular theme kept coming up in discussion when least expected: a sign of the times in a society in search of its 'roots'. In grandma's cupboard are to be found the things that really matter.

This is one of the routes which takes us to the very spot where the incompatibility of the concepts of ideology and mentality is to be seen in its starkest form. I am referring to the affirmation of the autonomy of the mental sphere and its irreducibility to the economic and social. This is an old idea, in case anyone thinks I am claiming that it is a recent discovery. But it is new in the way in which it finds expression today through concepts like the 'collective unconscious' or the 'collective unreal'.

To elaborate the former one has only to look at what Philippe Ariès said in his contribution to the 'New History' dealing with the history of mentalities. The collective unconscious to which he refers is defined neither in terms drawn from psycho-analysis - from Jung perhaps, in actual fact - nor according to the criteria of Lévi-Straussian anthropology. His notion is openly and avowedly much more empirical, based on the autonomy of a collective mental adventure which obeys its own rhythms and causation. In his special field of collective attitudes to death, Ariès deciphers the elements of an adventure which is apparently independent of all socio-economic determination, even through the mediation of demography. But the intermediary layer of gestures, collective attitudes and representations which he makes the object of his study is also defined without reference to constituted ideologies: neither religious discourse - whether Catholic or Protestant - nor philosophical discourse is given its due, or even really taken into consideration: these hypotheses are superflous in a history whose lines of force are woven in the collective unconscious.

I have said elsewhere, on more than one occasion, why this rarified history, which shies from manifest correlations for fear of falling into a reductionist or mechanistic approach, leaves me perplexed and dissatisfied. In the present state of research I have fewer reservations about using, as others have done, like G. Duby in his most recent works, the term 'collective unreal' which in my view is more malleable and, above all, less susceptible to dangerous extrapolations from the field of psycho-analysis.

In both cases, in the current state of controversies surrounding the history of mentalities - to say nothing of psycho-history, which I have ignored - one has the distinct impression of the creation of a field in which the Marxist historian is being directly challenged. The ball is in his court.

4 IN WHICH THE MARXIST HISTORIAN BECOMES HISTORIAN OF MENTALITIES

Of course, he is well aware of the fact and is not remaining inactive. For my part I have entitled one of my recent books *From the Cellar to the Attic*, after a conversation I had - now a long while ago - with Emmanuel Le Roy Ladurie: the subsequent author of *Montaillou*, who expressed astonishment at the journey which had taken me from the 'cellar', or social structures, to the 'attic' - my researches on de-christianisation and attitudes to death - and declared his intention not to leave the cellar. Everyone knows with what success he has subsequently gone back on his words.

But we are not the only ones to have made this journey: other historians, both Marxists and non-Marxists, between 1960 and 1980 have passed from social history to the new site of mentalities: Georges Duby, Maurice Agulhon, Pierre Chaunu in his own way ... each with his own particular reasons and by his own route. For some, a complete break with their past; for many others, on the other hand, it is part of an awareness of a continuum, evident in their firm resolve to remain in control of both ends of the chain - running from the history of structures to one concerned with the most worked out ideas.

One might ask oneself the reason for this collective movement whose significance and non-contingent nature is shown by its scale, and which, as we have seen, has involved historians of very different allegiances (if not formations). There is no shortage of answers, perhaps the most elaborated being that of Pierre Chaunu who, in the course of remarks on 'quantification at the third level', analysed the great waves which over the last decades have affected historical study. We may endorse his view that each phase of historiography has confronted the problems which imposed themselves upon it most forcibly. And this explanation - everyone guarding their own particular reservations - will just about suffice.

I will allow myself to add a personal reflection at this point - going back to when I was starting out some time in the early 1960s. A whole generation of historians was being schooled then in the procedures of social history as taught to us by Ernest Labrousse: social history of the quantifying kind which 'counts, measures and weighs'. Then came the time of confrontation over the nature of the ancien régime: a 'society of orders', as argued by Roland Mousnier and his school, or a society of classes? It was a dispute which might have been sterile and which doubtless was partly so, immobilising initiative and encouraging some of this generation to get on through guile.

In fact, seen with hindsight, it was a worthwhile detour. Without giving up their own methods of approach or working hypotheses, historians, via the analysis of social structures, came to grips with explaining collective options, attitudes and behaviour. In so doing they found they had taken on (but that is surely what they were after) a far more onerous brief.

Moving from social structures to collective attitudes and representations raised the whole problem of the complex mediations between the real life of men and the image, even the fantastic representations which they make of it; a problem which they invested in their approaches to the history of mentalities. Approaches which defy all mechanical reduction, confronting the interweaving of the different times of history, to use Althusser's expression, by which is meant the inertia in the diffusion of key ideas and the co-existence in stratified layers of models of behaviour drawn from different heritages.

Starting out with clearly delineated problems, they have found others along the way: it was because I wished to explain the counter-revolution in the south that I was drawn to study de-christianisation in its two aspects - violent and explosive in the Year II, spontaneous and gradual during the century of the Enlightenment. But while wishing to get to grips with the latter phenomenon, through the testimony of wills for eighteenth-century Provence, I discovered something else - more profound and more important perhaps - a changing sensibility to death, and hence a shift in the wider vision of the world of which Robert Mandrou spoke.

Arriving at the end of the road, at the point where the history of mentalities meets with (without becoming dissolved in) historical ethnography, the historian takes stock. Could it be that as a result of successive mediations he has lost the thread of the all too straightforward and linear history on which he started out?

In actual fact, he only appeared to abandon ideology in order, on the basis of more careful study, to arrive at a precise and refined reading of it. Of course, he must not make too much of the possibilities contained in the Marxian formula about the 'particular lighting' or 'ether' of a period. Such references would permit a loose reading if it were not for the fact that recourse to the theory of mode of production as all-embracing and ultimately all-determining restores it firmly within the unity of the historical field.

The history of mentalities is, then, the study of the mediations and dialectical relationship between the objective conditions of the life of men and the way they perceive them. At this level the opposition between the two conceptual networks we have been contrasting - ideology and mentalities - becomes blurred. Far from leading to mystification, the exploration of mentalities ultimately entails a necessary widening of the field of research not as some alien and exotic land, but as the natural extension and culmination of all social history.

Some debates are rewarding. All the argument over the elite and the nature of the old-style bourgeoisie has led to an enormous advance in conceptualisation. Even if the flowering of the history of mentalities over the last twenty or thirty years were only a welcome digression - which I do not believe - it would at least have rendered the enormous service of causing us to face more directly reality in all its complexity.

Translated by John Dunne

2 THE IDEAL IN THE REAL

Maurice Godelier*

> The journey of a thousand leagues starts with a single step (Lao-Tzu, *Tao-te-Ching*, Poem LXIV)

Why begin with these fine words spoken by Lao-Tzu, the 'Old Man' as Etiemble calls him? Not to impress people, but to make clear my aim in setting out - in the wake of countless others - to write about ideologies or, rather, about the ideological. I should like to break out of the rut in which most discussions of this theme become bogged down and to push on ahead.

For something is wrong in the state of the human sciences when it comes to ideology. Not that the field has been neglected or scorned. On the contrary, it has been one of the most consistently 'worked over' during the past three decades, and it seems even that interest in it is still growing. For France, suffice it to mention Lévi-Strauss's work on mythical thought in general and on the myths of the American Indians in particular, and the work of J.-P. Vernant, M. Détienne and P. Vidal-Naquet on the relations between mythical thought, philosophical thought and scientific thought in the evolution of ancient Greek society from the birth of the Polis, of the City-State, to its decline. Mention should be made, too, of investigations by J. Le Goff, G. Duby and R. Mandrou into the history of 'mentalities' in the Middle Ages or in modern times. But, needless to say, I ought to have begun with mentions of Benvéniste and Dumézil. My purpose in citing these names is not to draw up a list of the meritworthy, but to point to the contrast between the boldness of these people's work, their fertility, and the banality of the reported theses which these specialists occasionally dare to put forward when they stick out their necks to take a broader view of their field and of their approaches. On this point, though, they would gladly leave things to the philosophers, themselves specialists: specialists in general ideas.

Caricaturing outrageously, we may say that there are, by and large, two main contending theses in the age-old debate between ideas and social realities or history:

---

*Maurice Godelier is an anthropologist at the Collège de France, currently director of the CNRS (Conseil National de Recherches Scientifiques). He has recently published the first full-scale study drawn from his field work in New Guinea, *La Production des Grands Hommes*.

THESIS 1

Ideas govern the world because it is they which shape social realities in the first place and which drive societies and their history along a certain course over periods of thousands of years. In support of this, people point to Islam, Hinduism, Christianity, Maoism, in other words, all the great religious or political ideologies that seem to have shaped men in their image, to have been the living spring whence poured forth reality and not its point of arrival, the expression - in thought - of realities born independently of it and unaided by it.

THESIS 2

A society cannot be reduced to the ideas its members may develop about it. It exists independently of ideas about realities, which are distinct from it and which are of greater consequence than it in history, first among these being material realities and the social relations which organize them. In a word, in the order of social realities, infrastructural realities take precedence over superstructures and ideas. At all events, the latter are not just conjured up out of thin air: they must 'correspond' to some determinate society and epoch upon which they 'act in turn'. The gods of antiquity died with it. I expect everyone will have recognized in passing the theses normally attributed to Marx.

To which upholders of the first thesis reply that the gods on Olympus were not born with the slave mode of production, and that Christianity, with its ideology of one God in Three Persons, dead upon the Holy Cross to save mankind, is still alive and well today having traversed - though not without a number of crises and metamorphoses - two thousand years of history and three or four modes of production. How does this tie in with the economy, where is the correspondence between infrastructure, superstructures and ideologies?

Are not the specialists right? How could anything positive or new arise from problems stated as abstractly as this? Surely there is an element of truth in each of the two theses, so that neither can ever really hope to prevail over the other? And then, after all, since all the best work has shown the two to be correct at one and the same time - whatever their authors may have intended - wouldn't it be best to come down in favour of both of them, one *after* the other? Maybe, but in which order? It becomes a question of dosage, depending upon whether one prefers to be more 'materialist' or 'realist', or more idealist or formalist. Which is what Lévi-Strauss does when he insists upon the 'primacy of infrastructures' in *The Savage Mind* but then concludes, in *Honey and Ashes* that the retreat of mythology in the face of philosophy in the ancient Greek City was 'an historical occurrence *signifying nothing*, except that it happened in that place and at that time,' and adds that 'if history remains in the forefront it is that this is the place belonging to irreducible contingency as of right'. How are we to give an account of the logic of forms of thought and of their emergence and development if history is considered as the erratic work of 'the irreducible contingency of events'? How are we to accept the primacy of infrastructures as a governing law of reality while at the same time proclaiming the irreducible contingency of history?

Of course, we are no longer so naive as to believe that the contradictions of a system of thought are merely the outcome of a given state of Science, of a shifting and uncertain relation between our knowledge and our ignorance. We are well aware that behind thought lie thinkers, with their biographical roots, their positions and their contradictions, which they share with many others in their society. So, theoretical progress alone will never suffice to resolve theoretical contradictions entirely, at least, not in the field of the human sciences.

Having said that, I shall now return to the central point here, and it is a fundamental one. What is at issue is the question of the existence and of the nature of an internal order, of a logic in the functioning and evolution of societies. That an order does exist would appear to be an idea that is accepted by everyone, for experience denies that all social activities or all social relations have *equally important* consequences upon the organisation and the reproduction of societies. All societies have something like an explicit hierarchy of different social activities. But is it this explicit, conscious hierarchy - which is visible in the arrangement of institutions - which really governs the reproduction and the keeping of this society in being?

That is the crucial point of the argument. To the Marxists' primacy of the economy in all societies, non-Marxists answer with the primacy of kinship among the Australian aborigines or the Nuer (Radcliffe-Brown, Evans-Pritchard), or the primacy of religion (L. Dumont) in the Indian caste-system, or the primacy of politics in fifth-century BC Athens (K. Polanyi, Ed Will). It should be remarked that by objecting to the primacy of kinship, politics or religion, one is not only objecting to the primacy of systems of ideas: one is rejecting the primacy of ideas that are embodied in institutions, thereby becoming social relations, social structures, in a word, what Marxists would call 'superstructures'.

Taking a closer look, there is every chance that this discussion is going to continue for a long time to come, even though there is little likelihood of its progressing, i.e. of 'allowing us' to progress. For the two camps start from irreconcilable, irreducible theoretical assumptions; hence they can *never argue at other than cross-purposes*.

What, after all, are the non-Marxists really doing? Despite the fact that each of them answers the Marxists with a different primacy, depending upon the society to which he is referring, they all proceed in the same manner and from the same assumption: they refer to *facts*, the existence of a viable social order, the fact of the *visible, apparent domination*, in the social practice and consciousness of members of any given society, of activities that the Marxists would call 'superstructural', in order to refute a *hypothesis concerning the existence of an order of causalities which is not, cannot be immediately visible*, apparent, and/or known to the individuals and groups making up these societies. In this respect, they may agree that there is a certain measure of truth in the Marxist thesis, namely that it corresponds to the logic of capitalist society, this being the only one in which the economy apparently, openly dominates both the organization and the workings of society. After allowing for this particular case, the Marxist hypothesis is regarded as devoid of any explanatory value or scientific consequence. It could only be for other reasons, for partisan ones, that Marxists so obstinately insist on taking an exception for the rule, for a law, and doggedly strive to fit all societies, and history, past or present, into it.

And yet this argument, which in appearance confines itself to facts alone, drawing therefrom its strength and justification, rests upon a theoretical thesis that is assumed to have been demonstrated whereas in point of fact it has not. The thesis is well-known, namely empiricism: it assumes that the visible *order* of things furnishes a *self-evident* demonstration of their *reasons* for being, that the order of facts makes them intelligible. This thesis thus implies that there is no point in hunting behind the visible order of facts in search of some hidden order capable of refuting it or of subsuming it under a different explanation produced by science. So, on the basis of this undemonstrated thesis, the empiricists refer to the domination of some social activity or other in a given society as though this reference alone were sufficient to refute the Marxist thesis.

As for the Marxists, they start out from the opposite thesis: that the appearance of facts does not reveal their essence. They are not the only ones to hold this view, which is why they have been joined by Lévi-Strauss and the structuralists, who are also anti-empiricist on principle. As a result, the Marxists are under obligation not only to show that the fact of the 'domination' of a given 'superstructure' in no way refutes the hypothesis of the primacy of infrastructures, but also to show how the primacy of infrastructures 'explains' the domination of a given superstructure. Is this a little like asking them to square the circle, is it their crown of thorns? One sees the cross a Marxist has to bear if he wants to sustain the validity of his approach in the human sciences. But he won't get out of it by attacking in order to defend himself. For even if he can reply to the empiricists that they too need to provide an explanation for the domination of this or that superstructure and that talking of the strength of an idea is inadequate, for, where does this idea come from, where does it derive the strength to impose itself, to shape men and society? For these questions concern him as much as they concern the empiricist, and he is under the same obligation to reply. And these questions merely reformulate the problem of the nature, the role and the functions of ideas and ideologies in the working and evolution of societies.

Why then, since we are aware of the issue, which is crucial, aware of the fruitlessness of a debate around irreconcilable theses capable of resulting only in a shouting match, aware too of the challenge, of the gauntlet flung in the Marxists' faces, of the cross they have to bear (and which they have made with their own hands), why then have we embarked on this course by citing Lao-Tzu and the prospect of a thousand-league journey? Would it not have been sufficient to write this handful of pages and to have sat back, satisfied with having untangled a particularly knotty theoretical discussion?

If we have done so, it is not due to any suicidal or masochistic tendencies on my part, but to the conviction that a step has been taken, a first step which may carry us, if not a thousand leagues, at least out of the dead-end street where, in my view, thinking on the question of relations between ideas and social realities has become stuck. This step consists in transforming the terms of the debate themselves with the aid of two theoretical findings enabling us to do so. I shall summarize them as follows:

1 The distinction between infrastructure and superstructures is not, in our view, a distinction between levels or instances, nor is it a distinction between institutions, although it may be one in certain cases. In its underlying principle, it is a distinction between functions. In the last analysis, the notion of causality, of the primacy of infrastructures refers to the existence of a hierarchy of functions and not to one of institutions. A society does not have a top and a bottom, and it is not a system of 'levels' piled one on top of the other. It is a system of relations between men, relations that are hierarchized according to the nature of their functions, these functions determining the respective impacts of each of their activities upon the reproduction of society.

2 We have reached the conclusion, moreover, that any social relation whatsoever contains *within itself* an *ideël* element, an element of thought, or representations that are not merely the form that this relation assumes in our consciousness, but are a part of its content. Do not confuse ideël with ideal or imaginary. These representations do not present pre-existing realities to the mind 'after-the-event' as it were (where these realities are thought of as having been born independently of and unaided by these representations), much as one might 'present' a new-born baby to family, friends and neighbours. On the contrary, these representations appear to be an integral part of social relations as soon as the latter begin to take shape, and they

are *one* of the conditions of their formation. Ideas are not here an 'instance' separate from social relations; they are not merely appearances, nor are they deformed-deforming reflections in social consciousness.

But, while there is an element of ideël everywhere, this in no way implies that everything that is (socially) real is ideël. Does this mean, however, that all ideël reality, all ideas, are ideological? And if so, are there any criteria for distinguishing from among ideas those that are ideological and those that are not? Certainly not if we confine ourselves to dubbing any representation of the world that is in the least bit organized 'ideological'. Ought we then to conform to another, more current, usage and to stick the label 'ideological' on those 'illusory' representations which men elaborate concerning themselves and the world, and which serve to 'legitimate' an existing order after the event, so to speak, hence legitimating the forms of domination and of exploitation of man by man which this existing order may contain. This restrictive definition seems 'Marxist', but is it really, and how does it tie in with the idea we have just put forward, namely that any social relation necessarily contains an element of thought that is not necessarily either 'illusory' or 'legitimizing', and which forms part of this relation from the moment of its formation?

In order to make progress in solving these problems, we shall come back to these different points and analyse the following problems in turn:

1 The nature of the distinction between infrastructure and superstructure.

2 The relations between economic determination and the domination of a given 'superstructure': the problem of the foundation of this domination.

3 The problem of the 'ideël' element of reality and of the distinction between the ideological and the non-ideological.

THE DISTINCTION BETWEEN INFRASTRUCTURE AND SUPERSTRUCTURE

The first point, which clouds all that follows and which condemns the protagonists to total mutual incomprehension from the outset, is that both sides of the argument mean the same things, i.e. see in the distinction between infrastructure and superstructures a distinction between institutions and not between functions. But, to start with, what do we mean by 'infrastructure'?

The infrastructure is the combination of the different material and social conditions which enables the members of a society to produce and reproduce the material means of their social existence. These comprise:

1 The determinate ecological and geographical conditions within which and from which a society extracts the material

means enabling it to exist.

2 The productive forces, that is, the material and intellectual means that members of this society utilize, after having invented, borrowed or inherited them, within the various 'labour' processes through which they act upon nature for the purpose of extracting their means of existence, these means thereafter constituting a 'socialized' part of nature.

3 The relations of production, that is, the relations between men - no matter which - which fulfil the triple function of:

a determining the social form of access to resources and of the control of the means of production;

b redistributing the labour time of society's members among the different labour processes and organizing these different processes;

c determining the social form of the circulation and distribution of the products of individual or collective labour.

For us, as with Marx, the social relations of production alone constitute, strictly speaking, the 'economic structure of a society'. 'Die Gesamtheit dieser Produktions verhältnisse bildet die Ökonomische Struktur der Gesellschaft' (K. Marx: Introduction to *Contribution to the Critique of Political Economy*). It is worth recalling, however, that productive forces and relations of production, though distinct, *never exist separate from each other* but *always combined*, hinged together in some *specific* way or other. The various specific forms of these combinations constitute so many 'social forms of production' or 'modes of production'. These modes of production cannot be reduced to the different forms of division of labour. There is no such thing as an agricultural, pastoral, artisanal, etc. 'mode of production'. These are modes of subsistence. It is perfectly possible to practice stockbreeding, agriculture and handicrafts all within the same relations of production, be they feudal, capitalist or socialist, etc. The specific characteristics of each of these productive activities may entail particular forms of division of labour without implying different forms of ownership of the means of production and of the product.

Let us take another look at these definitions for a moment. They are formal: but they are not empty. Just as in reality one finds only particular forms of production and particular products, so 'general' notions of production, relations of production, etc. are merely an abstract and convenient shorthand for aspects that are *common* to all economic structures while characterizing none in particular; these definitions are therefore both positive yet general items of knowledge and formal conditions for the analysis of empirical realities which are always specific. They enable us to seek, though alone they will not allow us to find.

Such as they are, however, these definitions entail consequences which are normally passed over in silence and which contradict the usual (Marxist) conception of relations between infrastructure, superstructures and ideology.

Productive forces
I shall start by examining the definition of productive forces: material and intellectual means, etc. Material means are, in the first place, man himself, his own body and his physical capabilities. Then come the means which man interposes between himself and nature in order to act upon the latter. These means may be found ready-made or else may be manufactured. All this, however, use of the body and material means, implies the existence and the application of a complex body of representations, ideas and idealities: representations of the goal pursued, of stages, effects, of activities which we call 'work' but which rarely appear as 'such' in a good many primitive or pre-capitalist societies. And these representations themselves connect up with rules governing the manufacture of tools, body attitudes, the use of tools and, needless to say at a deeper level, with indigenous conceptions of nature and of man's relations with nature.

We thus find *inside* all man's material activities upon nature a complex body of *ideël realities* whose presence and intervention are essential if this activity is to occur at all.

Documenting these ideël realities contained within the various material activities and differing from culture to culture and from epoch to epoch, is a vast and difficult undertaking, one on which historians and anthropologists have long been involved; despite revivals due to ethnoscientists such as Conklin or of a historian of science and technology such as Joseph Needham, this remains a particularly neglected branch of the human sciences. To keep this discussion general, it seems to me that the different ideël realities that one comes across within a given labour process can be classified according to two main types, depending upon the functions that these representations fulfil.

On the one hand, we have taxonomies of plants, animals, soils, climatic phenomena, etc., of manufacturing rules and rules governing the use of tools, plans of material action and of symbolic conduct. These representations and these principles are also interpretations of reality whose effect is to *organize the forms* taken by the different material activities (labour processes) *and the phases* in which they take place.

But there are also representations which 'explain' why this or that task *must* be reserved for men, women, young people, slaves, commoners, masters, aristocrats, the king and so forth. In other words, these are representations which *legitimize the position and the status* of individuals and groups in terms of the realities that are permitted them, forbidden them, imposed upon them, etc.

Of course, this distinction only exists for us, and it is purely analytic in value. It is absurd to see Hesiod's *Works and days* as a treatise on agronomy as people often do just because the peasant-poet includes a great deal of technical advice to his brother concerning harvest dates, the selection of soils, etc.

In fact, Hesiod wrote this religious and political poem right in the middle of an agricultural crisis in Greece in the eighth century BC. For him, the crisis was the result of man's overweening nature, which had driven the gods to heaven. Through his brother, he was advising all Greeks to observe scrupulously the rituals demanded by the cultivation of the fields. Practised thus, agriculture would become a source of 'merits', a school of 'virtue', and the gods would once more deign to communicate with men and to call down their blessings upon them.

To appreciate the full import of this example, I should add that there is no word for 'work' in ancient Greek. The word πονος is used for all unpleasant activities, like the word *labor* in Latin, and while there are two verbs ποιειν and πραττειν for 'make' and 'do, act', there is none for 'work'. It is also important to recall that the term τελνη was not used by the Greeks for agriculture as they did not regard this as a 'trade' as they did crafts or commerce, these latter being activities involving 'trade secrets' or special techniques and servile activities, since the craftsman and the tradesman worked not for himself, but for some outside customer who provided him with his living. Agriculture, on the other hand, at least in ancient Athens (as well as in Rome, during the archaic period, if we are to believe the beginning of Cato the Elder's *De Re Rustica*), was regarded as an activity 'worthy' of a 'citizen', on a par with war or politics. We have here an effect of the relations of production upon the organization of the division of labour, since only citizens who were members of the πολιτεια, of the community of members of the πολις, were entitled to own land in the city and were thus duty-bound to defend this sacred earth by bearing arms. It should be borne in mind, however, that the placing of a high social value upon agriculture in no way implied that social value was placed on 'work' itself, that it did not exist in Sparta or in the cities of Beotia; in fact it disappeared gradually in Athens as the citizens gave up cultivating their land themselves, leaving this task to their slaves. For Aristotle, in the fourth century BC, agriculture had become a 'servile' activity, like handicrafts.

Hence, right at the heart of the most 'material' area of societies' infrastructure, at the very heart of the productive forces available to them for acting upon nature, we come across an ideël element ('knowledge' or abstract representations of all kinds, with their extensions in the form of know-how which is also a system of body techniques). This ideël element constitutes a sort of 'internal skeleton', the internal organizing plan behind their 'activation'. But productive forces are only 'activated' within the framework of determinate social relations, which imposes a determinate form of division of labour by *attaching* a specific *value* to a specific task and by *linking* that task to a specific social category (men/women, elders/young people, master/slave, etc.). These bonds, these links also contained an ideël element consisting of representations legitimizing the values attached to different social activities.

But these representations do not exist in the mind alone. They are also ideas that are expressed in a language. This is one of the essential conditions of learning techniques and of their transmission from one generation to the next, of the conservation of productive forces. These representations have to be *communicated* from generation to generation via language and/or through body learning. So, we are going to have to count among the productive forces not only the idealities which we have enumerated, but also the means - whether linguistic or otherwise - required in order to express them socially and to transmit them within a given society and 'culture'.

This analysis thus brings us to conclude that thought and language belong, of necessity, to the productive 'forces'. Thus the distinction between infrastructure, superstructures and ideology is not a distinction between material reality and immaterial reality. It is a distinction between functions, and not a distinction based on 'substances' or institutions, whether material or otherwise. Finally, if we find thought lying at the heart of the most material aspect of social activities, this shows *a fortiori* that there can be no social relation that does not contain within it an element of thought, an ideël element. Seen thus, thought ceases to be a 'level' that is separate from other levels. By demonstrating its presence everywhere in social reality, we can progressively diminish or even abolish the notion of 'level' or 'instance'. Of course, these are not the conclusions one normally finds in standard accounts of the 'basic concepts of Marxism-Leninism'. But examination of the definition of the 'social relations of production' is liable to hold yet other surprises in store for us.

Relations of production

Professional economists, and with them the general public, spontaneously represent the economic structure of all societies in the image of what happens in our own society, as a body of *institutions that are distinct* from other relations, whether social, political, family, religious, etc. In the capitalist mode of production, the production process takes place inside 'firms', which are social units distinct from family, church, parties or racial communities. This is neither the case in the pre-capitalist or non-capitalist societies of the past nor in those of today. On this point, Marx (if not the Marxists) was the first to condemn the temptation to apply our own peculiar view of the economic to all societies. A century later, after Max Weber, we find the same position in the writings of Karl Polanyi and the 'substantivist' tendency in economic anthropology.

Historians and anthropologists have noted that when one attempts to isolate the economic structure in pre-capitalist societies, one is obliged to look among those social relations which the Marxists class among the superstructures: kinship relations, political relations, religious relations. To illustrate these different possibilities. I shall select three examples from among the many which history and anthropology offer.

Most ancient Australian aborigine societies, which lived from hunting, gathering and sometimes fishing, were divided into kinship groups which exchanged wives among them, these wives circulating from generation to generation in the same direction (divisions into moieties: sections or into sub-sections practising a restricted or generalized form of exchange). These social divisions not only regulated marriage and descent, which is the explicit and universal function of kinship relations; they also served as a framework for the exercise of power and for ritual practices designed to act upon the conditions of reproduction of the universe and of society, upon the sun, the moon, the rain, etc. Political and ritual powers and authority were gathered into the hands of the old men who were masters of the initiation rites, married to several wives and representing the different kinship groups making up each 'tribe', each society.

These kinship relations also served as a social framework for the appropriation of the territory of each tribe and of its natural resources. This worked in two ways, one abstract, the other concrete, (distinctly yet complementarily employing the two indissociable aspects of kinships: descent and alliance). On the one hand, each kinship group inherited from its ancestors (real or mythical) 'rights' to the use of certain portions of territory, rights which the young learned from the mouths of their elders in the course of long initiation journeys, during which they would cover every inch of the tribal territory, discovering all its diverse aspects and its resources (water, vegetation, etc.) and all the dangers liable to arise in case of prolonged drought. These rights were held in common by all the members of each kinship group; in common, but not exclusively, for in certain circumstances other groups, allies in particular, were allowed access to territory and resources. In practice, the 'concrete' appropriation of these resources occurred within the framework of local bands roaming over different portions of the tribal territory. These were the units of direct, everyday 'production' and consumption, and not the sections (referred to above). These bands consisted of a small number of families and individuals belonging to several sections though centred around a patrilineal and patri-local 'core' of families belonging to the section on whose territory the natural resources were normally exploited. The band took advantage of the presence of these allies in its midst to exploit the resources of several patches of territory when circumstances required. Relations of kinship, descent and alliance thus served as a framework for the abstract (ownership) and concrete ('labour' process) appropriation of nature. These relations, combined with relations between the sexes and between generations thus formed the social framework of the various material processes of production, functioning both as a social condition of the abstract appropriation of nature and its resources, and as the basis of the social organization and of co-operation among individuals and groups in the various concrete processes of the material exploitation of resources (hunting, gathering, fishing), and as the framework for their distribution. So, kinship relations in these societies filled the three functions defining the relations of production: they constituted the *economic structure*, they were *the locus and the form of the economy* in these societies.

If, on the other hand, we turn now to Oppenheim's work on ancient Mesopotamia, we find that in Assur most of the city's lands were regarded as the property of the god Assur. In the centre of the city stood the temple, dwelling place of the god and his priests. The economy functioned as a vast centralized system within which local communities and individuals were subject to the authority of the temple and the priests, to whom they were obliged to make over a portion of their labour and their products. Here, religious relations, or religion, form the framework for the appropriation of resources while at the same time constituting the society's economic structure; they were also social relations of production.

Finally, as my last example, I shall take a Greek city-state, a πολις such as fifth century Athens; this time we can observe that it is the political relations which are, deep down, relations of production. One became a citizen as of birth, because one's father was an Athenian and because one therefore belonged to a πολιτεια, a community of free men who, together, formed a πολις, a city and a state. To be a citizen was to have an exclusive right to own a portion of the city's territory, to be owner of a κληρος, a landowner. Citizenship thus entailed both being a free man and a landowner who either did or did not cultivate his farm, depending upon whether or not he owned slaves to do the job for him; it entailed entitlement to the magistracy and political responsibility, to bear arms and the duty to defend the sacred soil of the fatherland; finally, only citizens could enjoy the protection of the gods of the city and officiate at their worship. Clearly, here, the political - the fact of belonging to a πολις, extends everywhere, engulfing what we now understand by having political rights and the right to engage in politics.

Foreign freemen, residing in the city and doing business there, aliens in other words, were prohibited from owning land (except in the case of rarely accorded exemptions, since this was tantamount to becoming a citizen), from acceding to the high offices of state, from entering temples and places of worship of the gods of the city, nor were they entitled to fight side-by-side with citizens. This gave rise to an initial division of labour, since they were confined to such activities as handicrafts, trade, banking, these being considered unworthy of citizens, even though the latter could also exercise these activities and indeed had to if they owned no land. But freemen, whether citizens or aliens, could have themselves replaced in all these 'economic' activities by slaves, even in banking. Under these circumstances, certain slaves could grow rich and purchase their freedom or even own slaves themselves.

Slavery existed well before the advent of the city-state regime. It had existed in the form of domestic slavery, but it underwent a change of form and began to affect the evolution of ancient society increasingly when it came be to associated with commodity production and became an essential factor in the accumulation of wealth and the creation of inequalities among citizens. Slavery came to be the most dynamic and most contradictory characteristic of the Greek economic system in the fifth century BC. In order to grasp the originality of this system, however, one should avoid jumping to the conclusion that it was the forms of division of labour that engendered the forms of ownership of the means of production and of products. For it was the reverse that was true. It was because personal membership of a πολις, of a community, functioned simultaneously as a social condition of land-appropriation that all those activities which we regard as 'economic' were distributed along a *hierarchy of personal relations and statuses* and thus enjoyed greater or lesser social value by comparison with the highest status-level, that of full citizen.

It should be noted in passing that in ancient societies, as in a good many primitive ones, by the very nature of the relations of production, the primary aim of production is not the accumulation of wealth but the preservation, the reproduction of the status of individuals or groups within the community, the reproduction of their relations with the remainder of this community and hence the reproduction of the community itself and its structure. If we compare these situations, in which membership or non-membership of a community serves as the point of departure for 'economic' relations, with the situation which arose in China after the socialist revolution, then the contrast is striking. If indeed the workers and peasants, and workers as a whole, in socialist China do own the land and the means of production and their products, then we shall have here a new example of economic relations which would at the same time be political relations; this time, though, the 'community' constituting a socialist 'nation' would be the point of arrival and not the point of departure for the economic relations existing within it. But this new type of fusion between what we call the political and the economic bears no resemblance whatever to that of the ancient Greeks for its continued existence and development do not entail domination by a minority, a minority of freemen and citizens over the remainder of society, nor the exploitation of slaves. But for social development to occur without exploitation or without constantly recreating hierarchies, one needs, in addition to political and cultural revolutions, a tremendous increase in the material means capable of being made available to each through the intermediary of all.

At the conclusion of this analysis of three examples in which, in turn, we have seen kinship relations, 'religious' relations and political relations forming the economic structure of society, we reach the same findings as in the case of our analysis of productive forces, namely that in their content itself there is an ideël element, a thought (and language) component: *the distinction between relations of production and superstructures is, in its underlying principle, a distinction between functions and not institutions.* We have clearly seen this in all three cases, though particularly so in that of the Australian aborigines. On each occasion, the distinction was one based on functions *inside the same* social relations, the same institutions. In certain societies, including our own, there are distinct institutions corresponding to distinct functions, but this is an exception rather than the rule, an exception that has enabled western thought to perceive with greater clarity the role of economic relations - i.e. social and material relations between men and nature and among themselves in their appropriation of nature - in social evolution.

We can thus see that, in the course of history, *relations of production, or economics, do not occupy the same locus and consequently do not take on the same forms nor is their mode of development the same, and hence they do not have the same effects upon the reproduction of societies.*

The first theoretical question that needs to be answered in building a comparative scientific analysis of socio-economic systems, of 'social forms or modes of production', concerns the *discovery of the reasons and the conditions* which have led relations of production to change places - and hence forms and effects - in the course of history. Needless to say, neither one man alone, nor even a single discipline, could carry out this analysis; furthermore, it no longer corresponds to what we understand by or practise as economic history and economic anthropology. It is already hard enough to isolate and define the economic structure of a society, and it is a measure of the greatness of Malinowski, Firth, Audrey Richards, Gluckman and many others that they managed to do so for the societies they studied. But it is extremely difficult to answer the following question: why is it that in a good many primitive and peasant societies kinship relations between groups and individuals at the same time serve as social conditions of the production of their material means of existing socially (not of surviving, but of accomplishing all those things that are materially demanded of a member of society)?

I shall not attempt an answer here. I shall merely say that as a Marxist I shall be seeking for some of the major reasons for this among the constraints imposed by the level of the productive forces available to these societies, and especially in the fact that *living labour power* counts for more in these societies than the accumulated labour power existing in the form of tools or developed resources, in other words, means that are external to man yet which extend and enhance his action upon nature. It should be borne in mind that while the means of production used by hunters and gatherers or by primitive farmers and stockbreeders are usually easy to make - within everyone's capabilities - men actually reproduce themselves with life and that life, in all societies, 'reproduces itself' within the framework of kinship relations, by marrying and having children, through alliances and consanguinity. It may be that kinship relations served as the principal support for relations of production because they were the place of reproduction of man's principal means of production, namely himself. But this would draw us into a discussion of the theory of male domination, of the 'exchange' of women and a Marxist analysis of the incest taboo. To return to my main theme: have I not just thrown open my own analysis to those who reject Marxism, since they are inevitably going to conclude hastily that with the exception of capitalist societies, economics has not played a determinant role in history? It was always something else which 'dominated'. Am I then hoist with my own petard? Is it possible to mistake determination for domination and to infer the non-domination of the infrastructure from the dominance of a 'superstructure'?

THE PROBLEM OF THE FOUNDATIONS OF THE DOMINANCE OF NON-ECONOMIC STRUCTURES

Let me begin by making one important point clear. The dominance of a given social activity and of its corresponding institutions within society cannot be deduced or hypothesized. It is something one observes. In the first place, it is evident to the members of the society in question. They can observe it concretely around them, in the configuration of their institutions, in their social relations; they may think it and experience it as such; in a word, recognize it in and about themselves, in their individual practice and in the general practice of other members of their society. They are thus able to point to it as such in their explicit and implicit accounts to outsiders visiting their society and questioning them as to their customs. We can imagine the traveller of antiquity visiting Egypt or Athens one day. He could hardly have failed to note the importance of religious activities in the one case, of 'political' activities in the other.

Herodotus travelled through Egypt in the middle of the fifth century BC and noted in his ιστοριαι that the Egyptians are an excessively religious people. A century later, Aristotle, a Macedonian lured to Athens by the glory of that city, placed at the head of his treatise on *The Politics* these remarks characterizing the Greeks as men par excellence, beneath the gods, like all men, yet well above all other men, whether barbarians or savages, ignorant of the πολις, the city-state regime, in other words, not citizens: 'Man is naturally a political animal, a being destined to live in a city, and he who, by nature and not through the effect of some circumstance or other, does not belong to a city, is a creature either inferior to or superior to man.'

And at the beginning of the present century, Radcliffe-Brown, investigating among the Australian aborigines, was struck by the dominance of kinship relations among them: 'Wherever the Australian native goes all the persons he meets are his relatives by the working of the kinship system. These are further classified for him by the section system.' And it is clear today that this division into sections was not only applicable to humans but also to the entire universe, that the sun, the moon, the rain, sperm, lightning, kangaroos, etc. were also supposed to 'belong' to one or another of the sections which divided up men for the purpose of the accomplishment of rites.

However, I should not like to give the impression that it is always as easy as this to pinpoint the activity, the 'superstructure' which dominates within a given social formation. Often enough, the face of dominance is far more tangled, less easily discernible. To give but one example, historians still find it difficult to measure and explain the very important part played by christianity in the functioning of medieval society. Had it not become the dominant institution and ideology in feudal society when, at the turn of the tenth century, the church was still the premier landowner in Europe and the theory of the three orders had just achieved its most complete formulation, sanctioning the domination of the *oratores* and the *bellatores*, of those who prayed and those who fought, over those who worked, placing men in the service of God, the priests, at the summit of the human order.

Christianity, unlike religion in ancient Assur, was not the *direct* framework for the control and exploitation of men and land. In this sense it did not control the reproduction of society as a whole. This took the form of an immense hierarchy of personal relations of dependence which subordinated lords to each other and peasants to lords; the substructure, the matrix of this hierarchy was the seigneury or lordship in all its forms, domestic, landholding, or banal. It was within this framework and on this basis that the lords spiritual and temporal were able to pre-empt from the work of their peasants the means of glorifying God, of making war, and of glorifying themselves. Such was the dominant institution in feudal relations and it was born before even the peasants and barbarians had been completely evangelized, before Europe had become Christendom. It was the fruit of the efforts of a warrior aristocracy slowly organizing the different forms of its domination following the close of the age of the great invasions, at the end of the sixth century AD; this lay aristocracy was to remain the dominant element in the new dominant class. In our opinion, it is in relation to the growing dominance of this institution that we ought to seek to measure and explain the growing dominance of christianity in people's minds and in society, and not the reverse. I shall go no further in this attempt to analyse this case of dominance, as it is rather more difficult to determine; I prefer to return to our initial examples, since they are clearer, and I shall attempt to clear things up a little. How are we to account for the dominance either of kinship, politics or religion, and how are we to explain changes in dominance over the course of time?

We can reject the argument which 'explains' first of all that social relations dominate a society's functioning because they fulfil several functions, and which then goes on to explain that they assume several functions because they dominate society's functioning. This is a strange, tautological argument.

A lot more interesting is the argument which some put forward, *starting from the mind* and from the ideas capable of dominating it in order to account for the dominance of social relations founded upon kinship, or religion, etc., in the functioning of certain societies. It should be pointed out here that we are not concerned with ideas which dominate a society's thinking for a while and then 'go out of fashion'. What concerns us are ideas that seem in some way to be 'embodied' in lasting social structures or whose appearance seems to entail a deep, lasting alteration in the social relations existing between men and with nature.

Yet it is easy to show that one cannot take ideas alone as one's starting point in order to explain the content and the relative strength of ideas. Unless one assumes that ideas arise *completely* arbitrarily in thought or, what comes down to the same thing, are introduced into thought from the outside (i.e. by forces external to man and for reasons specific to these forces), unless, again, one assumes that the *whole* force of an idea depends purely upon the fact that the majority if not all members of a society in which it dominates *believe* it to be 'true', then *one element among the reasons* for its content and its power to dominate exists *independently of thought* and in the very nature of the social relations existing among men and between men and nature. For saying that an idea is 'true' means saying that this idea has the capacity to 'explain' the order or the disorder reigning in society and in the cosmos, and it entails claiming that this 'explanation' allows us to 'act' effectively upon the problems connected with the maintenance of this order or with the abolition of this disorder. 'Proofs' of the veracity of an idea can never be reduced merely to a question of thought or to an effect of thought. This idea has to 'correspond' to something outside of or beyond thought in social and/or cosmic reality. Ideas never in themselves contain all the reasons accounting for their influence and their historic role. Thought alone can never produce these reasons, for this influence never comes from ideas on what they *are* but from ideas on what they *do*, or better still, on what *they get done* in society and on society or on the world outside it.

This is why any analysis that begins by isolating thought from the other components of social reality (the ideël from the non-ideël) and then attempts to deduce the latter from the former (the idealist approach), or the former from the latter (the vulgar materialist approach) will, by virtue of its underlying principle, inevitably box itself into a corner. Of course, one may set out from thought alone in order to analyse the dominance of social relations (just as one may set out from the material aspects of these social relations alone), but one ought not to do so since, if ideas dominate as much because of what they *do* and *get done* as because of what they are, then the causal relation which emerges is one of *a hierarchy of functions* existing *simultaneously* and *mutually self-assuming* rather than a relation founded on linear causality and on a logical and chronological priority between a cause and effects that are external to it. But saying that there is a functional relationship between an idea and its dominance is not just saying that the reason why kinship relations and ideology dominate inside many primitive and peasant societies is because problems of consanguinity and alliance arise more frequently than elsewhere; or that the reason why political relations and ideas dominated in Athens was because problems of personal status and of power arose more than elsewhere. One would still have to explain what it was, in each case, that made these particular problems more important than elsewhere.

To return now to our three examples, in these three societies, kinship governs descent and alliances as it does in all societies; and yet it does not dominate in all of them. Wherever one looks, religion organizes relations with the supernatural, and yet it is not dominant in all societies. We may therefore logically and legitimately put forward the idea that the explicit, universal functions of kinship, namely the social regulation of the reproduction of life via the regulation of marriage and descent, *do not suffice* to *explain its dominance* in cases where it does so. We may say the same for politics or for religion where they dominate the thought and the functioning of a society. We thus need something more, a function which *is not present in all cases* of functioning of kinship, politics or religion, but which *is present in each case* where these social relations and the corresponding ideas *dominate* the functioning of society.

We know what this function is: in each case, the *dominant relations function simultaneously as social relations of production*, as the economic structure of society, and as a framework for the material appropriation of nature. I thus propose to render this observation more general by offering the following hypothesis:

for a social activity - and with it the ideas and institutions that correspond to it and organize it - *to play a dominant role in the functioning and evolution of a society* (and hence in the thought and actions of the individuals and groups who go to make up this society), it is not enough for it to fulfil several functions, *it must necessarily directly fulfil*, in addition to its explicit ends and functions, *the function of a relation of production*.

Of course, it takes more than three cases to verify a hypothesis, on top of which, one needs to be sure that these three cases do in fact verify it. Let us take it as it is for the time being and now turn straight away to the theoretical consequences which it entails.

1 This hypothesis says nothing as to the *nature* of the social relations *that may function as* relations of production. It contains no prior judgment, whether ethnocentric or otherwise, as to what the economic 'ought' to be.

2 This hypothesis says nothing as to the *specific reasons and conditions* which cause relations of production to shift in locus and form in the course of history. It merely contains a *general indication* to the effect that there is a close relationship between these changes in the place and form of relations of production and existing material conditions. *There is a relationship between the topology and morphology of relations of production and the level of productive forces.*

3 This hypothesis tells us something about the reasons accounting for the relative influence and the unequal importance of social relations in the functioning and reproduction of societies, and this influence depends less upon what they are than upon what they do. It comes down to saying that of all the social relations that go to make up a society those which, among other functions, determine access to resources and to the means of production and which constitute the social form of appropriation of nature have greater influence than others upon the functioning, and the transformations of that society. It thus assumes the *universal existence of a hierarchy among the functions that have to be fulfilled by social relations in order for a society to exist as such and to reproduce itself.* The role of a given social relation is more or less determinant depending upon the functions it fulfils, and the relations that are 'determinant in the last instance' are always those that function as relations of production; the fact that they function as relations of production means that they dominate the reproduction of society; dominating society in association with them are the representations which organize them and express them.

This brings us to Marx's hypothesis concerning the role of economic structures and of the material conditions of history, which he regarded as 'determinant in the last instance'. It is clear, for me, that this notion of 'instance causality' has nothing to do with a hierarchy of 'levels' or 'instances', nor even of 'institutions' which would somehow be the same everywhere; what it refers to is the existence of a hierarchy of functions which in all cases lends greater 'influence' to those social relations that are relations of production.

It thus becomes impossible to attempt to counter Marx with the fact of the dominance of kinship (Radcliffe-Brown), of politics (Ed Will) or of religion (L. Dumont), since each of these examples serves to confirm his hypothesis, it being a hypothesis designed to enable us to carry on searching and not a law from which facts or reality could be 'deduced' mechanistically.

I am perfectly aware, moreover, that my approach to Marx is not the one normally encountered among Marxists, even among the most sophisticated ones, such as Althusser. Normally, they represent relations of production in terms of the way in which they exist in our own capitalist mode of production, *isolated* from kinship, religion, politics, and they ethnocentrically project this form onto all societies. They are led to conceive of last-resort causality first and foremost as a twin action of the infrastructure *upon* superstructures, and of *selection* of one of the superstructures which is then *elevated* to a dominant position (Balibar, Terray). But this assumes that relations of production and superstructures are always distinct institutions and it takes our own society, which is an exception, to be the rule.

But it was this exception which, for the first time, enabled humanity to perceive more clearly the role of economics and the material conditions of production (nature and the effectiveness of productive forces) upon the evolution of society, and of history. This was Marx's real 'epistemological break' and, beyond him, it lay in the new and unique character of the capitalist mode of production which enabled people to see other forces in history than those that had been apparent and evident to the actors in this history themselves up until that time. In any case, it is better to say that one sees these evident forces differently than to say one sees something other than these apparent forces. For, in antiquity, there was no 'class' hiding *behind the visible 'orders'* among which the population of Athens was distributed - the manner of this distribution being comprehensible to all - citizens, aliens, slaves, freed men, etc. A 'class' that managed to remain concealed not only from the Greeks themselves but also from all non-Marxist historians would in any case be something of a paradox. The problem is one of *interpretation* of social reality, of its intimate *order*, of its conditions of emergence and disappearance.

Is this to say that people's own interpretations of the reasons for the dominance of politics in their society and for the dominance of certain citizens over the rest of society were mere illusion, that the Greeks were living in an imaginary relationship with themselves? But illusion for whom? For the Greeks or for us? And how would this illusion have arisen? Because *someone* deceived them, because they deceived themselves, or because they *wanted* to deceive others? All these are the kind of questions that usually crop up as soon as one attempts to distinguish 'ideological' ideas from those that are not. Does the fact of having acquired a different vision of the reasons for the dominance of superstructures and of the ideas that organize them help us to see things any more clearly?

THE IDEËL ELEMENT OF (SOCIAL) REALITY AND THE DISTINCTION BETWEEN THE IDEOLOGICAL AND THE NON-IDEOLOGICAL

In analysing the most 'material' aspect of social realities - the forces of production available to a society for the purpose of acting upon the surrounding nature - we observed that these contained two intimately interwoven components: a material element (implements, man himself...) and an ideël element (representations of nature, rules governing manufacturing and the use of tools, etc.). These representations are indispensable in the utilization of these material means. And this utilization takes the form of connecting sequences of action constituting what we call the 'labour process'.

We have also seen, in the case of Hesiod, that a labour process often involves symbolic acts through which one acts not upon visible nature, as with implements, but on the invisible forces which control the reproduction of nature and which are thought to be capable of granting or refusing man his wishes: a good harvest, good hunting, etc. This symbolic element in the labour process constitutes a *social* reality that is every bit *as real* as material actions upon nature; but its end, its reasons for being and its internal organization constitute a set of ideël realities arising from thought that interprets the hidden order of the world and organizes action in the direction of the forces controlling it. The accomplishment of these rituals often involves material means (sacred objects, clay for body-painting, etc.), but these have no meaning or effectiveness other than within the system of interpretation of the social order which selects them.

Next, when we analysed the significance of the absence of a term to designate 'labour' in ancient Greece and the representations connected with the practice of agriculture, handicrafts and commerce in ancient Athens, we saw the emergence of another type of ideël reality: representations which *attach a positive or a negative value* to an individual or group depending upon the material and/or symbolic task which it accomplishes, *conferring upon it a status* within the social hierarchy. And these representations only have meaning within a system of representations that *defines and legitimizes* a certain distribution of all those tasks essential to the reproduction of a society among the individuals and groups making up that society (men/women, elders/younger people, masters/slaves, aristocrats/commoners, priests/laymen, etc.). This value system is an effect of the relations of production within the 'division of labour'. Finally, in analysing the example of the Australian aborigines, we saw that their kinship relations were at the same time relations of production, and we detected a series of rules covering the 'abstract' appropriation of nature, these rules being transmitted from generation to generation through relations of consanguinity. These ideël realities here *defined and legitimized* individuals' and groups' concrete access to the material resources and the supernatural realities composing their territory.

We could go on with this analysis, but we would just go on observing the emergence - in the midst of the manifold facets of social life - of ideël realities *that are distinguishable through the functions they fulfil.* And these ideal realities appear not as the effects of social relations in thought, but as one of their necessary internal components and as a condition just as much of their formation as of their reproduction. Whichever kinship system we choose to look at, we immediately find that it can *neither exist nor reproduce itself* without manipulating ideël realities that are well-known to anthropologists, such as rules of consanguinity, of alliance, residence, the terminology of kinship, a body of principles defining and legitimizing the personal rights and duties attaching to these relations and delimiting what is meant socially by the term 'relative' as opposed to non-relatives, friends or enemies, foreigners, etc. Far from suggesting that kinship relations exist independently of these ideël realities, they constantly presuppose them. Of course, kinship relations cannot be reduced to this ideël element since they are also a series of personal relations of dependence or obligation - whether material or not, reciprocal or non-reciprocal. They are not only what they are in thought - ideëlly - but also what they get done concretely.

This is even more visible in the case of religious activities. The fact that the Pharaoh was regarded as a God reigning among humans, that he was lord of the earth and of the lives of his subjects, temporary incarnation and permanent resurrection of Horus, son of Osiris, all these were ideël realities, representations which both *legitimized* his power and served as principles underlying the *organization* of the realm, dividing up tasks and material and spiritual obligations, getting the peasants to work for the glory of the gods, of the Pharaoh and of all those who received power and wealth from him.

In short, there is an element of ideël everywhere, which does not mean that everything in (social) reality is ideël. Ideas are not an 'instance' isolated from social relations, re-presenting them, after-the-event as it were, *in* consciousness, *to* thought. The ideël then is thought in all its functions, present and at work in all of man's activities, capable of existing only in society, as society. The ideël cannot be opposed to the material, for thinking involves setting matter in motion: the brain. An idea is an impalpable reality, a reality that is not immediately sensible. The ideël, then, *is* what thought *does*, and its diversity and its complexity corresponds to the distinction and the complexity of the functions of thought. These functions have just been demonstrated in the case of labour, kinship and religion.

Which are they?
Representations:
1 they *make* 'realities' external or internal to man - including thought itself - *present* in thought. These 'realities' may be material and/or intellectual, visible and/or invisible, concrete and/or imaginary, etc.
2 But 'representing' a 'reality' *to* the mind always involves the mind in *interpreting* this reality. Interpreting means explaining, *defining the nature, the origin and the functioning* of a 'reality' that is present in the mind. There can be no such thing as a representation that is not at the same time an interpretation and that does not at the same time assume the existence of a *system* of representations, i.e. of a body of representations governed by a specific logic and coherence, whichever these may be. These interpretations have no existence other than through and in the mind. The moment they represent an invisible world or law, this invisible world starts to exist socially, even if it corresponds to *nothing* existing in represented reality.
3 On the basis of these representations-interpretations, the mind then *organizes* relations among men and between men and nature. Representations serve both as an internal framework and as an abstract end. They then exist in the form of rules of conduct, principles of action, things permitted or things prohibited, etc.
4 Finally, representations of 'reality' are interpretations which either legitimize or illegitimize relations between men and between men and nature (see Table 2.1).

These, in my view, are the four main functions of thought. It is these which, whether distinctly or interwoven, are assumed by the various types of 'ideël' (= 'ideëlities') dealt with in my examples. These functions are present in differing degrees in all social activities, and they combine with other functions of social relations that cannot be reduced to the ideël: producing and controlling the material means of existence, ensuring the unity and permanence of human groups in spite of and through the inevitable contradictions (of interest, of power) that arise, acting upon the visible and the invisible order of the world, and so on. These functions cannot be carried out without thought, but are not reducible to thought-acts, nor can thought deduce them of its own accord. They are not born of thought alone: their roots strike more fundamentally in the fact that we are a social species *capable* of acting upon its social and material conditions of existence for the purpose of transforming them. Consequently, man is the heir to nature's pre-human evolution. Thought *exercises* the possibilities of the brain, but it does not *create* them.

However, interpreting, organizing, and legitimizing are all different ways of *producing meaning*. All the functions of thought flow together in this result: producing meaning and, on the basis of meanings produced, organizing and reorganizing mutual relations between men and between men and nature.

Table 2.1

The functions of thought and of the 'ideël' realities 'produced' by thought.

'to present' any kind of reality, including thought, to the mind. F1	*to interpret* what is presented, i.e. to define its nature, origin and functionning. F2	*to organize*, on the basis of this interpretation, relations between men, and between men and nature. F3	*to legitimize* or illegitimize the existing social and/or cosmic order. F4

But at the same time, nature and man - as a being capable of living *in* society and of *producing society* - are realities which *precede* the meaning that thought is capable of giving to them *and which do not depend upon this meaning for their existence.*

This analysis now enables us to distinguish from among ideël realities those that are ideological and those that are not. Is there a 'formal' or 'functional' criterion capable of enabling us to distinguish the one from the other? Not if we confine ourselves to labelling 'ideological' just any *system* of representations simply because it contains a principle of organization, however vague. Is it conceivable that there could be representations having no links with any other - if only to oppose it - living in a 'free' state, like particles wandering in the interstellar void?

We need a rather more restrictive definition of ideology, and the most usual one seems to be a sort of 'Marxist' definition of ideology, which we shall state briefly as follows: ideological refers to those 'illusory' representations which men have of themselves and of the 'world' which serve to legitimize an existing social order born independently of them, thus leading to the acceptance of the forms of domination and of oppression of man by man which this order contains and upon which it is founded.

What happens to this definition when we match it against our analysis of the four functions of thought and against the fact that all social relations contain an ideël element which organizes it from the inside, and which is one of the very conditions of its formation? Are we to consider representations that 'legitimize' the social order as ideological (F1 + F2 + F4) and those that 'organize' it as non-ideological (F1 + F2 + F3)? In addition, though, we are going to have to bear in mind the fact that legitimization is based on 'illusory' interpretations. In F2, therefore, we shall have to distinguish illusory interpretations ($F2^{i}$) from non-illusory interpretations ($F2^{non-i}$).

The complete formula is shown in Table 2.2.

Table 2.2

non-ideological ideël	ideological ideël
$F1 + F2^{non-i} + F3$	$F1 + F2^{i} + F4$

Seen thus, religious representations to some extent become the 'paradigm' for all the illusory representations man has developed, develops and will develop concerning himself and the world - differing on each occasion - in which he lives. Let us take a closer look at all these points.

First, obviously, not all the representations man has evolved concerning himself and the world, when fishing, hunting, farming, etc., and which help him to organize these activities, are illusory. They contain an immense treasure-trove of supposedly and genuinely true knowledge constituting a veritable 'science of the concrete world', as Lévi-Strauss puts it when speaking of the 'savage' mind. But for whom, then, is what is illusory in them illusory? Not for those who believe in it, but for all those who either do not or no longer believe in it. Hence, they are illusory for others, for ourselves, for example, we who are capable of countering them with other representations of the world that strike us as better verified, more true, if not as the only true one. By definition, a myth is only a 'myth' for those who do not believe in it, and the first to believe in it are those who 'invent' them, in other words who think them out and formulate them as fundamental 'truths' which they imagine to have been inspired in them by supernatural beings such as gods, ancestors, etc. So, it is only to others that ideological representations appear as *such*, i.e. as mistaken interpretations that are not recognized as such. We may thus straight away turn down the narrow eighteenth-century notion that religion was just a pack of lies invented by the priests - who never believed a word of it - in order to deceive the good, ignorant people and bend it to their domination (cf. Condorcet).

Not that I would deny that there have been, and shall be in the future, a good many priests or 'ideologists' who do not believe or who have ceased to believe in the ideas they profess, nor shall I deny that lies have always been one of the means employed by the dominant in order to preserve their domination. And, in addition to declared lies, there are also lies by omission, silences, bits left out, deliberately or otherwise, of discourse, all of these being highly revealing. The problem then is not merely to account for the fact that foreign observers of a society, whether contemporary or not, may not share the beliefs held to be true by that society and consider them to be false, but how to account for the fact that in a given society and at a given moment in time ideas held to be true by the majority of this society's members can come to be considered as false by various minorities. Where do these contradictions spring from, can they be reduced to opposing views on the same things, or do they express opposing interests, contradictions that break beyond the bounds of thought and lie within the functioning itself of social relations among men in this society, and with the nature surrounding them? In Athens, Aristotle was certainly expressing the dominant opinion when he stated that barbarians were 'naturally' born to 'be slaves', but he was opposed on this by certain Sophists such as Antiphon, who declared that men were all identical by nature and in all things, and that one was not destined to be either free man or slave at birth. This critique of slavery then did not boil down to a difference of ideas. Its foundations lay in the very contradictions in the slave relations of production, despite the fact that never in antiquity did the vast majority of free men imagine seriously for a moment that their society could exist without slavery.

We thus come back to the conclusions reached in our analysis of the foundations of the dominance of social relations. No single formal criterion can *suffice* to distinguish ideological ideas from those that are not, and the fact that certain ideas seem 'truer' than others in a given society stems not only from their abstract veracity but also from their *relationship* with the various *social activities*, which are hierarchized according to the nature of their *functions*, in the forefront of which stands the function of relation of production. And this relation is such that these ideas seem to be even truer inasmuch as they appear to 'legitimize' existing social relations and the inequalities they contain, in other words, inasmuch as they express and defend the ruling order in society. Is this the ultimate criterion distinguishing ideological ideas from those that are not? Are ideas that 'legitimize' the existing social order ideological because of this very function? Once again, unfortunately, this is a biased and a partial approach to the question, for it entails concentrating upon those representations which legitimize an existing social order while forgetting all those which regard this order as illegitimate and which either legitimate a return to an older order now no longer existing or else the advent of a future order not yet in existence. It also means forgetting all those Utopias which, right from the outset, are thought of as 'realities that have never existed and that will never exist anywhere (U-topia), but which make it possible to raise up a "principle of hope" against the existing order' (Ernst Bloch, *The Principle of Hope*). Here again, what distinguishes these representations is not only that the content of the ideas is different, but also entails a different relationship with the existing social order, *a relationship that is born of contradictions entailed* by the functioning of this order.

Consequently, when we look at ideologies in all their diversity, we cannot possibly say that they are nothing but *illusions* developed *after the event, as it were, in order to legitimize* concrete social relations supposed to have come into existence *prior to* and *independently of* them. It is when they do not appear to the exploited as illusions or as instruments of their exploitations that they contribute effectively to persuading these people to accept their exploitation. So, ideas have to be considered fundamentally 'true' by the majority of a society's members, by both dominant as well as dominated groups, in order for them to become dominant themselves.

3 THE HISTORIOGRAPHY OF EVERYDAY LIFE: THE PERSONAL AND THE POLITICAL

Alf Lüdtke*

I

For some time, the history of 'everyday life' has attracted wide attention in Germany, both from professional historians and from the public at large. Family life in feudal or bourgeois societies, the history of sickness or of death and the transformation of eating habits have been accepted by the history industry, and are increasingly regarded as 'relevant'. Outside the 'profession' the new interest is nourished by books, films and exhibitions.

The evidence from projects in schools shows that it is the active investigation of the realities of everyday life, past as much as present, which is crucial; for it is this which allows participants to imagine and work out such realities for themselves. Active participation in the investigation of the everyday life of the past creates the most effective barrier against the uncritical consumption of pre-fabricated interpretations. It sets up a creative dialectic between the familiar and the strange, between one's own experience and that of the other; discovery of oneself and of others are thus both means and ends of study. Thus 'learning by research' is a very pertinent formula, at least for teaching. Here, a remarkable initiative was the 'President of the Republic's prize for German history in schools'. The dry, official name should not fool us: the competition,

*Alf Lüdtke is at the Max Planck Institute, Göttingen, researching on the police in nineteenth-century Prussia.

along with the 1974-6 programme entitled 'Movements for Freedom' (in one's locality) which was sponsored by the then President, Gustav W. Heinemann, touched and sometimes offended the sensibilities and prejudices of pupils, teachers and parents. From 1977 the general heading became the 'Social History of Everyday Life': pupils studied work-processes, relations in the home and leisure. In 1980 the organisers sought, for the first time, to join 'everyday life' to politics in the traditional sense; the theme was provocative: 'Daily life under the National Socialists'. A press and letter campaign instigated by the *Frankfurter Allgemeine Zeitung* rapidly broadcast the various work-projects and objectives far beyond the classroom and incited a predictable controversy: might not the grandchildren question their grandparents with undue energy? Might not their insistence cause much distress? Was not, moreover, a critical confrontation the only possible object of such an exercise?

My own observations, as member of a regional jury, make me rather sceptical on these points. From much of the work, it seemed as if 'Daily life under the National Socialists' had little to do with the politics of the Nazis. One of the exercises in the competition was to conduct interviews with contemporaries. Thirteen-, fourteen- and also eighteen-year-olds asked grandparents, great-uncles and aunts, 'what was it like, then?' - for them personally, at their place of work, in the neighbourhood or in the local community. The questions 'Why?' and 'To what purpose?' were all too frequently not asked. Should we then conclude that 'everyday life' is the agency of de-politicisation?

The problem does not only arise in this context: I have had to face this same question in my own investigations of the everyday life of workers. Its force, however, will perhaps be especially clear in the case of daily life under fascism. Therefore, an example from this area may be useful.

II

In the most recent schools' competition, one of the tutors, a seasoned local historian, together with his group of schoolchildren chose the Nazi District Authorities in Göttingen. Without doubt, this was an excellent idea: by concentrating on a single, local case it might be possible to make the system of domination under German fascism palpable. And, no less important, many of the one-time members of this particular party office could be found and were even willing to be interviewed, itself, an unusual situation. The outcome was a number of long, thoroughly professional reports of interviews. Together with extensively documented abstracts from official files, they give a panorama of everyday life in a Nazi District Office during the 1930s. But what is the significance of these results? What is revealed of the practitioners of a terrorist domination? The daily office-life of the employees appears hardly to have distinguished itself from that of the neighbouring revenue office - it certainly did not in those employees' memories. Here as there it was difficult to stick to the work itself: people offered information about the morning coffee-break and what filling the rolls used to have; it was recalled who normally had to open which post and who else was sometimes allowed to; and of some importance was whether the section manager was friendly or distant and awkward, and also how the office outing went. And this went not only for the secretaries, but also, for example, for the head of the personnel department. Was there any contact with the SS and the Gestapo? 'Well, perhaps..., no, probably..., but only occasionally.' Were hints ever given that certain unco-operative persons should be observed and checked up on by the police? No, it had not come to their notice, and anyway the SS had always acted independently.

Such answers do not reveal simply bad consciences or poor memories. In fact, the preoccupations recorded have the ring of truth. The National Socialist system of 'authoritarian anarchy' or 'polycratic' domination was characterised by bitter struggles for power and prestige both within each party agency and between party authorities and the SS. Such contests were often the motive of much activity. This can be verified from other sources. Research on the political system and of the 'logic' of fascist domination have confirmed this fundamental pattern.

If, however, it always remains necessary to draw upon conventional, historical research then one's misgivings about the significance of even meticulous accounts of everyday life can only be strengthened. At least three objections will be considered here. These, moreover, complement one another and guide us to a more fundamental criticism.

Our first concern is that the primary or even exclusive attention to detail may be motivated purely by antiquarianism. In what way, we must ask in the above case, do the details of office organisation enable us to analyse fascist terror and domination in a more appropriate manner? Secondly, the central aim of reconstructing the 'inner perspective' of those very people involved must ignore the social processes which take place behind their backs. Surely the result of this is a neo-historicism which is no longer, sure, or insufficiently so, of what its aims are and what conclusions it hopes to come to. And in the case of the recalling of office monotony, where the quite unspectacular opening and writing of letters could only occasionally offer anything of any excitement, does not such a method already excuse the participants and thereby neglect the task of historical and moral evaluation?

The third objection concerns the endlessness of the task. We may take 'everyday life' to mean something more than merely the 'sameness' of each passing day, and suppose it to include the 'production and reproduction of daily life' in all its fullness. But this denies us all rigorous thematic boundaries and banishes all analytical guidelines. There is a danger of sinking into an endless mire of stories and dates, which cannot be simply dismissed. As an example of this, the bulky dossiers, such as those brimming with the local and regional research of the french *Annales* school, are a doubtful example if not a deterrent. In order to know our everyday office life, must we not investigate every possible department at all levels? To complete the description it would presumably be necessary to record the daily life of the neighbouring revenue office and other local and regional agencies, nor could businesses, private households, youth groups or schoolclasses be excluded. In short, 'everyday life' comes to imply the whole totality of social relations in all their many facets.

The central criticism boils down to the view that an interest in 'everyday life' and its 'reality' serves only to over-emphasise details of secondary importance. What, in fact, have daily cups of coffee or the success of the office outing in a district office to do, for example, with the National Socialist Jewish policy in Germany as a whole, or even, for that matter, in Göttingen? Are we perhaps being informed only of *apolitical* or even *sub-political* forms of behaviour? From this it would follow that 'privatisation' is the only factor common to all these everyday activities of office and elsewhere.

III

At this point, it seems to me necessary to insert a remark about the purpose of the example just given. The intention is not to elaborate upon the state of research into German fascism; in particular, we are not concerned with strategies for the investigation of the acceptance of authoritarian domination before 1933 by broad sectors of those dominated, nor that of fascist domination after 1933.

My quite different intention is to discuss the difficulties that arise from attempts to capture the 'inner perspective' of full-bodied social structures or of long-term changes. My question is about the usefulness or redundancy, or even danger, of the interest in 'everyday life'. The problem is familiar to me not only through the school competitions but also and primarily in my own research into the conditions and experiences of first- or second-generation industrial workers in the latter half of the nineteenth century. Is not their behaviour often one of dumb 'accommodation', to use P.N. Stearn's expression, and mere political apathy?

The uses and disadvantages of the history of everyday life have fuelled professional debates about the concepts and development of the discipline. The doubts raised here are more often matters of principle than any result of personal experience of this kind of project. The advantage of such debates is that they are free of the need to defend investments of work and effort. Thus, Hans-Ulrich Wehler, one of the initiators and spokesmen of 'historical social-science', in his contribution to a German survey of contemporary thought, remarks curtly that the concept of everyday life is extremely 'woolly!' As a remedy, he recommends intensive study of the 'history of families, towns, education, women and sport'. Presumably Wehler is alluding to the already mentioned multiplication of topics; in any case, it is clear that for him such topics are 'second-order questions'.

Everyday life is only of marginal interest even to those historians who are by no means committed to the conventional histories of state and politics. It is Wehler and his colleagues who call for a 'historical social science', a 'synthetic ... history of society'. As ever, a decidedly 'critical' intention is declared, and, at least in 1969, 'the enlightenment of political practice' was explicitly accepted as the aim of historical study. If, however, one inquires what is meant by a 'synthetic history of society' it transpires that society is, despite the demand for synthesis, parcelled off into the 'dimensions' of 'economy, authority and culture'. According to this view, everyday life is almost necessarily marked by its distance from the forces and battlefields of the historical process; everyday life comes to signify merely the 'private' sphere.

There certainly are studies which seem to accept this view. These, it is true, are frequently of the kind characterised by rigorous quantification. The investigation of secular changes in birth and death rates and of rates of migration between old and new towns is clearly necessary; but often such projects remain isolated and abstract: the question 'for whom' is at best implicit and otherwise unasked. Of course, the 'production and reproduction of real life' cannot be comprehended without thoroughly exact figures on, for example, productivity, trade cycles, real wages, subsistence wages, the consumption of beer and potatoes and differential mortality. All these, however, only become meaningful together with a qualitative account of the various modes of production and of the nature of the social relations of production.

The history of everyday life is less concerned with the classic debates on the above themes. Its special feature is its attempt to expose the contradictions and discontinuities of both the modes and relations of production, in the context of the lifestyle of those affected; to make these evident and to explain them.

The general transition to wage labour and the 'silent compulsion' exerted by the production of commodities and by the cash nexus in the agricultural and industrial regions of Germany from the late eighteenth to the late nineteenth centuries was indeed a transformation of economic structure; and it is appropriately designated as 'commercialisation' and as the 'development of capitalism'. This obviously encompasses those quite specific interests of the afflicted that could be articulated in public protests or strikes. But were there not other interests? What of the demands that as yet found no common or public expression: the sufferings and joys, the fears and hopes of the economically and politically dependent? Were the impositions of authorities no more than a fabric of organisation and norms - both in the case of direct attacks, such as the brutal paternalism manifested in the treatment of servants, and in the case of a mixture of physical and non-physical force, such as that exerted by the police, the military and schools? These silent struggles were just as crucial as those observed in direct protest. A mode of life, therefore, is in no way a sharply delineated 'superstructure'. For all the very different groups of the wage-dependent and the subjugated, work organisation or authoritarian violence is present only in the form in which it is perceived, expressed or suppressed or even rejected and transformed in their own social practice. Manorial servants, factory workers in machine-building factories (such as those with Krupp or Gute-Hoffnungs-Hütte in the second half of the nineteenth century) and even the office workers in the above-mentioned district office all interpreted the forces they faced according to their own social experience. The only 'objective' existence of work-time regulations was quite literally on paper. It was, in every case, only the attention and the action of those involved that made them real. Work-time regulation was, in addition, always a process of conflict between one's own needs, those of one's colleagues and, of course, the lenient suspicion of the supervisor. For the historian, this will often be reduced to a single result and the subjective significances vanish. In the end, the 'synthesis' turns out to be nothing more than *either* a submission to *or* an evasion of the relevant pressures; at the most it is also 'insubordination' and maybe even 'resistance'.

In a more theoretical language we might say that 'social reproduction' is made possible by the *mutual* production of 'objective' and 'subjective' components. This demands a point of view that considers neither 'meaning' as against 'socio-economic position' nor vice versa. Only thus are the contradictions of society released and therewith the disposition and opportunities for alternative projects - for the overturning of society. The many implications of forms of authority and communication, especially their multiple interconnections, are only visible if they are not reduced to their final resultant. Only with this approach can 'tangential' Utopias be anything more than disreputable surface phenomena, predestined to be crushed by the mainstream of history. The analysis of historical and social interaction into single compartments - as, for instance, in the program outlined by Wehler - fails to do justice to the complexity of particular situations; it conceals the *concurrence* of submission, distance and insubordination. If one clings to the proven guidelines, as laid down by the latest historical offering, then the dynamics of history is lost.

IV

The fundamental question at issue in the debate about the importance of everyday life concerns the historian's criteria for singling out certain phenomena only as political.

According to one view, the 'political' has to do with 'official reality' and the more public arenas. Something will be dubbed 'political' if it impinges upon the ruling norms or the official definitions, either to use them to buttress domination or to repudiate it. Any other forms of expression or kinds of statement are taken to be 'private'. From this it follows, in the first place, that the nature of everyday modes of behaviour should be examined in its real context. Had, perhaps, the office coffee-break in the Göttingen district office anything to do with the unsuccessful attempt of an assistant in the criminal department (documented in the files) to have a 'Jewish home', emptied by the 'Final Solution' of 1942, allocated to himself? The data cannot tell us. Did the evidently fairly informal manner of address in the district office disturb the party chiefs, who were active Nazis? But perhaps the resemblance to a state or private office was taken as a sign of the much desired *Volksgemeinschaft*? There are no answers to these questions. Nevertheless, the drawing of simple or sweeping boundaries is evidently no solution.

Another common approach is to associate 'political' with the long-term pursuit of interests through a collective organisation, e.g. in a 'political' party. This view cuts the knot of conceptual and methodological difficulties. In practice, it leads to no more than that 'synthetic' approach which merely adopts the perspective of the 'victor' (W. Benjamin). In this situation there is good reason to take individualistic and especially 'affective' expressions of interests as being, for those affected, very much 'political' expressions. Certainly this makes it easier to recognise concealed ways in which demands are raised and pursued.

It is important to include within 'the political' more than simply strategically calculated action. If we do not, we divide the totality of emotional expressions and symbolic meanings; we ignore the fact that it is these which transform 'ideal types' into (inconsistently) acting individuals and groups. It is a fair assumption that the supposedly resigned or apathetic who do not participate in collective action or organisation have their own quieter - and for them equally effective - ways of satisfying their needs, stilling their hopes and longings and avoiding or compensating for their fears. In the case of factory workers in nineteenth-century Germany, one example would be sexual 'licentiousness'. Another would be the presence of family members at the midday break. In each case power relations are involved.

If one attempts in this fashion to take account of the motives and stimuli of all those involved, quite new cases spring up. This I hope to make clear with the help of the results of my own research into work-breaks in factories in the late nineteenth century. I was concerned with the conflicts around work-time, and around the management and control of time. The problem was not the 'classic' theme of the eight-hour day, but one of everyday life in the factory.

It is generally taken as self-evident that factory work requires a mechanical time discipline and, indeed, did in fact bring one with it. Such was also the opinion of the factory masters and their economists. However, in the work processes themselves such a mechanical imposition is not to be found. And this is true not only of the initial introductory phase. For factory masters and supervisors time discipline had a clear purpose: to establish the uniform pace of the machines. Only thus could these be made to yield profits. Accordingly, it was necessary that during work-time the work-force was directed exclusively to the production of commodities and not to the creation of use value.

The efforts of the factory supervisors were guided by the following thought: non-work was pleasurable to the workers but profitless 'expenditure' to themselves and should be separated from work with the aid of rigorous time regulations; during work-time and at the work-place it must be suppressed. Consequently, factory production must necessarily control the whole daily activity of the workers.

The expectations and demands of the factory chiefs were mirrored in the factory regulations. If one follows their development over a number of decades, at, for example, Gute-Hoffnungs-Hütte (GHH) in Oberhausen and Sterkrade or at the Gusstanl-fabrik Friedrich Krupp in Essen, one observes how each of the numerous revised versions was more voluminous than its predecessors. Regulations stipulated not only the time but also the details of when and how work should begin. At GHH, according to the regulations of September 1870, 'By the time the bell (or alternatively the clock tower) has ceased to ring every worker should be at his place and should begin his work.' But the actual daily practice prompted the following, typical complaint from a factory supervisor: 'We have discovered that the commencement of work will often be delayed for several minutes, even the steam machines will not be in motion.' Here, in the reflections of the supervisors, it is clear that the introduction of factory regulations fixed neither the extent nor the content of work-time. For the workers (usually men in these factories) pursued a varying and an evidently almost ceaseless struggle to control the expenditure of their labour power - their social and intellectual as well as their manual capabilities. These battles were extensively concealed and almost always unspectacular.

The factory owners and their directors sought in two ways to prevent workers recovering the control of their own time. They intensified controls and at the same time granted a midday or midnight break (usually of half an hour) and often, for the day shift, a quarter of an hour for breakfast; occasionally there was even another fifteen-minute break in the afternoon. Additionally, many supervisors tolerated or encouraged the taking of 'refreshments' during work - for example, the drinking of tea or mineral water.

The interest of the factory masters was not, therefore, generally to prevent all breaks. They were far more concerned to establish an enforceable minimum of work interruptions which was just sufficient to permit physical reproduction (and daily bodily necessities). It was clear that nobody could survive the workshops or the furnaces without some minimal opportunity for recovery and refreshment. The concessions by the owners and directors were always calculated and prophylactic in intent. Thus, for furnace workers, even strictly forbidden 'pleasures' like beer or schnapps would sometimes be permitted.

Concerning physical recreation, it seems that the workers, largely responded in the way the factory masters had calculated. It is clear, at least from the memories of workers and from 'interviews' with old workers at Krupps (1907-12), that the official breaks were intensively used for physical recovery:

> A great deal of eating went on: a great slab of bread and butter and always something with it, sausage, raw meat, cheese, sometimes boiled eggs and gherkins. The further it got from the last pay day the more cheese there was to have. There would always be something to drink, which, as a consequence of our work [in an engineering works], was just as necessary as good food. Hot or cold coffee or buttermilk were available with equal frequency.

So reported the theologian, Paul Göhre, who in 1890 worked for six weeks in an engineering works in Chemnitz, Saxony as a 'participant observer'. Such pauses were a time of silent communality. The noises of eating were joined only by the rustling of newspapers as they were turned or passed around. Everyone sat beside one another, reports Göhre, 'relaxed and unspeaking'. These official breaks were truly for the purpose of the 'reproduction of labour power', the laborious gathering together of one's powers for the following hours of toil at the drills and milling machines.

There was something quite different during informal breaks: a relaxed and sometimes even merry conversation. Göhre observed 'continual, two-sided intercourse ... between men of the same age, neighbours at work, those from the same sector, the same assembly line and under the same masters'. In these informal and mostly illegal exchanges, it seems, the practices of 'breaking' the work rules were not tamed at all. In many ways workers actively distanced themselves from the demands of work. Here indeed was 'expenditure'. These frequent exchanges, sometimes long, sometimes short, were not always about the necessity of securing one's job, of trying to hold the fluctuating wage rate stable or even of attempting to raise it. They were not always concerned to communicate something: 'Above all one joked, teased and was always keen for a friendly scuffle...each was all heart to his mates: some men embraced each other and rubbed a usually bristled face against their cheeks.' The re-appropriation of time during work was not therefore always an individual refusal, expressed perhaps through 'disappearance'. An essential element was social exchange, playfulness and physical contact at least with one's mates who worked within sight and earshot, with whom one had to co-operate and even fight. Truly, these were little more than moments, even if they were repeated, in which needs could be expressed and satisfied - moments of 'political' action.

The permitted breaks served mainly the function of physical reproduction and so were directly related to the business of physical survival. Even here, though, there were moments of 'mere' togetherness, the beginnings of personal and collective identity. In the illegal breaks such moments became predominant: the capacity for action and the possibilities of expression could be tested and developed; there were further opportunities to be alone and to be with others - to push back the forces of the factory, even while not directly fighting them.

V

Of course, the problems of the politics and the control of time could be pursued further. Changes in the work process would have to be discussed, for example the introduction of rigorous work rhythms and the assembly line, as would the whole process of Taylorisation. But we have enough material to answer the question: What is 'political' in or about the everyday life of workers in the factories? I shall summarise my answer in two points and then comment upon them.

1 According to conventional distinctions, workers *either* pursue, in a strictly 'instrumental' fashion, their own interests, namely their own wages and subsistence, *or* they struggle to transform the relations of production, and only in this latter case do they act 'politically'. This one-dimensional mode of analysis has very little to do with the lives of workers in the process of their daily production and reproduction.

2 The arena of the 'political' cannot be defined in all generality and abstraction, for the political is bound to the everyday realities in the lives of those involved. At least in those more developed capitalist societies one can make out differentiated, though not fully isolated, political arenas. Our present-day hue-and-cry about an intermittent or even long-term 'de-politicisation' of the subordinate classes in capitalist society, over a 'privatisation of politics' testifies only to the relativisation of the arena of central decision-making, of politics at the level of the state. The formula of 'de-politicisation' is only the mirror image of the 'politicisation of the private'.

Comment on 1

A minute investigation of work processes, for example in relation to work-breaks, reveals many kinds of connection between the orientation towards subsistence and the discovery of identity. These work-breaks are themselves part of the experience of self-preservation and at the same time produce such experiences.

A precondition for daily survival was the overcoming of manifold uncertainties, at home and at work. At the work-place one was not only always vulnerable to accidents and in need of protection against decisions 'from above'; dependence on calculations about economic cycle and upon economic change was another central experience. And between these daily and yearly risks, there was the further uncertainty, no less important, shaped by fluctuations in wages. Take-home pay fluctuated fortnightly for individuals, sometimes from between 300 per cent to 400 per cent; wage differentials between workers fluctuated too, sometimes from one pay day to another (see wage lists of the GHH from the early 1870s and autobiographical records from the 1890s). Such fluctuations were only calculable to a very limited extent, for they remained dependent upon levels of production and the delivery of the goods (and thus upon the successes of workers elsewhere).

The resulting logic of survival for the individual and his family economy was, however, bound up with the preservation of personal dignity and social respect. In the everyday politics of the workers, physical survival could not be wholly separated from social prestige, nor could the one be traded off against the other. The ideal of both men and women to become and remain 'respectable' was neither simply the imitation of a petty bourgeois idyll nor distorted 'class-consciousness'. In fact, the ideal was a reflection of the daily uncertainties, anxieties and resignation, but also the the daily successes.

Surviving implied both: physical replenishment *as well as* (re)assurance of personal dignity and communal respect. Thus, endeavours to survive by illegal means, e.g. the common practice of pilfering in the Hamburg docks, were not perceived as disgraceful or non-respectable. And also 'labour aristocrats' (using the term in E.J. Hobsbawm's interpretation) had to rely on a variety of heterogeneous material resources: In 1900 almost 60 per cent of the 'skilled metalworkers' in Chemnitz could not feed a household of two adults and three children (the figures for construction workers and for textile workers were 82 per cent and 85 per cent, respectively). Not only unpaid domestic labour, but women's wage-work and wage-work of children remained a basic economic need for sustaining one's family. The men themselves re-appropriated time, pilfered tools and residues; simultaneously they strived for extra earnings. Göhre reports that one of his fellow-workers did wood cuttings on Sunday mornings and sold them by sending his children to local fairs; somebody else tailored late at night, a driller worked as a coachman on Sunday afternoons, a smith was a waiter almost every night in a workers' pub - and all of them tried to get overtime. But only a few usually got a chance depending upon the masters' mood and interest.

Success in terms of survival, of material and social improvement fostered that demonstrative pride which became visible in encounters with neighbours and workmates but also before, as Marx puts it, 'commissioned and noncommissioned officers' in the workshops or on the streets or in the inns. These *everyday politics* were by no means always a matter of defence. Again and again one can detect a free but persistent purposefulness: whether in the company of colleagues, friends or relations, in groups of people of similar age, in the mens' sports' groups and drinking circles or the womens' gossip parties, there was always the opportunity to be oneself and to speak for oneself. There the attacks and the threats of the powerful were far away and could for a time be forgotten, against all kinds of impositions and in the long term, of social and material ascent. The desired 'decorum' was crystallised into an occasional demonstrative pride, which might be directed against other inhabitants of the house, against workmates and even against their superiors in the work-place or policemen on the streets and at meetings.

In the struggle for physical survival, as in that for one's own 'person' and prestige, successes and failures were bound together, whether in the field of the work-place, within or outside the family. However, in the face of continual risk a sceptical caution was no more than rational, especially with respect to promises and expectations which transcended their immediate experience.

Comment on 2

Does not the importance of everyday politics in the 'production and reproduction of real life' demand that the interdependence of the 'private' and the 'political' should be systematically included in a historical reconstruction? No doubt, but this is no more than a formalistic evasion of the substance of the problem. For in step with the 'politicisation of the private' there was, in imperial Germany after 1871, a society increasingly under the sway of monopolistic capitalism, a persisting separation of the broad and diffuse 'masses' from the politics of the central state, a separation which becomes unmistakable in such spectacular examples as the mass participation of workers, who had previously been ready enough for strikes and other action, in the imperialistic war of 1914-18 or the similar mass acceptance of German fascism in 1933, which accompanied the collapse of communist and even more of social-democratic organisations, the failure and 'betrayal' by party and trade union leaders. Yet perhaps more instructive than the dramatic events of 1914 and 1933 are the less conspicuous details such as those once observed by Karl Korsch. After a journey to England, Korsch, from his youth a socialist and close to the 'youth movement', and later a decidedly Marxist analyst, examined in the newspaper, *Die Tat*, 'the technique of public debate in England'. In this article of March 1913 he reported how, at the political speeches at Hyde Park and elsewhere, there was always a lively to and fro of questions and answers, of assertion and ripost. Korsch then turned to look at the situation in Germany:

> Let us suppose that improvised political speeches in the open air were not forbidden in Germany or that in excited times of excitement they took place despite the ban. Only two outcomes are conceivable: either the mass of the audience are well disciplined (social-democratic workers) in which case the speech must remain a pure monologue, the masses being wholly passive and silent except to give applause; or alternatively, a wild hubbub of speeches and cries, where no one can understand anyone else.

We are not here concerned with the comparison of differently textured national 'political cultures'. Important are, however, Korsch's reflections upon the probable behaviour of the organised and unorganised workers. In the case of organised workers in Germany, the separation of the 'private' from the 'political' or 'public' took the form of frequently expressed, highly stereotyped expectations with regard to the party leaders. For the non-organised, the separation of arenas had a different consequence: their everyday politics always carried with it individual isolation and Korsch claimed that all mutual comprehension was made impossible. Neither group of workers, therefore, was able to bundle together their heterogeneous needs and interests into a common position without coming under an enormous practical pressure that greatly curtailed their powers.

The polarity of 'private' and 'political' in developed, capitalist industrial societies is by no means obsolete. Such an approach will, of course, tend to emphasise the - supposed - function of an event rather than the perspective of those involved. For their experiences and interpretations point not to a separation, but to a connection, an exact concurrence between apparently private 'small happinesses' (especially in the nuclear family) and perspectives that are more global and long-term. Consequently, the fact that the ruled ignored the arena of state and party politics does not prove that they did not, in their own way, perceive and experience it.

Whether the limits of everyday politics (in the work-place or at home) were or were not seen by the many affected must remain an open question. One needs to know which of those implicated in the 'privatisation of politics' were committed to the view that only everyday politics was or could be legitimate. However, 'privatisation' should on no account be assumed to be a compensation for frustrated efforts and disappointed hopes of national politics. At the very most, this is plausible only for a small group of the politically engaged; for them alone may the emptiness of the revolutionary rhetoric before 1914 and then the rapid collapse of revolutionary action after 1918-20 have taught them the lesson that they should in the future avoid all contact with a politics which had become literally distant.

Further, one may ask whether political 'passivity' represented a repudiation of local or national social democratic leadership. The patent complaisance of the masses in the arenas of state and party politics is a proof neither of their faith in the ruling elites nor in the oppositional elites, nor can it be evidence of the 'rationality' of those who simply complied with the supposed organisational imperatives of capitalism. A more differentiated analysis of the shifting boundaries of the 'personal' and the 'political' might save us from the rigid alternative: *either* there was acceptance *or* silent protest. Perhaps, though, non-participation, silence and deafness were all nothing more than the expression of pure disinterest, a sign of how very little organised politics meant to many.

VI

The central question remains unanswered: what is the relation between everyday politics and the politics and domination of society and the state at large? For, a careful examination of the examples given makes the problem clear: on the one hand a conspicuous submission to the state and organised politics; on the other, frequently great political sensitivity and active independence in the work-shops, the offices, the tenements and the streets.

The separation of the 'personal' and the 'political' served the function of preserving structures of power and domination. And this operated not only in the interests of the rulers but also of the oppositional organisations such as the SPD after 1914. Was then this separation part of a calculated strategy? Certainly, the strategies of the ruling classes and, more importantly, the operative form of hegemony in society need to be examined. Through this process society is shot through with cultural patterns that make subjection appear as necessary or unavoidable. It was not only bourgeois 'culture', such as was generally imitated in the work of the education movement, that furthered conformity. In the context of daily production and reproduction, the demand for a 'just wage' was much nearer the bone for most people - but the wage-relation itself was not a subject for dispute!

An analysis of the way in which wage-earners and their dependants were disciplined up to 1914 and how their organisations were smashed or crippled before and after 1933 is necessary but insufficient. Firstly, because this can only lead to historical subjects becoming, once again, merely the victims of treacherous machinations or of brute suppression. And, secondly, there is an empiricist blindspot: in fact, there was fierce and persistent conflict between the dominant groups as to how they could secure their interests. Moreover, though

I can do no more than mention them, there is the history of the recurrent changes and realignments of 'alliances' within the ruling classes and cliques (such as the industrialists, the big landowners, the bureaucracy and the military).

This view 'from above' can only be adequately countered when the social experiences affecting the subordinated classes and strata are reconstructed. Such experiences direct our attention to relationships of daily practice. In these experiences, the interconnection between life circumstances and subjectivity is accomplished - and so therefore is that between the strategies of domination and the patterns of hegemony. In the context of experience the conditions of action obtain significance for those involved; here then is the basis for their politics.

To understand modes of experience we must comprehend the reciprocal transformation of 'objective' conditions of action into cultural meanings or rules, in the context of daily production and reproduction. The contradictions and fractures of experience, in particular, demand our attention; the flow of experience is evidently irregular and at many levels. Its various contours and depths mark the possibilities of knowledge and action for the different types of worker. Pessimism as to the possibility of politicisation, such as Korsch acquired 'from experience', may lead us to overlook everyday politics; it is then an easy step to trivialise the connections between the task of survival and the quest for personal identity or between the capacity for resistance and intellectual independence. Nevertheless, that same pessimism reminds us of the difficulty of the question we face: how can a kind of politics be possible where the actions and wishes of its agents and recipients are not to be reduced to an either/or of readiness for action or complacency. For, in such politics, collective action and the articulation of individual needs would have to be bound together.

A BIBLIOGRAPHICAL NOTE

On the problem of fascism and everyday life, I have found the following sources helpful.

For the example of the local Nazi party organisation see: Arbeitsgruppe (Klassenstufe 11) des Felix-Gymnasiums Göttingen: NSDAP-Kreisleitung Göttingen. Alltag in einer Universitätastadt 1933-38/45. Göttingen 1981 (Masch.); write to: Schülerwettbewerb Deutsche Geschichte, Postfach 800660, 2050 Hamburg 80; for a general outline of the power-structure and especially the fissures between Nazi-apparatuses cf. P. Hüttenberger, 'Nationalsozialistische Polykratie', in *Geschichte und Gesellschaft*, 2, 1976, pp. 417-42; aspects of working-class resistance as well as governmental strategies to cope with those, and even more, to prevent them are richly documented by T.W. Mason, *Arbeiterklasse und Volksgemeinschaft*, Opladen, 1975; mechanisms of 'Ästhetisierung der Politik' (W. Benjamin) are helpfully introduced in the study of the widespread quiescence among the German population (even among large groups of the industrial proletariat) by E. Hennig, 'Faschistische Öffentlichkeit und Faschismustheorien', in *Ästhetic und Kommunikation*, 6, 1975, no. 20, pp. 107-17; indispensable for the phenomenology and as well for the analysis of the ways in which the majority of the dependent 'immediate producers' in town and in the countryside seem to have been accommodated during fascism is the recently published collection of contemporary reports produced clandestinely by social democrats, see: *Deutschlandberichte der SPD, 1934-1940*, Frankfurt 1980.

The examples of coffee-breaks in factories in the late nineteenth century are drawn from my current research; for more detailed information on the struggles over the definition of work and non-work see my article: 'Arbeitsbeginn, Arbeitspausen, Arbeitsende, Skizzen zu Bedürfnisbefriedigung und Industriearbeit im 19. und frühen 20 Jahrhundert', in G. Huck (ed.), *Sozialgeschichte der Freizeit. Wuppertal 1980*, pp. 95-122; the parallel changes in the length of daily and weekly working hours in the German factory industry are convincingly analysed by W.H. Schröder, 'Die Entwicklung der Arbeitszeit im sekündaren Sektor in Deutschland 1871 bis 1913', in *Technikgeschichte*, 47, 1980, pp. 252-302; autobiographical material is collected by W. Emmerich, *Proletarische Lebensläufe*, 2 vols, Reinbek, 1974-5; cf. also the survey A. Levenstein did in 1910, cf. *Die Arbeiterfrage*, München, 1912; protocols of interviews with 'Arbeiterveteranen' Essen are kept in the Historisches Archiv Krupp from about 1907-1972 and Historisches Archiv der Gutehoffhungshutte, Oberhausen; the 'tastes' and 'colours' of working-class experiences, especially at home and in public places or in pubs, are provided from the anecdoal richness of O. Rühle (a left-wing KPD dissident of the 1920s) in his *Volkskunde des Proletariats*, 2 vols, Berlin, 1930, Giessen, 1978.

On the problems of 'control of the work-process', 'meaning of work and non-work', and 'modes of experience', see the following:

On questions of control, see in particular, D. Montgomery, *Workers' Control in America: Studies in Work, Technology and Labor Struggles*, New York/London, 1979; J.R. Barrett, Work and Community in the 'Jungle', Chicago's Packing-house Workers, 1894-1922', unpublished Ph.D. dissertation, University of Pittsburgh, 1981. Aspects of work and non-work are discussed and described in a manner which avoids the traps of the common formalistic distinction between 'work' and 'leisure' by J. Ehmer, 'Rote Fahnen - blauer Montag. Soziale Bedingungen von Aktions und Organisationsformen der frühen Wiener Arbeiterbewwegung', in D. Puls (ed.), *Wahrnehmungsformen und Protestverhalten*, Frankfurt, 1979, pp. 143-74. The 'state of the art' regarding the multi-faceted problems of 'experience' is not very stimulating. Usually 'experience' gets used as a quite unspecific and general denominator of the mediations between societal 'conditions' and the agency of classes, groups or individuals. Fresh thinking, especially on the non-linear aspects of experiences, and on the relations between cycles of experience and political acticity (or passivity), could be triggered off by F. Brüggemeier, 'Soziale Vagabondage oder revolutionärer Heros? Zur Sozialgeschichte der Ruhrbergarbeiter 1880-1920', in L. Niethammer (ed.), *Lebenserfahrung und kollekttives Gedächtnis*, Frankfurt 1980, pp. 193-213; L. Passerini, 'Arbeitersubjektivität und Faschismus. Mündliche Quellen und deren Impulse für die historische Forschung', in L. Neithammer (ed.), *Lebenserfahrung*, pp. 214-48.

Culture

4 WOMEN AND THE FAITH IN ICONS IN EARLY CHRISTIANITY*

Judith Herrin**

The cult of icons presents several paradoxes. It runs directly counter to the Old Testament prohibition of 'graven images', which was binding on early Christian communities, and it represents an essentially pagan art form, the commemoration of the dead, ancestors, rulers, heroes and divinities both mortal and immortal. This prompts the question: how did icons come to hold such a central position in Christian art? Had the church simply ignored the heathen roots and Mosaic interdiction of this type of representative art? Or had it justified a Christian adaptation and re-employment of older art forms by theological argument? One answer was given in the eighth century, when the Byzantine empire tried to resolve the apparent contradiction built into this early Christian art by destroying icons and figurative art. A different one was developed by the western church, which was not prepared to do away with its own tradition, supported by no less an authority than Pope Gregory the Great: 'For what writing [*scriptura*] presents to readers, this a picture [*pictura*] presents to the unlearned who behold, since in it even the ignorant see what they ought to follow: in it the illiterate read. Hence, and chiefly to the nations [*gentibus*], a picture is instead of reading.'[1] The challenge of iconoclasm revealed a deep commitment to Christian art, both in the East where icon veneration finally triumphed and in the West where destruction was rejected outright. When under attack the icons found intense support throughout the church, although this iconophile response differed in important respects. In this paper I shall be primarily concerned with the eastern response, that faith in icons which represents a more personal type of dedication to Christian images.

Posing this problem means, in effect, seeking the origins of Christian art, a topic far too large and complex for a short paper. But within this long development the role of the icon is significant and merits special consideration. Icons centre

---

*This paper owes much to the disagreements and critical points raised by David Freedberg in particular, and by Anthony Barnett, Averil Cameron and Robin Cormack, all of whom I thank and absolve from any responsibility for the final version. I should also like to acknowledge the assistance of the 1980/1 Fellows and Staff of the Society for the Humanities, Cornell University, and of Francine Wynham and Jon Halliday.
**Judith Herrin is a member of the editorial board of *Past and Present*.

attention on one of the basic problems of the early church, the representation of holy persons, while simultaneously revealing features of the non-Christian antecedents of this art. I am concerned with this tradition. My approach will not be that of an art historian, nor will I deal with the theological debates over the propriety of figural imagery. I will discuss the place of icons in worship, their character and the way they came to symbolize the holy and mediate between earth and heaven. In particular, as icons became a vivid focus of devotion, they began to embody human relations with God the Creator and Ruler of the entire Christian world. And I will argue that women played a notable part in this developing cult of icons.

So without denying the theological dilemma of Christian representational art, I want to concentrate on some features of Late Antique Mediterranean culture, shared by Jews and Gentiles, pagan and Christian alike. These provided a common social experience within which the artistic evolution of the Christian church took place. In particular, the first part of this chapter will be devoted to a discussion of funerary art, for this represents one of the most striking ways whereby Christians transmitted pagan rituals and artistic forms to their new faith. In the second part, I will examine some of the reasons for the preservation of these forms, once assimilated to a Christian mode, when they came under attack in the East, and will ask how much that response informs us about the role of women in the cult of icons.

I

It is characteristic of human societies to treat death, the possibility of life after death and obligations to dead ancestors as a major concern. The finality of material existence in this world is regularly contrasted with more eternal values and the completely immaterial hereafter. Burial rituals and funerary monuments everywhere reveal a basic concern shared by societies as different as nomadic Siberia and Pharaonic Egypt. While some leave more direct evidence in the form of written accounts of mourning or in particularly impressive tomb architecture, none totally discount the needs of the dead in whatever other world they have passed on to.

In the pre-Christian Mediterranean world a variety of beliefs was attached to the fate of the deceased, but the maintenance of family shrines and the perpetuation of the memory of ancestors through prescribed ceremonies was widely observed. The early Christian communities cannot have been unaware of their contemporaries' customs in this respect: from the Gospel of St John (ch. 19, 40) they would have known that Christ's body was embalmed with spices and bound with strips of linen in the Jewish fashion. In addition, the existence of classical mausolea and tombs must have been as familiar as the Egyptian habit of mummifying (which had been adopted by the first-century AD Jews of Palestine) and the Greek preference for cremation. The commemoration of dead rulers in funerary monuments and living emperors through images to which respect had to be shown, extended this practice into the daily political sphere. Tomb stones, funerary urns, sarcophagi and burial portraits provided proof of the ubiquitous concern to record and cherish the dead. The chief differences lay in the manner by which this was to be effected. Preservation of the body was naturally abhorrent to those who believed that the soul was released by death, but even they marked the final resting place of the ashes. Others, who did not practise incineration, built tombs which sometimes became public shrines. In the case of emperors, in particular, the distinction between private and public burial was almost impossible to maintain, and these tombs were rarely restricted to immediate kin.[2]

As the first few generations of Christians were almost all converts from other faiths, they must have brought direct knowledge of traditional burial methods with them into the church. These were strengthened by subsequent missionary activity, for even in the fifth and sixth centuries non-believers of many varieties were still adopting the faith. The influence of such customary practices and means of commemorating the dead should not be underestimated. Christian burial customs, using both cemeteries and catacombs, marking graves with a portrait of the deceased and celebrating the good fortune of ancestors with annual feasting at the tomb, followed normal, heathen practice. Only by their belief in the resurrection and the life to come did the Christians set themselves apart from their contemporaries.[3] And this distinguishing feature of the faith did not preclude funerary representations considered traditional in all cults. So it is hardly surprising that Christian art is found precisely in those places reserved for graves, often next door to examples of pagan and Jewish art on the graves of non-Christians. It is possible that the private houses where these early Christian communities met to celebrate their faith were also decorated, but if so this type of art has not survived. Only one building adapted for the specific function of baptism is known from the first three centuries AD - the baptistery at Dura Europos, an eastern frontier town destroyed by a Persian army in 256 and fortunately preserved under sand in the North Syrian desert. Interestingly, this small monument is completely overshadowed by other cult buildings in the same town: the spectacular frescoes of the synagogue, large statues of Palmyrene gods in their temple and the decorated Mithraeum.[4] Even if the paucity of other evidence has attributed undue prominence to the tomb art of the early church, great significance was attached to the burial rite, not only in Christianity but in most other Late Antique religions. Viewed in this perspective, catacomb art proves extremely revealing not only of Christian attitudes towards visual representation, but also of the long pre-history of burial ceremony which deeply influenced the early church.

Another aspect of funerary art which made it suitable for the early communities was that it avoided some of the most obvious, official, pagan forms of art, works displayed in public places throughout the Roman world. Greek excellence in the field of free-standing statuary and the survival of many ancient statues of gods, athletes, rulers and philosophers, often naked, may have prevented Christians from using this medium. A fourth-century emperor, on the other hand, could re-use a statue of Apollo as his own. Imperial statues and portraits in every city of the empire reminded the early Christians of the temporal rulers of the world, often persecutors, who demanded a secular worship. Recognizing this public cult celebrated in life-like paintings and life-size monuments, they shunned material images, reinforcing Christ's command to worship their heavenly Lord in spirit and in truth. Although attempts are occasionally made to argue that the early church was not implacably hostile to human representation, attention has more often been given to the apparent reluctance to portray the Founder of the faith and the preference for symbolic decoration. Evidently there was some anxiety associated with Christian figural art which could easily be mistaken for its pagan equivalent.[5]

The earliest surviving Christian graves are marked by shrines where offerings could be made, and by symbolic representations of the faith, doves of peace, loaves and fishes, the IXΘYC anagram and the chi-rho sign. In addition, Christian families sometimes displayed a portrait of the departed and an inscription recording the name and genealogy.[6] For all the faithful, the duty of honouring the dead was such an important one that Christian graves were bound to attract the type of art normally set up at tombs. In this respect the Egyptian tradition of preserving the body in mummy form and the Roman practice of depicting the deceased in a most life-like fashion were very influential. The former required that the mummy should contain a portrait painted during the individual's lifetime, usually in encaustic (wax) on wood; this was inserted into the mummy over the face (see plates 1 and 2, the complete mummy of Artemiodoros and the portrait of a young woman, pagan works of the second century AD). The latter custom identified the grave with a sculpted bust or a portrait in low relief, painting or gold glass. Both seem to have been employed by Christians with sufficient means. For the poor humbler imitations were used. There was no hesitancy about such funerary portraiture, it was the accepted manner of naming a grave and was widely adopted for private family tombs.[7] In this way pre-Christian art forms were put to use in the church by those who converted from other faiths, and by those whose families had been Christian for generations. This art avoided the most obvious pagan associations of ancient statuary, but it was none the less rooted in ancient custom shared by many cults.

The tombs or places of martyrdom attached to the Christian

heroes of Roman persecution naturally attracted particular attention and these gradually developed into cult sites. In their determination to honour and revere those who had suffered death for the faith, Christians of the third and fourth centuries created new centres and new forms of worship. The traditional places of death and burial of the martyrs, tombs already set apart both by their physical setting and by the character of the deceased, begin to serve a public function as martyria. Pilgrims visit these sites with a heightened sense of awe, recording in graffiti their belief that the figures enshrined would intercede for them, protecting and guiding their lesser co-religionaries.[8] In the slow transition from plain grave to cult shrine a variety of means for indicating divine approval, ranging from the saint's halo to the Hand of God receiving the martyr, were employed to emphasize the proximity of such heroes to God himself. Thus, by the early fourth century the cult of martyrs had established both the main type of Christian building and its artistic decoration (churches were still a rarity). These patterns were inherited by the first Christians who benefited from Constantine I's decision to grant the church an official status, tolerated and equal to the many other cults of the empire.

This fundamental change in the position of the Christian communities was responsible, by and large, for the development of Christian art. Once the faith could be celebrated openly and above ground, it needed larger buildings and these required decoration. Constantine led the way in commissioning new monuments and a whole range of wealthy patrons followed his example. I should like to stress just one aspect of the growth of this official art: the importance of Constantine's 'discovery' of the site of Christ's martyrdom, Golgotha, and the associated holy places of Jerusalem and Bethlehem. The fact that this was carried out under imperial instructions and with the active support of Constantine's mother, Helena, does not mean that it was different from the established tradition of identifying and celebrating the sites of martyrdom. It was simply more significant and achieved with greater resources. Once the actual tomb had been found, Constantine endowed the most magnificent church, setting aside revenues from provincial taxation and instructing the bishop of Jerusalem to acquire the costliest and most splendid building materials. The stress on luxurious and lavish decoration of the church of the Holy Sepulchre, intended as a demonstration of the wealth both worldly and spiritual of the Christian faith, stood in marked contrast to the meagre resources of the provincial episcopal centre.[9] Imperial investment in this construction, which set an altar directly above the holy spot, reinforced the tradition of martyria. For centuries to come, churches would be founded on the tombs of the saints.[10]

While Constantine's building activity in Palestine adorned the *loca sancta* (holy places) and unearthed the few relics of Christ's martyrdom (the True Cross, crown of thorns, nails, lance and sponge), the revolution in the status of the faith permitted Christians to express their beliefs without restraint. The combination of these factors produced a rapid increase in pilgrimage to the sites of the Passion, as well as the settlement of individual holy people and entire monastic communities close by. Reading the accounts of these early pilgrims, there is an overwhelming impression of the importance attached to physical contact; Christians sought to touch, to kiss and to embrace objects associated with their Founder's earthly existence - the manger at Bethlehem, the place of baptism in the Jordan, the spot from which Christ ascended. All the associations of the cult of saints and martyrs were here magnified. The same desire for proximity to the holy places and actual contact with the relics, plus the longing for some reminder of them, contributed to the development of cult objects which had been placed close to the source of holiness, which contained oil from lamps in particular shrines or water from holy streams. Frequently these souvenirs were decorated with scenes from the life of Christ, the Baptism on a flask of Jordan water, the Ascension on one containing dust from the very spot at which the Apostles had witnessed the event. Small pilgrim flasks in metal or clay were most commonly used to transport this precious contact home to those Christians who were unable to make a pilgrimage. But in addition, holy objects such as stones from Calvary were carried off in great quantities: the trade in relics had begun.[11]

This public commemoration of the Founder of the church and its first heroes was rapidly extended to its fourth-century leaders. In Antioch after the death of Bishop Meletios (381), the inhabitants called their sons after him and set up his image in their homes, in public places, on their rings, seals and bowls.[12] The double consolation of hearing his name and seeing his image everywhere was enhanced by the belief that he would protect and look after his flock. Such local cults consolidated and expanded the traditional role of martyria, emphasizing the significance of visual representation. For shrines were identified partly by the images in them and these in turn generated a standard iconography of the saints, recognized by their attributes and scenes from their lives. The great column saint, Symeon the Stylite, was another local patron of Antioch, but was also celebrated in Rome, where craftsmen set up little images of him in their workshops for protection. His cult, like that of St Menas, was spread by pilgrim flasks and visual depictions of his column.[13] Bishops of Constantinople, painted on panels displayed in the Forum, were destroyed during fourth-century battles between Arian and Orthodox supporters. Portraits of Roman pontiffs are also known to have existed.[14]

In this context of proliferating personal representations, the question of depicting God in other than symbolical or allegorical form became more pressing. Two factors in particular appear to have helped to resolve this problem: the identification of the holy places, which drew attention to Christ's incarnation and life on earth, and the debates over His nature or natures, which were concluded at the Council of Chalcedon (451) in a decisive statement of the union of the human and the divine. The divine being uncircumscribable, artists found a legitimate way of representing God through the human Christ. This was not, of course, a straightforward procedure. Doubts persisted as to the propriety of such portraits and the actual depictions. In the sixth century an ecclesiastical historian could claim that the type with short frizzy hair was more authentic than the long-haired type that resembled Zeus.[15] Pagans had observed this Christian adoption and by this period they employed the same device to hide their continued devotion to Zeus through apparent pictures of Christ. According to Christian sources, such devious means were always revealed and the pagans exposed, by some miracle worked by the image itself or by a fearful retribution administered to the pagan painter.[16]

It is often forgotten that traditional classical forms were maintained in imperial and pagan portraiture, statues, tomb stones and public monuments side by side with Christian art. Neither had an exclusive control over the established media, which were also used by adherents of other cults. What we think of as being an unmistakably Christian style was achieved more by the official suppression of pagan and oriental beliefs than by the conscious development of specifically Christian art forms. In the case of encaustic panel paintings from Egypt, there does appear to be a decline in their production from the third century, possibly indicating that this medium was not favoured by the church.[17] Instead, the earliest Christian art from Egypt seems to have employed sculpture in low relief for its personal representations (plates 3 and 4). In this, it adapted another pagan form and maintained the traditional concern for a frontal portrait, drawing attention to the eyes and face of the holy person. On the tombstone of Apa Shenute from the White Monastery near Sohag, we see the abbot in his monastic robe carrying a staff with the long pallium of his office over his shoulder. He was a disciple of Pachom, who founded the first communities, and he spread this organised ascetic way of life through his own monasteries in Upper Egypt. The carving probably dates from shortly after his death in 451 and was made at the request of his monks to commemorate his pioneering role.[18] The earliest surviving icons, which seem to date from the sixth century (plates 6 and 7), introduce a much greater sophistication through the use of encaustic, paralleled in the continued production of secular portraits. The church could not make this medium its sole preserve until the whole tradition of classical portraiture had died away.[19]

One of the consequences of the church's new role in society and overt Christian worship can be seen in the determination to identify all the sites mentioned in the Bible and to track down every tiny relic of Apostolic times, however small. The researches of Origen, Jerome and Eusebius, whose *Onomastikon* lists biblical place-names with their fourth-century equivalents, represents the former.[20] The tracing of 'real' portraits of Christ and the Virgin reflects the latter. Although St Luke's painting of the Virgin and Child is a purely apocryphal story, this very picture was allegedly discovered by Eudocia, the wife of Theodosius II, who lived in Jerusalem from 443 to 460, and was sent to Constantinople. There were already two important relics of the Virgin in the Byzantine capital, the veil and the girdle, housed in splendid shrines which were later decorated with large votive images; the 'portrait' by St Luke may have been set up in one of them.[21] Similarly, the legendary stories of towels on which Christ had imprinted His features seem to go back to the same period. King Abgar's request for a painting of Christ had proved to be an impossible task for the artist, but one such towel supposedly carried back to Edessa in Christ's lifetime was rediscovered in the sixth century as a precious relic. A comparable 'authenticity' was occasionally claimed for images known as *acheiropoièta*, icons not made by human hand, of which the Kamouliana icon of Christ was a famous sixth-century example (it was also based on a miraculous image on a cloth and thus had a double pedigree).[22] For some images of great beauty angels were held responsible, for instance the Kiti mosaic made by angels, *aggeloktistos* (see plate 5), while other non-human hands guided craftsmen in the execution of particular representations of Christ. In all artistic activity divine intervention was possible and certain images could therefore be invested with holy authority.[23]

However they were supposed to have been produced, all these representations of Christ, the Virgin, Apostles and Saints, took as their model the human form. If God had originally made man in His own image, the same was true of fourth- and fifth-century Christian artists: they painted Christ in their own image, with the most natural and familiar human attributes.[24] This principle applied equally to votive images set up by people in their own homes, for example pictures of a particular saint or holy man whose aid had benefited the individual, and to monumental images erected by emperors and commissioned by bishops to adorn churches. In both private and public buildings Christian art presented its chief figures in the guise of friends, spiritual leaders and benevolent helpers in the world of the living, that is, in exactly the same way as the Christian dead. Although none could claim the Holy Family as their direct ancestors, in an important way the Christian community had always cultivated the familial sense of being one with Christ, and this feeling was perpetuated by such cult images. This identification of fifth- and sixth-century believers with the founders of their faith can be traced through many literary sources, which reveal the depth of feeling generated by Christian art. In dreams, frequently the medium of communication between the divine and ordinary mortals, saints are recognized by their resemblance to portraits in churches and homes.[25] Images of the Virgin and Christ are responsible for the conversion of stubborn pagans, often through some potent display of power to chastize or cure. This evidence suggests that the relatively novel role of the saints as intercessors was gaining strength, precisely because of the approachability of well-known and well-loved holy persons.

For women the Virgin appears to have filled this role most effectively. Their identification with the maternal anxieties and sufferings of Christ's Mother, the *Theotokos* (who bore God), developed in parallel with Her special cult, first elaborated at the Council of Ephesos (431).[26] A female model of holiness was probably appealing to those who had been characterized and condemned as so many duplications of Eve. It was certainly responsible for the conversion of St Mary the Egyptian according to the traditional account of her repentance at the sight of the Virgin's image at Jerusalem. Another icon of the Virgin in the church at Sozopolis (in southern Asia Minor) was held to be capable of miraculous cures and attracted women who were unable to conceive. A couple from Amaseia made the pilgrimage to Sozopolis and were cured by the application of some holy oil from the lamp which hung in front of the icon; they later returned with their son, Peter, to give thanks to the Virgin.[27] This cult was not limited to the East, or to women. The fresco panel erected in the Catacomb of St Comodilla in Rome to commemorate the widow Turtura in 528 illustrates its appeal in the West. It shows the Virgin seated on a jewelled throne holding the Child on Her lap and flanked by saints. At the bottom left stands Turtura in black, with a scroll recording her gratitude to the Virgin.[28] Apart from a slight difference of scale, the holy figures being larger than the donor, there is no distinction in the humanity of all persons represented. But by Her central position, Her attributes and Her direct frontal gaze, the Virgin is set apart - close enough for the identification between women to be made yet distant in the same way as all the dead; beyond the world yet within reach of the living. In the Christian devotion of the sixth century this painting fills the same role as the icon in the East. It is also remarkably similar to one of the earliest surviving icons, an enthroned Virgin and Child with saints preserved in the monastery of St Catherine on Mount Sinai.[29]

Of course, the cult of the Virgin was by no means restricted to female adherents, as male devotion to the icon of Sozopolis shows, nor were women unable to express their religious emotions in front of male figures of sanctity. In the early years of the seventh century an icon of St John the Baptist, housed in a church in Constantinople, commanded the attention of a certain lady called Anna who lived nearby. Following her parents' tradition, she lit a lamp in front of this icon every evening, sending a young girl to do this for her if she was too busy.[30] The Virgin, however, represented a meaningful example of female holiness, which does appear to have been appreciated by women.

By the middle of the sixth century the literary evidence for a cult of icons is so strong that no one could doubt that figural representation was approved by the church. It was employed by ecclesiastical leaders such as patriarchs of Constantinople, especially during periods of doctrinal warfare when rival candidates sought to impose their control over the church. It also appears to have been used by bishops who were perhaps prevented from residing in their episcopal sees. The appointment of Abraham, abbot of the Phoibammon monastery at Luxor in Upper Egypt, to the see of Hermonthis probably occasioned the painting of his icon (plate 7). Owing to his great holiness, Abraham is here shown with a halo; he wears episcopal robes, carries a Gospel book and appears as the archetypal Egyptian monk, dedicated to ascetic practices. From written sources Abraham is known as a contemporary of Patriarch Damianos of Alexandria (578-605), and was a famous monastic leader and writer, as well as the fourteenth bishop of Hermonthis. It is likely that he continued to reside at this monastery when appointed to the see and that the icon was made and sent to his episcopal church to be displayed (it has holes to facilitate mounting on a wall). It probably dates from the beginning of his episcopate, *ca.* 590/600, and may have been returned to his monastery after his death in *ca.* 610/20.[31] As no other portraits of bishops have survived, it would be rash to assume that this display of icons of living churchmen was customary. Indeed, other sources would seem to indicate a continuing ambivalence about portraits of contemporaries.

Under Patriarch Sergios of Constantinople (610-38), the monks of the *Romaion* monastery were visited by St Theodore of Sykeon, a famous holy man (who was, incidentally, devoted to the Sozopolis icon). He succeeded in curing a monk possessed by an evil spirit, and as a reminder of this blessing on their community the monks wanted a picture of the saint. Realizing that this wish might not be granted, they instructed a painter to observe Theodore through a small concealed opening, so that he could capture the holy man's likeness in an icon. Afterwards they showed the image to Theodore who smiled, and told the painter that he had stolen something; but he agreed to bless the object and pardoned the artist.[32] Several features of this story are interesting: Theodore's reluctance to be painted, his characterization of the painting as theft, and his final blessing of it which clearly gave it greater authority. The first appears to be related to an understanding of the power of icons; the second to their extremely life-like quality, while the third typifies the manner in which such portraits painted in the lifetime of the subject were sanctioned as a substitute. This was to become the standard way for people of extreme sanctity to be venerated both while they were alive and after their death.

To understand the power generated by these cult images, it is necessary to look at them closely. Fortunately a few painted in the sixth and seventh centuries have survived, most of them housed on Mt Sinai where they escaped outbreaks of iconoclasm both Christian and Muslim.[33] An analysis of these artefacts brings us much closer to the faith experienced by the early Christians.

The word *eikôn* means any image or representation, but these early icons generally show a portrait of Christ, the Virgin and Child, Apostles or Saints, in pairs or singly, and scenes from the life of Christ. Occasionally full-length standing figures are shown, alone or in groups as in the Gospel scenes, but there is a marked preference for the head and shoulders portrait which concentrates attention on the face of the holy person. This is further intensified by the regular use of a plain gold background, comparable to the tradition of early Christian mosaics (e.g., the Kiti apse mosaic, plate 5). For the moment I shall leave aside the narrative icons, which do not occur amongst the earliest examples, and which are not devotional objects of prayer in the same sense. Three of these sixth-century icons have a background of classical architectural features, reminiscent of the sculpted portrait bust placed in a niche, but this appears to be a feature of one particular workshop, possibly an imperial one in Constantinople. In size the early icons which have survived range from 92 x 53 cm to 20.1 x 11.6 cm.[34] They are all painted in encaustic on thin pieces of wood, that is using the ancient technique of heating wax until it is malleable, adding the colour and applying it in layers on the wooden base.[35]

It is this technique which determines the first characteristic of such portrait icons: their uncannily human quality. This is produced by the blending of different shades of coloured wax to imitate life-like flesh tones and to depict highlights in the eyes, on hair and garments. Even on a plain gold ground the halo of a saint may be marked out by a slightly raised surface, emphasized by almost undetectable red spots, which catches the light (see plate 6). The sophisticated and subtle qualities of encaustic had been used throughout the ancient world for portrait painting and was adapted in the sixth century, possibly earlier, for Christian imagery. This development of encaustic icons, however, had a very much wider appeal and rapidly gained prominence as the preferred medium of Christian art. It was probably the highly naturalistic and convincing representations of the Holy Family and saints, who appeared more familiar and closer to the viewer through their evidently personal quality, that encouraged this spectacular growth. Proximity, accessibility and recognizability were all stressed in these icons, qualities most necessary for the role of intercessor which Christians hoped to find in Christ, the Virgin and saints. While God Himself was never depicted, these holy persons who could intercede with Him on man's behalf took up a station midway between the world below and heaven above. The icons created a new focus for the worshipper, bringing the divine into his own home in an approachable and comprehensible fashion.

The second characteristic of these portrait icons is that they address the beholder very directly, frequently through a marked frontality.[36] The holy figure looks at the believer with an intentness which emphasizes the personal relationship between them and the immediacy of their communication. Whether the former is delivering a message, or the latter is making a prayer, their contact is intensified across the space that separates them. This is especially noticeable when the icon is displayed at eye level and gives rise to the well-known optical illusion of the gaze which appears to follow the beholder, the all-seeing eye from whom nothing can be hidden. Although this phenomenon is documented from ancient times onward and could not have been new to the Byzantines, the frontal icon employs it in a manner which commands attention from a wide arc. When the figure seems to direct itself personally to each and every viewer, its authority is greatly enhanced, and they all feel themselves recipients of a special message. The force is strongest with a totally frontal pose, but even the figure which does not look straight at the spectator can arouse similar feelings of immediacy, for the life-like quality suggests that he or she has just glanced aside and might turn back at any moment. Normally an unswerving communication is established at first glance. This is effectively illustrated by the Sinai icon of Christ (see plate 6), previously assigned to the thirteenth century and now re-dated in the sixth, since under the overpainting an original deposit of encaustic layers was revealed in cleaning.[37] Christ is here shown raising His right hand in blessing and holding a gemmed Gospel manuscript in His left, but the viewer's attention is immediately drawn to the face and particularly the eyes. Although this is a majestic and awe-inspiring figure, it has an emphatically human aspect achieved by the subtle treatment of the flesh, the shading on the throat and under the cheek bones and the piercing quality of the eyes. These are not of equal size; the left eye is larger and more widely opened; and this asymmetrical arrangement possibly reflects the ancient *topos* of dual expression. One eye is the calm approving one, the other a hostile and rejecting one.[38] While the tradition was to be developed into the rather terrifying Pantocrator images of Daphni and Cefalù in the eleventh and twelfth centuries, on this icon it lends itself to a more benevolent visage. This is a very human God.

These two characteristics give rise to a third consideration: the private nature of personal devotion before an icon. In accounts of the earliest use of icons it is clear that they were displayed in homes, very often when an individual wished to give thanks to a particular saint or holy person for assistance or consolation. After being cured by Saint Symeon Stylites, women and men made shrines in their homes with images of their benefactor. These sometimes proved to be healing agents themselves. In other cases, persistent faith in saints with special powers, such as Artemios and Febronia and their images, was rewarded by cures.[39] Similarly, people going on journeys often carried an icon with them, partly for their prayers but mainly for the protection it would provide.[40] Such portable icons were probably small, had lids to protect the painted surfaces, and were produced in large numbers, unlike the costly and unique icons commissioned by rich patrons for their churches. Local saints were depicted on these lidded icons; for instance, people from Galatia in central Anatolia might carry an icon of Saint Platon (see plate 5). In a colourful story related by a monk on Mt Sinai, a pilgrim from Galatia, who was captured by desert brigands, was released by his local saint, whom he recognized as Platon from his likeness to portrait icons. However unlikely the story seems, one of these icons has survived in the Mt Sinai collection and provides an instructive illustration of this type.[41] Saint Platon is shown together with an unidentified female companion or martyr on his left, both gazing out from the icon to the beholder. Between them, faintly delineated on the gold ground, is a cross studded with gems indicated by circles. Both figures have large staring eyes, long noses and oval faces which are disproportionately large for their bodies. They occupy only the lower half of the icon leaving an extensive background space unfilled. Clearly, the execution of this icon is rough and primitive in comparison with Constantinopolitan works of the same period, but it strives to create the same impression.

Both the literary evidence and the actual icons suggest that people found these domestic cult objects reassuring and protective. The individual's attachment to one special saint or holy person was deepened by the intense private devotion paid to his representation displayed in the owner's home. Freed from all public and prescribed rituals, the worshipper entered into an extremely personal communication with the saint, which seems to have satisified a basic need for divine approval. Possibly this need was no longer being met by the services of the ecclesiastical hierarchy; possibly churches were felt to be too crowded, too noisy or too large for such isolated acts of worship; or the domestic icon may simply have provided an additional means of communicating with the holy. Although no single explanation seems to account for the expansion of the personal icon cult, its domestic character and privacy of direct communication must be significant components.

II

In connection with this cult I should now like to examine one aspect of icon veneration which is not adequately understood, its importance for women. When I first read Byzantine accounts of female devotion to icons, I dismissed them as yet another example of the common slurs on womankind perpetrated by uniformly male writers. After closer inspection, I feel that this opinion should be revised. For what we read about their attachment to icons is surely a reflection of their homebound situation, their restricted access to churches and their frustrated religious passion. Not all women could aspire to the monastic ideal, and their expression of faith within the confines of the secular world was limited. Since their existence required some divine sanction to make it more bearable, they clung to the icons tenaciously. Through these at least they had an outlet for their pent-up feelings. Hence, the association of women and iconophiles (icon-lovers) may not be only a disparaging male comment on female weakness and incapacity to understand the higher points of theology: there may be a real connection between icons and the way Byzantine women worshipped. This is not to claim that all icons functioned in an identical fashion; some were used as palladia, paraded around the walls of besieged cities, or as standards at the head of a fighting force going out into battle. Nor is the devotion to icons restricted to women; as we have seen, men shared this cult, but they had additional and alternative ways of expressing their belief in public ritual and through the ecclesiastical orders. For women, however, the icon offered a special approach to religion, an individual contact with a particular holy person, which could be exercised without restriction (as in the case of Anna and the icon of St John the Baptist). It is in this context that I wish to examine the female defence of icons under attack.

Of the known cases of such devotion dating from the period of icon destruction (iconoclasm), several women are empresses,[42] many are related to iconophile saints and others reflect the attitude of the women of Constantinople. The most famous are undoubtedly Irene and Theodora, who restored the official worship of icons in 787 and 843 respectively. Irene came from Athens as the chosen bride of Leo IV, the third iconoclast emperor of the Syrian dynasty; the couple were married in the capital with great pomp and ceremony in 768 and one year later their son, Constantine, was born.[43] Irene's iconophile sympathies can hardly have been recognized at the time of the marriage, and may only have developed later. They must, none the less, have been strongly felt, for it was not an easy task to undo forty-five years of iconoclast domination within the church and restore the icons to their former position, as Irene did after Leo's death. After one premature attempt in 786, this was achieved at the Council of Nicaea held in 787. Irene was, of course, assisted by able theologians and ecclesiastical administrators, as well as an impressive circle of persecuted monks, who returned enthusiastically to the capital as soon as the prospect of a restoration of icons became known. A good deal of the initiative in this process must be placed with the empress, however, as the church was firmly in the hands of the iconoclast party and the imperial administration had been purged of all with persistent iconophile views.

In the case of Theodora, we are again faced with the apparent female commitment to icon veneration in the wife of an iconoclast ruler. But the manner by which Theodora became empress was a rather singular one: she was selected in a beauty contest, with less concern paid to her origins or upbringing (she was in fact the daughter of a Paphlagonian landowner and quite a suitable match except for her iconophile beliefs). The emperor who chose her was the iconoclast, Theophilos (829-42), who persecuted icon worshippers without fully realizing his wife's secret devotion to the same cause.[44] But Theodora's protection of iconophiles and support for their party were concealed from Theophilos, taking advantage of the privacy of female quarters in the imperial palace (which had also served as a hiding place for some of Justinian's opponents in the time of the earlier Empress Theodora).[45] In this illicit support for iconophiles, Theodora was assisted and encouraged by her mother-in-law, Euphrosyne, who had arranged the bride show. Euphrosyne was the grand-daughter of Irene and daughter of Constantine VI; she had been brought up as a devout iconophile and had become a nun while her family faded into obscurity. Her marriage to Michael II was obviously one of political convenience, intended to strengthen the emperor's lack of imperial qualifications, and it ignored Euphrosyne's religious beliefs. These were maintained, however, and were responsible for the induction of her grandchildren into the iconophile cause. Together Theodora and Euphrosyne arranged for the imperial family to learn to venerate icons, while Theophilos continued to persecute iconophiles such as Methodios, the future patriarch.[46] Only after her husband's death in 842 did Theodora reveal her attachment to the cult and embark on a campaign of restoration. This time there was much less opposition and the re-establishment of icon veneration was more securely rooted by the *Synodicon of Orthodoxy*, a liturgical and theological innovation to justify and consolidate the position of icons in the eastern church.[47]

In the uniformly prejudiced iconophile sources which have survived, many iconophile women are related to monks and saints who suffered persecution for their faith in icons. This close association with the victims of iconoclast attack, which is documented largely in their *Lives*, renders their commitment rather conventional; it is almost like a *topos* (cf. the saints of other periods whose parents were humble but deeply religious and made special efforts to have their children taught the Psalms and Gospel stories). But sometimes the account documents a particular form which is interesting, for example the devotion which St Stephen's mother felt for the icon of the Virgin housed in the church at Blachernai, and the personal communication and aid which she experienced at this Constantinople shrine.[48] An outstanding example of iconophile piety is given by St Theodore of Studium in his funeral oration for his mother. Other women supporters are documented by his correspondence.[49] Throughout the saints' lives of the eighth and ninth centuries there are references to such women who protected icon worshippers, for instance, a lady whose estate near Constantinople was a hiding place and later monastery for Saint Nicholas.[50] But all these sources present a partisan view, denigrating iconoclasts

Plate 1 *far left* The stucco case of mummy of Artemiodorus, from Hawara, Egypt, early second century AD (British Museum)

Plate 2 *centre* Portrait of a young woman in wax, from Hawara, Egypt, second century AD (British Museum)

Plate 3 *left* Tombstone of Shenute, from the White monastery near Sohag, Egypt, shortly after 451 (Staatliche Museen zu Berlin)

Plate 4 Egyptian stele (upper part), relief of a bearded saint, fourth to seventh centuries (Dumbarton Oaks Collection)

Plate 5 Apse mosaic of the Virgin and Child flanked by archangels (detail), church of the Panagia Aggeloktistos, Kiti, Cyprus, late sixth century (Judith Herrin and Courtauld Institute)

Plate 6 *far left* Icon of Christ, monastery of St Catherine on Mount Sinai, sixth century (Michigan-Princeton-Alexandria Expedition to Mount Sinai)

Plate 7 *left* Icon of Bishop Abraham of Hermonthis, from Luxor, Egypt, *c.* 590–600 (Staatliche Museen zu Berlin)

Plate 8 Icon of St Platon and a female martyr, monastery of St Catherine on Mount Sinai, seventh century (from K. Weitzmann, The Monastery of St Catherine at Mount Sinai, Princeton, 1976, Vol. 1, plate LXI)

Plate 9 Gold coins of Empresses Irene and Theodora, obverse and reverse, of 797–802 and 842–3 (Dumbarton Oaks Collection)

and overpraising iconophiles to such a degree that we should treat them with caution. The only conclusion to be drawn from them with confidence seems to be that the iconophile party had female supporters, which is not entirely surprising.

A further association between female devotion and the cause of the icons is provided by the *Life* of St Stephen and concerns the inhabitants of Constantinople. The first instance occurred when Leo III ordered the icon of Christ which was displayed on the Bronze Gate of the imperial palace to be taken down: among those who protested against this action, women led the attack and killed one of the men sent to remove the icon.[51] Clearly, this decision, the first overt move against icons, directed against a prominent image well-known in the capital, would not have passed unnoticed. And it would have been natural for crowds near the palace at the time to have protested. Whether women in particular, hearing of the intended removal, rushed to the palace to try and prevent it is another matter. Stephen's biographer implies this in his description of their violent killing of a *spatharios* and subsequent stone-throwing attack on the patriarch's residence. Was he really exaggerating their role in order to claim them as the first iconophile martyrs, a claim not made explicitly in other sources?[52]

A second instance of metropolitan women maintaining the worship of icons occurs later in the *Life* when St Stephen is imprisoned in the Praetorium. Here the wife of a jailer not only provides sustenance for the iconophile prisoners, whom the saint has organized as in a monastic community, but also brings in her own icons so that they may make their devotions in the traditional manner.[53] This is a more convincing picture of female courage in resisting iconoclasm, as it takes place in the capital, generally understood as the bastion of iconoclast practice, and within a prison crowded with iconophile opponents, where imperial control must have been strong. It confirms the private and domestic nature of iconophile worship, recording the secret possession of three icons stored under lock and key in a chest, which the woman managed to conceal from her husband and the other jailers. One of these icons depicted the Virgin and Child, the other two were of Saints Peter and Paul. Although the episode may be an inflated account of some female support for St Stephen and his fellow prisoners, it seems to contain an indication of the ways in which iconophile practices were maintained throughout periods of persecution. In the 760s, when the saint was imprisoned, Constantine V had only just begun the violent campaign which would lead to Stephen's martyrdom. But the commitment to oppose iconoclasm had been made by women of no great means or education such as the jailer's wife, and at risk to their lives these people would continue to shelter the monastic victims of iconoclast attack.

Such evidence alone hardly provides a basis for analysing the relationship between women and icons, but taken in conjunction with the social restraints imposed on Byzantine women in the seventh and eighth centuries it suggests the following highly tentative conclusions. The cult of icons provided a suitable vehicle for the expression of female religiosity, being a very personal one which could be practised privately either at church or at home. For those who owned domestic icons there were no restrictions on their devotions. For others, icon veneration even in public places was less bound by particular ceremonies; it required no assistance from ecclesiastical officials and was not limited to the public celebrations of the liturgy; it could be performed at the individual's convenience and in an anonymous fashion. Given the limited participation available to women in regular church services, when they occupied special galleries or areas segregated from men, they may have found greater satisfaction in the worship associated with icons.[54]

Another factor in the attraction of icons lay in the very narrow ecclesiastical roles open to women.[55] In the early centuries of the church, before the so-called Edict of Toleration, Christian communities accorded their female members a higher status with greater equality than could be maintained in the fourth century expansion and organization of an official faith. From a position which included the potential role of martyr (and women were martyred for their Christian beliefs), their active participation was restricted to the order of deaconesses, which declined after the sixth century. There were no institutionalized female offices within the church. A male hierarchy dominated every public expression of belief, admitting men to certain lay positions but denying an equivalent role to women. Only in the philanthropic work of caring for the sick and supporting the poor were women permitted to excel, and such charitable work was largely dependent on private means and thus impossible for these without wealth. Similarly, it was harder for a Byzantine woman of average or less than average means to enter a nunnery than those with substantial dowries and land. Once established within a monastic community, however, women could express their faith fully and could attain a position of unassailable religiosity. Byzantium produced a number of female saints, many of them from wealthy backgrounds, very few of humble origins. So for the majority of Byzantine women, there were almost no outlets for religious expression apart from the cults associated with particular saints and protectors (especially the Virgin). In this context image veneration established an approved method of worship that was not dependent upon the authorities; it enabled women to find a personal and positive way of expressing their fervour.

The female devotion to icons is sometimes explained by the assumed susceptibility of women to all that is superstitious, to a particularly female belief in miracles and expectation of healing affected by cult objects. The Byzantine sources which document the growth of the cult of icons do not support this generalization; on the contrary, they reveal the universal spread of such beliefs and the equal participation of men in the veneration of icons. Of course, more men than women were literate and had some understanding of the theological debates of the times. But we should not assume that their education made them necessarily less susceptible to a fanciful interpretation of phenomena not understood until the sixteenth century. Nor did the development of icons with healing powers introduce an inevitable superstition: the church firmly believed that God could perform miracles through the medium of icons.[56] So the attraction of icons was not based solely on the illiterate and superstitious nature of women, but conversely female devotion to these images may have been related to their position in society. There may be a structural reason for their iconophilism.

We know very little about the personal beliefs of any Byzantine women. Even in the case of those individuals discussed above, there are no autobiographical records to assist us in reconstructing their views. They have to be judged by few documented acts. For Theodora there is clear evidence of her commitment to icons during her husband's iconoclast persecutions. She had her own icons in the gynacaeum of the palace and sent her children to their grandmother's monastery for instruction in iconophile veneration. Yet after 842 she did not immediately restore the image of Christ to the obverse of the gold coinage, preferring to establish her own authority as ruler in association with the young heirs, Thecla and Michael (see plate 9). In the case of Irene practically nothing is known.[57] She seems to have replaced the Christ icon on the Bronze Gate of the imperial palace and endowed some iconophile church decoration, as well as erecting a statue of herself and her son, the unfortunate Constantine VI.[58] After his removal from power, she commemorated her sole rule by placing her own image on both sides of the coinage - a new departure in Byzantine design (see plate 9). We do not know if she had harboured a deep commitment to the cause of icons during her short marriage to Leo IV, if she had domestic icons of her own, or if she adopted the iconophile position for purely political reasons. The latter cannot be ruled out for we are dealing with an untypical woman, who did not stop at the blinding of her own son, when he stood in the way of her ambition.[59]

Given their position in Byzantine society and the type of worship which the icon offered, I think that women were more probably iconophiles than iconoclasts. Precisely because the icon facilitated a private and personal form of worship, it was favoured by those excluded from public services. And their enthusiasm for the human depiction of holy persons increased the demand for icons, extended their use from tombs and churches to homes and private chapels, and emphasized the nature of direct communication open to all who venerated them. These developments might have taken place in any case; the medium of encaustic lent itself well to portraiture, and the necessary iconography had already been developed in other media, fresco and mosaic. But in Italy where the technique does not appear to have survived the fall of the Roman empire, icons were not produced until much later, when eastern models were copied.[60] The combination of early Christian practices with the encaustic portrait tradition occurred in the east, and it was in the east that faith in icons continued for many centuries, ignoring the artistic changes and religious upheavals of the Renaissance and Reformation in the west. It went through a series of alterations: the original encaustic technique was replaced by tempera, and the limited number of subjects portrayed on early icons grew to a wider range of imagery. Yet the icon retained a hold on the popular imagination for over a millennium.

This faith in icons had a very long prehistory. All the converts to the new faith were familiar with deeply ingrained customs relating to the care of the dead. In addition, many had worshipped images of deities in human form, personalized gods to whom their prayers had been directed, and practised an almost instinctive belief in the efficacy of tactile contact with these gods. These traditions were part of the common life-style of the entire Mediterranean world and the early Christians could not avoid or ignore them. From ancient funerary practice and the celebration of its martyrs, the church was predisposed to place confidence in familiar representations of holy persons. Roman portraiture and sculpture, both private and public, and the required veneration of imperial images formed a further step in the development of the early Christian encaustic icon. Pagan and secular skills were adapted, craftsmen inspired by works allegedly made under divine direction, and a new art form emerged in the later fifth or sixth century - the devotional icon.

The flexibility of this Christian medium is revealed in the great variety of functions performed by icons. They were equally suitable for large-scale images commissioned by rich patrons for the lavish decoration of churches and for small objects made in considerable numbers for a poorer market. They satisfied both public and private needs, serving to rally military forces and to protect beleaguered cities, to introduce an ecclesiastical dignitary to his diocese, to commemorate a miraculous cure and to facilitate personal prayer. In this final capacity we can see how they became especially significant for women, who were otherwise denied a full communication with the holy. Precisely because the smaller portable icons could be carried on journeys or from one house to another, they could be adapted for a purely domestic use by women. Through their particular qualities they could provide a powerful stimulus to private devotion, a visual aid to Christian worship. The larger, public icons housed in churches and shrines also exercised this capacity which attracted women and drew them into novel expressions of religiosity. The cult of icons thus grew both from a private and personal commitment, made by individuals and frequently by women, and from an institutional incorporation which recognized the power of the new art form. It was fanned by an imperial desire to control the most ancient and authentic representations of Christ and the Virgin, to house these objects and related relics in Constantinople and thus protect the imperial city.

Icons were therefore elevated to a revered position within the church while they continued to command immense popular devotion, a combination which ensured the cult's survival even through two long and severe bouts of persecution. And by the middle of the ninth century, when the second phase of iconoclasm ended, icon worship was more systematically embedded in the organized ritual of the church and re-established in the life of the ordinary Christian. The exact role of women in this historic triumph is unsatisfactorily documented. But from their positions on the throne and in the streets of the capital, they clearly played a militant part. Through their control over domestic organization, they inculcated a devotion to icons in children of both sexes, and it seems reasonable to conclude that in the East women were a major force in the preservation and reproduction of faith in icons.

NOTES

1 This fundamental justification of Christian art is given by Gregory the Great in a letter of October 600, to Serenus, bishop of Marseille, see J.P. Migne, ed., *Patrologia cursus completus*, series latina, 225 vols, Paris, 1844-64, vol. 77, col. 1128C; Eng. translation by J. Marmby, *Selected Epistles of Gregory the Great*, in *A Select Library of Nicene and Post-Nicene Fathers of the Christian Church*, second series, ed. P. Schaff and H. Wace, 14 vols, New York, 1890-1900, vol. 13, p. 53. Serenus had removed all Christian artefacts from his church because of the danger of them being worshipped. Exactly the same grounds were cited by the two Anatolian bishops who initiated the Byzantine outbreak of iconoclasm about 125 years later.

2 On the burial customs current in the first century AD, see J.M.C. Toynbee, *Death and Burial in the Roman World*, Ithaca, 1971; J. Jeremias, *Heiligengräber in Jesu Umwelt*, Göttingen, 1958; A.D. Nock, 'Cremation and Burial in the Roman Empire', in *Essays on Religion and the Ancient World*, 2 vols, ed. Z. Stewart, Cambridge, Mass., 1972, vol. 1, pp. 277-307; A. Rush, *Death and Burial in Christian Antiquity*, Washington, D.C., 1941; and in general, F. Cumont, *After Life in Roman Paganism*, New Haven, 1922; L.V. Grinsell, *Barrow, Pyramid and Tomb. Ancient burial customs in Egypt, the Mediterranean and the British Isles*, London, 1975.

3 And this belief was not always visibly recorded, leaving no positive Christian identification, see P.-A. Février,

'A propos du repas funéraire: culte et sociabilité', *Cahiers archéologiques*, vol. 26, 1977, pp. 29-45. See also, A.D. Nock, 'Early Gentile Christianity and its Hellenistic Background', *loc. cit.*, vol. I, pp. 49-133; M. Simon and A. Benoit, *Le Judaïsme et le Christianisme antique*, Paris, 1968; M. Hengel, *Property and Riches in the Early Church. Aspects of a Social History of Early Christianity*, English translation, London, 1974; H.C. van Eijk, *La Résurrection des Morts chez les Pères Apostoliques*, Paris, 1974.

4 C.H. Kraeling, *The Excavations at Dura-Europos conducted by Yale University and the French Academy of Inscriptions and Letters*, Final Report, VIII, pt. 1, *The Synagogue*, New Haven, 1956; *ibid.*, *Fifth Preliminary Report*, P.V.C. Baur, 'The Paintings in the Christian Chapel', New Haven, 1934; M. Rostovtzeff, *Dura-Europos and Its Art*, Oxford, 1938.

5 On the difficulty of distinguishing Christian from heathen art, see the texts quoted in C. Mango, *The Art of the Byzantine Empire, 312-1453. Sources and Documents*, Englewood Cliffs, New Jersey, 1972 (hereafter cited as Mango, *Art*), pp. 18, 40-1, and pp. 62-3 below. The gradual decline of ecclesiastical opposition to figural art is traced by E. Kitzinger, 'The Cult of the Icons in the Age before Iconoclasm', *Dumbarton Oaks Papers*, vol. 8, 1953, pp. 83-150; but Sister Charles Murray, 'Art and the early church', *Journal of Theological Studies*, N.S. vol. 28, 1977, pp. 303-45, claims that this opposition is much exaggerated, cf. the same author's *Rebirth and Afterlife. A Study of the transmutation of some pagan imagery in early Christian funerary art*, Oxford, 1981, pp. 13-36. For a helpful reappraisal of the literary evidence, see H.-G. Beck, 'Von der Fragwürdigkeit der Ikone', *Sitzungsberichte der Bayerischen Akademie der Wissenschaften*, Philos.-Hist. Klasse, vol. 7, 1975.

6 P.-A. Février, 'Le culte des morts dans les communautés chrétiennes durant le IIIe siècle', *Atti del IX congresso internazionale di archeologia cristiana*, Rome, 1977, vol. I, pp. 211-74; J. Pelikan, *The Shape of Death: Life, Death and Immortality in the Early Fathers*, New York, 1962; M.-L. Thérel, *Les symboles de l' 'Ecclesia' dans la création iconographique de l'art chrétien du IIIe au VIe siècle*, Rome, 1973; A. Grabar, *Christian Iconography. A Study of its Origins*, Princeton, 1968, esp. pp. 60-86.

7 K. Parlasca, *Mummienporträts und verwandte Denkmäler*, Wiesbaden, 1966; H. Zaloscer, *Vom Mumienbildnis zur Ikone*, Wiesbaden, 1969; A.F. Shore, *Portrait Painting from Roman Egypt*, British Museum, London, 1972; Toynbee, *op. cit.*, pp. 245-81; D.E.E. Kleiner, *Roman Group Portraiture: The Funerary Reliefs of the Late Republic and Early Empire*, New York/London, 1977. H.P. L'Orange, 'The Antique Origin of Medieval Portraiture', *Acta Congres-*

sus Madvigiani, Proceedings of the Second International Congress of Classical Studies, Copenhagen, 1954, vol. III, pp. 53-70; reprinted in the author's *Likeness and Icon. Selected Studies in Classical and Mediaeval Art*, Odense, 1973, pp. 91-102.

8 A. Grabar, *Martyrium. Recherches sur le culte des reliques de l'art chrétien*, Paris, 1946, reprinted London, 1972; H. Delehaye, *Les origines du culte des martyrs*, Brussels, 1933, reprinted New York, 1980; P. Brown, *The Cult of Saints. Its Rise and Function in Latin Christianity*, Chicago, 1981; W.H.C. Frend, *Martyrdom and Persecution in the Early Church*, Oxford, 1965. On the belief in St Peter's powers of intercession, see J.M.C. Toynbee and J. Ward Perkins, *The Shrine of Saint Peter and the Vatican Excavations*, London, 1956, pp. 135-62, 165-7, 170-2; P. Styger, *Die römischer Katakomben*, Berlin, 1933, pp. 341-4; R. Krautheimer, *Rome. Profile of a City, 312-1308*, Princeton, 1980, pp. 18-20; C. Pietri, *Roma christiana. Recherches sur l'église de Rome ... 311-440*, 2 vols, Rome, 1976, vol. I, pp. 272-95, 316-48. For the earliest representations of Sts Peter and Paul, which go back possibly to the second century, see Grabar, *Christian Iconography*, pp. 68-71.

9 J. Wilkinson, *Egeria's Travels*, London, 1971, pp. 158, 160, 162-3, 164-71; Mango, *Art*, pp. 11-14.

10 Brown, *op. cit.*, pp. 7-8, 42-3; but note that the practice depended on direct contact with the original tomb.

11 A. Grabar, *Ampoules de Terre Sainte (Monza-Bobbio)*, Paris, 1958; Wilkinson, *op. cit.*; on the early pilgrims and Christ's relics, cf. J. Wilkinson, *Jerusalem Pilgrims before the Crusades*, Warminster, 1977, pp. 35-6. The fact that the shroud was *not* found and commemorated in the early fourth century has given rise to a host of theories and beliefs, see the recent survey by Averil Cameron, *The Sceptic and the Shroud*, an inaugural lecture, King's College, London, 1980. The hunt for relics was to introduce a new possibility: that of bringing tombs to new cult centres, generally urban, see for example the extensive translation of relics to Constantinople, Averil Cameron, 'Images of Authority: Elites and Icons in Late Sixth-Century Byzantium', *Past and Present*, vol. 84, 1979, pp. 3-35, esp. 18-24.

12 St John Crysostom, *Homilia encomiastica in Meletium*, in J.P. Migne (ed.), *Patrologiae cursus completus, series graeco-latina*, 161 vols, Paris, 1857-94 (hereafter, Migne, *PG*), vol. 50, cols. 515-16; cf. Mango, *Art*, pp. 39-40.

13 On the cult of St Symeon and its role in the developing use of icons, see K. Holl, 'Der Anteil der Styliten am Aufkommen der Bilderverehrung', *Gesammelte Aufsätze zur Kirchengeschichte*, vol. II, *Der Osten*, Tübingen, 1928, pp. 388-98; on the Roman craftsmen, Theodoret of Cyr, *Historia Religiosa*, XXVI, in Migne, *PG*, vol. 82, cols. 1472D-1473A, cf. Mango, *Art*, p. 41.

14 *Parastaseis syntomoi chronikai*, ed. T. Preger, in *Scriptores originum Constantinopolitanorum*, ed. T. Preger, Leipzig, 1901, vol. I, para. 10, p. 25, cf. Mango, *Art*, p. 16. The Arians are also alleged to have burnt an image of the Virgin and Child. G. Ladner, *I Ritratti dei Papi nell'antichità e nel medioevo* (Vatican City, 1941) vol. I.

15 Theodore Lector, *Historia Ecclesiastica*, I, 15, in Migne, *PG*, vol. 86, col. 173A, cf. Mango, *Art*, p. 40, and Murray, *Rebirth and Afterlife* (as cited in n. 5).

16 See, for example, John of Ephesus, *Historia Ecclesiastica*, part III, ch. 29, English translation by R. Payne Smith, Oxford, 1860, pp. 214-15), and the instances cited by Mango, *Art*, pp. 40-1.

17 See the recent discussion in K. Hopkins, 'Brother-Sister Marriage in Roman Egypt', *Comparative Studies in Society and History*, vol. 22, 1980, pp. 303-54, esp. pp.348-51 and p. 353, where the mummy portraits are tentatively identified as gifts between courting couples. While this hypothesis is unlikely to account for the production of all portraits, e.g. plates 2 and 8 of Hopkins's article, their decline seems to be related to the increasing domination of Roman law and Christianity, two forces which introduced novel forms of marriage into Egypt.

18 A. Effenberger, *Koptische Kunst*, Vienna, 1975, p. 186; H. Zaloscer, *Die Kunst im christlichen Ägypten*, Vienna/ Munich, 1974, p. 118 (where the identification of the tombstone with Apa Shenute, who died in 451, is considered possible rather than definite).

19 None of these later portraits have survived, but their existence is clear from epigrams referring to the display of paintings of courtesans, commissioned by admirers, see for instance, Agathias, *Anthologia graeca*, ed. W.R. Paton, vol. 5, London, 1919, book XVI, no. 80, with a pun on the melting heart and the wax composition, cf. Mango, *Art*, p. 119. The adaptation of encaustic for religious subjects may have been promoted by imperial patronage in Constantinople.

20 Eusebius, *Onomastikon*, ed. E. Klostermann, Leipzig, 1904 (Die griechischen christlichen Schriftsteller der ersten drei Jahrhunderte, vol. 11; Eusebius *Werke*, vol. III), with Jerome's Latin translation facing. Cf. Wilkinson, *Jerusalem Pilgrims*, pp. 1-2, 47-52 (extracts from the letter of Jerome to Eustochium, ed. I. Hilberg, Leipzig/Vienna, 1912, pp. 306-51).

21 On the discovery, see Mango, *Art*, pp. 34-5; A. Wenger, *L'Assomption de la Très Sainte Vierge dans le tradition byzantine du VIe au Xe siècle*, Paris, 1955; and on the cult of the Virgin at Constantinople, Averil Cameron, 'The Cult of the Theotokos in Sixth Century Constantinople', *Journal of Theological Studies*, N.S. vol. 29, 1978, pp. 79-108.

22 On the Abgar image, see the discussion in Averil Cameron,

The Sceptic and the Shroud (cited in n. 11 above), and on the Kamouliana *acheiropoièton*, Mango, *Art*, pp. 114-15.

23 Examples of divine guidance in Mango, *Art*, pp. 144-5. On the Panagia Aggeloktistos (made by angels) at Kiti, Cyprus, see N.P. Kondakov, *Ikonografiya Bogomateri*, 2 vols, St Petersburg, 1914, vol. 1, pp. 231-40; A.H.S. Megaw and E.J.W. Hawkins, *The Church of the Panagia Kanikaria at Lythrankomi, Cyprus, Mosaics and Frescoes*, Washington, D.C., 1975, esp. pp. 168-9.

24 G.B. Ladner, *Ad Imaginem Dei. The Image of Man in Medieval Art*, Wimmer Lecture, 1962, Latrobe, Pennsylvania, 1965.

25 See the instances cited by Patriarch Germanos, Migne, *PG*, vol. 98, col. 184A, and by Bishop Theodore of Myra in 787, J.D. Mansi, *Sacrotum conciliorum nova et amplissima collectio*, 53 vols, Florence, 1759-98, reprinted Paris/Leipzig, 1901-27 (hereafter, *Mansi*), vol. XIII, cols. 33C-D. There are numerous examples in the *Miracles of Saint Artemios*, ed. A. Papadopoulos-Kerameus, *Varia graeca sacra*, St Petersburg, 1909, also publised in *Zapiski istor.-philolog. Fakulteta imperatoskago S. Petersburgskago Universiteta*, vol. 95, 1909, cf. notes 28 and 39 below.

26 M. Jugie, *La mort et l'assomption de la Sainte Vierge*, Rome, 1944, and Wenger, *op. cit.* (note 19 above).

27 On the conversion of St Mary the Egyptian, see the *Life*, ch. XVI in Migne, *PL*, vol. 75, col. 682A-C, and the late sixth-century tradition recorded by the Piacenza pilgrim, Wilkinson, *Jerusalem Pilgrims*, p. 83. On the icon of the Virgin at Sozopolis, see Eustratios, *Life of S. Eutychios*, Migne, *PG*, vol. 86, cols 2325-8. This same icon was held by Germanos to be responsible for many cures, see Migne, *PG*, vol. 98, cols 185A-B.

28 Colour reproduction in K. Weitzmann, *The Icon. Holy Images - Sixth to Fourteenth Century*, New York, 1978, pp. 48-9, plate 5.

29 K. Weitzmann, *The Monastery of S. Catherine at Mount Sinai. The Icons*, Princeton, 1976, vol. I (hereafter, Weitzmann, *Icons*), B3; also reproduced in *The Icon*, pp. 42-3, plate 2 (see note 26 above).

30 *Miracles of Saint Artemios*, no. 34, pp. 51-2; cf. C. Mango, 'On the History of the *Templon* and the Martyrion of St. Artemios at Constantinople', *Zographe*, vol. 10, 1979, pp. 40-3, to whom I am indebted for this reference. Another cure effected by St Artemios through the power of Christ was acknowledged by the invalid's mother, who gave thanks before an icon of Christ in the same shrine, see no. 43, p.72.

31 M. Krause, 'Zur Lokalisierung und Datierung koptischer Denkmäler. Das Tafelbild des Bischofs Abraham', *Zeitschrift für ägyptische Sprache und Altertumskunde*, vol. 97, 1971, pp. 106-10. Of course, the reverse may

also account for the icon, viz. that it was painted to be displayed in the monastery while Abraham was away as bishop.

32 *Vie de Théodore de Sykéôn*, ed. and trans. A.M.J. Festugière, Brussels, 1970 (Subsidia Hagiographica, 48), ch. 139; English translation in E. Dawes and N.H. Baynes, *Three Byzantine Saints*, Oxford, 1948, p. 178; cf. a similar occasion in the *Life* of St Daniel the Stylite, cf. 12, when a disciple had a portrait painted above the entrance to a chapel; the saint was furious and removed it, determined 'not to receive the glory of men', Dawes and Baynes, *op. cit.*, pp. 13-14. This fifth-century example reflects a stronger hostility to the veneration of living holy men than Theodore's in the seventh. J.D. Breckenridge, 'Apocrypha of Early Christian Portraiture', *Byzantinische Zeitschrift*, vol. 67, 1974, pp. 101-9, cites a similar opposition on the part of Plotinus. This must, however, be seen in the light of general opposition to the commemoration of the living in portraits.

33 G.A. and M. Soteriou, *Icônes du Mont-Sinaï*, Athens, 1956, 2 vols; Weitzmann, *Icons* (note 27 above).

34 Weitzmann, *Icons*, B5 and B27, respectively. There are about 30 which appear to antedate the onset of iconoclasm in 730. The three Constantinopolitan icons are B1, B3 and B5, of Christ, the Virgin enthroned with saints and angels, and St Peter.

35 Weitzmann, *Icons*, pp. 8-9; Shore, *op. cit.*, pp. 20-5.

36 Zaloscer, *op. cit.*, pp. 23-6, 59-69; M. Schapiro, *Words and Pictures. On the Literal and the Symbolic in the Illustration of a Text*, The Hague/Paris, 1973, pp. 38-49, 60 and note 79.

37 Weitzmann, *Icons*, pp. 13-15, and plates I-II, XXXIX-XLI.

38 Schapiro, *op. cit.*, p. 60; H. Maguire, 'Truth and Convention in Byzantine Descriptions of Works of Art', *Dumbarton Oaks Papers*, vol. 28, 1974, pp. 133-4; cf. Agathias' description of the eyes of an image of St Michael, Mango, *Art*, p. 115.

39 Examples of these votive images were cited at the Council of Nicaea in 787, to demonstrate divine approval of such practices, see *Mansi*, vol. XIII, cols 68A-D, 73C-76C. On the use of an icon of Saint Artemios, see the *Miracles*, no. 31, pp. 44-5 (as cited in note 23 above).

40 *Mansi*, vol. XIII, col. 65; Mango, *Art*, pp. 138-9.

41 Weitzmann, *Icons*, pp. 38-40 (on this icon, cf. p. 31 for another lidded one); *Mansi*, vol. XIII, cols 32C-33C; Mango, *Art*, p. 40.

42 I do not include Irene the Chazar, wife of Constantine V, although she is counted among iconophile empresses by Theophanes, see *Theophanis Chronographia*, ed. C. de Boor, 2 vols, Leipzig, 1883 (hereafter *Theophanes*), vol. I, pp. 409-10; cf. *Nicephori opuscula historica*, ed. C. de Boor, Leipzig, 1880 (hereafter *Nicephorus*), pp. 58, 59. She must have been a young girl at the time of her marriage (Con-

stantine was only twelve years old) and undoubtedly received instruction according to the new iconoclast theology (Leo III had just dismissed his iconophile patriarch and instituted the official destruction of icons), and she was probably kept under strict control in the imperial palace until the consummation of the alliance (her son Leo was not born until 749 and was raised as an iconoclast). So it seems extremely unlikely that Irene 'maintained the true faith' (iconophilism). Cf. S. Gero, *Byzantine Iconoclasm during the Reign of Constantine V with Particular Attention to the Oriental Sources*, CSCO, 384, Subsidia 52, Louvain, 1977, pp. 13, 22.

43 *Theophanes*, vol. I, pp. 444-5; *Nicephorus*, p. 77. From the fact that Irene was born in Greece, many historians have concluded that the whole Balkan peninsula was devoted to the cult of icons and that iconoclasm had no effects there. To generalize in this way from one isolated example seems quite unsafe; in addition, it is highly unlikely that the fervent iconoclast Constantine V would have permitted his eldest son, Leo, to marry an iconophile. A much more probable explanation is to be sought in the suitability of the alliance which Irene brought to Constantinople. Central Greece was not an area firmly controlled by the capital, and Irene's family, the Serantapychos, was obviously an influential one. On this, see the fascinating survey by P. Speck, *Kaiser Konstantin VI. Die Legitimation einer fremden und der Versuch einer eigenen Herrschaft*, 2 vols, Munich, 1978, Appendix III, vol. I, pp. 405-19; vol. II, pp. 821-30.

44 Symeon the logothete, *Chronographia*, p. 624; George the monk, *Vitae imperatorum recentiorum*, pp. 789-90; cf. Theophanes Continuatus, p. 89, all three ed. I. Bekker, *Corpus Scriptorum Historiae Byzantinae*, vol. 45, Bonn, 1838. For a useful discussion of the source material and the chronology, see W.T. Treadgold, 'The Problem of the Marriage of the Emperor Theophilus', *Greek, Roman and Byzantine Studies*, vol. 16, 1975, pp. 325-41.

45 Symeon the logothete, p. 629-30; Theophanes Continuatus, pp. 91-2 (both as cited above, note 44).

46 On Euphrosyne, who was the second wife of Michael II and step-mother of Theophilus, see *Josephi Genesii, Regnum Libri Quattuor*, ed. H. Lesmueller and I. Thurn, Berlin/New York, 1978, p. 35; Symeon the logothete, pp. 628-9; Theophanes Continuatus, pp. 78-9, 86, 89-90 (where Theodora's mother, Theoktiste, is confused with Euphrosyne); and Treadgold, *art. cit.*

47 J. Gouillard, 'Le Synodikon de l'Orthodoxie. Edition et Commentaire', *Travaux et Mémoires*, vol. 2, 1967, pp. 1-316, esp. 119-38, 160-82.

48 Migne, *PG*, 100, cols 1076 B-D, 1080A. Later in the *Life* of St Stephen the destruction of this icon is recorded together

with Constantine V's redecoration of the church, *ibid.*, col. 1120C. But the fame of the icon was such that in the eleventh century an encaustic painting of the Virgin found at Blachernai was immediately identified as the same one, see Gero, *op. cit.*, p. 112; note 5. Other icons survived iconoclast attacks through divine protection, for example, the mosaic icon of Patriarch Germanos, or the relics of St Euphemia; some were undoubtedly protected by being covered up, the mosaic decoration at the church of Hosios David in Thessalonike is a well-known example. The destruction of figural representation in the capital appears to have been quite thorough: until the archeological discovery of the Kalenderhane mosaic of the Presentation in the Temple no pre-iconoclast iconic decoration had been found.

49 Migne, *PG*, 99, cols 883-902; about twenty women feature in his two published volumes of correspondence, *ibid.*, cols 903-1607, cf. A. Mai, *Novae Patrum Bibliothecae*, ed. J. Cozza-Luzi, 8 vols, Rome, 1844-71, vol. III, pp. 1-244; J. Gouillard, 'La femme de qualité dans l'oeuvre de Théodore Stoudite', *Résumés der Kurzbeiträge, XVI Internationaler Byzantinistenkongress*, Vienna, 1981, 4/4.

50 Migne, *PG*, 105, cols 901 A-B.

51 Migne, *PG*, 100, cols 1085C. This detail is omitted in Theophanes' account, *Theophanes*, vol. I, p. 405, and further elaborated in the probably spurious letter to Leo III, attributed to Pope Gregory II, see J. Gouillard, 'Aux origines de l'iconoclasme: Le témoignage de Grégoire II?' *Travaux et Mémoires*, vol. 3, 1968, pp. 243-307, esp. p. 293, lines 218-25. Here the icon is identified as one of Christ called Antiphonites, which was in the Chalkoprateia; the women are held responsible for the death of an officer, a *spatharokandidatos*, called Julian.

52 Migne, *PG*, 100, cols 1085 C-D; cf. *Theophanes*, vol. I, p. 409, where the first record of Leo III's violent persecution of iconophiles is connected with his dismissal of Patriarch Germanos in January 730. Stephen the deacon, author of the *Life*, has conflated the two incidents of 726 and 730 in fact, for he places the removal of the Christ icon and subsequent martyrdom of the women of Constantinople in the year when Anastasios was patriarch, i.e., after January 730. The reason for this muddle is probably Stephen's desire to give greater honour to Patriarch Germanos, whose lack of protest over the 726 event was considered shameful by later iconophiles, see G.L. Huxley, 'On the *Vita* of S. Stephen the Younger', *Greek, Roman and Byzantine Studies*, vol. 18, 1977, pp. 97-108; M.-F. Rouan, 'Une lecture "Iconoclaste" de la Vie d'Etienne le Jeune', *Travaux et Mémoires*, vol. 8, 1981, pp. 415-36.

53 Migne, *PG*, 100, col. 1164A.

54 On the changing position of women in Byzantium, see my study, 'De Veranderigen in de positie van vrouwen in het

Byzantijnse Rijk', *Jaarboek voor vrouwengeschiedenis*, 1980, pp. 141-60; J. Beaucamp, 'La situation juridique de la femme à Byzance', *Cahiers de civilisation médiévale*, vol. 20, 1977, pp. 145-76; J. Grosdidier de Matons, 'La femme dans l'empire byzantin', in P. Grimal (ed.), *Histoire mondiale de la femme*, 3 vols. Paris, 1974, vol. III, pp. 11-43. A. Laiou, 'The Role of Women in Byzantine Society', *XVI Internationaler Byzantinistenkongress*, Part I/1, pp. 233-60, = *Jahrbuch der Österreichischen Byzantinistik*, 31/1, 1981.

55 J. Herrin, 'Women and the church in Byzantium', *Bulletin of the British Association of Orientalists*, vol. 11, 1980, pp. 8-14. D. Abrahamse, 'Women's Monasteries in the Middle Byzantine Period', and E.A. Clark '"Humble Leadership": A Conflict of Values in Early Women's Monasticism', two papers prepared for the Seventh Byzantine Studies Conference (Boston, November 1981), to appear in *Byzantinische Forschungen*. I am grateful to both authors for permission to read these texts.
authors for permission to read these texts.

56 See the categorical statement by Germanos cited in note 25 above.

57 Irene is certainly one of the most striking personalities of the eighth century and her proposed second marriage to Charlemagne one of the greatest might-have-beens of early medieval history, but of her personal beliefs we remain ignorant, see Speck, *op. cit.*, vol. I, pp. 323-88, vol. II, pp. 733-813.

58 On Irene's artistic patronage, see R. Cormack, 'The Arts during the Age of Iconoclasm', in A. Bryer and J. Herrin (eds), *Iconoclasm*, Centre for Byzantine Studies, University of Birmingham, 1977, pp. 35-44.

59 Speck, *op. cit.*, vol. I, pp. 283-321, vol. II, p. 705-31.

60 On the early medieval encaustic icons in Rome, some of which seem to have been introduced by eastern popes, see Krautheimer, *op. cit.*, (note 8 above) pp. 91, 100-5. In some respects relics served as the western equivalent of icons, see P. Brown, *The Cult of Saints*, and A. Grabar, *Martyrium*, vol. II, pp. 343-57, on the close relationship between relics and icons (both cited in note 7 above).

5 PLEBEIAN CULTURE IN THE TRANSITION TO CAPITALISM

Hans Medick*

EVERYDAY LIFE AND POPULAR CULTURE

Recent research into the social life of the lower orders and classes of town and country in early modern times has been marked by important, new initiatives. The pioneering work of Edward Thompson, George Rudé and Eric Hobsbawm, and also of the French social historians, such as Yves Bercé and Mona Ozouf, first draw attention to exceptional, spectacular manifestations of popular culture: food riots and price revolts, carnivals and politically rebellious festivals. Today, however, the history of the everyday cultural expressions, experiences and life-style of the common people in town and country seems increasingly to be attracting interest.

Essentially, popular culture presupposes a fully thought out materialistic concept of culture. For, in Marcel Mauss's words, the social life of the pre-capitalistic rural and urban lower classes from the sixteenth to early nineteenth century must be understood as a 'total social fact'; this social life is neither a quasi autonomous aggregate of cultural artefacts, beside or beyond politics, economics and class structure, nor an ideological superstructure derived from its determining base. Rather, the popular culture of the rural and urban lower classes should be conceived and investigated as a 'material culture', that is, as an integral and essential moment in the everyday production and reproduction of the social relations of production.

This said, 'popular culture' may be taken to be those symbolic and structured attitudes, norms and practices through which the lower orders experience, articulate and act in response to their own social relations. This matrix should not be regarded as being more or less outside class, as was the normal practice in traditional German studies of folk history and also in the early French studies of 'mentalité'. Rather, as the English Marxist historians have rightly insisted, popular culture in history is more the expression of a 'whole way of conflict' than of some kind of classless 'whole way of life'. It is true that popular culture does, on the one hand, function - perhaps in the familial and kinship systems, of village or of guild - as an

*Hans Medick researches at the Max Planck Institute, Göttingen University, and is engaged in a longitudinal study, over five centuries, of a Swabian village. He is co-author of *Industrialisation before Industrialisation*, Cambridge University Press, 1982.

agency of adjustment, tending to produce equality, in the sphere of production and reproduction. On the other hand, it is the abundant evidence of resistance, even when concealed or silent, which predominates in those social relations which are determined by the processes of surplus extraction and appropriation.

Gerald Sider has presented the thesis that the peculiar independence and capacity for resistance of early modern popular culture against the attacks and inroads of domination and hegemony was anchored in the domestic and familial mode of production and, in terms of class, relatively undifferentiated relations of production. Though this seems to be central to an understanding of popular culture, it is not sufficient. At least one further dimension of cultural resistance can be identified, namely the peculiar forms of experience and practice in popular culture. These are connected with and sometimes inseparable from oral traditions or ritual and customary behaviour.

In my opinion, it remains to be clarified whether changed forms of the capacity for resistance could not have become conscious, just at the time of the transition to capitalism, and then been passed on. This period - from the sixteenth to the early nineteenth century - is characterised, on the one hand, by increasing fragmentation of class relations in both town and country and the at least partial dissolution of the old household and guild organisation of production. On the other hand, Peter Burke has identified this period as 'the golden age of traditional popular culture'. Perhaps we should ask, putting Sider's theory to one side, whether it was not the particular modes of experience and the practices peculiar to popular culture, namely non-literary traditions, non-verbal communication and ritual and customary action, which constituted a decisive obstacle to the advance and triumph of the cultural norms of elite and civic culture?

In the study of non-European, primitive and peasant societies social anthropologists have established a close connection between a mode of experience which compounds irreducibly cognitive, emotional and active elements on the one hand and, on the other, modes of action and expression characterised by the predominance of ceremony and ritual. And this sort of combination, wherever else it may be found, seems to have been a fact for the popular culture of the lower orders at the time of the emergence of capitalism.

PLEBEIAN CULTURE AS THE 'PLEBEIAN PUBLIC'

The term 'plebeian culture' is taken to designate as a better, a more specific term the common people's ways of life and experience during the transition to capitalism, than the vaguer and much used phrase, 'popular culture'. 'Plebeian' evokes well that obstinacy of behaviour and expression characteristic of the 'lower orders', as it was seen with a mixture of contempt and fear 'from above'. It is this compound of simultaneous resistance and insurgency but also of dependence upon the ruling orders and classes and upon their 'civilised', elite culture that we are after. 'Plebeian' seems, therefore, most fit to capture the richness, the contradictions and the dynamic of those forms of experience and expression which constitute the socio-cultural reproduction of the urban and rural lower strata during the transition to capitalism. Characteristic of 'plebeian culture' was the twofold meeting of traditional ways of perception, social rules, morals and customs with, the new reality of early capitalist markets and production relations on the one hand, and with the politics of discipline in religion, morality and commerce, enforced by the police powers of the early modern state on the other.

The existence of relatively independent kinds of communication, their peculiarly 'communal' expression and their place as part of a concrete, historical class and power system is made clearer by 'plebeian' than by 'popular culture'. Plebeian culture appears to constitute a particular type of public.[1] It possesses that sensuous physical character which Basil Bernstein has termed 'expressive symbolism' and distinguishes itself both from the 'public realm of reason' of the educated bourgeoisie and from the seigneurial, ceremonial self-display of the aristocracy, 'the official public'. When Edward Thompson writes that symbolic and poetical meanings have always been most powerful at the popular level, when those showing popular belief systems felt no necessity to defend their opinions with rationalistic argument,[2] he means just the context of 'expressive symbolism', the plebeian public realm. Here, symbol and the experience that comprehends it are linked not by intellect but by ritual customary actions.

Jürgen Habermas in his book about the development of the liberal fiction of the bourgeois public space only touched upon our problem. He did, however, introduce the expression, 'the plebeian public' when speaking of suppressed alternatives to the dominant public, but limited it to one particular historical context:[3]

> In that stage of the French Revolution which is inseparable from the name of Robespierre there surface, for a moment, a public ... stripped of its literary costume and no longer belonging to the educated classes, but to the uneducated people. Nevertheless, this plebeian public, which lived on underground in the Chartist movement and in the anarchistic traditions of the European workers' movement, shared the intentions of the bourgeois public ... [for] like this it was an heirloom of the 18th century.

Thus, Habermas conceives of the 'plebeian public' as a self-contradictory association which emerged as a historical reaction to the 'bourgeois public' and yet remains fixed in its relationship to it. Oskar Negt and Alexander Kluge have - perhaps a little hastily - stripped the 'plebeian public' of this contradictory character. They regard the 'plebeian public' as merely a 'species' of the 'bourgeois public' and sharply distinguish it from the 'proletarian public'.[4] The 'proletarian public' is characterised by its 'direct', sensual and collective mode of experience in contradistinction to the 'mediated', intellectual mode of experience of the bourgeois. Further they speak of 'a concept of the public which is rooted in the process of production', something quite alien to the separation of 'public' and 'private' in bourgeois life. The 'plebeian public' is bound up with work and with socialisation through the family.

Such a characterisation, however, seems to me to point more to the similarity of historical and structural relationships shared by plebeian and proletarian publics than to what divides them. This provokes the question whether and to what extent the 'public' of the proletariat in the nineteenth and twentieth centuries shared the same modes of expression and contradictions as plebeian culture; whether proletarian culture was not only the successor to plebeian culture, but also, in important respects, its product. An analysis merely of the fixed or possible modes of experience and perception in each of the cultures - what Negt and Kluge call 'experience in the manufacture of experience' - could be important in this context. The question posed by a historically informed working-class history is, then, to what extent, if at all, do the particular modes of action and experience of plebeian life and culture correspond to, or find their continuation in, those of the proletariat?

PLEBEIAN CULTURE BETWEEN PLEBEIAN ECONOMY AND CAPITALIST ENTERPRISE

Our first task must be a detailed reconstruction of the forms and functions of plebeian popular culture. In his various works Edward Thompson has sought, in the case of England, to understand the social logic and the modes of expression of plebeian culture from the experiences of the lower orders themselves. In contrast to his first relevant work, *The Making of the English Working Class*, Thompson's later investigations exhibit increased efforts to comprehend general social relations, and, in conjunction with this, more attention to the limits to change in a plebeian culture embedded in 'tradition'.[5]

The decisive 'battlefield' in which plebeian culture was to develop was, according to Thompson, conditioned by the particular class formations of eighteenth-century English society: the simultaneous polarity and reciprocity of 'patricians' and 'plebeians'. This antagonistic symbiosis between a part of the ruling class and the lower orders was a historical consequence of the 'Glorious Revolution' of 1688, which split the upper classes into a Court and a Country party. In these circumstances, the representatives of the Country interests, the gentry or 'agrarian bourgeoisie', could only obtain a position of hegemony through concessions to the lower orders. This necessary consideration and the anti-absolutist politics of the gentry, to which they owed their domination, conditioned their use of power. They relied more on the techniques of symbolic domination, 'cultural hegemony' and the introduction of legal institutions - as Thompson has shown in his interesting study *Whigs and Hunters* - than upon active repression and constant police supervision of the masses. What was specifically 'rebellious' in the dynamic of plebeian culture was, on the whole, bounded by these limits.

Had this been the only perspective from which Thompson revealed the unfolding of plebeian culture, this great 'hunter of the Whigs' would at the same time have to appear as one of the last of the Whig historians. Plebeian culture seems to be a scion of old Anglo-Saxon freedoms and owes its existence to the liberality of the gentry. And Thompson is certainly not, in my opinion, wholly free from this viewpoint. Decisive, however, is his own emphasis of the independent dynamic of plebeian culture: a 'creative culture-forming process from below'.[6] This process, according to Thompson, had its basis in the changes in the agrarian and proto-industrial relations of production, which, on the one hand, had, especially since the seventeenth century, freed small producers from patriarchal, manorial control, and on the other, exposed them to the new restrictions of capitalistically structured markets.

From the collision of the traditional, socio-cultural rules and the bounded experience of the plebeians with these altered socio-economic conditions emerged, according to Thompson, the dynamic of English plebeian culture. And it is in the realm of the spectacular that he sees its chief agency of expression: in food riots and in price revolts, and in the theatrical and ritualistic mass action of fairs, festivals and holidays. This is indeed an autonomous sphere of plebeian culture. Thompson, however, seeks to explain these 'communal', symbolic and ritualistic modes of action and perception specific to the plebeian arena not from the internal structure of their experience, but from the reciprocity and antagonism in the class relations between gentry and commoners. These relations become stylised as if in theatre or anti-theatre; the struggle for power is upon a public and symbolic plane. Thus, the commoners acquire 'class-consciousness', but never that perspective which would challenge the hegemony of the gentry. For Thompson, this limitation of 'class-consciousness' is, in the last resort, a consequence of the cultural hegemony and symbolic domination of the gentry.

This, highly abbreviated, summary of Thompson's theses raises a number of critical questions and these in turn will serve to introduce my own interpretation. What is, in my opinion, questionable is Thompson's postulate of a throughly conscious and accentuated conflict between the forces of the new capitalist markets and relations of production, and the traditional norms of behaviour and socio-cultural rules which motivated and conditioned plebeian actions.

Thompson's 'rebellious traditional culture' of the plebeians is a 'conservative culture' whose strongest impulse in its activities and its resistance is drawn from a protest against capitalism:

> capitalist logic and non-economic, tradition-bound behaviour [of the plebeians] come into an active and conscious conflict as for example in the resistance of new modes of consumption ('demand'), or in the resistance to the imposition of clock discipline and against technological innovations and rationalisation in the work process which threaten to destroy the family based relations of production. Thus, we may read the social history of the eighteenth century as a succession of confrontations between an innovatory market economy and the tradition-bound moral economy of the plebeians.

Corresponding to this interpretation, it is the spectacular and confrontational manifestations of rebellious popular culture which, for Thompson, stand in the foreground, as, for example, when driven by 'the moral economy of the crowd' in food riots and price revolts. Thompson's work lacks an analysis of those quieter, but equally 'communal' characteristic manifestations of the everyday life of the plebeian lower orders, which developed - to a considerable extent in harmony with the growth of capitalistic markets - in consumption, fashions and especially in drinking culture. Here, in my view, is the crucial deficiency of Thompson's interpretation: in fact, the plebeian culture of the poor and propertyless is - as had been true of the culture of the propertied peasant from the sixteenth century - essentially a market phenomenon. This was true in a double sense and herein lies its central dialectic.

Plebeian culture is a market phenomenon in the first sense because there is a destructive contradiction between its bearers and the penetration of capitalistic markets into their traditional way of life, a contradiction that was publicly and spectacularly operative in food riots and price revolts. But it is also a market phenomenon in a positive, well adapted and dynamic sense. The plebeian producers invest not only 'enormous emotional capital' in their socio-cultural reproduction, as Thompson has highlighted, but also a considerable part of their usually modest monetary income.

In this 'economic' perspective it is the family economy that constitutes the hinge upon which 'plebeian culture' revolves. It is true that household and family do not directly determine the spectrum of symbols or modes of expression which characterise plebeian culture. Rather, these are firmly bound to collective practices, as dictated by morals and customs observed by peer groups, neighbourhood associations and the local market. Nevertheless, to use Daniel Thorner's terms, the 'labour-consumer-balance' of the small producers was anchored in the domestic economy, and regulated cultural practices through its own stubborn propensities, those of economic need. Thus, it was only through a 'labour-consumer-balance' centred in the domestic economy that the external economic pressures were, as it were, transformed into cultural energy. On the one hand, the relations of production were making the poor and propertyless of town and country increasingly dependent on wage labour, commodity exchange and a money economy. On the other, those same relations of production continued - well expressed in Olwen Hufton's phrase, 'economy of the last-resort' - to follow the social logic of the domestic economy, which demanded an immediate balance between work and consumption. Herein emerged the specific imbalance between long-term, scanty monetary incomes and short-term, extravagant expenditure, which defied all admonitions to thrift and prudence, and expressed a decided preference for the satisfaction of the growing needs created by a commodity economy. The frequent journalistic criticisms of what might today be called 'economic mismanagement' among the small producers points to such behaviour, even after we have allowed for class prejudices.

In comparison with the principles of bourgeois thrift and foresight, where wealth was due 'not so much to great income as to moderate expenditure'[7] the economy of the plebeian orders distinguished itself by the fact that their expenditure stood in no 'proper' relation to their revenue. In this respect the behaviour of the small producers was closer to that of the 'man of rank' than to that of the 'properly earning class, those of middle-rank'. As a contemporary observer, J.A. Günther, noticed:[8]

> Unaccustomed to the money economy; unfamiliar with the thousand essential or conventional needs of life which attended him, not knowing their true worth or the art of satisfying them with all possible thrift, strange to the whole business of accounting in a private economy, he never thinks of establishing a determinate budget which would set his expenditure in proportion to his income and order all his expenses, from greatest to smallest, under distinctive headings. Instead, he spends as long as he has, denies himself and others no pleasure of life, no gratification of some sensual whim....becomes prodigal in expenditure and everywhere becomes exposed to misfortune.

This behaviour, so negatively represented by upper and middle-class critics, in fact shows its own rationality and positive consequences. By no means irrational, it is simply the expression of preferences and priorities which were profoundly different from those which the moralising, mercantilist advocates of thrift and industry sought to impose. These priorities, however, were the conditions of the possibility of plebeian culture:[9]

> Those who are most familiar with the customs and habits of these persons report that they work for nothing beyond their bare upkeep, and never think to make provision for the future. And though they squander much of their earnings at horse racing, their families receive the same subsistence money as ever; the only difference being that they then work very much harder in order to meet the extravagant expenses occasioned by these festivities.

The lower orders of town and country continued to act according to the rules of a peasant or craftsman, family-based, subsistance economy, though their situation was one of increasingly dependent reproduction, as money income through piece-work, or at least wage-labour regulated by time, became the basis for their survival. It was an economy that reckoned with money income and the universal exchange and circulation of commodities, but still according to the norms of an economy with separated spheres of circulation, where goods were ordered into a hierarchy of usefulness and still endowed with symbolic meaning. The long-term needs of the household had a relatively low priority in the monetary sphere. By contrast, the demand for public consumption in the monetary sphere was extraordinarily high.[10]

Such 'economic' priorities produced a kind of behaviour in consequence that was typical not only of the plebeian lower orders, but also of the industrial proletariat of the nineteenth century. For that too united a fairly 'scanty' reproduction of its daily existence according to 'tradition' and custom with relatively high expenditure upon public rituals and funerals, upon festivals and games and, moreover, upon everyday forms of active public consumption - be they the pleasures of the pub or the carrying of a pocket watch. Money income did not yet play the role of a universal medium and intermediary for the whole field of needs and preferences. It did not serve as a continuous balance between the utility of the goods which satisfied daily needs against that of luxuries, nor to effect savings which could secure the former. A money income that exceeded the expenses of meeting the immediate, short-term demands of subsistence was, to some degree, viewed as a surplus above life's necessities. It could be invested in sociocultural reproduction, permitting the purchase of prestige and luxury goods and defraying the costs of demonstrative outlays for festivals, celebrations and other rituals of interaction. For the small producer money as a means of hoarding reserves was as remote as his chances of long-term accumulation, in the face of capitalistic exploitation and surplus-extraction. Money income, therefore, found its most 'rational' use in its relatively short-term conversion into the currency of sociocultural reproduction.

This type of activity should not be seen simply as the product of the structural dispositions of the family economy. For it was, to a high degree, caused by the material conditions of life and labour for the lower orders in town and country and by their position in their respective class structures. The everyday experience of particular forms of exploitation, which often arose more from the system of distribution than from the work-process itself, made money and money income in particular into what J. Moser has called an 'instrument of primitive class struggle' for the independent consumers and producers. Debts with moneylenders, tradesmen, shopkeepers and above all with landlords (who were frequently the source of work), excessive and 'starvation' rents, which bore particularly on smallholdings, and finally the tax demands of the state (of which excise duties on consumer goods were the most important) constituted an oppressive load. To this the small producers could only respond with renewed recourse to their traditional economic logic.

A strategy of money saving or, indeed, one of maximising earnings was, in such a situation, neither rational nor possible; what was rational was to minimise the continually threatened losses, and that implied the immediate spending of money income which was usually uncertain and by no means regular.

The 'social exchange', as it occurred in festivals, sports and celebrations, in the exchange of gifts, and also in the ordinary events of daily 'display', could, in such circumstances, be more sensible, even in an 'economic' sense, than the hoarding of money earnings. It did not matter whether the occasion was a marriage, a christening or a burial: the non-monetary giving and receiving which lay at the bottom of all these public rituals constituted a solid economic advantage for the lower orders; for their life and work situation during the transition to capitalism was one of fundamental uncertainty and unpredictability. In this way, the common people came nearest to a kind of 'social security' against misfortune and 'hard times'. Such an advantage would hardly have been achieved through individual saving and a 'middle-class' ethic of life and work. For the 'social exchange' that was so typical an expression of plebeian culture strengthened the bonds of kinship, neighbourhood and friendship. Thus, it produced or reproduced just that solidarity to which the small producers could, in times of dearth, crisis and need, most easily have recourse. Be that as it may, it did not lead to an 'egalitarian Utopia'. The forces of social distinction and of elevated claims to status made themselves felt even in plebeian circles. Brotherly help for the weak frequently found its limits, even in the plebeian forms of 'social exchange', in the barriers of respectability and prestige.

The above argument permits a number of conclusions to be drawn: the timely introduction of anthropology into history called for by Edward Thompson and practised by colleagues such as Natalie Davis, Gerald Sider and Keith Thomas[11] - should in one important respect be radicalised, along the lines indicated by Pierre Bourdieu. Bourdieu demands an abandonment of the 'dichotomy between the economic and the non-economic' and its replacement by a 'general science of the economy of practical action', so that 'the theory of properly economic activities is only a special case within a theory of the economy of human action.'[12]

In the analysis of plebeian culture this means that the symbolic action of the small producers, their conspicuous consumption in festivals, celebrations, sports and other forms of excessive 'expenditure' (G.Bataille) should be examined in the light of their economic grounds or economic significance. Above all else, therefore, attention should be focused upon the relationship between the spectacular and the non-spectacular moments of 'everyday' life. The question is, to what extent were both moments expressions of one 'economy', which in the context of increasing dependency upon money income still obeyed or partially obeyed the norms of the old subsistence economy?

Such an interpretation, however, must lead beyond Thompson's account of the 'social logic' of plebeian culture as a 'plebeian community'. Thompson seeks to illuminate this logic by setting it against the class rivalries of eighteenth-century England; he thereby overemphasises the communal public and spectacular interaction constituted by the symbiotic antagonism of gentry and commoners. His interest in the political and rebellious forms of plebeian community blind him to its other dimension. These contain all those features which were a consequence of the new capitalism and of the markets and class relations resulting from it.

This side of the plebeian arena should be investigated in the context of the consumption of luxuries, fashions, the 'prodigality' of festivals and celebrations, and also in the habits, precepts and expressions of daily life.

To press the point we may say that what P. Bourdieu's 'symbolic capital' did for the lord, 'ready coin' did for the working man. His money income found its meaningful expenditure - as did the symbolic capital of the lord - far more in public display and appearances than in precautionary savings. 'Ready coin' realised its worth - as did the capital of the lords - primarily in the transformation of economic goods into those symbolic and communicative acts, i.e. into socio-cultural actions and manifestations, which first and foremost gave meaning to the plebeian existence. The ambiguous symbols of this kind of 'expenditure' manifested themselves above all in drinking culture, but also in fashions and jewellery and in the consumption of colonial goods such as sugar, tea, coffee and tobacco. These symbols had a strong, socially associative and compensatory function. Especially at the local level, they constituted an important medium for the resolution of class oppositions, and not only with peasant proprietors, but also with the urban bourgeoisie.

The observations of a Thuringian country-dweller, probably an administrative official, provide a good example from the end of the eighteenth century: he complained vigorously that the 'outward culture of refinement of the higher and middle ranks' had spread to the 'meaner classes of people'. In the age of the French Revolution, he, with especial alertness, perceived such consumption as a potential threat. His remarks, however, contain more than his own fears; they also reveal the plebeian wilfulness that was united to the desire for 'refinement' of the 'meaner classes of people':[13]

> Also the less wealthy, yes even the poor allow themselves ever more wants and even suppose, thanks to their distorted idea of a universal equality of mankind, that they must join their wealthy fellow citizens or the higher ranks in expenditure and in lifestyle, in order to fulfil the rights of man that he claims to have been born with. This, however, very often exceeds his powers in an economic respect....At a festive occasion where people of rank were dined according to desire....I saw a poor, but proud day-labourer take a meal of Bremen Bricks [river lampreys from north Germany, a fashionable, marketed fish of the time] and drink down a bottle of malaga with it just because he wanted to join in with the so-called people of rank. Before this day he knew neither the fish nor the wine by name. This single meal cost the man more than he could earn in two full weeks....I know of persons in the country who are so proud in this respect that they willingly stint themselves of necessities only in order to be able to assert their right to mix with the wealthy at public amusements.

In this ambivalent way consumption functioned as a vehicle of plebeian self-consciousness. True, such a consciousness cannot be seen as an explicit manifestation of class-consciousness in the sense that Thompson means when he speaks of the 'active and conscious conflict between the capitalist process and traditional, non-economic behaviour'. Nevertheless, it contains a social expression of wants which frequently bears undertones of class-consciousness. This form of plebeian consciousness manifests itself primarily outwards as an aspiration to status through the public and symbolic demonstration of a 'superior' life-style. This was hardly an attempt to transcend the existing class relations. Even when plebeian culture precipitated some action which clearly and self-consciously ran against the norms of the ruling class, it seldom challenged the received status system. Plebeian self-consciousness was unable to develop an autonomous potential for hegemony. It remained, even in its most extreme forms, on the plane of social exchange or competition. The concept of a 'displaced class struggle', coined by Louise Tilly to describe food riots and price revolts, may therefore have more general application.[14]

Forms of 'derived class-consciousness' were also common; here the antagonism against a local or regional ruling elite received expression through recourse to the example of a rival ruling elite. An example of such explicit antagonism between plebeian determination and a regional ruling-class is offered by the East German ethnologist Bernd Schöne in his recent interesting, work. It shows how domestically employed ribbon weavers in eighteenth-century rural Saxony attained a class-consciousness in their conflict with the dominant peasant environment by adopting the clothing fashions of the urban bourgeoisie. Schöne summarises his account as follows:[15]

> By dressing themselves as others...the independently producing ribbon weavers departed from peasant modes of dress and chose as a model those fashions favoured by the urban bourgeoisie...It was above all the striking clothing worn by female relatives of the ribbon weavers that was so different from customary peasant costume and expressed so conspicuously the desire of the weavers to exhibit their self-conscious social position. The ribbon weavers' endeavour consciously to dress themselves differently from the peasants was part of their struggle for social recognition in a peasant dominated world. Greater regard and more esteem within their society was what they wanted. They believed that increased prestige was due to them in virtue of their contribution to the rural economy.

This example, to which many others could be added, indicates a central dimension of plebeian consciousness. It was strongly determined by such norms as respectability, prestige and distinction. And under conditions of extreme poverty and need, a 'raised' consumption was the medium in which the plebeian orders could achieve such distinction. The remarks of a contemporary observer at the beginning of the nineteenth century make this clear. He wrote of the lower orders of the little town of Sulz in Württemberg: 'Even those who eat nothing but potatoes at breakfast and midday would consider themselves less than human if they were compelled to give up their morning coffee.'[16]

In this and like cases, frequently orientated through social exchange within a single social order, plebeian consciousness resembled that conception of respectability which Gareth Stedman Jones described as an essential characteristic of the 'inward-looking culture' of London's working classes as late as the second half of the nineteenth century.[17] However, the behaviour which resulted from this consciousness was not necessarily 'inward-looking'. It could, with the aid of shared symbols of consumption, turn itself aggressively outwards; as it did, for example, with the 'tobacco, drinking, smoking, chewing and eating' of men and women from the lower orders around Zurich at the end of the seventeenth and the beginning of the eighteenth centuries. 'To the great disgust and disapproval of pious and honest people' these men and women regularly smoked 'publically and shamelessly' on their way to church 'and the Godless even during the preaching'.[18] For these and similar manifestations of plebeian culture and the plebeian arena, Rudolf Braun's remark is pertinent: 'If up till then, social position had been the basis for luxury, now luxury became the basis for social position.'[19]

The forms in which plebeian culture expressed itself in the extraordinary consumption of luxuries were certainly influenced by capitalist (but by no means industrial) laws of market and utilisation, but they cannot be reduced to them. The use which the plebeian lower orders made of these new luxuries did not conform to such laws. Even if the forces of the new capitalism did, objectively and permanently, 'socialise' and subordinate the plebeians, the potential of their new system of demands and its articulation remains undecided. How fixed or how variable? How hermetically closed or how open to memories and change were those, in a quite essential respect, experiences and insights essential to the plebeian arena? It may be that the plebeians in their cultural life received only a counterfeit of these dreams, wishes that could never be realised in their repressed and 'needy' life-circumstances. Indisputable, however, is that they exploited the advantages of inchoate capitalism, without acknowledging its limitations.

A NEW THIRST AND ITS BACKGROUND: HOGARTH, *GIN LANE* AND *BEER STREET* (Plates 10 and 11)

An example of the complex and at once functional and contradictory relationship in which the material culture of the plebeian masses stood to the politics and economics of mercantile capitalism is to be seen in the change and constancy of plebeian drinking customs. The decline of beer as a popular drink and source of nourishment and the rise of spirits as both plebeian and proletarian daily drink and solace cannot be seen in isolation from the significance of other drinks, stimulants and luxuries; nevertheless, the changes in the consumption of alcoholic drinks play a central role in the early modern 'revolution of Europe's diet'. This revolution was in no way a child of industrial capitalism. An acute contemporary and early social historian, Professor August Ludwig Schölzer of Göttingen (1735-1809) described its consequences at the end of the eighteenth century as already epoch-making. 'It is indisputable that the discovery of spirits, the arrival of tobacco, sugar, coffee and tea in Europe have brought about revolutions just as great, if not greater, than the defeat of the Invincible Fleet, the Wars of the Spanish Succession, the Paris Peace etc.'[20] What role did beer and spirits play in this 'revolution', and what did they signify in the life of the common people in the context of emerging capitalism? I should like in the following section to unravel these problems by means of an example which is both concrete and specific in time and place. From this two things should become clear: first, the limited state of research on the social history of alcohol and, more generally, of the patterns of consumption of the plebeian strata and classes in early modern times - research which has often not yet recovered the level of inquiry and insight of the eighteenth century; and second, the significance of exemplary, intensively described cases - as customary in social anthropology - for historical understanding.

William Hogarth (1697-1764) was neither historian nor ethnographer,[21] but he was in his own way a master of 'thick description'.[22] He was an engraver in the most developed country of his day and both an observer, whose powers were unrivalled, and a moral critic of the plebeian masses of eighteenth-century London. At the climax of the so-called gin epidemic around the middle of the century he produced two striking allegories, *Gin Lane* and *Beer Street*, which, from Hogarth's own middle-class perspective, express the contemporary significance and evaluation of beer and spirits.

Gin Lane and *Beer Street* are not merely topical illustrations of two different drinking habits of the day. They also draw attention to different and opposing economies and life-styles, to profoundly different societies and class-determinate cultures, in which the two drinking habits are embedded. Hogarth set his Gin Lane in one of the then London slums, the parish of St Giles in the City of Westminster.[23] Life in Gin Lane is marked by death, apathy, hunger and the physical decay of people of the lower orders, who have all, in some way or another, sold themselves to the demon gin. There is no bourgeoisie in Gin Lane; the ruinous state of the houses and the buildings alone forbids all 'bourgeois' settlement. For the occupants of Gin Lane the community of the street is the necessary form of existence.

Only a cellar pub, the Gin Royal, offers any visible (and cheap) lodging; its legend reads 'Drunk for a penny, Dead drunk for twopence. Clean straw for nothing'. Certainly, a few houses stand up against the ruin. They record the prosperous circumstances of those who dominate 'Gin Lane' economically: small businessmen, all of whom, each in his own way, draw their profit from the misery of the gin drinkers. 'Killman', the distiller, distils the gin neither secretively nor only for home consumption. He plies his trade quite legally and, as the numbers on his barrels show, vigorously. He is one of the countless 'compound distillers'[24] of eighteenth century London who secured custom directly without the intermediary of traditional pubs and without any social restraint with respect to children and adolescents.

Next door to the gin shop is a barber's, the barber has been compelled through lack of customers to give up his business and has just taken his own life. His neighbour to the right, an undertaker, is more successful; the coffin which advertises his trade to his future customers hangs before his intact house. Opposite, on the other side of the picture is Mr Gripe's, the pawnbroker's. All the ways of Gin Lane lead to him. He holds the disintegrating world of Gin Lane together in so far as he controls the economy of debt and poverty which makes the consumption of gin possible - and indeed necessary. The 'honest' craftsman and the 'honest' housewife appear solely in a state of downfall: a carpenter exchanges his last possessions, his saw and livery, for cash with Mr Gripe. On the same spot a housewife pawns her kettle, fire-hook and teapot, the symbols of her status and duties. What Hogarth shows us here, is not 'the autumn of the traditional handicrafts'[25] nor 'the displacement of the traditional housewife' (in the sense of the old peasant household), but the absolute end of both in the economy of debt that is the ruling economic principle of Gin Lane.

A short look at the social origins of the gin-drinking members of Gin Lane's population is enough to show that the classificatory apparatus of experienced historians of class will not apply here. Despite death, isolation and apathy, there is indeed social movement in 'Gin Lane'. It is, however, more readily decipherable through the clues that fill the detail than through borrowings from the results of research into social mobility and stratification. The drinkers of Gin Lane belong to the lower orders in that they are beneath all those strata which through property, work or family might retain any identity and respect. What traces of social, economic and human identity remain, are being destroyed through intoxication, perverted into their opposites.

In the centre of the picture is a bare-breasted, drunken mother; her body carries the marks of syphilis, a consequence of prostitution. For a pinch of 'fine' snuff she lets her child fall. In her drunkenness she is indifferent to her child, but not to the refinement of consumption. A maternal role and a mother's duties fall victim to the mania for new habits of consumption. This disease, however, infects not only mothers and women, but both the sexes together, young as well as old; it destroys, according to Hogarth, not only the honest home but also the proper relationship between the domestic and the public, the former the family-centred privacy of the woman, the latter a primarily masculine community. So it is not only mothers who become child-murderers; drunken fathers cause brutal deaths: a delirious cook in the background strikes himself on the head with his bellows instead of fanning the fire. Instead of meat, he has stuck his own child on the spit. The helping hand of the mother, rushing forward, is powerless to save her child. These key scenes represent, in a drastic way, the destruction which gin has wreaked on 'good' family life. Perversion and catastrophe thrust so deeply that sexuality, the household economy and the relationship between parents and children are all affected with equal severity.

The scenes to the side of the picture explain and supplement those in the centre and foreground. They also refer to the perversion of social norms and behaviour through the economy of 'Gin Lane'. Gestures of intended aid and solidarity from the young to the old, turn out - when performed through the medium of gin - to be not life-preserving, but lethal: a London

Plate 10 Gin Lane (Mansell Collection)

Plate 11 Beer Street (Mansell Collection)

haulier or coal carrier, one of the most exploited and, because of the publican's monopoly as an employment agency, most dependent workers in 'Gin Lane', fills his idle time with the transport of fragile, human freight. Gin is being dispensed to the old woman in the wheelbarrow, by way of help and fortification.

In these scenes Hogarth lets us see a double reality. For an instant we see behind the surface of social decay which otherwise determines his picture of Gin Lane and its population. For the kindly intentioned woman handing a glass of gin to the feeble old woman reveals evidence of popular belief and practice: here, the old folk-belief in alcohol as a medicine and as a tonic.[26] Hogarth, however, was not concerned simply to confirm an old 'custom'. He also draws our attention to the perversion of this custom in the socio-economic context represented. Here, good intentions are transformed into their opposite. An old custom and a traditional tonic have come - under the impact of the distillery - to be the vehicle of a strength-sapping, fatal addiction.

The only place of intensive sociability in Gin Lane seems to be in front of Mr Killman's gin distillery. On closer examination, however, this sociability turns out to be riven by perversion, conflict and antagonism. Two beggars lay about one another with their stools - gin has not increased their mutual compassion. Youths are swinging sticks, not against Mr Killman, but against one another. The only peaceful gin-drinkers in this place are two young girls from the orphans' home or paupers' house, identifiable from the paupers' badges, GS (back-to-front for St Giles) on their arms.

The isolation of the drinkers' 'anti-social sociability' is developed in the loneliness of the dying and the destitution of those left behind. Whether we consider the dying gin and ballad salesman in the foreground, who has pawned his last shirt, or the orphaned child at its mother's coffin, near whom stands a wholly disinterested parish overseer, the message is the same: traditional plebeian sociability and solidarity, which had embraced birth, life and death, has been destroyed by the economy of Gin Lane. Mothers, fathers and housewives have, in the inverted world of Gin Lane, quit their roles and introduced a state of affairs (or perhaps a nightmare in the mind of the engraver?) characterised by the extinction of family, home, legitimate sexuality and honourable work. Moreover, the forms of collective consumption and amusement in the plebeian arena appear altered and destroyed. Isolation, apathy, violence and death take its place, without, however, building any community whatsoever.

Where, one might ask, does Hogarth see the origins and the forces behind this history of destruction through consumerism? Who, according to him, is responsible for this shocking picture? After what has been said so far, one would suppose that it was the bankers and businessmen, i.e. the loan capital of Mr Gripe and the murderous distilleries of Mr Killman, who stand in the dock. And truly, Hogarth is not shy to name them as guilty, as the real rulers and power-wielders in Gin Lane, who exploit the 'social slavery' of poor drinkers and the drinking poor for their own profit, and who are the axis around which the economy of Gin Lane turns, both literally and pictorially.

However, though such a view is not inappropriate it is not, in fact, Hogarth's more comprehensive one. The economy of Gin Lane reveals itself as 'political economy' in a somewhat unexpected sense: the true culprits must be looked for in the sphere of politics. Hogarth marks them out precisely as being half-absent and indifferent, representing them as uninterested figures in the background, like the parish overseer by the coffin, or practically planting them in the air, where to a visitor or stranger to Gin Lane they are almost invisible, like the royal law-giver on the church spire. This minute detail, pointed out by Ronald Paulson,[27] puts us on the right track; it is the only London church with an authentic king on the spire, St George's Bloomsbury (with George I). Through an easily detectable trick of perspective Hogarth replaces the pawnbroker's sign with an inverted cross, which serves by way of a substitute for the cross missing from the church spire. The inverted cross has become an unmistakable pointer to the inverted politico-economic and also ethical relations which Hogarth here and indeed elsewhere criticises: the false trinity of church, state and usury. It is this which explains the absence of a benevolent, paternalistic authority in Gin Lane. For the only authority in Gin Lane is a perverted one; it is not the overseer of the parish and its poor with his rod who represents political and moral authority amongst corruption, no, it is the representative of loan-capital with his spurious cross, Mr Gripe.

In opposition to the debt, deprivation and isolation of *Gin Lane*, work, amusement and sociability fill the sunny scene of *Beer Street*.[28] Hogarth locates Beer Street in the London parish of St Martin-in-the-fields, in the immediate neighbourhood of Hogarth's own home in Leicester Fields. The hoisted flag on the spire of St Martin's in honour of King George II's birthday (30 October) and the royal proclamation on the table in the foreground which commends the 'advancement of commerce and the cultivation of the arts of peace', unite the custom of beer-drinking not only with the industry and amusements of Beer Street, but also with the positive development of the 'national economy' in general. The economic influence of beer culture is, at least in the picture, so mighty that of all the houses in Beer Street only the pawnbroker's is, in the fullest sense of the word, ruined. The economy of debt has, in one respect, been turned on its head: Mr Gripe must close shop. He has fallen from the status of exploiter to that of common consumer. For, at the bolted door of the pawnshop, it is the Beer Street salesman and not Mr Gripe who determines the direction of the exchange operation. He delivers the goods and Mr Gripe, like everyone else, must pay with 'decent' money.

The liberal sociability of Beer Street appears as a Utopia, built upon a harmonious balance of work, nourishment and pleasure. Its inhabitants are honest and respectable craftsmen: the butcher (with whetstone), the wheelwright (with tongs) and the plasterer (with a phallic worktool) and his lover in the foreground and the toasting, cheerily working tailor and roofers in the airy heights of the upper storey and roof in the background. Even the bearers of a sedan chair, containing an important lady dressed in panniers, indulge themselves without any concealment in an innocent and unexceptionable pleasure when they use a pause in work not simply for idleness, but to down a mug of beer. Simultaneously they supply a commentary on the corresponding scenes of 'assistance' in *Gin Lane*, the child beside its mother's coffin and the removal of the feeble old woman in the wheelbarrow. While beer nourishes all classes and promotes class harmony, gin is an instrument of death and self-destruction for the lower orders and remains so even when subjective, i.e. class or group, solidarity is attempted.

According to Hogarth, the 'economy' of Beer Street is based upon a mutually beneficial interaction between industry, sociability and amusement, including an appropriate quantity of 'healthy' and legitimate sexuality and sensuality. Here, the fruits of nature, the rewards of industry, count for more than the profits of mercantile gain or of the bitter and destructive economy of debt which so dominated Gin Lane. Admittedly an insolent and feeble artist attempts to make propaganda for the opposite by replacing the word 'health' in the pub sign motto, 'Health to the Barley Mow', with the new trade-mark of a brimming gin bottle and glass. But his furtive advertisement has yet to have any influence on the solid craftsman's community of Beer Street. Hogarth, together with friends like John Fielding, fought a great moral and propaganda campaign against the alliance of rural capitalists and urban distilleries. Yet despite the terrible and massive experience of the contemporary gin epidemic he seems to have believed that Beer Street, though threatened, was not in danger of destruction. Hogarth did not intend Beer Street to represent a backward-looking Utopia but a forward-looking economic project. The direction of this project is indicated by the two fishwives in the foreground who are studying a ballad by Hogarth's friend Mr Lockman about the advantages of British herring fishing. In 1751, the same year in which Hogarth's engravings appeared, Lockman, who was secretary of the 'free British Fishing Society' published a pamphlet on *The Shetland Herring and the Peruvian Goldmine* which contrasted the solid profits of the native fishing industry and native hardwork with the groundless promises of the mercantile overseas speculators. In contrast to the fishwives' 'sensible' reading, Hogarth has little use for the dry products of the academic learning and enlightenment of his day. The address on the book basket in the foreground indicates what end Hogarth thought them fit for, though he allows that they are a useful side-product of the London packaging industry.

What, however, has brought these 'educated' fishwives to Westminster, to a place which even today does not count as their own? What motivates them to turn to their education instead of pursuing their normal trade and crying out their wares? What has driven them to leave Billingsgate fishmarket in the City, their home market? There, it is true, they have fallen into second place behind the big fish-buyers and the monopolistic 'fishmongers' who dominate the market. But what has brought them near to Parliament, into the neighbourhood not only of evidently comfortably living craftsmen, but also of superior ladies who travel in sedan chairs? It can hardly be the hope to find customers for their second-rate cheap fish; Gin Lane would promise more in that respect. No, the fishwives, and Hogarth with them, are pursuing a directly political goal. For they are in fact refugees (as was well more evident to contemporaries than it is to historians) from the old market of Billingsgate, now dominated by monopolistic buyers and dealers. They have gone towards Westminster because it was there that enlightened parliamentary reformers and their poetical friends like Mr Lockman wished, around the middle of the eighteenth century, to found an officially protected and regulated 'free' fishmarket. This being after the failure of all the attempts to secure a law 'for making Billingsgate a free market for the sale of fish'.[29]

Hogarth's allegories *Gin Lane* and *Beer Street* are concerned not only with loan-capital and its effects, but also with an established monopoly of contemporary commercial capital. Hogarth shows himself as a firm advocate of the 'free market', by which he meant not freedom for capitalist dealers and sellers, but a market which - under the protection of judicious mercantile legislation - served the interests of small producers and salesmen and promoted the health and welfare of consumers.

Of course, the question which must now demand our attention is whether Hogarth's pictures correspond to any historical reality? Are the death scenes of *Gin Lane* the product of accurate, ethnographic observation of actual plebeian decay and its economic causes, or are they simply the fantasies of a bourgeois moralist, reflecting his anxieties about plebeian excesses and expenditure? Similarly, with respect to the healthy socio-economic relations of *Beer Street*: to what extent are they based on a realistic evaluation of the role of beer in the life of upper-plebeian craftsmen? Perhaps Hogarth's vision was determined by nothing more than a wish, his faith in a harmonious union of the traditional industry of craftsmen and mercantile capitalism. Such an ideology found strong support in the political and economic thought of the time, but given the state of the old crafts in Hogarth's London was this anything more than a retrospective idyll?

Finally, one would like to know what in these engravings refers specifically to the experience of the English gin epidemic and what goes beyond that? Are we looking upon socio-critical portraits or upon an artistically generalised iconography of the norms and attitudes of the contemporary upper and middle strata: their judgment of the drinking habits and life-style of the plebeian classes and the way they were changing? And last but not least, how far is the artistic accumulation of socio-cultural experiences, as exemplified in Hogarth's work, susceptible to generalisation, *viz*. of application to and comparison with other historical situations?

A sketch of an adequate answer to these questions must begin with those problems posed by Hogarth himself. The pictures draw our attention to the interaction of economy, politics, social position and culture, and how this may vary - taking as a particular instance the change in plebeian drinking habits which involved the at least partial replacement of beer by gin as a festive and daily beverage.

W. Schivelbusch and in a similar way J. Roberts, W.R. Lambert and U. Jeggle have already sought to give answers to these problems.[30] Schivelbusch has described the emergence of the mass consumption of spirits as a 'genuine child of the industrial revolution'.[31]

> It [i.e. spirits] is for drinking what the mechanical weaving stool was for weaving. Like the industrialization of weaving, the industrialization of drinking was initially devasting for traditional forms of life. Indeed, in 18th century England spirits and the mechanical weaving stool worked hand in hand to annihilate the traditional modes of life and work.

A not immediately apparent historical error on Schivelbusch's part - the assumption that the mechanical weaving stool was already broadly established in the eighteenth century - points up the weakness of most of the existing research into the social history of alcohol. This is the unsupported construction of a far too direct link between the deprivations and imperatives of proletarian conditions of existence as determined by industrial capitalism and the onset of the mass consumption of alcohol. Alienating factory work and miserable living conditions in towns are seen both as the goads which drove men to gin and as destroyers of the old common culture where beer was the universal drink and an important source of nutrition. Even those historians who do not adhere to such a strictly linear view, like Roberts, maintain that it was industrialisation that opened the flood gates of gin; though it is admitted that its culturally destructive effects must not be presupposed.

The date alone and the circumstances of the first great gin epidemic between 1720 and 1751, which stimulated Hogarth's engravings, are a warning against such theses. They point to another set of relationships: increasing agricultural production under nascent rural capitalism, special and brutal 'free-market' forms of mercantile capitalism in the production and marketing of gin, the fiscal interests of the state and the spreading of the consumption of spirits among the wage dependent strata in towns, who were below the order of craftsmen - all this at a time when industrial capitalism had not yet begun.[32]

Important information about the true pattern of development in the production and consumption of gin in the first half of the eighteenth century is contained in some of T.W. Ashton's statistics.[33] Ashton shows that gin consumption and production in England at this time rose sharply and continuously, from 1.23 million gallons in the year 1700 to a peak of 8.20 million gallons in 1743 and 7.05 million gallons in 1751, and then fell drastically in the second half of the century. G. Rudé gives an estimate of average gin consumption for an adult, male Londoner at the height of the epidemic: 14 gallons (63 litres) per annum.[34] Though this figure may seem exagerated, even when compared with the higher averages of today, the frequent references of contemporary observers to the use of gin especially by the wage-dependent poor of London, and to gin having replaced beer as a daily drink tend to confirm it. Dorothy George has summarised these observations and at once picked out one of the essential commercial origins of gin as well as some of the everyday situations in which it was so important:[35]

> The sale of gin in the small shops was one of the chief causes of this evil. London had myriads of such shops. They supplied the poorest classes with their standard daily meal: bread, beer and cheese, which now became a meal of bread and gin... Marketwomen and street-sellers went to such a shop to breakfast, when an alehouse was too expensive; there also one bought one's pennyworth of necessary foodstuffs and also one's half-peck (5 Kilos) of coal; there the youth who carried torches sold his all-night torches and there too went the chambermaids to buy soap or candles and let themselves be persuaded to take a drop of gin.

The extent to which spirits in the first half of the eighteenth century had already become a daily necessity is recorded by Ashton's observation that the quantity of gin produced and consumed (mostly in London) did not decline during these relatively lean years of drought, grain-shortage and famine, but on the contrary leapt upwards. 'It appears almost,' concludes Ashton, 'as if the people wished to drown their sorrows in gin.'[36]

What makes these findings remarkable is that they pose a serious question to one thesis, both global and optimistic, of the historians of the eighteenth century. This thesis culminates in the claim that it was mainly rising 'real wages' - a consequence of cheaper grain - which, in the first half of the eighteenth century, caused an expansion of consumption and, in particular, of the consumption of gin by the economically dependent classes. It is surely true that the emergence of the mass production and consumption of spirits does have its origin in the relatively low grain prices of the agricultural depression of the first half of the eighteenth century; but this by no means implies what one of the optimists has written, that 'the buyers of grain and of products derived from grain [including gin] profited more than its producers' so we may speak of a 'shift in income in favour of the poorer orders of society'.[37] The history of the gin epidemic at the time of the commencement of agrarian capitalism shows how, on the contrary, producers, dealers and sellers were able to find devious and effective ways to turn the potentially beneficial effects of cheaper grain to their own advantage. Of a weekly turnover of 12,000 quarters of wheat (1 quarter = 290.91g.) on the London markets 7000 went to the gin distilleries. Thus, we see, at least in the case of London, how an unholy alliance of surplus producing landlords, urban distillers and gin-sellers, faced with low grain prices, not only responded to a growing plebeian taste for gin, but also encouraged, indeed 'manufactured' this taste.[38] At the very least, it is clear, contrary to the opinion of the optimists, that the dynamic of production and consumption was so powerful that it persisted even in times of famine and relatively high grain prices.

The traditional 'moral economy', that Edward Thompson has described, was not only undermined by external forces, capitalist relations of production in agriculture, the organisation of agricultural markets and urban distilleries, but also from within by the changes in demand and taste on the part of the lower orders themselves. Beer consumption, which we may take as an index of the well-being of the working people, declined or stagnated during this time,[39] and only recovered in the second half of the century and then more because of heavy taxation and consequent price rises of gin than from any independent change in plebeian tastes. In 1758, a reform-minded official could with satisfaction assert, 'Gin is now so expensive that good porter-beer has recovered its former pre-eminence.'[40]

However, movements in price and the history of the relations of production in the strict sense are not enough to explain the change in plebeian tastes. Of equal importance, in the case of gin at least, are the special relations of distribution, the social context of consumption and the peculiarities of the plebeian 'economy'.

During the years of the gin epidemic the free-trade in gin ignored the traditional pubs, alehouses and taverns; gin was mainly sold through a special chain of mobile and fixed gin salespeople, who thereby constituted an essential socio-economic link between gin producers and consumers. As well as the smaller 'compound distillers', such as the one represented by Hogarth, small food shops and a host of other gin sellers plied their trade of sweetened, spiced and frequently adulterated varieties of gin:[41]

> Every small grocer, many tobacconists and even the people who sell fruit and vegetables on stalls and barrows sell gin as well; many petty merchants keep gin at hand to sell to

their customers; and for seamen, soldiers, wage-earners and others of this rank it is hardly possible to go anywhere without being fastened upon by one of these salespeople or by acquaintances whom they have met on the street and who invite them to come and share a glass or two.

Along with the small shop owners and the itinerant salespeople an abundance of others pursued the gin trade as a sideline. The 'free trade' of gin penetrated deep into the heart of metropolitan society: cobblers, carpenters, dyers and above all the many weavers in the parishes of Spitalfields and Bethnal Green were all mentioned as sellers of gin. 'The one half of the town,' remarked a contemporary observer of the gin business, 'seems to be determined to supply the other half with poison.'[42]

In the parish of St Giles, where Hogarth, with some justification, located Gin Lane, there were in 1750 according to official police figures, 506 places where gin was sold for only 2000 houses. These figures are surely no exaggeration; for it was the public outcry at gin consumption which produced the survey, and the police, who were frequently mixed up in the gin trade, would certainly not have erred against their own interests. Against this background it is hardly surprising that even England's greatest prison for debtors, London's King's Bench Prison, was a centre of gin consumption. In 1776, 120 gallons of gin and 8 barrels of beer were recorded as the weekly ration.[43]

The crucial importance of this system of distribution, in which the small gin shops dominated, showed itself clearly in the initially unsuccessful attempt to attack gin consumption through parliamentary reform. Only when that system of distribution had itself been brought under control could the moral appeals of a William Hogarth or a Henry Fielding come to fruition. Walpole's Gin Act of 1736, which introduced sharp increases in taxes upon gin and high licensing charges, was the first serious attempt to deal with the problem through the price mechanism; it, however, suffered defeat through the organised resistance of distillers and sellers. The injunctions were ignored and tax officials and informers were murdered to intimidate the administration; furthermore, wakes were organised under the mantle of the plebeian community on behalf of 'Mother Gin' or 'Madam Geneva', who languished on her death bed, and the regulars were drawn in with offers of 'free' drinks and appeals to the 'Anglo-Saxon freedoms' now threatened by the excise. A 'turning point in the social history of London'[44] was not reached until the Gin Acts of 1743 and 1751, when the gin shops were compelled to submit to the rigours of policing by the justices of the peace and reform through local officials. These restraints were not achieved by radical prohibition but by an 'enlightened' compromise, which had been first proposed to Parliament by one of the big gin producers of the day. The compromise satisfied both the unchanged fiscal interests of the state and the interests of the really big 'industrial' producers. The disadvantages were borne mainly by the small gin-shops and the 'compound distillers'. For the production and sale of gin were only brought under control by making them respectable; production and distribution were separated, the latter being limited to licensed pubs. Only thus could the price rises for gin from 1750 have their moral effect and beer - at least transitionally - recover its old rights.[45]

None of these perspectives, however, reveals those forces which either compelled or simply encouraged plebeian consumers into the arms of 'Mother Gin'. One answer, though one 'from above', was given by John Fielding, the magistrate, writer and ally of Hogarth, in his essay *Of the late Increase of Robberies* (1751). Fielding sees excessive gin consumption as a part of the new commercialised culture of artisans, apprentices and Common Labourers especially in the capital. This sets 'luxuries' in the place of the traditional 'extravagances' as ordained by the year's seasons and the festival calendar. Lumped together with gin, lotteries and gambling are the principles of the new monetarisation and commercialisation of pleasure.

Fielding is therefore in agreement with later writers such as R. Southey and the German traveller R.W. Archenholtz, who saw the puritanical absence of festivals and holidays as the cause of the at once commercialised and excessive life-style of the 'common people':[46]

> They criticize the Catholic religion because of the multitude of its holidays, but they fail to see that it is precisely the shortage of holidays here at home which brutalises and destroys the working classes and that where holidays are infrequent they are invariably desecrated. At Christmas, Easter and Whitsun, the only festivals in England, the handworkers and peasants devote themselves only to boozing and riots.

For Archenholtz the boredom of the English Sunday is a product not only of the ban on work and trade, but also of dancing, music and other traditional pleasures; it is, furthermore, a direct cause of the Sunday 'excesses' at the commercial drinking places: the laws from the time of Puritan governments contributed in no small way[47]

> to the sombre character of the English....For on the only day which the common man may use to his own amusement there shall, according to this law, be neither dancing nor music; instead, there are tea gardens, taverns, brothels and other public houses all full of people who, without dancing a step, indulge themselves in every debauchery, which this senseless law can never prevent.

So, the new thirst for gin was the bitter-sweet compensation for the loss of the old life-style with its rhythm of festivals and holidays? Perhaps. Given the magnitude of the social transformation going on in early eighteenth-century London, the disintegration of social relationships amongst the lower strata and their certainty of an early death, such an explanation is certainly not to be written off. Nevertheless, this explanation is not free from the myopia of observers from the upper strata. Here is neither Hogarth's comprehension of the relationships of economics, politics and class which lie behind the new drinking, nor any perception of the day-to-day relations of life and work - yet all these were a precondition of the 'craving for pleasure'.

Fielding's reference to the spread of money as a vehicle of demand and to the supposed 'luxuries' of the working classes, under which he includes their intoxication through gin, is nevertheless a clue. What was so important was less excessive wages - as Fielding thought - and far more the experience of fundamentally uncertain conditions of life and employment, especially for the unskilled. Such people may well have been inclined to obtain sporadic enjoyment of luxuries, such as gin, in exchange for money: for many, this was the only 'luxury' attainable. For unskilled workers (such as carriers), out-of-door servants and apprentices and even skilled craftsmen who worked as wage labourers or for piecework rates, merely surviving from day to day was a continuous struggle where the risks were incalculable. When Fielding mentions in passing and with disapproval the compensations of gin, that it temporarily removes 'all sense of fear and shame' for the 'poorer sort', he perhaps hit upon an elemental necessity of life for the working people of the 'other London'. For those beneath the social and economic threshold of 'honest handicrafts', gin was - as Hogarth implied - the only 'medicine' which offered even temporary respite from ceaseless toil and uncertainty. Neither the old solidarity of the neighbourhood nor, increasingly, the guilds any longer provided the framework in which offers of employment, demand for work and 'livelihood' could be balanced out. In their place was only the fleeting sociability of the street, the gin shop and, of course, the pub, which as 'house of call' was the centre of a fluctuating and seasonal labour market and to some degree an *ersatz* for established modes of life and labour.

It seems then that the mass consumption of gin in eighteenth-century London had its home and origin in a certain segment of the plebeian arena, and then became an 'ascendant cultural value' for other strata of the emerging working class, a role that was by no means always negative.

NOTES

1 Gunther Lottes, in his important but still largely unknown work, *Politische Aufklärung und plebejisches Publikum: Zur Theorie und Praxis des englischen Radikalismus im späten 18. Jahrhundert*, Munich, Oldenbourg, 1979, *Ancien Régime, Aufklärung und Revolution*, vol. 1, p. 110,

proposes a distinction between a traditional 'plebeian culture' and a later 'plebeian public', the latter of which he sees as a variant of a middle-class public whose social preconditions have been suspended. This separation, however, cannot be accepted for historical reasons. This, however, does not touch the most important results of Lottes's work, which in crucial points corrects Edward Thompson's representation of the English Jacobin movement as the 'advance guard' of the early nineteenth-century workers' movement.

2 See E.P. Thompson, 'Anthropology and the discipline of the historical context', *Midland History*, 1971-2, pp. 41-55; here, p. 49.

3 J. Habermas, *Strukturwandel der Öffentlichkeit: Untersuchungen zu einer Kategorie der bürgerlichen Gesellschaft*, Neuwied, Luchterhand, 1962, Politica: Abhandlungen und Texte zur politischen Wissenschaft, 4, p. 8.

4 O. Negt and A. Kluge, *Öffentlichkeit und Erfahrung: Zur Organisationsanalyse von bürgerlicher und proletarischer Offentlichkeit*, Frankfurt, Suhrkamp, 1972, pp. 8f, n. 1.

5 See especially E.P. Thompson, 'The moral economy of the English crowd in the eighteenth century', *Past and Present*, no. 50, 1971, pp. 76-136, 'Patrician society, plebeian culture', *Journal of Social History*, no. 7, 1973-4, pp. 382-405; 'Eighteenth century English society: class struggle without class', *Social History*, vol. 3, no. 2, May 1978, pp. 133-65; *Whigs and Hunters: The Origins of the Black Act*, London, Allen Lane, 1975.

6 Thompson, 'Patrician society, plebeian culture', p. 393.

7 J. Beckmann, *Anweisung, die Rechnungen kleiner Haushalte zu führen: Für Anfänger aufgesetzt*, Göttingen, 2nd edn, 1800, p. 3.

8 J.A. Günther, *Versuch einer vollständigen Untersuchung über Wucher und Wuchergesetze (und über die Mittel, dem Wucher durch Strafgesetze Einhalt zu tun, in politischer, justizmässiger, und mercantilischer Rücksicht)*, vol. 1, Hamburg, 1790, p. 162.

9 Anon., *Remarks upon the Serious Dissuasive from an intended Subscription for Continuing the Races*, 1733, cited in A.P. Wadsworth and J. de Lacy Mann, *The Cotton Trade and Industrial Lancashire*, Manchester, University Press, 1931, (Economic History Series, 7), p. 392.

10 See the excellent resumé in M. Douglas and D. Isherwood, *The World of Goods: Towards an Anthropology of Consumption*, London, Allen Lane, 1979, ch. 7; 'Separate Economic Spheres in Ethnography', pp. 131-47. See further the works of M. Godelier, *Rationality and Irrationality in Economics*, London, Monthly Review Press, 1972; *Perspectives in Marxist Anthropology*, Cambridge, University Press, 1977 (Cambridge Studies in Social Anthropology, 18); '"Salt money" and the circulation of commodities among the Baruya of New Guinea', pp. 127-51.

11 E.P. Thompson, 'Folklore, anthropology and social history', *Indian Historical Review*, vol. 3, no. 2, January 1977, pp. 247-66. N. Davis, *Society and Culture in Early Modern France*, London, Stanford University Press, 1975; K. Thomas, 'History and anthropology of religion and magic 2', *Journal of Interdisciplinary History*, no. 6, 1975, pp. 91-109 (the latter is an answer to the critique by the ethologist Hildred Geertz of his book *Religion and the Decline of Magic: Studies in Popular Beliefs in Sixteenth and Seventeenth Century England*, London, Weidenfeld & Nicolson, 1971, Geertz's critique was publised as 'An anthropology of religion and magic 1', *Journal of Interdisciplinary History*, no. 6, 1975, pp. 71-89); G. Sider, 'Christmas morning and the New Year in Outport Newfoundland', *Past and Present*, no. 71, 1976, pp. 102-25.

12 P. Bourdieu, *Outline of a Theory of Practice*, Cambridge University Press, 1977, ch. 4: 'Structures, habitus, power: basis for a theory of symbolic power', pp. 159-97.

13 'E.A.H.' *Über die öffentlichen und gemeinsamen Vergnügungen der Landleute: Ein Versuch, Polizeidirektoren und menschenfreundlichen Obrikeiten und wahren Volksfreunden zur Prüfung vorgelegt*, Altenburg and Erfurt, 1804.

14 Discussion comment by Louise Tilly, 1978.

15 B. Schöne, *Kultur und Lebensweise Lausitzer Bandweber, 1750-1850*, Berlin, 1977 (Akademie der Wissenschaften. Zentralinstitut für Geschichte. Veröffentlichungen zur Volkskunde und Kulturgeschichte, vol. 64), pp. 107f.

16 C.A. Wunderlich, *Versuch einer medizinischen Topographie von Sulz am Neckar*, Tübingen, 1809, p. 40.

17 G. Stedman Jones, 'Working class culture and working class politics in London, 1870-1900: Notes on the remaking of a working class', *Journal of Social History*, no. 7, 1974, pp. 460-508.

18 Sources quoted in H. Strehler, 'Beiträge zur Kulturgeschichte der Zürcher Landschaft: Kirche und Schule im 17. und 18. Jahrhundert', PhD Dissertation, Zurich, 1934, p. 59.

19 R. Braun, *Industrialisierung und Volksleben: Veränderungen der Lebensformen unter Einwirkung der verlagsindustriellen Heimarbeit in einem ländlichen Industriegebiet (Zürcher Oberland) vor 1800*, 1960, new edition, Göttingen, 1979, p. 115.

20 'Professor Leidenfrost' (i.e. A.L. Schlözer), 'Revolutionen der Diät von Europa seit 300 Jahren', *Briefwechsel meist historischen und politischen Inhalts*, no. 44, 1781, pp. 93-120, here, p. 93.

21 Definitive critical edition of Hogarth's graphic works: R. Paulson, *Hogarth's Graphic Works*, 2 vols, New Haven, Conn., Yale University Press, 1965; monographs: R. Paulson, *Hogarth, His Life, Art and Times*, New Haven, Conn., Yale University Press, 1971, and his *Popular and*

Polite Art in the Age of Hogarth and Fielding, Indiana, Notre Dame University Press, 1979.

22 See Clifford Geertz, '"Thick description": Toward an interpretive theory of culture', *The Interpretation of Cultures: Selected Essays*, New York, Basic, 1973, pp. 3-32; Peter Linebaugh wrote a short 'poetical' interpretation of Hogarth's series 'Industry and Idleness' of 1747: 'Prints of William Hogarth - Crime, Labour and Capital in the 18th century', *N.E.P.A. News*, April-May 1979, pp. 1-6.

23 An exact description of the facts, but not of the interpretation given here, is in Paulson, *Hogarth's Graphic Works*, vol. 2.

24 For the 'compound distillers' and their role, see M.D. George, *London Life in the Eighteenth Century*, Harmondsworth, Penguin, 1965, p. 43.

25 M. Stürmer (ed.), *Herbst des Alten Handwerks: Quellen zur Sozialgeschichte des 18. Jahrhunderts*, Munich, 1979.

26 See the article, 'Branntwein', *Handwörterbuch des deutschen Aberglaubens*, vol. 1, Berlin and Leipzig, 1927, cols 1504 ff.

27 Paulson, *Popular and Polite Art*, p. 5.

28 Description of the facts in Paulson, *Hogarth's Graphic Work*, vol. 2, pp. 207 ff. We do not share Paulson's interpretation of *Beer Street*, which holds that Hogarth intended to criticise the new ideal of 'supply and demand in a free market', according to the maxim 'this is the way things work or would work if the state did not interfere' (see Paulson, *Popular and Polite Art*, pp. 6 ff). On the contrary, Hogarth's *Beer Street* seems to advocate explicitly the ideal of mercantile advancement on the basis of the old craft system, in a state which is free of corruption and not dominated by usurious capital. The excessively well-fed artisans, however, hint at Hogarth's conscious portrayal of the characteristics of an ironic Utopia.

29 'An Act for making Billingsgate a free Market for the Sale of Fish' (10 and 11 William III, cap. 24, ss. 11-12), 1699. For the fight for a second, 'free' fish market in London in the eighteenth century, see W.M. Stern, 'Fish marketing in London in the first half of the eighteenth century', D.C. Coleman and A.H. John (eds), *Trade, Government and Economy in Pre-Industrial England: Essays Presented to F.J. Fisher*, London, Weidenfeld & Nicolson, 1976, pp. 68-79.

30 W. Schivelbusch, *Das Paradies, der Geschmack und die Vernunft: Eine Geschichte der Genussmittel*, Munich, 1980, espec. pp. 159 ff, 'Die Industrielle Revolution, das Bier und der Branntwein'; J.S. Roberts, 'Der Alkoholkonsum deutscher Arbeiter im 19. Jahrhundert', *Geschichte und Gesellschaft*, no. 6, 1980, pp. 220-42; W.R. Lambert, 'Alkohol und Arbeitsdisziplin in den Industriegebieten

von Sudwales 1800-1870', in D. Puls (ed.), *Wahrnehmungsformen und Protestverhalten: Studien zur Lage der Unterschichten im 18. und 19. Jahrhundert*, Frankfurt, Suhrkamp, 1979, pp. 296-316; U. Jeggle, 'Alkohol und Industrialisierung', in H. Cnacik (ed.), *Rausch, Ekstase, Mystik*, Düsseldorf, 1978, pp. 78-94.
31 Schivelbusch, *Das Paradies*, p. 165.
32 The best short account is still D. George, *London Life*, pp. 41-55; for the political discourse on the gin problem at the time of the gin epidemic, and for the relation between politics and economic interests, see S. and B. Webb, *The History of Liquor Licensing, Principally from 1700 to 1876*, London, 1903, reprint: London, Frank Cass, 1963, espec. ch. 2; 'A period of laxness', pp. 15-54; for a special episode, see G. Rudé, '"Mother Gin" and the London riots of 1736', *Guildhall Miscellany*, no. 10, 1959, pp. 53-63; see also G. Rudé, *Hanoverian London, 1714-1808*, London, Secker & Warburg, 1971, pp. 17, 91 ff, 152 ff, 210.
33 T.S. Ashton, *Economic Fluctuations in England 1700-1800*, Oxford University Press, 1959, p. 36; *An Economic History of England: The Eighteenth Century*, London, Methuen, 1955, pp. 6 ff, and the tables concerning the production of strong beer and gin, pp. 242-3.
34 Rudé, *Hanoverian London*, p. 70.
35 George, *London Life*, p. 49.
36 Ashton, *Economic Fluctuations*, p. 36.
37 A.H. John, 'Agricultural productivity and economic growth in England, 1700-1760', *Journal of Economic History*, no. 25, 1965, pp. 16-34, here p. 20; for the consumption of gin and other luxury articles p. 22.
38 See George, *London Life*, p. 42; and S. and B. Webb, *History of Liquor Licensing*, pp. 19 ff; the information about the weekly volume of corn sold on the London markets and its disposition can be found at p. 43.
39 Ashton, *Economic History*, p. 242.
40 Sir John Fielding (half-brother and successor of Richard Fielding), cited in Rudé, *Eighteenth Century London*, p. 91.
41 Order Book, Middlesex Sessions, January 1725-26, cited in George, *London Life*, pp. 45 ff.
42 'Theophilus', in *Gentleman's Magazine*, vol. 3, 1733, p. 88.
43 The constables' returns are discussed in D. George, *London Life*, pp. 53 ff; for the conditions in King's Bench Prison, see ibid., p. 291.
44 G. Rudé, 'Mother Gin', pp. 59 ff.
45 S. and B. Webb, *History of Liquor Licensing*, pp. 28 ff; for the 'turning-point in the social history of London', see George, *London Life*, p. 49.
46 'Alvarez Esperiella' (i.e. Robert Southey), *Letters from England*, London, 1807, vol. 2, p. 169.

47 J.W. von Archenholtz, *A Picture of England*, London, 1797, pp. 166 ff.

6 PILGRIMS AND PROGRESS IN NINETEENTH-CENTURY ENGLAND

Deborah Valenze*

It is hard to tell how villagers measured being 'out of date' in the nineteenth century. In Burslem, in the Potteries, a local expression summed it up. One person might notice another's coat and say, 'Why, it's as old as Tregortha!' The village 'symbol of antiquity' was not a building or a place, but a person. John Tregortha, former Methodist local preacher turned tract-seller, had somehow achieved a status of Methuselah even though he never lived much beyond the age of fifty. By Burslem standards, he personified obsolescence. His changeless, Quaker style of dress, his endless supply of god-given prophecies, and his devotion to dispensing homely wisdom won him a wide reputation. Though people thought him strange, they nevertheless honoured him with a mixture of impatience and understanding.[1]

Historians seldom use religion to gauge a strictly popular mood in nineteenth-century England; usually religion is seen as a conventional force pulling together conflicting interests under banners of worn-out Victorian virtues. A conservative-radical framework, however, limits our understanding of popular religious behaviour. What can we say, for example, about the village scold who occupies a prominent place in local affairs because of her Methodist principles, but who fits into no particular category, either social or political? Too often the tags of 'respectability' and 'self-help' have overshadowed less practical traits associated with religion, traits which, though personal and sometimes peculiar, can illuminate the larger world of the village labourer. During the industrial transformation of England in the first half of the nineteenth century, sectarian Methodism gave expression to significant aspects of the labouring experience. While specific political, economic, and social factors undoubtedly played a part in labourers' lives, they

*Deborah Valenze teaches history at Worcester Polytechnic Institute, Worcester, Mass., and researches on popular religion in eighteenth-century England.

will not enter into this brief discussion. More germane to an overall picture of popular religion, one applicable to other contexts, are general changes in work and social relations that came to bear upon villagers' lives. Sectarian Methodists developed a mode of expression rooted in contemporary issues of status and deference, independence in earning a living, and displacement and migration. This period was, in a sense, the golden age of sectarian Methodism in England, though scattered incidences of the same form of activity occurred later on as the effects of modern industrial development spread unevenly throughout Britain. Indeed, the role of sectarianism described below is not unique to England. The following discussion hopes to suggest alternative ways of analysing similar movements in non-European settings where the transformation of traditional ways of working uncover religious belief resistant to change.

Sectarian Methodism in late eighteenth- and early nineteenth-century England was a distinctly popular faith.[2] The principal offshoots of Wesleyanism - Primitive Methodism, Bible Christianity, and Independent Methodism - thrived not only outside chapel walls but out of the hands of designated leaders as well. What followers considered 'real religion' was simple in theory and free in style. The sects derived ideas concerning self-expression, sexual equality, self-government, and a priesthood of all believers from seventeenth-century Quakerism and early Methodism. As each group broke away from the Wesleyan Connexion (fast becoming a rigid institution), more pronounced forms of popular religion appeared. By 1820, a considerable number of societies were meeting in cottages, houses, and out of doors, led by local talent in local style. Cottage religion became a recognized working-class alternative to the religion of the church. As a shrewd gossip in George Eliot's 'Amos Barton' observed, labourers and stockingers in search of religion 'never came to church, [but] come to the cottage instead', where religion was free from clerical and upper-class influence.[3]

Eventually certain characteristics of sectarian Methodist worship became identified with lower-class status. Primitive Methodists acquired the name 'Ranters', reminiscent of political radicalism and religious heresy, but more directly referring to their loud praying and relentless singing. Followers of Independent Methodism, Bible Christianity, and the other sects usually wound up with the loose epithet 'Methody'. The pious worked hard to earn such recognition. Two notorious forms of Methodist behaviour, loudness and constant reproof of neighbours and kin, demanded an aggressiveness backed by ready convictions. Both practices violated codes of propriety and privacy even within the familiarity of small villages. Truly good Methodists were vocal rebels against convention.[4]

Such outspoken behaviour assumed greater significance in the context of work relations. Methodistic traits could bring about heated confrontations between domestic servants and their masters or mistresses. No doubt some Methodist servants fulfilled their duties with god-fearing efficiency; but others found their loyalty to one Master interfering with duty to the other. Piety itself thus became a weapon in private conflict, as servants used religion as a bludgeon against sinful masters. Obituaries triumphantly recounted loud competitions in grace-saying at dinner-tables, and righteous protests against curses hurled by masters. Preacher Billy Hickingbotham (b. 1789), 'champion bag-racer of all of England' and one-time poacher, never accepted any abuse from any master. When one employer swore at him for his involvement in so much 'Methody' work and ordered him to stop, Billy reproved him and in turn threatened to quit his job. Billy stayed on until his master - perhaps as proof of providential judgment - died.[5] Sectarian Methodism could also provide servants with a defence against the religious influence of masters and mistresses. It was no accident that a servant to the Duke of Devonshire, Peter Bond (b. 1796), became a Primitive Methodist preacher in spite of his trying position, which threatened to 'draw him...into spiritual slavery'.[6] In a distinctly upper-class, Established Church atmosphere, sometimes the most pointed response was a Methodist one.

The life of preacher Elizabeth Smith offers a vivid illustration of subtle domestic warfare between servant and mistress. Elizabeth was born in Ludlow, Shropshire, in 1805. Like many servants, she emerged from unstable circumstances. Her father, through recklessness, lost everything he owned in a small glove business and, in despair, enlisted in the navy. He was reported dead soon after, leaving his widow with six children and no income. Elizabeth became the charge of her 'industrious and moral' grandmother of the same village. After attending a National (Church of England) School for a short time, Elizabeth assumed an apprenticeship with a dressmaker. But new acquaintances, including theatre people, began to undermine the careful efforts of her anxious grandmother. Abruptly, when she was sixteen, Elizabeth was sent to London to work as a servant.[7]

Servanthood offered no prescribed guarantee of elevating Elizabeth Smith's manners and morals. Obviously domestic service could lift young women from lowly circumstances into better environments; homeless girls made ideal candidates for improvement, especially when thrust into the hands of middle-class mistresses intent upon preserving the tranquillity of their households. But service also heightened a country girl's awareness of class differences, and sometimes she arrived at the job with a wilfulness that a benevolent mistress could not always subdue. For Elizabeth, self-assertion took a religious form. The struggle that ensued involved more than simply internalized turmoil: religion inspired rebellion against employers, public avowal of a separate working-class faith, and ultimately, renunciation of worldly success.

At first, religious ruminations played a minor part in Elizabeth's life at the McDonald home in London. She was dutifully reverent but hardly zealous. Periodically, however, the McDonalds sent her to work at the home of their relative, a vicar of West Stratford in Buckinghamshire, and there her religious inclinations took a turn for the worse. 'Influence' from above brought about rejection from below. Elizabeth 'began to entertain atheistical thoughts', and whenever twinges of conscience troubled her, she sought to escape in romances and novels. Upon her return to London, she adopted a different strategy of repudiation. Renewed reading in the Bible led her to formulate a private ascetic religion that effectively separated her from her employers. An odd ritual appeared in her behaviour: every evening she denied herself supper, an act which remained undiscovered presumably because she dined apart from the family. She was inspired, she recorded, by *Matthew* vi. 16-18: 'Moreover, when ye fast, be not, as the hypocrites, of a sad countenance....That thou appear not unto men to fast...'. She sought spiritual counselling when visiting her grandmother in Ludlow in 1825, but not from any member of the Church of England. Instead, she consulted a local Primitive Methodist woman who put her in touch with a travelling preacher. While continuing to work at the McDonalds' in London, Elizabeth drew encouragement from correspondence with the Primitives and prayed in solitude until she was converted.[8]

Her first test of strength occurred in the spring of 1826. For her exemplary service, the McDonalds chose Elizabeth to accompany them to the races on 'the most noted day' (Derby Day). Elizabeth refused to obey. Her puritanical stance betrayed religious beliefs intolerable to the McDonalds. 'I do not want any Methodists about me,' her mistress said. A series of confusing events followed. Elizabeth wished to leave her situation; at the same time, her health began to fail. Mrs McDonald hit upon a solution acceptable to all. 'Smith,' she said, 'I am afraid you are in a consumption.' She then dismissed Elizabeth 'out of fear lest the children should be thereby injured'. Elizabeth returned to Ludlow and to dressmaking, and, with greater freedom and miraculously restored health, began preaching later that year.[9]

The female preachers of sectarian Methodism were perhaps the greatest flaunters of propriety. All three major sects employed them, and a smaller group, the Female Revivalists, obviously made them the centerpiece of their religion. Their right to preach was one of the primary issues that precipitated a break between Primitive and Wesleyan Methodists. But in spite of their status as a *cause célèbre*, the sects reneged from promoting female preachers in an explicit way. Primitives discreetly concealed most female appointments on their preaching plans with asterisks or initials, and Independent Methodists kept no straightforward account of ever having engaged them. Though Bible Christians occasionally posted notices of their appearances (without announcing names), the leaders of the sect actively encouraged men preachers to marry - and thus legitimate - their 'sisters'. Leaders apparently concluded that publicizing women preachers travelling about alone on foot exposed them - and the sect - to unwanted slander.[10] Consequently, before the public eye, preachers soberly recounted the feminine virtues of female counterparts like Elizabeth Smith. Sarah Kirkland (b. 1794) 'proved a great blessing', recalled one contemporary, 'for...by her prudence, modesty, circumspection, neatness, and plainness of dress, was a pattern for [many young females]'. His description, ironically, referred to Kirkland's highly successful tour through Nottinghamshire at the peak of Luddite violence.[11]

The role of women in general, and female preachers in particular, did not always conform to such pleasing patterns of femininity. In fact, women capitalized more often on the mythical image of their sex as uncontrollably vociferous and overbearing.[12] When a congregation squirmed in protest against a long sermon (an especially heinous offence among Primitives), a woman might speak for her more cautious neighbours. Reprimanding the preacher conferred a certain badge of heroism. Mrs Caroline Duffield (b. 1804), a 'veteran' of Yarmouth Primitive Methodism, recalled such an instance in her own career. Preacher John Smith (notoriously long-winded) had announced his text, 'Come ye to the waters, and he that hath no money; come ye, buy, and eat; yea, come buy wine and milk...', when Mrs Duffield called out impatiently, 'Without money and without price!' 'Be quiet, sister Caroline!' retorted the preacher, 'we haven't come to that yet!'[13] Habitual loudness could distinguish a member for posterity. Hannah Broomhead, a class leader of Calver, Derbyshire, joined the Primitives late in life and with few inhibitions. 'At public worship she was lively, and by her loud and sudden exclamations she occasionally gave offense to some,' read her memoir. 'Having tried and failed to suppress her emotions without spiritual loss, she at length determined to worship God her own way, taking *Isaiah* 12th chapter and 6th verse for her motto.' Her neighbours no doubt knew the text: 'Cry out and shout, thou inhabitant of Zion: for great is the Holy One of Israel in the midst of thee.'[14]

Evangelists built their reputations upon such behaviour. Their ability to deliver burning assaults straight from the heart qualified them as quintessential popular preachers. The antithesis of learned and polite clergymen, preachers - particularly female preachers - often made their mark by communicating in an unsophisticated and penetrating way. Priscilla Lambden (b. 1802), of Hurstbourne Tarrant (Hants), was considered 'too harsh, and her language too heavy and pointed'. Nevertheless, her exhortations had an appealing, if somewhat unorthodox, quality. 'I want to see you warm-hearted one way or the other,' she reportedly said, 'either hearty sinners, or hearty Christians'.[15] Elizabeth Gosling (b. 1789) 'imitated no one; studied no foreign phrases, or hard words....Her sentences were frequently unconnected, but she constantly dwelt on the great and important doctrines of repentance and faith, conversion and holiness.' Her attitude was winningly trenchant. When questioned about election, she replied, 'Are you converted to God? Do you feel Christ in your heart, the hope of glory? If not, don't talk to me about election.' Like other successful preachers, she possessed a special knack for invading the private corners of her listeners' lives. Whether by exploiting the advantages of superior spirituality or by assuming a tone of domestic intimacy ascribed to their sex, women attacked members of their congregations with endless reprimands. According to the author of Gosling's memoir, she demonstrated an outstanding 'faithfulness in reproof'. 'I am not aware,' he confessed, 'that in all my travels, I ever met with one that excelled her in this part of her duty. She would reprove, rebuke, and exhort. And she reproved the more wealthy as well as the poor.'[16] Similarly, Mary Bate Adams (b. 1797) was 'so zealous...in reproving sin, that as they afterwards confessed, persons avoided meeting her.'[17]

What motivated such aggressive, outspoken behaviour, which surely exacted its price from the preacher in the form of social ostracism, and in some cases, economic and political harassment? The experiences of servanthood have suggested a few possible answers; but in order to comprehend the broader intentions behind popular preaching, it is necessary to uncover the long road to sainthood travelled by other labourers. Like Elizabeth Smith, many came from broken homes and experienced personal losses early in life; compounding these private hardships, their occupations inevitably schooled them in misfortunes of another kind. In rural areas where changes in landholding and land use destroyed traditional village communities, small farmers and agricultural labourers became leaders of cottage societies. A number of preachers followed trades that were threatened or eliminated by factory industry. Handloom weavers, for example, played a major role in sectarian Methodism in Lancashire and West Yorkshire. The decline of many small domestic industries also affected the daily lives of preachers. In a diversity of circumstances, popular preachers and their congregations faced rapidly diminishing economic security - a diminution which undermined the household economy and called into question customary forms of behaviour.

Cottage religion preserved the world of the cottage economy. For handloom weavers resisting the decline of domestic industry, perseverence was essential. '"Stand fast as the beaten anvil to the stroke",' a Lowton (Lancs) weaver exhorted his listeners, at other times intoning, '"Finally, brethren, be ye steadfast, immovable, always abounding in the work of the Lord."'[18] The 'spirit of freedom and independence'[19] often celebrated in the character of weavers manifested itself in his or her religious affiliation as well. Independent Methodism in Lowton provided a community for the displaced, the dissatisfied, and the unadaptable. Weaver William Birchall (b. 1824) spent his life in Lowton, first working at handloom weaving while preaching and playing a leading part in the local Independent Methodist society. Determined to withstand economic hardship, he embraced the rigorous code of morality and individualism of Independent Methodism. Birchall was known for 'the high stand which he took to maintain the purity of the church, when discipline had to be enforced'. Only after suffering 'greatly straitened circumstances' and 'protracted afflictions...in his family' did Birchall abandon weaving in order to teach school - another occupation that allowed him considerable personal autonomy and freedom to work at home.[20]

The scattered town of Lowton itself was transformed during the formative years of Independent Methodism. When the society began meeting in 1780, the inhabitants of Lowton worked in agriculture and domestic handloom weaving. Over the next half-century, farming and domestic industry declined and Lowton began to lose its population to nearby factory towns. Numbers slowly rose and then fell after 1831. All textile production, besides a limited amount of domestic silk-weaving, died out. Lowton weavers responded to these changes in different ways. Many, including some Independent Methodists, became involved in radical politics during the 1830s and 1840s. A group of Owenites also attracted a sizeable following.[21] Throughout this time, the small Independent Methodist society steered a changeless course. Unlike local Wesleyans, who advanced to chapel status as early as 1788, the Independents remained a cottage society. Originating at the Gilded Hollins Farm, meetings continued in domestic quarters for nearly seventy years. When a member donated land in 1793, the society built a school rather than a chapel. Numbers increased over the next few decades, so in 1834, the Independents replaced the old Sunday school with a larger building. In 1849, after generations of cottage meetings, the society finally erected a chapel.[22]

The preservation of cottage meetings throughout the economic transformation of Lowton was no coincidence. Chapel-building entailed unwanted expense: the society was small, members were poor, and funds first went towards supporting the indigent and to Independent Methodist missions. Cost, however, explained only part of the unwillingness to build a chapel. The decline of cottage industry incited Lowtonites to cling more tenaciously to traditions associated with domestic-based life. Their allegiance to cottage meetings, like their continuance of handloom weaving, grew out of a determination to protect a personal domain. Organized along family and neighbourhood lines and stressing equal participation of both men and women, Independent Methodism created a stable household of believers. Preachers repeatedly returned to the alternating images of serenity and violence of the Psalms to express the ideal of domestic security against the threat of economic upheaval. In the midst of constant struggle, temporal as well as spiritual, the 'house of the Lord' offered refuge and reward.[23]

More often than not, the transformation of village economies uprooted labourers and cast them out into earthly pilgrimages. Through the experiences of displacement, they arrived at similar precepts of sectarian Methodism, but with a different emphasis: while adopting the rugged individualism and domestic solidarity of cottage religion, they capitalized on its portable potential rather than its stabilizing power. The idealization of the *domus* became the source of a wealth of pilgrim imagery for those who were completely deprived of material security. One weaver enacted a heroic pilgrimage. John Holgate (b. 1811) abandoned handloom weaving at Barrowford (Lancs) in 1841, and in the following fourteen years, worked at four different jobs in five different places. Throughout that time, he passed through as many Independent Methodist societies, preaching all the while.[24] The formulation of portable cottage religion made possible an extraordinary exchange of preachers between localities. Despite differences in occupations and backgrounds, preachers promoted goals that had a general appeal. The desire for self-sufficiency and autonomy - spiritual or otherwise - underlay the proliferation of sectarian Methodist societies across all of England.

One clear case of shared interests occurred in Filey, Yorkshire, where 'Praying Johnny' Oxtoby, an agricultural labourer from Warter, became the leading figure in the religious revival of a fishing village in 1823. Praying Johnny displayed all the features of a self-made popular preacher. Born in 1767 at Little Givendale, near Pocklington, Oxtoby was still very young when his family was forced to give up their small farm. His parents sent him to live with an uncle in nearby Warter, where he was raised 'in the midst of very humble surroundings'. Oxtoby's education was meagre. After a short stint at a village school, he began work as an agricultural labourer and led a poor but secure life. He reportedly attended the village church (but never got 'true religion') and adopted the habit of steadily saving a small portion of his salary. The accumulation continued for over twenty years, so that by 1804, Oxtoby was 'the master of his own movements'. Then came a spiritual crisis of sorts: having encountered travelling Wesleyan Methodists in a neighbouring village, Oxtoby began to ruminate about religion and finally experienced conversion under a sermon entitled 'Saving Faith'. His awakening moved him to visit every home in the surrounding area 'to talk and pray with families', and eventually, he left Warter to extend his efforts (now under the aegis of Primitive Methodists) through Lincolnshire and the East Riding.[25]

Oxtoby arrived at Filey at a timely moment. The small village was feeling the sharp effects of modernization in the fishing industry. Over the last two decades, population increases had slowly produced a vast surplus of labour for an unchanging number of village boats. Trawling, meanwhile, was threatening to eliminate the Filey fishing coble (hardly changed since Norman times) from major market competition. Recent government intervention further unsettled the village by interfering with the traditional pattern of seasonal fishing excursions. The household economy of the Filey fishing families, interlaced with local folklore and customs, began to disintegrate under the pressure of external influences.[26]

Oxtoby's brand of popular piety encouraged the villagers to examine their own lives for solutions to troubled times in Filey. Instinctively, he appealed to their sense of local community and their attachment to a way of life threatened by growing towns and trawlers. 'His external appearance,' commented his biographer, was 'more like one of the old prophets than a modern minister of the gospel.'[27] Oxtoby's 'prayers and homely exhortations were couched in the broad East-Riding dialect'.[28] According to Hugh Bourne, founder of the Primitive Methodist Connexion, Oxtoby's speech[29]

> was very provincial; and much of his preaching consisted in giving accounts of what he had seen of the work of God when he was at this place, and that place; and as the work was frequently breaking out under him, he was constantly furnished with something fresh.

Filonians responded to his strong language, his occasional prophetic stance, and his dabbling in the art of healing. With each conversion, he strengthened the collective traditionalism of the village.

Oxtoby's greatest talent, house-to-house visitation, proved wonderfully effective in Filey. After large meetings taking place outdoors or in houses, Praying Johnny circulated among villagers' households in order to attend to 'convicted' hearers, much as a doctor might make housecalls during an epidemic. The enthusiasm for domestic services of every kind grew in Filey and ultimately outweighed formal services in the new chapel. One preacher reckoned that more souls were saved in class meetings (always in houses) than elsewhere. 'There has always been a strange social element in the Church-life of Filey,' he observed years later, 'and a marked domesticity in its devotions.'[30] By appealing to the household unit, an economic necessity in Filey, cottage religion provided means of preserving traditions and rites of the old fishing village.

The mendicant popular preacher was a bearer of traditionalism in the face of change. While at times revitalizing declining villages, sectarian Methodists also brought village values into new factory towns. Transplanted into 'modern' settings, preachers projected a double image: their connection to cottage religion was both reminiscent of a tradition-bound, stable past and remindful of a turbulent present. Their clothing often marked them as ordinary country folk; it was more suited to work than 'church', and in some cases, it betrayed everyday occupations. The plain and humble image cultivated by female preachers also identified them with country customs. In rejecting fashionable frills for plain poke bonnets, they opted for the attire of rural labouring women over modern dress imported from distant cities. Speech identified preachers according to their native districts as well as their class. With scant education, most likely administered in dialect, preachers (particularly women) had few opportunities to develop oratorical skills that would soften harsh sentiments and disguise social origins. Armed with irreverent reproofs, cottage evangelists confronted the anonymity of modern towns with standards of accountability belonging to the rural past.

The sects produced a legion of country-to-town evangelists. Thomas Haslam (b. 1813), a spinner from Egerton (Lancs), became celebrated as 'a willing horse' among the Independent Methodists. Haslam was already converted when he came to Bolton at the age of fifteen to work in a factory. His involvement in religious activities grew at a tremendous rate, until he 'was well known in that half of town in which the chapel is situated, and was frequently called upon to visit their sick and dying, baptize their children, to marry, and to bury'. Haslam's greatest strength, however, lay in his tireless determination to monitor the lives of every society member, reproving and rebuking them so much that 'he was not always admired'.[31] Another cottage evangelist, James Benton (n.d.), succeeded in establishing a Primitive Methodist society in the factory town of Belper (Derby). Using hymns and verses of his own composition, he accosted townspeople with specific accusations designed for missioning 'at close quarters'.[32] Female preachers showed particular acumen in securing a foothold in large towns. Ann Carr (b. 1783), Elizabeth Tomlinson (b. 1775), and Sarah Kirkland (b. 1794) penetrated the very households of followers around Nottingham and Derby. As Ann Carr proudly noted after visiting families around Nottingham, 'No place would have held one-third of them.'[33]

As champions of village virtue in mid-Victorian England, cottage evangelists confronted trying times. Large-scale movements appropriated many of the aims of sectarian religion; practices once conceived of as religious means of protecting the household - temperance, careful attention to children, and avoidance of debt - appeared in secular dress. Popular preachers also fell under the shadow of both the modern mass revivalist and the upper-class philanthropist. Face-to-face evangelizing, 'ranter-like', was out of style. Few townspeople understood Primitive Methodist preacher Billy Hickingbotham when he railed against the new 'fashion...of wearing cap-borders' in the 1850s. 'The women wear'n something called caps, but they arn'na caps,' he complained; 'and some folks have something like religion, but it in'na religion.'[34] The phenomenal industrial growth of the Potteries in Staffordshire, the birthplace of Primitive Methodism, witnessed the passing of small sectarian chapels. At Hanley, around eighty working men purchased an abandoned Primitive chapel and turned it into a 'People's Hall for lectures and public meetings' in 1850. Four years later, the building became a theatre.[35] New aims and interests had displaced village religion as an organizing force in industrial cities.

Cottage evangelism nevertheless continued in isolated parts of England and Wales. In rural areas, villagers preserved the traditional arrangements of cottage societies despite the national trend towards chapel-building. Primitive Methodists in Preston (Wilts) met in cottages belonging to two eighteenth-century farmhouses from 1830 until 1907, when members finally decided to erect a corrugated iron chapel.[36] Around Lancashire, Independent Methodists founded several new societies at the end of the century. Increasingly, their ventures gave expression to a vanishing way of life and declining village fortune. At Skelmersdale, a mining village near Southport, a society originated in a double cottage in 1884. Once celebrated as 'the cradle of all the Free Churches of Skelmersdale', the cottage housed the society throughout the next few decades as the local population declined owing to flooding of the collieries.[37] The Welsh Revival of 1904-5 gives similarly suggestive evidence of the persistence of sectarian Methodism in industrializing societies.

Thus religious movements in cities and towns tried to answer the cry against modern times and the call for customary village accountability. Even when fewer town-dwellers had first-hand knowledge of village life, the message of cottage religion remained symbolically significant. To the discerning eye, promoters of plebeian righteousness, humble virtue, and village concerns were still at work in late nineteenth-century cities. The Salvation Army took up similar causes and at its peak outnumbered the Primitive Methodist Connexion in the 1880s. As an international movement, the Salvation Army also points to a wide-reaching, even global context for considering this form of religious activity and its relation to labouring experience. Primitive and Independent Methodists can claim a peculiar kinship with sectarians in developing nations today. The Shakers of St Vincent (W.I.), for example, often worship in cottages called 'praise houses' and also engage women as leaders in improvised, domestic-styled religious practices. In Brazil, the Umbanda spiritualist movement has emerged in response to rapid industrialization in southern regions; like cottage religion, it has gathered strength from substantial rural-to-urban migration.[38] Religions of the dispossessed and oppressed continually appear where traditional nativist cultures confront modern industrial capitalism. Nineteenth-century cottage preachers would have little trouble comprehending their insistent demonstrations.

NOTES

1 F.F.B., 'John Tregortha', *Proceedings of the Wesley Historical Society*, 1939-40, vol. 22, pp. 15-20. I owe thanks to Susan Amussen and the lunchtime discussion group at Brown University for their comments on an earlier version of this essay.
2 For the earlier period, see John Walsh, 'Methodism and the Mob in the Eighteenth Century', G.J. Cuming and Derek Baker (eds), *Popular Belief and Practice*, Cambridge University Press, 1972, pp. 213-27. See also E.J. Hobsbawm, *Primitive Rebels*, New York, Norton, 1959, ch. 8; James Obelkevich, *Religion and Rural Society*, Oxford University Press, 1976.
3 *Scenes from Clerical Life*, 1858, Harmondsworth, Penguin, 1973, p. 50; H.B. Kendall, *History of the Primitive Methodist Church*, 2 vols, London, n.d.; Arthur Mounfield, *A Short History of Independent Methodism*, Wigan, 1905; F.W. Bourne, *The Bible Christians*, Devon, 1905.
4 Walsh, op. cit., pp. 224ff. See also MSS. Journal of Hugh Bourne, vol. 1, March 20, 1808; 'Memoir of Mrs Mary Lea', *Primitive Methodist Magazine* (hereafter *PMM*), 1856, pp. 198-9.
5 Rev. John Barfoot, *A Diamond in the Rough; or Christian Heroism in Humble Life*, London, 1874, pp. 46-7.
6 'Memoir of Peter Bond, of Beeley', *PMM*, 1826, pp. 333-7.
7 Most of the following biographical information was extracted from the six-part 'Memoir of Elizabeth Russell', which first appeared as a commemorative obituary in the *Primitive Methodist Magazine* for 1837. The memoir was later published as a pamphlet by the author, Thomas Russell, the husband of Elizabeth Smith. It included substantial excerpts from her personal journals.
8 Ibid., p. 96.
9 Ibid., p. 97.
10 Wesley F. Swift, 'The Woman Itinerant Preachers of Early Methodism', *Proceedings of the Wesley Historical Society*, 1952-3, pp. 89-94, 76-83.
11 G. Herod, *Biographical Sketches of Primitive Methodist Preachers*, n.d., p. 313.
12 See Natalie Z. Davis, 'Women on Top', in *Society and Culture in Early Modern France*, Stanford University Press, 1975, pp. 124-51.
13 A.H. Patterson, *From Hayloft to Temple*, Great Yarmouth, 1902, p. 23.
14 'Memoir of Hannah Broomhead', *PMM*, 1861, pp. 322-3.
15 'Memoir of Priscilla Lambden', *PMM*, 1837, pp. 17-19.
16 'Memoir of Elizabeth Gosling', *PMM*, 1837, pp. 177-80.
17 'Memoir of Mrs Mary Adams', *Bible Christian Magazine*, 1865, pp. 451-6.
18 'Memoir of John Birchall, of Lowton Common', *Free Gospel*

Magazine (hereafter *FGM*), 1871, p. 246.
19 R. Guest, *A Compendious History of the Cotton Manufacture*, Manchester, 1823, reprinted, London, Frank Cass, 1968, p. 38.
20 'Memoir of William Birchall', *FGM*, 1871, pp. 167-70.
21 See 'Memoir of John Birchall', op. cit., pp. 245-7; 'Memoir of John Roughly', *FGM*, 1874, pp. 300-3.
22 A. Mounfield, op. cit., p. 67; *The Connexion*, March, 1980, p. 5. I owe thanks to Mr Thomas Abel, President of the Warrington Independent Methodist chapel, for bringing the latter article to my attention. J. Corry, *History of Lancashire*, 1825, vol. 2, p. 682; E. Baines, *History, Directory, and Gazetteer of the County of Lancaster*, 1825, vol. 2, p. 718; *Victoria History of the County of Lancaster*, ed. W. Farrer and J. Browbill, London, 1906, vol. 4, pp. 150-1, 154.
23 See 'Memoir of Jepheth Thompson', *Free Gospel Advocate*, 1852, p. 88, for one illustration. On the imagery of the Psalms in 'religion of the non-privileged classes', see Max Weber, *The Sociology of Religion*, Ephraim Fischoff, translation, Beacon, Boston, 1964, p. 111.
24 'Memoir of John Holgate, of Dewsbury', *FGM*, 1877, pp. 355-7.
25 'Memoir of John Oxtoby', *PMM*, 1831, pp. 9-13, 44-8, 142-8; G. Shaw, *The Life of John Oxtoby*, Hull, 1894; Kendall, op. cit., vol. 1, pp. 365-70.
26 D.M. Valenze, 'Aspects of Popular Evangelicalism in Britain, 1790-1850', unpublished PhD dissertation, Brandeis University, 1982, ch. 6.
27 Appendix, 'Memoir of John Oxtoby', op. cit., p. 143.
28 Kendall, op. cit., vol. 2, p. 106.
29 'Remarks by Hugh Bourne', *PMM*, 1831, pp. 46-7.
30 Rev. R. Harrison, quoted in Kendall, op. cit., vol. 2, p. 106.
31 'Memoir of Thomas Haslam, of Bolton', *FGM*, 1871, pp. 247-9.
32 Kendall, op. cit., vol. 2, pp. 182-4.
33 Martha Williams, *Memoirs of the Life and Character of Ann Carr*, Leeds, 1841, p. 40.
34 J. Barfoot, op. cit., p. 78.
35 *Victoria History of the County of Stafford*, ed. R.B. Pugh, London, 1963, vol. 8, p. 171. The theatre was described as 'dingy and inconvenient' (p. 172).
36 *Victoria History of the County of Wiltshire*, ed. E. Crittal, London, 1978, vol. 9, pp. 93, 103.
37 A. Mounfield, op. cit., pp. 179-80.
38 Esther Pressel, 'Umbanda Trance and Possession in Sao Paulo, Brazil', *Trance, Healing, and Hallucination*, by Felicitas D. Goodman, *et al.*, New York, 1974, pp. 113-225; Jeannette H. Henney, 'Spirit-Possession Belief and Trance Behaviour in Two Fundamentalist

Groups in St. Vincent', op. cit., pp. 3-108.

7 TENNYSON, KING ARTHUR, AND IMPERIALISM

Victor Kiernan*

Tennyson was a great English poet, far the most richly gifted of the past century and a half, who failed to write great poems. If he ever, like the young Wordsworth, made 'rigorous inquisition' into his own qualifications, he might well have seemed to himself to be endowed with every requisite. He had extraordinary verbal felicity, a mastery of English words and sounds never surpassed and scarcely ever equalled, with an inexhaustible flow of imagery, and minutely delicate observation of nature. He had besides a keen interest in the widening horizons of knowledge. Concern for social and public questions came to him less spontaneously, at the prompting of friends and critics and, no doubt, of a wish to enrol more readers. But by 1835, when he was twenty-six, he was anxious, as his son and biographer Hallam records, to grapple with broad human issues. How to capture them in words and rhymes was another matter. His wrestlings with it were to beset him all his life, and made him curiously ready to resort to advisers for subjects. A story got about of Tennyson ruefully declaring: 'I have the best command of English since Shakespeare, only I have nothing to say.' Since long before his time the artistic impulse and the themes of art had been separate things, brought together in a variety of ways, often with the patron as matchmaker. In the nineteenth century the connection between them was becoming acutely uneasy. Poetry had outlived its old community functions, except at the humble level of weavers' or miners' songs, and fears were expressed that in a steam-driven world there was no room left for it. 'The genius of this time is wholly anti-poetic', Bulwer Lytton wrote in 1833.[1]

Many had no fault to find with this new age; others accepted it, as sensible men, because it had its good side, and nothing better was conceivable; but among the more imaginative there was a compulsive turning away in fantasy, in a variety of

---

*Victor Kiernan, a member of the editorial board of *Past and Present* and for many years lecturer in history at Edinburgh University, is author of works on Spanish, British and imperial history, and a translator of Urdu poetry.

directions, from a society emotionally starved and bewildering. Repelled by the squalid greed of what they had not yet learned to call capitalism, they were very apt to counterpose to its values, as a noble opposite, those of war. Rome and its army and empire were a staple of secondary education. Carlyle extolled violence; Ruskin, in his 1865 lecture (in *The Crown of Wild Olive*), preached a cult not unlike Nietzsche's of war as fountain of culture, mother of the arts, which could not draw breath in a money-grubbing environment. Some military men came to romanticize their profession as the upholder of true manhood against base materialism and effeminacy; T.E. Lawrence ended by shaking the dust of civilization off his feet and joining the air force.

In all this there lurked a fatal blindness, to the fact that capitalism, so far from being tamely pacific, would, as it evolved, bring far greater wars than ever seen on earth before, and that whatever their high-sounding pretences they would be wars for gold. This was so above all with imperial wars, and to Britain, far more than to any other country, war and its elevating devotion to duty meant empire-building. Writers were often in the lead of Victorian readiness to hug the empire as a balm for nagging dissatisfaction with the rat-race at home. Carlyle recommended a return to colonial slavery, Dickens had strongly authoritarian attitudes and close family connections with the colonies. Yet the record of the earlier, merchant-capital imperialism, the wars for spice trade and slave trade, ought to have been warning enough of how false was the antithesis of noble war and ignoble money-making.

Many rays of light were deflected onto British banners from the Roman eagles; many also from medieval shield and plumed helmet. Idealizing of war drew on the admiration for chivalry kindled by Scott and the rest of the feudalizing romantics. Its first thought, like Spenser's, was of a gentle knight pricking on the plain, a plain in the Punjab or Kaffraria for example. In its most archaic, absurd form chivalry was a nostalgic daydream of aristocracy conscious of sinking into futility or derogation, the baron turning into the *bourgeois gentilhomme*. Of this the Eglinton Tournament in 1839 was the most melodramatic ebullition. More widely, it was a daydream of a heterogeneous middle class, never fully and frankly belonging to the industrial age, easily ashamed of 'low' connections with 'trade' instead of glorying in 'business' like Caleb Garth in *Middlemarch*. A good part of it, professional especially but drawing in more and more sons of prosperous businessmen, was turning into a caste of *bourgeois gentilhommes*, learning from genteel Oxbridge tutors to assimilate itself to the gentry. But historians were making their unwelcome appearance, and throwing a more realistic light on the Middle Ages and their chivalry. For English fancy a ready retreat was open from Middle Ages into Dark Ages, or Arthurian Britain filtered through the halo of chivalry, an unreal but captivating past where feudalism itself had found a magic mirror to reflect its features in knightly guise. There chivalry could live on, disembodied, in a Camelot 'never built at all, and therefore built for ever', as Tennyson wrote, in a setting very unlike the more autochthonous Celtic twilight frequented by Irish writers.

With Tennyson the struggle to transmute reality into art began with painful personal experiences. Tennyson's father was a clergyman embittered by being baulked of the inheritance which went to a younger brother instead, with a dangerously violent temper inflamed by drink. His large family grew up in a shabby-genteel condition, looked down on by their flourishing cousins. To kindle radical stirrings in a young writer some such private irritant may be useful - the Wordsworth family's grievance against the Earl of Lonsdale was another - but it cannot be relied on to keep a blaze going. In Wordworth's case it was quickly fuelled by the French Revolution. Tennyson had a similar but much more limited phase. He got into a student set at Cambridge, the 'Apostles', who discussed very advanced ideas, and he took part with some of the members in a brief Spanish adventure on behalf of a Liberal conspiracy; one of them and all the Spaniards were caught and shot. In the same year 1830 there was the fall of Charles X in France, and then in England rioting farm labourers, of whom Tennyson saw something, and the agitation for the first Reform Bill.

All this ought to have been invigorating, but the chaotic family existence of his childhood and adolescence seems rather to have infected him with a lifelong dread of social disorder. He was capable of warm indignation at social evils, but those he attacked were too narrowly of the sort that individuals like himself on the fringes of the upper classes were exposed to; in particular, the mercenary and snobbish prejudices which prevented him for long years from marrying. Anti-aristocratic feeling of this kind may be at least as forcibly expressed by writers like him or Thackeray or Trollope, growing up on the edge of gentility, desiring entrance to the charmed circle, thinking how much worthier they are of a place in it than most of its occupants, as by men whose affiliation is with a consciously non-aristocratic middle class, men like Cobden or Bright. In Tennyson it outlasted his days of poverty and frustration. But he was not finding a way to transform personal resentment into a more generalized indictment of injustice. In a letter of 1847 he complains of the dullness of the English country gentry and their rustical conversation, but he only goes so far as to add: 'I wish they would be a little kinder to the poor.'[2] Here in a nutshell is his social doctrine: not to get rid of those in power, but to invite them to turn over a new leaf. Smouldering inner fires found their outlet not in opposition to the established order, but in religious or philosophical doubts and questionings, of the governance of heaven rather than of earth.

Already in the early 1830s, an old head on young shoulders, he was an advocate of slow, cautious, imperceptible progress.

His ideal was peace between classes, an end to 'the feud of rich and poor'. To bring this about he could at times contemplate some vaguely grand transformation of society, and recognize that it must involve strain and upheaval.[3] But that 'the old order changeth' was easier to admit in the abstract, or on a stricken field in ancient Britain, than to come to terms with in his own time and place. Professionally, he achieved success with his poems published in 1842. A pension followed in 1845, marriage and the Laureateship in 1850. He went on to make a fortune out of writing, handsomer probably than any other English poet ever achieved. It was a story of success that Samuel Smiles must have approved, but prosperity did not do away with all his uncomfortablenesses. There was madness, dipsomania, and drug addiction in his family; he himself suffered from hypochondria, and ailments with, it may be surmised, psychological causes, and was tormented by fear of blindness, and soothed his nerves with incessant smoking and a daily bottle of port.

On the literary plane, Tennyson's infirmity of nerves could be more beneficial, by keeping alive a restlessness, a sense of irreconcilabilities. He remained in old age what he had been in youth, a brilliantly accomplished versifier and often something far better, and an experimenter to the end. Poetically as well as politically, there was no such rapid ascent to glory, and then rapid and prolonged decline, as in Wordsworth's case.

Many traces of painful experience can be seen or guessed at in *Idylls of the King*, as well as in poems more transparently self-concerned; of long-delayed marriage, for instance, in Arthur's cry of longing for Guinevere, in 'The Coming'.

What happiness to reign a lonely king,
Vext-O ye stars that shudder over me,
O earth that soundest hollow under me,
Vext with waste dreams?

No one has more poignantly expressed the leaden forebodings that lie heavy on a nervous temperament, thrown much on its own resources. At Vivien's flattery Merlin - Tennyson's poetic *Doppelgänger* - fell mute,

So dark a forethought roll'd about his brain,
As on a dull day in an Ocean cave
The blind wave feeling round his long sea-hall
In silence.

Few have found an image as keen as the one in 'Guinevere' where the very thin-skinned Tennyson speaks of the resentment stirred up in Modred by an affront which

Rankled in him and ruffled all his heart,
As the sharp wind that ruffles all day long
A little bitter pool about a stone
On the bare coast.

Because of the uncertainty and insecurity of his early social position, as well as personal morbidities and chronic pessimism, Tennyson could never be the confident spokesman of any class, with a clearly focused political outlook. His conservatism was not that of a stout, solid John Bull, but of an anxious, anchorless individual, who had grievances of his own against the social order, liked to think himself a progressive, but was held back by spectres of chaos which a neurotic fancy, legacy of a frightened childhood, too easily conjured up; dread of a relapse into dark-age barbarism which beset all propertied Europe in times of social dyspepsia like 1848.

Committed to poetry's social responsibility, he set out to be his country's Public Orator; more than that, to be the voice of the people, or such of the people as he had any comprehension of. It was one asset that he had in himself so much of the Victorian contradiction between energy and confidence, hesitancy and pessimism; but it was the doubts and perplexities that he entered into more readily. When he tried to be outspoken and positive he was too likely to be more a mouthpiece for what the man in the street was already thinking than an instructor, and more influenced than influencing. This sometimes landed him in attempts to revive poetry by injections of crude excitement which could only make its languor more obvious. It would be wrong all the same to think of the Laureate turning out such wares to order, like a bespoke shoemaker, or espousing accepted notions for the sake of his position. He had his own need of the thrills of war or empire, like his hero or other self at the end of 'Maud', to rouse him from the spider-webs and shadows of his inner landscape. Sounds of distant bugles could stir in him a stronger confidence in national and human destinies. Like most patriots, he had no liking for most of his countrymen, and he could think of them with most satisfaction far away in time or space, like Sir Richard Grenville's bulldog crew in the *Revenge* or the garrison of Lucknow, though as a rule the commander had more of his attention than the men. He could admire men of action the more because he was very little capable of it, and and by putting himself into his heroes' shoes could rise above his customary inertness. Here too was justification for his art -[4]

The song that nerves a nation's heart
Is in itself a deed.

Compared with social anarchy, war could appear to him, as it has to so many others from Shakespeare down, a lesser evil, a controlled outlet for violence. An exceptionally humane man, he did not upset himself by thinking too realistically about mangled corpses. War was with him a mainly cerebral affair, fought with toy soldiers, lance and sabre not often smeared with real blood. Highly imaginative though he was, there was apt to be a certain want of practical or human realization in his flights. In a marvellous passage in 'Morte d'Arthur' Sir Bedivere 'swiftly strode' down from battlefield to shore:

Dry clash'd his harness in the icy caves
And barren chasms, and all to left and right
The bare black cliff clang'd round him, as he based
His feet on juts of slippery crag that rang

Sharp-smitten with the dint of armed heels -
And on a sudden, lo! the level lake,
And the long glories of the winter moon.

As word-painting these lines, with the sudden modulation in the last two from harsh to liquid consonants and from short to long vowels, are incomparable; they recall the sound-painting that nineteenth-century musicians strove after in their tone-poems. Yet anyone who has scrambled over wet slippery rocks knows that an iron-shod man in armour could not possibly stride downwards across them in that fashion - even without a wounded man on his back.

It was always possible, moreover, to think of England as on the defensive, a small nation surviving by quality and courage. 'Lucknow' is about the dogged British defence of the Residency, not the savage British assault on the city. In the Wellington funeral ode the duke wins the day in India 'Against the myriads of Assaye'. In the patriotic tradition of the thin red line Englishmen were always, like Macaulay's Romans, facing fearful odds. The *Revenge* is swallowed up in the maw of a Spanish fleet, the three hundred of the Heavy Brigade are engulfed in 'Russian hordes'. Tennyson could with a better conscience repel the charge of militarism, as he does in an 'Epilogue' to 'The Charge of the Heavy Brigade', in the form of a dialogue with a reproachful young lady. Man must be ready to fight for the sake of 'true peace'.

England's combats might be righteous and unsought, but they were gaining for it the widest-ranging empire in history, for Tennyson a bastion against his haunting sense of mutability and impermanence. It was something tangible and vast, which could be admired from every point of view from commercial to moral, and was coming to be seen almost as God's final bequest to humanity, the labour of His eighth day. It had, of course, the warrant of Roman precedent, and of Virgil and Horace, whose poetry he had at his fingertips. His tribute to Virgil dwells mostly on peaceful themes, common humanity, but it does not fail to catch an undying echo of 'Imperial Rome' in the Mantuan's 'ocean-roll of rhythm'. Before the caesars there was Alexander. A youthful sonnet in his honour began with the same words - 'Warrior of God' - as the epitaph decades later on Gordon.

His interest in the empire and its fortunes dawned betimes. About 1842 he was all for putting up with no nonsense from the Afghans,[5] and he contemplated a poem on the battle of Miani which won Sind in 1843. (Meredith's first poem was on the battle of Chilianwala in the Punjab in 1849). But his verses dealing directly with episodes of this kind were to be not very numerous, for so prolific a writer, and not very good. He found it simpler to put all such themes into disguised, mythic form. We may suspect him of doing this with his Ulysses, weary of ruling 'a savage race' who - strangely enough - know him not: they are his own islanders, but he sounds for all the world like a bored colonial official somewhere in the back of beyond. Tennyson's friend Spedding (of the Colonial Office) observed in him when still quite young an 'almost personal dislike of the present, whatever it may be'.[6] In *Idylls of the King* he made his most ambitious effort to render the feelings of the present more lucidly by transposing them into the past.

Poets were groping not only for subjects which might come home to men's business and bosoms in an unpoetical climate, but also for modes of expression worthy of them. Forced to justify its existence, only by great creations could poetry hope to survive; but these called for grand forms, which music, free to soar on wings instead of walking, was proving much better able to invent. Wordsworth was condemned to a lifetime of unrealizable aspiration by Coleridge's incitement to compose a majestic Philosophical poem; Tennyson, equally consumed by his vocation, was tantalized by the mirage of an epic. As his reputation rose he was increasingly sensitive to the appeals of friends and admirers for some masterpiece to immortalize him, much as Brahms was harassed by summonses to come forward as the symphonic successor to Beethoven. The outcome, produced disjointedly at intervals during nearly twenty years, was the cycle of connected narratives about ancient Britain known as the *Idylls*. 'There is no doubt that he regarded this poem as his chief life-work.'[7] Its Saxon simplicity of diction was not long in being noticed; it may be that here more than usually he was trying to live up to his image of himself as poet of the people, in the spirit of the Wordsworth of *Lyrical Ballads*.

Clearly the central idea of the Arthurian legend, of benign ruler and highborn followers vowed to protect the weak and right wrongs - a social inversion of Robin Hood and his foresters - has had a tenacious attraction. Rabelais might burlesque the knights of the Round Table as tatterdemalions earning a pittance in the next world by ferrying devils across the Styx,[8] Cervantes might banish all knight-errantry to the realm of farce; yet for centuries it went on casting a Celtic spell over the hard-headed Sassenach. Milton thought of King Arthur as the subject for his great work; Blake made a symbolic interpretation of the myth as a version of the Fall, from Eden or innocence;[9] Scott, Matthew Arnold, Swinburne, William Morris, all wrote Arthurian poems. From early in the century interest was reinforced by study of mythology. G.S. Faber, whose work may have coloured Tennyson's 'Morte d'Arthur', conceived of the ancients as believing in a cycle of eras, each in turn relapsing into chaos.[10]

Tennyson grew up reading the stories. He was fascinated by Merlin, seeing in him a type of the spirit of poetry; thinking thus of poetry as a species of magic, potent to alter the world, as Shelley believed it could. At twenty-four he was meditating an epic or drama about Arthur, and it was about then that he wrote the splendid fragment 'Morte d'Arthur'. He published this with an awkward fiction of its being a relic of a long epic, all the rest destroyed, which revealed his mistrust of his darling project as too archaic and remote from the contemporary mind. Years later, on the point of bringing out the first Idylls, he declared that one would have to be 'crazed' to write an Arthurian epic in the mid-nineteenth century.[11] By writing it in bits he could try it on his public by stages, as Byron had done with *Childe Harold* and *Don Juan*; and the breath of applause might fill his hesitant sails.

Only a third of the dozen tales have happy endings, and it is significant that their final dénouement was the first fragment to be written, a gloom-laden picture of two survivors, one dying, of two dead armies. Tennyson might have chosen to write of Hengist and Horsa bringing Saxondom into Britain; or (another theme that occurred to Milton) of Alfred valiantly defending their descendants against the Danes; or of William conquering England. Ancient Britain by contrast was a dying civilization, which appealed far more to his inner self, and could set many chords in readers' minds vibrating. Camelot is a candle in a naughty world, soon quenched, as the *Revenge* is overwhelmed by the mass of its enemies. In its remote shadows he could allow himself to see man and his world as he feared they really were. His villains, or evil-doers, like Milton's are far more vital than most of his virtuous men and women. But he was withdrawing into this far-off realm in order to deliver warnings to his countrymen from it, as well as in quest of affinities with his own self. For this purpose he had to import into it some incongruous migrants, ideals and idealists from his England, or his own corner of it, or this corner as he tried to see it, and it to see itself. They are marshalled by an Arthur turned into a Victorian gentleman, refined and rarified, but a muscular Christian too, a king on horseback; a type of the heroes like General Gordon who were building the empire, liberating its peoples supposedly from the darkness of bondage and superstition. Gazing at the empire, Tennyson could feel a simple certitude of rightness, a simplification of moral and political issues, unattainable in his own over-complicated country. Of the realities of empire he knew as little as of ancient Britain; of the connection, for instance, between City usurers and the occupation of Egypt which he lauded. Arthur remains unnatural, unconvincing, because Victorian standards of behaviour, within the family notably, contained so much over-strained pretence and deceit; but also because the idea of the empire as benevolent and disinterested was more than half a figment of fancy, or deception.

As later when writing his historical plays, Tennyson took great pains to get up his subject, even to the point of learning some Welsh. His materials were gathered from a variety of sources, beginning with Malory and the *Mabinogion* Likewise, the reflections on his own times, the new wine poured, often incongruously, into these old bottles, must be looked for in diverse quarters. He talked of the work as having many meanings. 'Every reader must find his own interpretation.' For him, its essential meaning was human endeavour ruined by temptation and sin; or 'the world-wide war of Sense and Soul, typified in individuals'.[12] It was an elastic enough formula. Soul and sense could modulate smoothly into the conflict of civilization and barbarism, which had a powerful hold on the European and above all the British mind. Empire meant in ideal terms the bringing of order and peaceful progress to lands beyond the pale. It would be strange if this notion did not find its way, however obliquely, into the *Idylls*. Three centuries earlier Camoens had written an epic on the expansion of Portugal in his own epoch. But he felt obliged to mix up history with classical mythology, and sculptors went on presenting captains and kings in Roman garb. In an age of telegraphs and newspapers, high events were far too heavily clogged with everyday associations to be treated without disguise in a long poem.

Tennyson's first musings produced a prose sketch and an allegorical framework in which Arthur stood for religious faith, the Round Table for 'liberal institutions', Modred the traitor for scepticism.[13] But more than two decades passed, like Wordsworth's long delays over *The Excursion*, before he was ready for these 'public' themes, or could work out a less unmanageable plan. When he had any scheme ready he was remarkably rapid in execution for a writer of such highly finished work. The *Idylls* were composed in two spells, the first from 1856, with a stay in Wales that year to encourage inspiration, to 1859, the second from 1868 to 1874. They were thus the performance of a man travelling from the age of forty-seven to sixty-five. Four narratives, one of them later divided into two, came out in 1859; taken in order of composition they stand in the final sequence of twelve as numbers 6, 3 and 4, 11, and 7. There was then another lengthy spell of hanging fire. His wife pressed for further progress with the grand design in which he seemed to have lost faith.[14] So in 1868 did Jowett, one of his chief mentors.[15] Four more were published in 1869 (in the sequence, numbers 9, 12, 8, 1); 'The Passing of Arthur' incorporated the fragment of many years earlier. 'The Holy Grail' was done in a fortnight, and was followed at once by 'The Coming of Arthur'. At the beginning of 1870 the poet was feeling 'extraordinarily happy' at the prospect of reaching his goal;[16] and the last three (10, 2, 5) were completed in 1871-4, though one ('Balin and Balan') was kept unpublished until 1885.

By the bulk of the reading public in their own time the reception of the *Idylls* was enthusiastic, and set the seal on Tennyson's success, partly because of the factor discussed by Bagehot in his *Literary Studies*, the entry of lower middle-class elements seeking culture as a part of their certificate of naturalization in respectable society (though they could scarcely be more uncritical than Byron's largely upper-class admirers).

More discriminating readers had reservations, much like those piled up against Tennyson later on; among them were the faithful Fitzgerald, Elizabeth Browning, Hopkins, Meredith, Swinburne, Bridges. As narratives the poems suffer from Britain's failure to take on the semblance of a living, breathing country. Their actors declaim in an empty theatre. In style too, in the effort to rise to the height of his great argument, or to convince us and himself of its height, Tennyson often labours, as if loaded with cumbrous armour; and he is always addressing us from a distance, from a pulpit or stage, instead of buttonholing us and talking man to man as writers are expected to do nowadays.

Yet moments of true drama come often enough. At the end of 'Gareth and Lynette' there is a sudden release of tension when the dreaded black knight,

High on a nightblack horse, in nightblack arms,
With white breast-bone, and barren ribs of Death,

is discovered to be a 'blooming boy'. At the end of 'The Last Tournament' the reader is taken by surprise in a very different way, when Tristram is in the act of presenting his trophy of victory in the lists to his mistress, King Mark's wife Isolt:

But, while he bow'd to kiss the jewell'd throat,
Out of the dark, just as the lips had touch'd,
Behind him rose a shadow and a shriek -
'Mark's way', said Mark, and clove him thro' the brain.

Amid much that today sounds unconvincing there are countless compelling touches, often of realistic imagery. Tennyson as well as Dickens knew what London roadways were like, and Merlin talks bitterly to Vivien of how unintelligible is virtue like Arthur's

To things with every sense as false and foul
As the poach'd filth that floods the middle street.

While Arthur looked sadly on at the last tournament

the laces of a helmet crack'd,
And show'd him, like a vermin in its hole,
Modred, a narrow face....

Tennyson's blending of ancient and modern is hinted at in the carvings on the gate of Camelot, stared at so long by the newcomer Gareth, where

Were Arthur's wars in weird devices done,
New things and old co-twisted, as if Time
Were nothing.

But whatever the meanings, intended or unintended, of the *Idylls*, there can be no gainsaying the quality of their workmanship. They are doubtless curate's eggs, only good in parts, but not seldom superlatively good, stored with echoing phrase, dazzling simile, hypnotic description.

The years of the first group of Idylls belonged, on the national scene, to the reassuring lull following the defeat of Chartism in 1848 and its ensuing decay, the Crimean War in 1854-6 helping to finish it off in with a burst of jingo enthusiasm from which the working class was not immune. In the colonial field excitements multiplied. Apart from skirmishings with Kaffirs in South Africa and Maoris in New Zealand, there was the conquest of the Punjab in the later 1840s and of Lower Burma in 1854. During the years of composition of the first Idylls there followed the second China War (1856-60), the attack on Persia (1857), and above all, in 1857-8, the greatest of all European colonial conflicts until after the Second World War, the outbreak and suppression of the Indian Mutiny, which, his son records, 'stirred him to the depths.' A brother of his friend Jowett died in India, the second to do so, in 1858.[17]

This was, for Tennyson as for most Englishmen and many other Europeans, a fearful display of barbarism revolting against Christian civilization, a land only narrowly prevented from 'reeling back into the beast' like Arthur's Britain. He was shudderingly reminded of it by the disturbance in Jamaica at the end of 1865, when the blacks were accused of planning, and the whites headed by Governor Eyre actually resorted to, a reign of terror. In the grand division of opinion in England Tennyson was one of an array of eminent writers who took Eyre's side. He would have done well to recall the moral of his poem 'The Captain', about a naval commander whose brutality brings his ship to disaster: the guilt of anyone in authority who 'only rules by terror'. His preconceptions must have been sharpened by one of his sisters having married a lawyer who went to Jamaica as chief justice. He was one of numerous writers with family links with the empire; a brother went to Tasmania, one cousin was in the navy, another, who died in the West Indies, in the army. He himself visited Ireland a number of times, and developed towards it an attitude, as an Irish historian who has studied it says, of 'naive hostility which became increasingly racialist with age....On Ireland his mind was one of angry, unhappy prejudice.'[18] So was his wife's; she considered the Irish 'a nest of traitors'.[19]

In 1866 came the Abyssinian expedition, Napier's march to Magdala on a rescue operation like so many Arthurian adventures, to liberate British captives of the half-crazy despot Theodore. A couple of years later Tennyson had as a visitor Theodore's young son Alamayu, in the custody of an English officer. In 1870 there was the repulse of the Fenian incursion into Canada from the USA, and the Red River fighting in the Canadian north-west. The next year Maori resistance was brought to an end; in 1874 the decisive campaign against the obdurate Ashanti kingdom took place. At home the agitation leading to the second Reform Act in 1867 was quite enough to flutter Tennyson, whose vivid fancy was always ready to magnify scuffles into cataclysms. On the Continent the Franco-Prussian war was followed by the Paris Commune, which threw all conservative Europe into a panic.

An epic must have a hero, and Victorian England believed, with help from Carlyle, as firmly in heroes and great men as in great works of art or engineering. Tennyson's Arthur is compounded from too many idealistic abstractions to be a convincing creature of flesh and blood. He is always a visionary, a stranger like Christ among his disciples. Somewhat like Tennyson himself, he has risen from obscure beginnings: his birth is shrouded in myth, and he has not inherited his throne but won it by prowess and a mysterious heaven-bestowed gift of leadership. He has no heir, no apparent interest in an heir; this is a childless realm altogether, built by one man, destined to perish with him. It is faintly illuminated by rays of Christianity lingering from Roman times, but the sudden advent of a highly religious and civilized reformer in the midst of primitive darkness is left as enigmatic as the white man's arrival must have been to Mohicans or Maoris. On this more workaday level, Tennyson may have owed something to his friend Carlyle's laudatory account of Dr Francia, dictator of Paraguay, as a solitary beacon of European enlightenment in the wilderness. On one side the *Idylls* are an encomium on monarchy, which in his own England the Laureate was doing much to refurbish. But Arthur is no constitutional monarch. In spite of Tennyson's early allegorizing idea of 'liberal institutions', there is no sign of the king sharing decision with anyone else. He sits at the Table with the rest, but the others are all sworn to obedience as unquestioning as the Light Brigade's.

Since Roman times Britain has been in turmoil, like the dark continents, Africa and Asia, as beheld from Europe. With Arthur's coming recovery begins, 'a nobler time' for the land. Pacification may seem for a while fairly complete, and Arthur's sway extends from the south to the Orkneys, Gareth's homeland, though we hear of no navy. But robber barons still infest the country, as Lynette complains to Arthur himself, each lording it over the neighbourhood of his tower, and bridge and ford are 'beset by bandits' 'Caitiffs' of all kinds abound - a Tennysonian archaism from the thirteenth century which could cover all undesirables.

Jeffrey and Borrow criticized Scott for resurrecting medieval-chivalric bric-à-brac, as a covering for conservatism. In their own day the first inventors of the code of chivalry were useful to feudalism by giving their feudal patrons a better look. That trampling young conqueror the Black Prince took the motto 'Ich Dien', and *service* has been the apologia of American capitalism. All fantasy-spinning is liable to turn into a grotesque caricature of itself. Tennyson can be taken as preaching the need for a conscientious landed aristocracy, doing its paternalistic duty to its humble neighbours or dependents. Carlyle had been preaching something much like this, moral rearmament of the upper class as prophylactic against a French Revolution on this side of the Channel.

In his own Britain Tennyson never knew what to make of common people. He was sorry for them, feared them, hoped they might be improved by education. In ancient Britain he could dismiss them to the wings, leaving the stage to their betters. We hear in 'The Coming' that they clamoured for a king, and Merlin presented them with Arthur, whom the 'great lords' rejected; but no idea of rousing commoners to resist oppressors could ever occur to Arthur, whose menials are 'thralls' or slaves. In Camelot itself we have a fugitive reference in 'Gareth and Lynette' to 'a healthful people' basking in their sovereign's protection, and in the 'Grail' a glimpse of them in the fields round about, in sight of the city's towers and grateful for royal guardianship against 'the heathen'. Their activity stretches no further than to turn out and applaud the knights at a tournament.

It is by warlike prowess that Arthur convinces admirers like Gareth of his right to be king. We see him in 'Lancelot and Elaine' wading in heathen blood, crimson from plume to spur, like a true crusader. He founds his Table as a substitute for Roman law and order, as he says in 'Guinevere', and to be 'a model for the mighty world' - as the British empire now was. In 'The Coming' he repulses the claims of an expiring Rome on Britain, not as a British nationalist or Fenian but simply because Rome is too feeble now to shelter the country from incursions; before Arthur comes to his aid Guinevere's father Leodogran, a harassed kinglet, is heard sighing over the disappearance of Roman power. Tennyson's unimpressive poem 'Boädicea', which belongs to 1859, carries evident overtones of the Mutiny: it is a very unsympathetic presentation of rebellion, full of wild bawling and brawling and religious hysteria, and the threat of ferocious revenge.

> Boädicéa, standing loftily charioted,
> Mad and maddening all that heard her in her fierce volubility,
> Girt by half the tribes of Britain, near the colony Cámulodúne,
> Yell'd and shriek'd between her daughters o'er a wild confederacy.

Very likely Tennyson thought of the Rani of Jhansi, the Indian heroine of 1857, as a similar virago. Metrically, the poem is one of those he called 'Experiments', and the freely handled trochaic lines of eight feet labour, with imperfect success, to echo the pandemonium of revolt. On the other hand the Romans are depraved and decadent; another warning against ruling-class misbehaviour, in this case in a colonial setting.

An imperial dimension of the Arthurian story is visible throughout. Arthur's expanding kingdom is itself a small empire, subjugating or overawing less civilized areas and bringing them within the pale of Christian manners. In the same style modern Britain was carrying fire and sword, light and sweetness, into the dark places of Asia and Africa. It may even not be irrelevant that Arthur has an exceptionally fair complexion, as if to typify the White Man (though Lancelot is raven-haired, as Tennyson was), and one of the latest-written Idylls ('The Last Tournament') gives us a remarkably Nordic vignette of a victorious Arthur on his throne, with golden hair and 'steel-blue eyes'. In 'Geraint and Enid' he sets off to improve a neglected district, remove bad officials, break 'bandit holds', and even, less distinctly, extend agriculture, just as a commissioner in a newly annexed province of India might do. He reproaches himself with not having assumed direct control of this region sooner, instead of allowing it to become, in 'delegated hands', the 'common sewer' of the realm; very much as, in the same year 1856 when this was written, the Governor-General of India, Lord Dalhousie, annexed the ramshackle kingdom of Oudh, on the strength of Sleeman's highly coloured report on its lamentable condition.

Many casual touches in the *Idylls* suggest empire parallels. Those in power before Arthur behaved like 'wild beasts', we are told in 'The Coming', and rulers like them were still at large in Asia and Africa. Mark of Cornwall is refused membership of the Table, as a princely black sheep in India might be refused a coveted decoration. Like the British there, Arthur stops petty royalties from fighting among themselves, keeps the better of them as tributaries, takes their sons into his service, like those of King Lot of the Orkneys. Exalted by his vision of the Grail, Galahad rides about overthrowing 'Pagan realms' and 'Pagan hordes', single-handed apparently, and 'Shattering all evil customs', very much like the long arm of modern Britain quelling Mad Mullahs or abolishing suttee. Among Gareth's opponents the 'Morning Star', waited on and armed by 'three fair girls' barefooted and bareheaded, has a markedly Oriental look. He is derived from a knight of Malory, Sir Persant of Inde; in medieval romances longitudes and latitudes were often wildly mixed up. Balin has been banished from court for striking a servant, and must learn to control his hasty temper and cultivate courtesy to high and low; Tennyson might well be admonishing his countrymen in India, who with all their sterling qualities were much given to beating their servants, and very little to winning native goodwill. There is a far graver breach of the code of chivalry in 'The Last Tournament', when moral decay has gone far. Arthur is leading in person an expeditionary force against a malefactor in his fortress. In the days of his 'Coming' he had been able to halt bloodshed as soon as the enemy turned tail, but now his men run wild, and after breaking into the enemy stronghold go on killing indiscriminately,

Till all the rafters rang with woman-yells,
And all the pavement stream'd with massacre.

Such scenes disfigured the conclusion of many sieges by British and other colonial forces, and were looked on by professional soldiers as often inevitable, if regrettable. Multan in the Panjab in 1849, Delhi and Lucknow during the Mutiny, were among the sufferers.

Each nation which has in turn felt itself the strongest - Revolutionary France, Victorian Britain, and in our day America - has wanted to impose its will on others, but to think of itself as their warden or rescuer. To Englishmen their long series of colonial wars might quite naturally seem to resemble the labours of Hercules, ridding the earth of its scourges. Theocritus's set of poems on the legends of Hercules were among Tennyson's models.[20] Arthurian myth fell neatly into the same pattern, and damsels in distress and their paladins lent a romantic appeal. Thanks to the Romantic revival, chivalric notions were in the air; a titular Archbishop of Carthage helped to launch King Leopold's private fief in the Congo by proposing a new order of chivalry to serve in Africa. But links are not hard to find between the special Arthurian attraction for English writers in that age, and England's spreading dominion over palm and pine. On the more serious-minded among those who were building and guarding the empire, the *Idylls* may well have had a considerable influence.

Sir George Grey, a notable Governor and enthusiast like Tennyson for imperial federation, noted in his collection of Maori legends a tale that reminded him of the finding of the child Arthur.[21] An Englishman teaching in a college in India wrote a book on the *Idylls*, and found them full of 'moral significance'.[22] A poetaster lauded Outram, 'the Bayard of India', as[23]

Prompt to redeem the helpless in distress,
And for the weak his lance in rest to lay.

Canon Tyndale-Biscoe, very much a devotee of the trinity of army-navy-empire, wanted the boys of his school in Kashmir to act like knights errant, always ready to spring to the aid of victims of injustice.[24] In the same spirit Conan Doyle's explorer in Amazonia, Lord John Roxton, set himself to act as 'the flail of the lord' and wipe out a gang of murderous slavers.[25] Possibly Tennyson looked back on his own Spanish adventure as an exercise in knight-errantry. In 1895 Sir G.C. Carter at Lagos criticized his subordinate, Captain R.L. Bower, who had bombarded the town of Oyo, as over-impetuous, too much inclined to pose as a knight errant.[26] The group of empire intellectuals active early in this century round Lord Milner, High Commissioner in South Africa, had been connected with a new Round Table, 'an Arthurian dream of a new Camelot as the focus for a dedicated British Empire'.[27] In America Walt Whitman, a warm admirer of Tennyson, admired the *Idylls* pre-eminently.[28] Unlike his countryman Mark Twain, he was an imperialist himself. Some of Tennyson's large following in America may have recognized a popular counterpart to the *Idylls* in the swelling literature of the Wild West, with its sheriffs and vigilantes battling against Indians, brigands, and other caitiffs of the New World.

Tennyson believed in God and immortality, not very positively in anything more of religion; but he deplored the decay of religious convictions as jeopardizing social bonds, and his England needed a crusading faith overseas, a broad practical creed for men of action. He was with difficulty, and only by ducal and royal persuasion, brought to include the Holy Grail among his quests, and in the poem common sense struggles with mysticism and incense-fumes. With regard to sex he felt less objection to excess of virtue. All the knights were pledged not to exceed the limits of monogamy, but some high-fliers, we hear in 'Merlin and Vivien', choose celibacy. Again, however, it may be worthwhile to look outward from Britain to the empire, where, even after English women became more generally available, it was often financially impossible for men to marry before middle age, as it had been for Tennyson himself; so that the only alternative to total abstinence was resort to prostitutes, or, at the peril of white prestige and racial purity, to native concubines.

Gladstone's private philanthropy was the rescuing of fallen women, who abounded in all big towns, a bleak reproach to the Victorian conscience. To his friend Tennyson thinking of such human degradation brought painful doubts about the condition of England. In the hall of the barbarous Earl Doorm, in 'Geraint and Enid', at sight of the captive Enid and their amorous lord

> Some, whose souls the old serpent long had drawn
> Down, as the worm draws in the wither'd leaf
> And makes it earth, hiss'd each at other's ear
> What shall not be recorded - women they,
> Women, or what had been those gracious things....

In women in high places a high moral tone was an indispensable requisite of a healthy society. All the Idylls of 1859 were studies of good and bad women, and of the devastating influence of the bad. A lurking sensation of insecurity in a class may show in the individual as a nagging fear of infidelity in the home. Society in England, that is to say the propertied classes at their then stage of evolution, could be stable only if women were prepared to accept the honorific but cramping place allotted to them. In Tennyson's long poem 'The Princess', respectable ladies had been seeking liberation in one way, claiming freedom of the mind and turning their back on men, an extravagance from which they had to be reclaimed. In the *Idylls* bad women were bent on a different freedom, of the body; to Tennyson a far more fatal deviation. In our time women have been following both paths of emancipation, the second hitherto with rather greater ardour and success.

As seducer of the wise Merlin, in the Idyll first written, Vivien is the embodiment of Sense working against Soul. As agent of the rascally King Mark, sent to Camelot in 'Balin and Balan' to make mischief, she resembles the courtesans who had a place in the diplomatic practices of Tennyson's *bête noire* Napoleon III, and Mark's licentious court is contrasted with the purity of Arthur's as Napoleon's might be with Victoria's. She too can be viewed in an empire setting as well, as a native siren with the voluptuous, insidious charms that white men in torrid lands had to be on their guard against. She is an avowed pagan, and in 'Balin and Balan' prophesies revival of the 'old sun-worship' and overturning of Christianity. Yet against the moral chastity-belt of Victorian virtue she represents something like a real revolt of womanhood, escaping from her creator's control like a miniature female Satan. Unlike Guinevere, she suffers from no guilty conscience; she preaches the life of the senses, and dismisses all Arthurian idealism as mere humbug or folly.

Old priest, who mumble worship in your quire -
Old monk and nun, ye scorn the world's desire,
Yet in your frosty cells ye feel the fire!...
The fire of Heaven is lord of all things good,
And starve not thou this fire within thy blood,
But follow Vivien thro' the fiery flood!

It is not surprising that she startled some readers. There was a 'pagan' admixture in Tennyson himself, as there must be in every artist, and memories of his first love, and Rosa Baring's physical attractions, may have come back to life in Vivien, stirring some lingering regrets, and driving him to take refuge in his dualism of flesh and spirit.

That a hopeful kingdom should fall to pieces through the contagion of a queen's adultery was a central point of his Arthurian conception from the beginning. Guinevere was to be another Eve, bringing death back into the world. Arthur's knights at first 'worship' her, as their emblem of truth and purity, Balin declares. (Victoria, if not worshipped, became a genuine cult figure for Englishmen in the outposts of empire: her death was shattering.) But rumours are soon heard, and alarm husbands like Geraint. Later on her liaison with the always conscience-stricken Lancelot has a cruder parallel in that of the more scandalous Isolt, Mark's queen, with the burly sensualist Tristram. Demoralization is spreading among the elite, and must lead to national ruin.

In the Dedication to the queen of the 1859 Idylls the poet could strike his optimistic note, as one singing 'in the rich dawn of an ampler day' ushered in by science and industry. In the springtime of Camelot, when women were still 'pure' and 'shy', a future of perpetual brightness could seem to stretch before the knights, with the exhilaration of service in a great cause. But radiant beginnings were soon clouding over. Heroic values flourished best in the pristine days, amid the 'heathen wars' when Arthur was laying his foundations. As in 'Maud', peace and prosperity seem to breed decay, and an atmosphere of over-ripeness hangs over the scene. There is a reaction, voiced by Tristram in 'The Last Tournament', against Arthur's puritanism, as only 'the wholesome madness of an hour', usefully nerving men to great exertions while these were required, but the time has come for them to enjoy themselves. Simplicity gives way to over-sophistication - 'too much wit Makes the world rotten', the Fool tells Tristram. The final tournament ends in disorder, and riotous festivities with women taking part.

In fact the moral stamina of Arthur's chosen few proves feeble enough; which hints at an uncomfortably low estimate by

Tennyson, hard though he must have tried to repress it, of the ruling classes of his England. Modred as faction-chief is a weasel of a villain, destitute of any greatness. His tactics consist of fomenting feuds within the Order and conspiring with the 'heathen'. In the closing catastrophe, the 'weird' battle in the western mists, he has 'the Heathen of the Northern Sea' for allies; they may be credited with some kinship with the French whom Tennyson was always expecting to see landing on England's shore.

In artistic design the *Idylls* are tragic, 'the great Arthurian tragedy' in his son's words.[29] Their completion left him preparing to devote the best of his remaining energies to a set of tragic dramas, mainly from English history. He was revealed in the *Idylls* as the poet of decay and change, penetrated by a sense of the unreliability of men and things which was always at odds with his longing, bred by a disturbed childhood, for reassurance.

With these forebodings and his fears of moral bankruptcy, all Tennyson's publications were in favour of a linking or fusion of the new bourgeoisie with the old aristocracy or gentry, or at any rate an amalgam of what seemed to him best in both. His nostalgias lay with the older class, his moral standards, like most of his readership, joined him to the newer. Belonging to the professional fringe of the gentry, he was well placed to aid in promoting communications between the two. He was doing so in one important way by recommending the empire, of which the new middle classes or their radical spokesmen were for long suspicious, as a joint investment. In the later decades of the century it was contributing greatly towards bringing the two propertied groups closer. But instead of being the sustainer of high resolve and rugged simplicity that he looked so expectantly to, it was a siren leading England astray, another Vivien learning the secret of a spell and using it as a fetter.

There was emerging, in short, the plutocracy whose greed and depravity Tennyson, along with other censors, contemplated with disgust. Not the best, but the worst, of two epochs was being combined. For him there could be no hope of a political or social order surviving for long after exhausting its moral capital. He could never shake off his fear of lost virtue bringing with it harsh penalties. Shakespeare's Henry IV in old age foresaw an England sinking into 'a wilderness again, Peopled with wolves';[30] and if we read into his words a premonition of the fate of the monarchy as it was in Shakespeare's day, and all that went with it, we may find in Tennyson's very similar language a warning that the death of Property might be at hand. The 'red ruin' Arthur accuses Guinevere of bringing on the land is a compound of many evils, not all explained; but it must include something of 'the red fool fury' of revolutionary Paris which was Tennyson's grand political phobia.

His long, deep plunges into the past, and returns to his own day, may be compared with those of other writers who took the time-machine back to Rome, like Kingsley in *Hypatia* and Pater in *Marius the Epicurean*, or into the Middle Ages like Bulwer Lytton in *Rienzi*, or into the Renaissance like George Eliot in *Romola*, and Browning, all in search of other vistas and of an observatory from which to survey their own epoch. The most revealing contrast is with William Morris and his pilgrimage into the far northland. Morris was fascinated by the sagas, and set about translating them, in the 1860s; in the early 1870s he made two visits to Iceland, as Tennyson visited Wales. He was profoundly impressed by 'the cold volcanic island and its fierce mythologies', finding there a secret 'strong enough to carry him out of his despair to the greatness of his last years'.[31] Like Tennyson going back beyond medieval chivalry to its fabulous Celtic ancestry, Morris was going back beyond the Saxon and Dane of an era coming under the scrutiny of historians eager to demonstrate the Saxon origins of the British Constitution, Cambridge University, and all other good things, to a mysterious Nordic twilight. There human grandeurs could be found enshrined in the sagas, as those of the Celtic mist could be found in the *Mabinogion*.

It was an opposite world, not of king and lord and lady of high degree, but a rough democracy of warrior farmers, leading a simple, rugged life where each man's fortunes rested on his own hardihood, his single courage and endurance, and on his own fate. Instead of a paternalist Arthur creating an aristocracy of merit to protect the helpless, what set Morris afire was the sturdy readiness of every man to protect himself, in a harsh endless feuding of individuals and groups, and of men against nature. In Morris's Iceland as in Tennyson's Britain, we are aware of the pressure of a writer's feeling about his own England; and we glimpse 'the imminence of his own participation in political life'.[32] In the Norse myth of the downfall of the gods he saw a presage of revolution, and after composing his version of the Volsunga saga in 1875-6, a few years after the last Idylls were finished, he was ready to advance to revolutionary socialism. To Tennyson the collapse of the Christian firmament in ancient Britain was an omen not of a better but of a far worse future. He too was soon to participate in politics, by joining not a socialist party but that aristocracy of merit, the House of Lords.

What Tennyson accepted exultingly in the progress of his age was chiefly its less human side, its scientific soarings; in various other ways it was deeply and, despite personal success, increasingly uncongenial to him, as materialistic and without faith. His mind moved away from it in time, backward into the past, and in space, outward into other continents: in each case into spheres from which economic calculation could be banished. Camelot and empire were above vulgar thoughts of pelf, the money cares that so oppressed his own youth. For him the two spheres were complementary. In the first his poetic imagination could work, if not altogether freely, towards a tragic vision.

From Camelot he judged his own England, and found it wanting. From the vantage-point of empire he could admire and applaud his England, and reassure himself that beneath all appearances it was still inwardly sound. There the civilizing mission, dutifully performed, vindicated the rightness of English principles and English religion; and the story had a happy ending, or rather no ending, to satisfy his craving for political stability. Camelot's great hall had fallen, but the Residency at Lucknow stood, and would stand, like Horace's Rome,

dum Capitolium
scandet cum tacita virgine pontifex.

Celebrating empire victories he could strike a note not tragic, but triumphalist.

In the Epilogue to the *Idylls*, addressed to the queen, Tennyson expressed a not very sanguine hope that England would get the better of its maladies - materialism, sloth, cowardice, impiety, libertine French ways; as if offering a cure for them, he blew the empire trumpet loudly, with indignant repudiation of those soulless Little Englanders who wanted to save money on defence by cutting Canada adrift. This elicited a response by a Canadian poetess,[33] and an assurance from Lord Dufferin, then Governor-General, that it had made a fine impression in 'this most powerful and prosperous colony'.[34] Some years later a Canadian named Harper, drowned while endeavouring to save life, was commemorated by a statue at Ottawa of Sir Galahad, and a memoir by his friend the later prime minister, Mackenzie King, who held him up as a model of all the virtues and 'above all a Tennyson man'.[35]

Tennyson's youthful confidence in Europe had faded, leaving him with a stereotype of a continent sunk in dark despotism and blind revolutionism. By contrast, the empire could stand for orderly progress. Having for a while dreamed of a 'federation of the world', he was ready to content himself with imperial federation. He seems to have thought of the white settlements as healthy offshoots of a good old England, which might better preserve the old heritage because less infected by the germs now creeping through England's veins. He made friends with Sir Harry Parkes, premier of New South Wales, entertained him on a visit to England, and in 1890 hastened to congratulate him on his firm stand against the 'monster' of a strike movement[36] - a stand all the more praiseworthy because Parkes was English-born and came of a working-class family. Hallam Tennyson would one day be Governor of South Australia, and then Governor-General of Australia.

The very prosy song 'Hands all round!' (an 1882 adaptation of some juvenile verses) called for brotherly union between England and its colonies, and might be taken to imply at the same time the harmony of classes which ought to prevail at home. It gave this reserved man, a sufferer from childhood from an isolating estrangement, and ill at ease with all but intimates, a chance to indulge in a bout of hearty good fellowship. In a way his friendliness towards Canada or Australia, peopled with emigrants mostly plebeian, was a democratic sentiment which found little scope at home; and the same might be said of his good will towards America. But in 'The Fleet', a fiery accusation of neglect of British naval strength, Tennyson displayed a less sentimental side of his thinking; if the country were hindered from importing food there would be mass hunger and social anarchy, 'the wild mob's million feet' trampling civilization down. An ode of 1886 for the opening of an Indian and Colonial Exhibition, winding up with another appeal for imperial solidarity, had as its refrain: 'Britons, hold your own!' To 'their own' another kingdom was being added that year, Upper Burma.

An admirer of Tennyson as bard of empire felt that he sometimes 'loved to dally too long in that strange, mystic atmosphere of bygone history', and to overlook heroes of the present in his preoccupation with those of antiquity.[37] During the years of the *Idylls* he was not, in fact, writing much about imperial achievements in the visible world, as opposed to his imaginary one. There was some recoil of public feeling after the Mutiny. Possibly an uneasy awareness that Britons in India had not been blameless led him to bring into 'Aylmer's Field' an unpleasant 'Sahib', a retired officer from India with a train of dusky attendants, and lavish of 'oriental gifts'. He is fond of running 'a Malayan amuck against the times', and, unforgivably, extolling French progress; he is, in short, a Nabob of the bad old days, not perhaps left so far behind as they ought to have been. But when the *Idylls* ended in 1873 the climax of European competition for colonies was at hand, and Tennyson's part in ensuring approval of Britain's renewed exertions must have been appreciable. No question of right or wrong is allowed into his lines on the occupation of Egypt in 1882, addressed to General Hamley; it may even seem deliberately excluded, since they start with a pretty picture of autumn in Sussex and end with another of stars paling in the dawn and the glory over Tel el Kebir. Their author was not a close enough student of military affairs to know that Hamley and his commander-in-chief, Wolseley, had the very worst opinion of each other.[38]

That the empire was an intensification, not negation, of capitalist greed, or that British privates in India were villainously treated, and British officers always grumbling about their pay and jockeying for promotion, as jealous of one another as any artists, were matters equally beyond Tennyson's ken. Nevertheless, misgivings crept in even here in his late years, and with them an uneasy feeling that Europe as a whole, or Christendom, was going the way of Camelot. He can hardly have been able to shut his eyes completely to the fact that the later stages of European expansion were not always so edifying. Machine-gun massacres did not lend themselves so well as earlier contests to romanticizing rhymes; and too many foreigners were taking a hand now, whose principles could not be anything like

King Arthur's. In 'Columbus' the explorer is seen in despised old age, and is commended as a good Christian and spreader of light and knowledge, who has brought the world closer together; but Tennyson idealizes no less the old native America, as an abode of golden-age simplicity, and regrets the villainous behaviour of the Spanish intruders. An unpublished poem of his youth, 'Anacaona', had pictured a Haitian princess in her idyllic tropical glades just before the Spanish irruption.[39]

There is a sombre contradiction at the heart of imperialism, even if Tennyson cannot admit it of his own empire. 'Locksley Hall Sixty Years After' dwells on the ferocity of other conquerors of olden times, 'iron-hearted Assyrians' and Tamberlane's 'wild Moguls', adding an allusion to Christians throwing defeated fellow-Christians into the flames. 'The Victim', a tale of the 1860s about human sacrifice to Thor and Odin, recalls both Arthur's resistance to heathen invaders and enormities of paganism in Tennyson's own day, notably those cults of human sacrifice in West Africa which were made a prime justification for European intervention. But if Dahomey is painted in 'The Dawn' as full of brutish savagery, so also is Europe, with its 'Christless frolic of kings'; the human race is still in its infancy, and the poet can only gaze longingly at what it may be a million years hence. In 'Kapiolani' (not much of a poem, though of some technical interest) it is left to a native chieftainess, a high-minded convert to Christianity, to deliver her Hawaii from the evils of idolatry. Clearly, Tennyson could no longer think so unquestioningly of the white man as fit to carry civilization into dark places. England itself might be gaining the whole world and losing its own soul. In the new 'Locksley Hall' it seems in danger of sinking 'back into the beast again'. Tennyson might be myopic at identifying social ills and cures, but he was at any rate no complacent optimist. His last poems show him sometimes struggling with despair. Already in 'Merlin and Vivien' thoughts hovering over

The sad sea-sounding wastes of Lyonesse

can be seen drifting towards the Waste Land of our own inwardly-crumbling world.

NOTES

1 Cited by D.J. Palmer, in *Tennyson*, ed. D.J. Palmer, London, 1973, p. 36.
2 Hallam Tennyson, *Alfred Lord Tennyson, a Memoir. By his son*, London, 1897, vol. 1, p. 243.
3 *In Memoriam* (1850), cv, cxii.
4 Epilogue to 'The Charge of the Heavy Brigade at Balaclava'.
5 Hallam Tennyson, op. cit., vol. 1, p. 185 n.2.
6 Ibid., vol. 1, p. 154.
7 J.H. Fowler, *Idylls of the King*, annotated edn, London, 1930, p. ix.

8 *Gargantua and Pantagruel,* bk 2, ch. 30.
9 H. Adams, *Blake and Yeats: the Contrary Vision*, Cornell University Press, 1954, pp. 58-9.
10 W.D. Paden, *Tennyson in Egypt. A Study of the Imagery of his Earlier Work*, New York, 1971, pp. 75 ff.
11 C. Ricks, *Tennyson*, London, 1972, p. 264.
12 Hallam Tennyson, op. cit., vol. 2, pp. 127, 130.
13 Ibid., vol. 2, pp. 122-6.
14 J.O. Hoge (ed.), *The Letters of Emily Lady Tennyson*, Pennsylvania State University Press, 1974, p. 27.
15 Hallam Tennyson, op. cit., vol. 2, p. 55.
16 Ibid., vol. 2, p. 93.
17 Ibid., vol. 1, pp. 431-2, 435.
18 O.D. Edwards, 'Tennyson and Ireland', *New Edinburgh Review*, nos. 38-9, 1977, p. 50.
19 Hoge, op. cit., p. 162 (a letter of 1861).
20 P. Turner, *Tennyson*, London, 1976, pp. 164-5.
21 J. Milne, *The Romance of a Pro-Consul*, London, 1911, p. 254.
22 H. Littledale, *Essays on Lord Tennyson's Idylls of the King*, London, 1893, pp. 10-11.
23 A.J. Trotter, *The Bayard of India*, London, 1909, p. ix.
24 *Tyndale-Biscoe of Kashmir. An Autobiography*, London, n.d., p. 240.
25 A. Conan Doyle, *The Lost World*, London, n.d., ch. 6.
26 J.A. Atanda, *The New Oyo Empire*, London, 1973, p. 63.
27 H. Tinker, *Separate and Unequal. India and the Indians in the British Commonwealth 1920-1950*, London, 1976, p. 24.
28 See *Democratic Vistas*.
29 Hallam Tennyson, op. cit., vol. 2, p. 134.
30 *Henry IV, Part II*, act 4, scene 5.
31 E.P. Thompson, *William Morris*, London, 1977, pp. 181-2.
32 Ibid., pp. 186, 189.
33 W. Greswell, *Tennyson and our Imperial Heritage*, London, 1892, p. 21.
34 Hallam Tennyson, op. cit., vol. 2, p. 143.
35 H.S. Ferns and B. Ostry, *The Age of Mackenzie King*, London, 1955, p. 92.
36 Hallam Tennyson, op. cit., vol. 2, p. 382.
37 Greswell, op. cit., p. 7.
38 J.H. Lehmann, *All Sir Garnet. A Life of Field-Marshal Lord Wolseley*, London, 1964, pp. 303, 308.
39 Hallam Tennyson, op. cit., vol. 1, pp. 56-8.

8 HOBSBAWM AND JAZZ

Tony Coe*

Some twenty odd years ago, when I first started working in London as a jazz musician, I soon became aware of a man of benign aquiline appearance and of a certain quietly commanding presence who frequented jazz clubs and concerts, and who would often be found in the company of jazz musicians with whom he enjoyed a drink and a chat at such places as the, now defunct, Downbeat Club, in Old Compton Street.

Most of us jazz musicians knew him, in fact still know him, as Francis Newton, staunch supporter of and writer about jazz, although the more one saw of him the more one felt that there was another side to him. This impression was reinforced by hearing the odd person, obviously 'in the know', call him 'Eric' and people referring to him as what sounded like 'Eric Osborne'.

Of course, we now know how well-founded those feelings were. Although perhaps it would be more accurate to describe his jazz interests not as a 'side' but as organic to the man as a whole. After all, is it not natural that a historian, deeply aware of social and political issues and with a real love of jazz, should seek to investigate and illuminate this unique musical and social phenomenon, as he does in his many writings on the subject? His book, *The Jazz Scene* - one of the most important ever written about this music - does this with obvious passion and insight: 'I do not think that any form of art has been developed which can transform ordinary emotion, as felt by all of us, into artistically valid statements more directly and with less loss of intensity.'**

As I am sure is the case with many others, I opted for jazz rather than a symphony orchestra as a career because I was attracted by this aspect of spontaneous composition. Where the symphony player is the middleman, so to speak, being the medium through which the composer (source) delivers his goods to the listener, the jazz player, when improvising, cuts out the middle-man, although the jazz player might be more accurately described as both source and medium. As a jazz drummer friend of mine, Harvey Burns, aptly put it when I asked him why he loved jazz: 'It's a kind of musical Heineken; it reaches parts that other musics don't.' Of course, we must consider the possibility that some would prefer those parts left alone, perhaps without even knowing why!

---

*Tony Coe is a jazz musician.

**Unless otherwise stated all quotations in this article are taken from *The Jazz Scene* by Francis Newton.

Newton wrote *The Jazz Scene* in 1959 and fortunately, since then, jazz has become steadily more accepted as an art form, receiving attention from non-jazz musicians, supporters of the minority arts and the general listening public although much of the latter's acceptance is undoubtedly due to the pill having sometimes been sugared by the use of devices, or even, one might say more strongly in many cases, gimmicks, which are borrowed from the pop idiom, for example the many electronic effects that are available these days and in particular a relentless sledgehammer beat which leaves nothing to the imagination, lacking the subtleties of rhythm and timbre that we associate with the best jazz drummers.

There are several reasons for the growing acceptance of jazz by the first two groups mentioned. Firstly, we have a growing number of jazz musicians who as well as a virtuostic mastery of their instruments also have a broad knowledge of other music, many having studied composition at music college. These days it is not uncommon to find a jazz musician attending a concert of music by, for instance, Schoenberg or Webern, who knows more about it from a technical point of view than the musicians who are playing it. The jazz musician draws upon any source he pleases to enhance his language, and twentieth-century European music is a very fertile one.

Secondly, there has been a growing tendency to bring together musicians from both camps in, for instance, recording sessions and in some *avant-garde* music, especially that which requires some improvisation.

Thirdly, many symphony musicians realize that there are benefits to be obtained from a working knowledge of jazz music. Clarinet virtuoso Alan Hacker, who was largely responsible for getting jazz accepted as a subject on the curriculum of the Royal Academy of Music, believes that involvement in jazz and exchange with jazz musicians can benefit straight musicians: 'I think it's very good, sometimes, to be involved in music where you don't have the "dots" in front of you and you have to use your initiative and invent - and it needn't necessarily be jazz.' And he finds that it is very strengthening to commune with fellow artists who are active in the same medium as oneself, but whose technique, language, outlook and goals are different. Robert Cornford, a highly respected musician in many, varied fields and a conductor of vast experience, contrasts the quick, trained ear of the jazz musician who, when playing in an ensemble, will be likely to know the relationship of the note he is playing to the chord sounding and the nature of the chord, to the comparatively uneducated ear of many orchestral musicians who perhaps don't even care as long as they are playing the written note correctly. There is surely a parallel here with the factory worker who does the same job all his life without any particular interest in the product as a whole. It is a fact that when jazz and non-jazz musicians play together in, for instance, a show and there is some kind of musical crisis (perhaps one of the singers misses a beat or two, for example) it will usually be the jazzman who saves the situation by his improvisational ability and hard-gained experience in dealing with such contingencies.

Fourthly, there has been an increase in financial aid for jazz in the form of subsidies for performances, tours and recordings and in grants for jazz compositions. In this country the Arts Council of Great Britain and the British Council have given considerable support, thanks to the efforts of certain individuals who have recognized the value of jazz as an art music. I have benefited through this myself, having received several bursaries for composition and travel grants towards European tours.

Newton, in his introduction to *The Jazz Scene*, has some very illuminating words to say about the increasing acceptance of jazz in minority culture - the 'official arts': 'As we shall see, until recently it has had only a marginal place among them, partly because the official arts were ignorant of it, partly because they resented it as a sort of populist revolt against their superior status and claims, or as an aggression by philistines against culture. It is both these things, though it is a good deal else. In so far as jazz has been absorbed by official culture, it is a form of exoticism, like African sculpture or Spanish dancing, one of the 'noble savage' types of exoticism by means of which middle-aged and upper-class intellectuals try to compensate for the moral deficiencies of their life, especially today when they have lost the nineteenth-century confidence in the superiority of that life.'

The Jazz Scene, which is indispensable to any jazz-lover's library, has, after its introduction, an excellent, informative chapter entitled 'How to recognise Jazz', in which Newton discusses, among other things, such musical peculiarities as 'the use of scales not usually employed in European art music, but derived from West Africa, or from the mixing of European and African scales; or from the combination of African scales with European harmonies'. He makes the point that jazz is a player's music: 'Everything in it is subordinated to the individualities of the players'. 'Every jazz player is a soloist, and just as the operatic listener ought to be able to recognise the voice of Flagstad or Schwarzkopf after a bar or two of the aria, so the jazz listener ought to be able to identify Armstrong or Hodges or Miles Davis.'

Since *The Jazz Scene* was written we have seen the advent of what is known as 'free jazz', which, in its purest form, has no restrictions such as tonality, harmony, tempo or form. This leads to the question, 'when is it jazz?' I would suggest that free jazz is jazz inasmuch as the players are rooted in the jazz tradition and their improvisation shows essential evidence of these roots. If there is none, then it is more properly called 'free improvisation'.

Also, there has been an extensive increase in the use of modes, such as the Dorian and the Phrygian, in jazz composition and improvisation largely due to pioneers like Miles Davis and John Coltrane. On the negative side, this modal bandwagon has been welcomed by some would-be jazz musicians who found running up and down Dorian scales much easier than improvising over the much more complex harmonic structures that we find in standards and in be-bop compositions of people like Monk, Parker and Gillespie. To illustrate this: try playing the open fifth (D - A) on the bass of the piano and use this as a pedal point to improvise above, playing absolutely anything you like on the white keys. This will always be acceptable, in a sense, to the ear, even if you let your cat run over the keys instead of your fingers!

Nevertheless, the introduction of modes to the jazz language has served to broaden it considerably and there have been many fine jazz improvisations on modal sequences, but almost invariably by musicians who are rooted in the jazz tradition of blues, standards and be-bop.

'Free jazz' has also its fair share of opportunists or fellow-travellers as Derek Bailey, one of the most celebrated exponents of free improvisation, calls them. For instance, one particular school cultivates a way of playing the instrument as though no degree of mastery has ever been attained on it - almost like a child dabbling. Perhaps it is Dada come lately. Of course, this style is very convenient for those who do not have a mastery of their instrument anyway! But one must be wary of dismissing a player out of hand. Although his technical and musical ability may be lacking, his motivations may be honest.

As a jazz musician, I can only say that Newton has got it just right:

> The blues is not a style or phase of jazz, but a permanent substratum of all styles: not the whole of jazz but its heart...and the moment when the blues ceases to be part of jazz will be the moment when jazz as we know it ceases to exist....It is to jazz what the earth was to Antaeus in the Greek myth. If he lost contact with it, he lost his strength. Whenever in the blank patches of some session a musician calls out 'Hey, Charlie, let's play the blues' this contact is renewed.

Both the spirit and musicality of the blues will be evident in a performance of a standard tune, which is not a blues, when it is played by such as Armstrong or Parker. To cite my own development as a jazz player, when I joined Humphrey Lyttelton's band early on in my career, my playing was suffering from an imbalance in that it was rather too feminized and lacked a certain aggressive masculinity which is essential. I believe that a jazz player should have both feminine tenderness, sublety and finesse, and masculine aggression, earthiness and what is known as 'balls'. Humph and his band were (and still are) deeply rooted in the classic jazz tradition which is permeated by the blues and his influence and taste had a decisive effect on my playing in correcting the aforementioned imbalance. In uniting the feminine and the masculine sides of artistic expression, jazz can be seen as a unifying activity.

The jazz public has been, for historical and social reasons, rather sharply distinct from the rest of the public for the orthodox arts, even when it did not keep itself aloof from them. Newton makes the following observations in *Jazz and the other Arts*: 'It is therefore not surprising that until recently jazz has had very little echo indeed among the rest of the creative arts.' He tells how the blues are concerned with truth, this word being the one which recurs often when blues singers attempt to differentiate their art from songs which are mere money-makers. 'This is no doubt why British adolescents listen to the voice of blues singers as they would not to those of parents, teachers or other poets....Nobody beats about the bush in the blues; neither about life, death, money or even love.' And he describes how Tin Pan Alley has used the word 'blues' to describe sentiments of a much lower order than what the real thing is about 'for self-pity and sentimentality are not in the blues'.

Of course, since *The Jazz Scene* was written popular music has seen many changes and some very interesting and worthwhile music has been created. Certain rhythmic procedures of rock music have been absorbed into the contemporary jazz armoury, but there are also melodic and harmonic influences; many jazzmen being attracted, for instance, by the Beatles songs which broke away to a large extent from the usually stereotyped harmonic progressions to which the jazzmen had been accustomed. Of course, pop music's debt to jazz is very much greater. If, for instance, you could by some means remove all blues influence from most present-day pop you would have a spineless and gutless music. What has happened in a lot of cases, unfortunately, is that the blues has been distorted and/or castrated, as has been thought expedient by the all too powerful capitalist entrepreneurial element seeking to appeal to the widest public possible. Let us take a specific case - Elvis Presley. Here we have a media-made star who took the blues idiom and exaggerated and distorted certain characteristic musical procedures and gestures which are the stock-in-trade of the great blues singers (for example Joe Turner or Big Bill Broonzy) resulting in a travesty of the real thing which one could even call offensive. As Newton says: 'The recent rock and roll vogue rests entirely on the invasion of such catalogues (original rhythm and blues) by "Tin Pan Alley".' Is one being too cynical in suggesting that Presley at that time was chosen as the star material above people who could have sung him into the ground because he happened to be the right colour? A related situation obtained with the swing bands in the 1930s and the 1940s. Such bands as those of Count Basie and Duke Ellington had to work against disadvantages not suffered by the white bands unless, like Benny Goodman and Artie Shaw, they courageously hired black musicians. This was a kind of jazz apartheid, but happily this state of affairs has greatly improved.

The uneasy symbiosis of jazz and pop music is poetically expressed by Newton: 'Jazz overlaps and interpenetrates with pop-music, lives within it as waterlilies live in ponds and stagnant streams; it may even, without ostensible change, become pop-music if sufficient people are moved to buy it.' The pity of it all is that, had the money that has been invested in pop music, been invested into other music, of a more deeply rewarding nature, we would have a discerning listening public with a more highly developed musical sense. But the financial powers-that-be, presumably influenced in no small measure by their own tastes in music (the oft-uttered expression, 'I know what I like', really meaning 'I like what I know'), have brain-washed the public into accepting their product by bludgeoning their ears with it day in and day out through the media of radio, television, discos and in places where they have no choice such as supermarkets and pubs - an enforced mediocrity!

Newton also makes a very good point about the jazz record industry when he tells us that: 'The only consolation for all concerned is that the demand for jazz records (unlike ordinary pop discs) is permanent. If a company is willing to tie up space and capital in them, they continue to sell to a new generation of fans.' As the late lamented British jazz drummer, Lennie Hastings used to say: 'They [the pop stars] are like ocean going liners, their careers being short, whereas we don't see that kind of glory, but are like dinghies, little bits of shit, that keep afloat much longer.'

'Secondary poverty', says Newton, 'is built into the world of jazz, because it is like acting or other types of show business, a world of casual labour which encourages free spending and discourages rational behaviour.' He goes on to say how a few manage to take care of the future by, for instance, taking less artistically rewarding but more permanent jobs. Some governments have shown an enlightened attitude to artists when times have been hard. For instance, Sweden showed its appreciation of baritone saxophone star Lars Gullin's contribution to jazz by looking after him in very generous fashion when he was suffering ill health due, to no small extent no doubt, to his addiction to narcotics.

Let us consider the question of drug addiction in the jazz profession. As Newton states: 'The jazz public insists against all logic, on the impossible achievement of spontaneous creation to order.' Jazz being a spontaneous art, it is understandable that the desire for consistency should drive jazz musicians to alcohol or drugs on an 'off' night. What control can a jazz musician exercise to make his 'on' nights coincide with his bookings? Charlie Parker would undoubtedly have had a longer life if he had not felt this pressure but had felt instead that the patrons would accept him as he was on any given occasion. Newton, in the chapter entitled 'Transformation' describes one of the perennial wishes of jazzmen: 'all jazz players still dreamed, and continue to dream of small "combos" in which they could both play as they please and please the public; or at any rate earn their living and play for a public which does not get in the way too much.'

In the Musicians Union, jazz musicians are in a minority and it is natural that certain blanket union rulings do not work particularly to our advantage. For instance, at a time of recession, like the present, the jazzman finds the going particularly rough for bad times must decimate any industry which depends on the spending of spare money, and one of the possible resources he has is to seek work abroad. Many of the continental unions are very easy-going about foreign musicians coming to work in their domains, and for this we are very thankful, but the same cannot be said of our own union which has been particularly obstructive in this area, ostensibly for the benefit of its members, but one cannot help thinking that we are seeing another manifestation of the well-known inherent insularity of the British for which we are ridiculed and despised by not a few people of other nations. Surely a special ruling is needed for jazz musicians who, because their music has minority appeal, comparatively speaking, need to spread their wares as opposed to those who can still survive at home because they play music of a more commercial nature and/or have permanent positions in subsidized institutions such as the BBC and some orchestras. If this very unjust attitude continues, the chances are that the unions in the countries concerned will put their foot down and deny jazz musicians the same facilities that their own have been denied.

As for the use of the word 'serious' to distinguish European music from jazz, jazz is, in the words of McCoy Toyner, from which a book gets its title, 'As serious as your life'! Alongside this, the general public's idea of the nature of the jazzman is sadly awry, laden as it usually is with prejudice, erroneous preconceptions and a certain amount of envy for the kind of life it imagines a jazzman leads. One such illusion is that, apart from his engagements, the jazzman leads a life of leisure - where the opposite is usually the case. He must obviously devote much of his time to music whether it be in the form of instrumental practice, or adding to his musical vocabulary and enhancing his language by, for example, listening to other players on record or studying other kinds of music via scores and recordings. Also he has to spend a fair amount of time taking care of the business side of things, touting for work, sending his brochures to possible bookers, sometimes the same ones year in, year out, for, as Eddie 'Lockjaw' Davis points out, even Coca Cola still carries on advertising, so why should we be any different? Then, of course, in the daytime, he must take care of the everyday chores that the 'nine-to-fivers' do when they arrive home from work but he probably doesn't have time for because he is preparing for his gig. Of course, when he is on tour, much of his day is probably spent in travelling anyway. I must admit that I got so fed up with the question 'What do you do in the daytime?' that I invented the stock reply: 'I do a paper round and run a part-time surgery.'

The image of the jazzman as some kind of freak is perpetuated to some extent by media writers who look to certain superficial (and by no means universal) facets of the jazz lifestyle for the sake of producing a cheap sensationalism. Witness the following extract from the *New Standard* on the occasion of Ronnie Scott's OBE award: 'He [Ronnie Scott] was dressed in black and every movement of his hands sent shadows streaming up the walls. Jazz musicians like vampires [sic] do not like the light'! A more sensible approach is reflected in Newton's comment that:

> The good and permanent band is normally run by a martinet or a 'natural' front man with an eye to the public. Few jazzmen like this for their instincts are anarchist. All 'natural' sidemen dream of a combo in which nobody will be leader, and everybody will play as he feels, a band of brothers. But this as long experience has shown, is a certain guarantee of rapid failure and disintegration.

Since Newton wrote this I believe that things have changed for the better. There are many successful co-operatively run combos. Perhaps (and let us hope) this is a sign of the times, being a kind of microcosmic reflection of a strong tendency in mankind, the artist leading the way socially as well as in his art.

You will find most jazz musicians very politically aware, but more than a few of them will adopt an attitude of resignation to an oppressive regime. It is in the free jazz, *avant-garde* school that you will find more overt and articulated dissent on the whole, the latter almost invariably inclining to the far left. What all jazz musicians share in common is a loathing of mindless, centralized bureaucratic administration and its lackeys. And not a few see Schumacherism as a possible answer to the straits in which mankind finds itself.

One thing, among many others, that we find a strong protest about in jazzmen is the way they themselves tend to be treated. Take, for instance, the prejudice of the customs official who assumes that any jazz musician who passes through is fair game for him as a possible narcotics smuggler. He would not dream of giving the same attention to members of the medical profession although fairly recent statistics showed there to be a high level of addiction to and usage of narcotics in that profession compared with many others, (the accessibility being an obvious factor). Is it the fear of the unknown, of somebody who cannot be pigeon-holed, of somebody without a 'proper job', of somebody he senses is dubious of some who like himself are in certain uniformed occupations? Is it the same mixture of fear and envy that we find in a certain section of the public?

Yes, jazz has more than its fair share of vicissitudes. Take the jazz pub landlord or manager who becomes jazz critic, voicing what he thinks are the preferences of his clientèle. It has always been very difficult to find venues for jazz performances, and the most usual is the pub with its bar facilities, its space and its (often atrocious) piano. We have the very common syndrome of a jazz band who, having built up a good following and increased the landlord's takings considerably, are told by him that (for instance) he thinks the crowd would like a 'bit more dixieland' or something like that, or his greed may even lead him to kicking the band out and replacing it with a pop group or a disco.

But a jazz musician's life has its blessings, like the phenomenon which happens no more than about twice yearly, when a session, or even just a single piece, goes like a dream, often for one of the musicians only, more rarely for the whole ensemble. It is not easy to describe this feeling which is almost like being taken over by an exterior force, by the power of which anything is possible - technical problems disappearing along with a feeling of complete oneness with your instrument and a flow of inspiration that you feel would go on for ever if only the gig did not have to end at a certain time.

And another pleasure is a certain, rare beloved breed of jazz aficionado who will always be present when you come to play in his area, health permitting. He is very modest about his deep knowledge of jazz and touchingly self-effacing. He will always commiserate with you when the rhythm section is unsympathetic or you are having a tough time at home and will reassure you when you have, in your own estimation, played badly. He will be the one, in an otherwise indifferent crowd, who makes it all worthwhile, listening attentively to the music. You will always be welcome to stay in his home, whatever the inconvenience. He is one of the true constants in your frequently insecure life. He is worth his weight in solid platinum. Without him there would be no *Jazz Scene*!

And when such a man is a major historian, his outlook and knowledge informing his many writings on this most important of twentieth-century art forms to bring an enhanced awareness of it to the public, then we are truly fortunate. Such a man is Eric Hobsbawm, alias Francis Newton, after Frankie Newton, American trumpeter!

Ideology

9 FOURTEENTH-CENTURY PREACHERS' VIEWS OF THE POOR: CLASS OR STATUS GROUP?*

Maria A. Moisa**

> O infinite kindness of the Supreme Author! How you have attended to the support of the state and to the payment by the needy, and prevented the poor wretches from starving! True, the poor pay, but later they are paid back by the rich who succour them, relieving their poverty. One can see the hand of the poor paying, but then it is the rich who pay them.
>
> Pedro Diaz de Valdes, Bishop of Barcelona, 1793[1]

Medieval writers did not use the word class except in its Roman sense of kind or category. The nearest notion to our concept of class was expressed by the word status, used both in the vague sense of condition in life and in the more specific one of rank, dignity, degree, or hierarchy.[2]

From the twelfth century and throughout the *ancien régime*, the various status groups were institutionalized in the three, or sometimes four, estates of some parliaments, e.g. the French Estates General or the Castilian and Aragonese Cortes,[3] lasting until the collapse of the absolute monarchy. After the social upheavals of the nineteenth century, these estates were seen by some, and in particular by the Catholic Church, as a permanent and natural institution, in accordance with the divine order, wrongly and sinfully violated by the men of the age of revolution. The estates were identified with 'orders' into which the world was divided according to a pre-ordained plan, and in consequence the society of estates-orders was deemed to be unchangeable and viewed against the background of the whole of Christian history.[4]

The identification of Christian order and the society of estates was not new. It could be found in Catholic doctrine, almost undisputed, from at least as far back as the fourteenth century. Many of the conceptions expressed at that time were repeated, with hardly any changes, in seventeenth- and eighteenth-century preaching, nineteenth-century Restoration doctrine, and even in the social catholicism of the second half of that century. Twentieth-century neo-Thomism has reverted to some of the basic ideas of this conception, and its influence on fascist and falangist social and political tenets is clear. The image of

*I have to thank Rodney Hilton for his valuable comments and his patience in answering my questions.
**Maria Moisa is a lecturer in medieval history at the University of Leeds.

a hierarchically structured society, vertically segmented, with *ancien régime*-type inter-class solidarities, so dear to Mousnier, has an obvious appeal to the various supporters of law and order. By going back to medieval sources looking for a theory of corporations or an estate-based system of political representation, it was possible to blame the evils of the class society on the French Revolution alone, which 'has destroyed the order of things established by eighteen centuries of Christianity; it has broken the natural bonds formed amongst men by reciprocal duty, common interest, functions in society...',[5] bonds identified with a social order that should be restored.

That this conception of society was not permanent and had more to do with the monarchy than with Christianity has been recently demonstrated by G. Duby, who has dismissed the division into estates as one of the 'imaginary institutions' that do not symbolize any reality.[6] Reality, to Duby, is class; medieval society consists of two classes, warriors and peasants, and history is moved by exploitation and not by co-operation. Nobility and prelates have the monopoly of armed violence, of the possession of the land, the ultimate source of all income, and of the administration of war, justice, and the land. Peasants extract everyone's living from the land, and pay rent, fines, taxes, and tithes.[7] Duby has followed the transformations of the three-estate theory from its origin in ninth-century England to the beginning of the thirteenth century, showing the hesitations, detours, and contradictions of different schemas, gradually accommodated into one prevailing view, and the connection between theory and political reality. The function of this theory is that of acting upon reality, not reflecting it.[8]

It will be argued in this chapter that, although the uses of the estate theory to check social change are clear, views based on class have been put forward in sermons on poverty, when a certain economic effect was desired. Sections of the clergy were influential in the adoption of economic measures, due to their direct involvement in production, while another sector preached a status-based conception of man's duties.

THE STATUS OF THE MENDICANT ORDERS

The 'classical' three-estate theory has been summed up by Duby as follows:[9]

> God has assigned specific tasks among men; some were commissioned to pray for the salvation of all, others were pledged to fight to protect the mass of the people; it was up to members of the third order, by far the most numerous, to provide for the men of religion and the men of war by their labour. This design, which impressed itself very quickly on the collective consciousness, presented a simple picture in conformity with the divine plan, thereby sanctioning social inequalities and all forms of economic exploitation.

> Within so rigid and clear-cut a mental framework could freely exist the various dependent relations which had long since been established between peasant workers and landowners, and which governed the machinery of an economic system that can essentially be called 'feudal'.

Theologians, political theorists, canonists, and moralists emphasized the harmony amongst the different sections of the universe, which was reflected in the human sphere. These sections performed functions, and each of them necessitated the others for the fulfilment of its aims. The aims were thought to be moral and other-worldly. In the words of Thomas Aquinas: 'A virtuous life is the end of human society'; 'living in virtue, man tends towards an ulterior end...the enjoyment of God...', and it is for the king 'to lead men to that end'.[10] There are no individual aims other than those subordinated to the general aims.[11] But for the good of society different human conditions, with varied legal status, are required.[12] There is no order without 'orders', according to the functions (*officia*), otherwise there is only confusion in the multitude.[13] The picture is that of a harmonious society, with complementary functions and no contradiction or conflict, therefore a functionalist conception of the social order.

The functions were not necessarily three as in the three-estate theory, and could change in time with the addition of new groups. Thus, in the fourteenth century, many added the *mercatores* or the artisans to the feudal trilogy of *oratores, bellatores*, and *laboratores*. But there was resistance to the admission of new groups both in the social categories and in categories within the church. When a new *ordo* of churchmen, the mendicants, appeared in the thirteenth century, claiming a new role, discussions began as to their function, and the long dispute on poverty broke out in 1254 at the Sorbonne, the arena of academic rivalry between mendicant and secular clergy. In this context the discussion on status became entangled with that on poverty and the role of the poor.

So far, the 'orders' in the church - secular clergy, Benedictine monks, and twelfth-century ascetic orders - were possessionate, that is to say, they were landowners. The church and the orders held possessions in common, in spite of individual vows of poverty. They did discuss their respective degrees of perfection in connection with their asceticism. But in the thirteenth century, the mendicants took the claim to perfection to an extreme, contending that they had attained 'evangelical poverty' by living on alms. They were landless and propertyless, and their status was that of those who have nothing (*status nihil habentes*). Having no land, they had no class basis and no place in the productive process or in the feudal hierarchy of possessions and lordship, and did not live on rents and tithes but on fund-raising. They were, by definition, a status group. Very soon their teaching and preaching became overwhelmingly important; this meant that most of what was said and written in the church was the work of a group of classless intellectuals. A long conflict followed between mendicant and secular clergy, in the course of which some new social theory took shape. Both sides argued in terms of degrees of perfection and of status.[14]

If Christian perfection was begging poverty, why should abbots and bishops 'have treasures, administer justice like emperors and princes, counts and barons, have many valuables...and a large retinue...'?[15] This is why it was necessary to draw a distinction based on function, role, and aim. Prelates had different functions, and if they possessed so much, it was just because of their status consistency (*congruentia sui statui*). Those possessions were not possessions, since they were held in common and belonged to the church, and so to the poor:[16] only their duties, as charity providers to the poor, the charity recipients, justified that wealth. The Secular Masters of the Sorbonne adapted patristic ideas on primitive communism[17] in such a way as to show that they, the prelates, were living in evangelical poverty and thus had attained the highest degree of perfection. The arguments were sophistic. The controversy went on and on, involving the great figures of the Franciscan and Dominican orders (Bonaventura, Aquinas, and Pecham, among others), the semi-heretical Franciscan Spirituals at the turn of the century, and, on a different level, the political theorists of the fourteenth century: Marsilius, Ockham, and the Franciscan supporters of the empire, fighting papal ideas on church endowment and the supremacy of the papacy over the lay state. The issues were different, but the starting point was the same: if the possessionate church owns property solely for the benefit of the poor, why not give it to the poor, and disendow the church?[18]

The Secular Masters replied that it was the obligations of the church that justified those possessions. They had more duties than rights, and the duties defined their status.[19] On the other hand, they could argue that begging was not a status, and that the mendicants had no role and no function. If they had a status, it was a *status damnabilis*.[20] In the late fourteenth century, the poet John Gower said that the friars did not belong to any of the three status groups - the three estates -, and thus 'each estate leaves them wandering in the world'.[21] Their much criticized errancy and lack of stability earned them the label of *gyrovagi*.[22] They were not vagrant monks, they claimed, but 'wheels of God',[23] an allusion to the missionary function assigned to them by the Pope. Solutions to the problem of their errancy were suggested, ranging from endowing them with rents and tithes[24] to paying them a salary[25] or considering them able-bodied idlers, who should be put to work.[26]

In the fourteenth century, mendicants continued to claim that their status was based on poverty, while that of lay lords was based on possessions.[27] But by then the issue had been successfully got around by the secular clergy, with their image of the administrators of charity as stewards of the poor, who were as 'poor' as the mendicants, in spite of their wealth. This kind of 'poverty' the mendicants included in their categories as *paupertas ficta* - fictitious poverty.[28]

SERMONES AD STATUS

A by-product of the discussions on status was the genre *sermones ad status*, by and large a Mendicant creation.[29] Instruction manuals on how to compose sermons and preach more effectively multiplied in the thirteenth and fourteenth centuries. There, categories of sinners were classified and instructions on how to deal with each of them given. The French Dominican Humbert de Romans, among others, made a list of possible audiences and advised that 'it should not be necessary to preach the same thing to all, but that one should adapt his preaching to the different hearers....In fact, one should address in an entirely different manner men and women, young people and the aged, the rich and the poor, the joyful and the sad, simple subjects and their prelates, servants and their masters...'[30] A page of categories follows. They include considerations of wealth, success, character, rank, virtue, health, religious status, etc.

The experts on sermon-making were missionaries, who tried to obtain the conversion of the infidels and the repentance of sinners.[31] They preceded the modern anthropologist in mapping out new, previously undiscovered, areas of mankind. They studied groups. Once they catalogued them, the overall resulting picture overlapped with the categories of the three-estate theory. The three estates were also adopted by the writers of sermon manuals, but together with other categories. The sermons themselves and the instructions of how to prepare them were plagued with contradictions. An early fourteenth-century German Franciscan friar, known as friar Ludovicus, begins a classification in this way: 'There are twelve genera of men: princes, knights, magistrates, merchants, rustics, mechanics, prelates, common people, widows and beguines, Benedictines, Austins, Franciscans.' Later on he adds 'the poor', and even further down he reduces it to a four-estate list: 'miles, rusticus, mercator et clericus' (knights, peasants, merchants and clergy).[32] Bromyard was to classify social groups in one way or another according to the subject he was dealing with and even change categories within the same paragraph. Under the heading 'Accidia' he begins by adopting the typical list of three estates: labourers, knights, clergy; but immediately adds another one: rustics, merchants, knights, and clergy.[33] A simpler division of society into rich and poor, more in accordance with the early fathers, runs throughout his *Summa Praedicantium*, particularly under 'Divitiae' (riches), 'Eleemosyna' (alms), 'Paupertas' (poverty), and 'Mors' (death).

New social groups, like the merchant bourgeoisie, who had no place in the feudal hierarchy, were accepted, as the mendicant doctrine was finding them a niche, assigning them a role in society and determining their moral duties.

THE POOR AS A STATUS GROUP

The sermons did not give clear definitions as to what was understood by the poor and poverty. They included both those who needed alms to supplement their income and those who lived entirely on alms. Poverty and almsgiving were regularly connected; but references to the labouring poor - those who give rather than receive - are also made sometimes in the same paragraph.

What are the poor in a status-conscious society? If status-less, they would be excluded and directed to Hell, where there is disorder, since there are no orders.[34] To be assigned a status, they had to fulfil a role. In religious terms this was easy: they were the living sacrifice that had taken the place of the sacrifice of animals; the Christian sacrifice was 'communicating', i.e. charity (*Hebrews*, X, 10, XIII, 16). This role was the classical one of the poor as ritual recipients of charity, so that the rich could be saved by almsgiving.[35] Abundance follows charity and alms redeem sin. The rich obtain eternal sustenance and therefore a greater advantage than the receiving poor.[36] Almsgiving functions as a rite of increase whereby the temporal goods of the giver are multiplied in this life and his spiritual goods in eternal life.[37] So the rich are saved by the poor.

Thus it was clear that the poor had a function in society, whereby they were integrated into it. But what was their status? As charity recipients, it was a religious one, which could be assimilated to that of the *oratores*.[38] Such a status was sustained by the flow of alms and the possessions of the church, which belonged to them. Their duties were religious too: praying for their benefactors and taking part in certain ceremonies. 'Divites est erogare, pauperis est rogare.'[39] The rich pay and the poor pray. God has provided for the poor by giving to the rich.[40] 'God has given riches to honour God and support the poor.'[41]

Such an idea fitted in well with a 'society of orders' in search of harmony. God had provided for everything, concentrating 'all these possessions in certain families only in order that they might be duly distributed to all the others'; he has made 'those who possess in abundance' responsible for 'those who lack everything'; he has made the rich 'the stewards of his providence', echoes Bossuet three centuries later.[42] Even as late as 1891, Leo XIII felt he could say, in *Rerum novarum*: 'What an inexhaustible treasure of social peace is contained in Christian brotherhood, through the use of riches and almsgiving!'

THE STATUS OF THE LABOURING POOR

The poor also worked. They must work, said the thirteenth-century Secular Masters, who thought the mendicant friars should also work with their hands. Those who are poor and do not work with their hands are idle.

There was a shift in values then: work, *labor*, the curse of the fallen man, a punishment for sin, was being displaced by the curse of poverty. In a century of discussion on the merits of poverty, work was elevated to the rank of virtue and duty. In the Franciscan Rule, in the early thirteenth century, work was an unimportant alternative to begging; it had to be menial work and was not meant to produce any wealth. For monks, labour had been created as a means of avoiding temptation. In mendicant doctrine, *labor* could be morally irrelevant or even, in some cases, harmful.[43] But in the fourteenth-century manual work was seen as increasingly important, and the vice of idleness was pointed out more and more frequently. The Secular Masters' views had caused a scandal in mid-thirteenth century. In the 1330s, even a Franciscan, Nicholas Bozon, could warmly recommend the virtues of work: 'Work is the life of man and keeper of health. Work drives away occasion for sin...is a stay to illness, safety of the people, sharpener of all the senses, stepmother to idleness, duty to the young and merit to the old.'[44] Artisans as well as peasants were praised by another Franciscan in the first half of the fourteenth century, friar Ludovicus, because they worked night and day.[45] Both the Dominican Bromyard (1360s) and the secular Brinton, bishop of Rochester, (1370s) agreed that idleness was a vice and that the idle were excluded from salvation.[46] Up to a point, they had accepted the Parisian Masters' suggestion that idleness, even that of the churchmen, was a vice, and that poverty implied having to work.

In his well known sermon at St Paul's Cross on the mutual need of rich and poor (1377), Brinton showed that 'if the poor did not exist, nobody would work, and the world would decay.'[47] The rich were made for the poor, and the poor for the rich. A few years later (1388) a similar idea crops up in a sermon by Wimbledon, also at St Paul's Cross, a place that ensured a mixed audience: 'if the labourers were nought, both knightes and priests must become acre men and herdis, and els they shuld for defaut of bodily sustenance deye'.[48] Working men, said Wimbledon, not *pauperes*. Presumably, it was to these that Brinton also referred. The poor, if labouring, were not on the receiving end of charity. The poor *qua laboratores* paid rents, taxes, and tithes. In the same sermon, often quoted as evidence of Christian solidarity[49] or even 'Christian socialism',[50] Brinton tells us that among Christians 'taxes and tithes are not collected *for* the poor, but *from* the poor to support princes and rich men in their haughtiness'.[51] Therefore his poor were both giving as producers and then receiving through charity. He did not object to this or suggest a solution. The situation was not very different, in some places, at the end of the ancien régime, when many thought, like Bishop Diaz de Valdes, quoted in the epigraph, that class exactions would be remedied by the status duty of charity.

The begging poor and the *laboratores* were now one. The labouring poor had complex duties. The first, the functional one, which they shared with the well-to-do *laboratores*, was work. This is what they had to do in pursuit of the 'common good', as their part in the mutually rendered services. They were a status group in so far as they performed an activity useful to the common aims of society. The second duty of the labouring poor was, from the point of view of the preachers, obvious: they should pay their tithes both on their produce and on their wages.[52] The third duty, common to labouring and non-labouring poor, was that of being patient and resigned to poverty, avoiding envy, ambition, and pride.[53] Those who longed for greater riches were no longer poor in spirit. Peasants should not complain of poverty,[54] and *pauperes* should not be angered and complain.[55] Patience would lead all poor safely to the other world, where they would reap their reward in proportion to their suffering in this world.

It is not clear whether the labouring poor shared with the beggars the duty of praying for their benefactors. This duty was so important that the beggar who did not pray was status-less (*nullius congregationis*) and could not honour God.[56] The vice that made working men status-less was sloth or idleness.[57] Brinton's sermon of 1377 lumped the two categories together: the poor work and pay tithes, *and* pray for their benefactors. But it is likely that the adepts of voluntary poverty, the mendicants, were keener on keeping both groups separate, since they belonged to one of them, that of the begging and praying poor, but would not do, at that time, any manual work. They identified solely with the receiving poor.

STATUS SINS

Sermons also pointed out the moral dangers inherent in each status, and the resulting vices.[58] Those dangers and those vices originated in the very function of each group in society, and this is why sinners were functionally categorized. The sins were simply the negations of the status duties. They were sins because they were dysfunctional. Lords had to be good *qua* lords, peasants good *qua* peasants, the poor good *qua* poor. Being a good lord or peasant or poor person meant simply fulfilling the duties of the status, which were predetermined by the various conceptions about status groups. The *sermones ad status* and on status did much to define the notions of duty and sin for all admitted categories, but, on the whole, the view that they conveyed was functionalist and static, adjusting moral values to social categories rather than social categories to moral values. Keeping people within their respective status groups was one of the functions of the preacher, who would stress the evils of ambition and social mobility, and the dangers of the wheel of fortune. A new emphasis on the three-estate theory at the end of the fourteenth and the beginning of the fifteenth centuries in England was probably connected with the aspirations of a number of rising social groups,[59] including the subversive ones of 1381. The collection published as *Middle English Sermons* (1360-1410)[60] does not include the typical *sermones ad diversos status* which appear in thirteenth-century collections and fourteenth-century Mendicant manuals; but it contains a large number of references to the three estates, 'clerics, knights, and commonalty',[61] 'each of which should occupy the office that God has set him in'.[62]

The correlative vice of the virtue of keeping one's place and working for the common good was that of self-interest and private utility, and working 'circa honorem et commodo proprium'.[63] The vice of the glutton affects the needy, and the vice of the proud man destroys his superiors.[64] The vice of looking after one's own interests with disregard for the social function leads to social conflict, a situation in which 'each defends himself and accuses the others': the common people blame the lords for extortion and misrule, the lords blame the pride of the commoners, the laity the covetousness of the church, while the clergy say that the wrath and anger of the common people will be the destruction of the world.[65] Preachers were not to stress the vices of one group before an audience consisting of other groups, though it was known that denouncing the vice of the rich made the delight of the poor, as the description of the vices of women pleased husbands, etc.[66] To each sinner his sin.

CLASS PREACHING

There were cases, nevertheless, when the possessionate clergy preached and campaigned against the Christian inter-class solidarity bond. They preached the duty of not giving alms. This applied both to the mendicant friars and to the begging poor, now considered undeserving poor.

One can see 'the poor' gradually changing from passive recipients of alms to 'those without whose work the world would decay'. In some sermons, the poor and the *laboratores* appear to be identical. Where, then, were the non-labouring poor? Were they seen, on the whole, as working people? It is necessary to follow this development by having a second look at the anti-poverty campaign started by the Secular Masters of the Sorbonne in the 1250s. The secular clergy, landed and aristocratic, had reasons to react in terms of class. They were employers of wage labour. They formulated, in thirteenth-century Paris, as later in other places, the idea that poverty is a sin and that the poor must atone by work, thus eliminating the supernatural function of that status group, 'the poor'. The *milieu scolaire* around the Sorbonne, which Le Goff thinks was too mercantile to accept the three-estate theory without the merchant bourgeoisie, produced, in scholastics and in the literature that reflected the scholastic disputes (e.g. *Roman de la Rose*, Rutebeuf's poems), the first systematic attack on begging and idleness. The friars, the Parisian Masters said, were beggars, and beggars who were able to work; but as they did not work, they were idle. Their idleness deprived them of a function in society and within the church.

In the 1350s the controversy on poverty was revived in Ireland and England, with Archbishop FitzRalph as the central figure. This coincided with economic circumstances in which the same ideas could be applied to the common beggar (or alleged beggar) with some practical results. The mid-fourteenth-century drastic reduction in the supply of labour created a new interest in putting beggars to work. Regular and secular clergy were affected by shortage of labour as much as any other employer of wage labour. Their distaste for the idleness of the friars and the vice of idleness itself was heightened by their need for productive labour. In this context, between 1350 and 1357, Richard FitzRalph of Armagh waged his pulpit battle against the mendicants, backed by regular[67] and secular[68] clergy alike. The basic idea applied by FitzRalph, following the Secular Masters, was that the precept 'He who will not work, neither shall he eat' referred only to those who have no money and no other source of income.[69]

The fourteenth-century labour legislation enacted the same crude work ethic. Begging was forbidden, and so was 'alms-giving', in the Statute of Labourers. This would prevent workers from wandering around looking for higher wages, since nobody would feed them. Giving them food, as an act of charity (*sub colore pietatis et elemosine*), became a crime. If the workers had left the place where they would normally have been, and whither the Statute attempted to return them, they were considered beggars and idlers who preferred this life to earning their living by work,[70] provided they were able-bodied (*potens in corpore*) and had no other source of income.[71] The argument that 'false' (able-bodied) beggars were depriving the real (invalid) poor of the alms they deserved was also used by Parliament. The Secular Masters had thought that friars were 'usurpers' of the alms due to Christ's poor and this usurpation was the cause of the hunger of many.[72] The City of London *Proclamation against beggars* of 1359[73] considered that the idle poor were wasting alms which would otherwise go to the genuine poor, those who could not work. In a *Petition against vagrants* in 1376, the Commons were to speak of beggars who could not help themselves as opposed to 'false' beggars who were able to serve and work.[74] Alms were due to the former, not to the latter. The prohibition of giving alms to those who could work was inspired by the secular clergy's attacks on the mendicant friars. For a whole century, it had been said that the friars, guilty of the sin of idleness, should not be given alms, so as to starve them into working and thus atoning for their sin. Legislation applied to wandering labourers that which had been previously said of errant friars.

How did Parliament assimilate the ideas of the clergy? The secular clergy, with some exceptions, were not renowned for their preaching.[75] Most preaching was mendicant. Status notions typical of mendicant sermons were probably the most widespread, though great pulpit disputes, like the one between FitzRalph and the friars at St Paul's Cross in 1356-57 transcended church circles and were echoed in later preaching and literature.[76] St Paul's Cross was the most direct link between church doctrine and the City, and perhaps Westminster. But the secular clergy had another, more effective, means of putting forward their views, and this was Parliament itself. Being possessionate and landed, they were rural lords and, as bishops and mitred abbots, represented in the House of Lords. Their class interests were similar to those of the lay lords, just as those of the parish clergy were similar to those of the gentry represented in the Commons. It is not surprising then that the clergy were able to convey to Parliament and enact in legislation the formulae that had been used for a century in their own internal disputes.

They also preached to each other. They met at councils and travelled frequently. FitzRalph's most famous tracts against poverty and idleness, the Proposition *Unusquisque*[77] and the *Defensio curatorum*[78] were delivered at the papal Curia at Avignon. But the bishops were not on the roads, like the mendicants, and, indeed, were not looking for vagrants. They preached at churches, and it is well known that the poor were everywhere, except in church.[79] When the bishops thundered against friars, beggars, and vagrants, the friars were sometimes there, but the beggars and vagrants seldom. The aim of the sermon was not conversion, repentance, or atonement. They preached about someone else's sin, about the evils of the tenants, the labourers, the beggars, and about the vice of their idleness. To their equals, they preached the *duty of not giving*. They were encouraging measures that would induce a certain behaviour *in others*, measures that would force others to work for them, to work harder, or more cheaply, or more steadily.

At that moment the secular clergy were not using the three-estate theory, or any idea of a society of orders, where everyone was to keep his place, his rank, or his status. This would have meant accepting that the poor *had* to beg, the bishops *had* to give, the lords *had* to protect, and so on, fitting in with the image of a static, non conflictual society. The friars saw themselves as a status group, identified with the common beggar as ritual recipients of charity, who prayed for the salvation of the giver. They did not object to the existence of property and power, but these entailed special duties, and a certain social consciousness: social function of property, common property in case of need, and tolerance of theft, as in Aquinas. Christian solidarity cut across status barriers. The secular clergy had a more dynamic attitude. Poverty was bad - a new thought - riches were good, and work produced more riches. They assumed the possibility of multiplying riches even if it was only in the feudal manner, by putting more land into exploitation;[80] hence the permanent need for more workers, and not only in times of demographic collapse. The prelates were aware of the clash of interests between the potential workers looking for higher wages and themselves, the rural employers looking for a cheap and abundant work-force. At that time, their preaching was class-based. The image of society behind it was simplified to the point where there were only two categories of men: men of property and those who have no money. Either one had land, rents, or some other source of income, or one had to work.

Had the theorists been consistent - and successful - these two categories would have become exclusive of all others, brushing aside those idle rich who were not employers, that is to say, the retinues, mistresses and hangers-on so often denounced by moralists, together with the idle poor. This was not done overnight, and in Southern Europe at least, friars, beggars, and hangers-on resisted for centuries with success, protected by their status, their duties, and the status duties of others towards them.[81] But when mutual status duties could no longer conceal the reality of conflicting class interests, new attempts to check class aspirations were made with a modified, two-estate theory. Thus, in the encyclical *Rerum Novarum*, 'only the church could bring together the poor and the rich, and she repeats that they absolutely need one another, since there cannot be capital without labour or labour without capital; workers and employers have mutual duties...the worker must not harm the employer, must avoid violence and sedition, the employer must protect'.[82] This co-operation was illustrated in the activities of the Catholic Workers' Circles, founded in 1871 by a marquis and several counts, who pleaded for mixed worker-employer syndicates.[83] Christian solidarity principles regarding social harmony were applied in order to penetrate the trade union movement, in response to a working-class movement of socialist inspiration which took for granted the existence of classes and class conflict.

One of the direct descendants of this renewed version of the status conception of society was the Spanish Falange, who revamped medieval imagery with the avowed intention of eliminating classes and class conflict.[84] Christian democratic parties have incorporated this harmonious ideal into their programmes. But it was in Catholic syndicalism that a non-conflictual society of orders, other-worldly, moral, paternalistic, and deferential, where workers co-operated with bosses, combined explicitly with Christian charity to the labouring poor. The uses to which medieval imagery has been put in modern times to some extent suggest what the aims pursued by the initial proponents of ideas on status duties of and to the poor were.

NOTES

1 P. Diaz de Valdés, *El padre de su pueblo o medios para hacer temporalmente felices a los pueblos con el auxilio de los señores curas párrocos*, Barcelona, 1806, quoted in J. Fontana, *La quiebra de la monarquia absoluta*, Barcelona, Ariel, 1971, pp. 208-9.

2 P. Michaud-Quentin, 'Le vocabuliare des catégories sociales chez les canonistes et les moralistes du XIIIe siècle', in *Ordres et classes*, Colloque d'Histoire Sociale de St-Cloud, Paris, EPHE, 1973, pp. 73 ff; G. Duby, *Les trois ordres ou l'imaginaire du feodalisme*, Paris, Gallimard, 1978; R. Williams, *Keywords*, London, Fontana, 1976, pp. 51 ff and 251 ff.

3 R.W. and A.J. Carlyle, *A History of Medieval Political Theory in the West*, Edinburgh, Blackwood, 1962, vol. V, pp. 134-5.

4 One of the latest exponents of this view is G. Fourquin, in *Lordship and Feudalism in the Middle Ages*, London, Allen & Unwin, 1976, pp. 232-9.

5 R.P. Lecanuet, *Les premières années du pontificat de Léon XIII*, Paris, Alcan, 1931, p. 420.

6 Duby, op. cit. The expression 'institution imaginaire' has been borrowed from C. Castoriadis, *L'institution imaginaire de la société*, Paris, Seuil, 1975. The conceptual framework is that of Lévi-Strauss's anthropology.

7 For a Marxist analysis of Duby's system see R. Hilton, 'Warriors and peasants', in *New Left Review*, no. 83, 1973.

8 J. Le Goff, 'Les trois fonctions indo-européennes, l'historien et l'Europe féodale', in *Annales E.S.C.*, no. 6, 1979, p. 1191.

9 G. Duby, *The Early Growth of the European Economy*, London, Weidenfeld & Nicolson, 1974, p. 164.

10 T. Aquinas, *De regimine principum*, I, XIV.

11 T. Aquinas, *Summa theologiae* (*S.T.*), 2a 2ae, 58, 5.

12 *S.T.*, 1a 2ae, 91, 6; 95, 4; 97, 1; 2a 2ae, 40, 2.

13 *S.T.*, 1a, 108, 2.

14 For the most important works in this conflict see the table in Y. Congar, 'Aspects ecclésiologiques de la querelle entre mendiants et seculiers dans la seconde moitié du treizième siècle et le debut du quatorzième', in *Archives d'histoire doctrinale et littéraire du moyen age*, 1961, pp. 44-52.

15 R. FitzRalph, *De pauperie salvatoris*, transcript in H. Hughes, 'An Essay Introductory to De Pauperie Salvatoris', PhD thesis, University of Manchester, 1937, p. 192.
16 Gerard of Abbéville, *Contra adversarium perfectionis Christianæ*, ed. S. Clasen, in *Archivum Franciscanum Historicum*, XXXII, pp. 109, 110, 123, 183, 184.
17 See A. Lovejoy, 'The communism of St Ambrose', in his *Essays in the history of ideas*, Baltimore, Johns Hopkins Press, 1948.
18 Marsilius of Padua, *The Defender of Peace*, New York, Harper, 1967, p. 210.
19 'What defines the status of a man is the obligations he acquires.' T. Aquinas, *S.T.*, 2a 2ae, 183. This idea was not specifically Mendicant.
20 At the beginning of the controversy, William of St-Amour, *De periculis novissimorum temporum*, quoted in C. Thouzellier, 'La place du *De periculis* de G. de St-Amour dans les polémiques du treizième siècle', in *Revue Historique*, no. 156 (1928), p. 74.
21 J. Gower, *Vox Clamantis*, in E. Stockton, *The Major Latin Works of John Gower*, Seattle, 1962, p. 188, quoted in P.R. Szittya, 'The antifraternal tradition in middle English literature', in *Speculum*, LII (1977) no. 2, p. 312.
22 Thouzellier, op. cit., p. 77.
23 J. Pecham, *Tractatus tres de paupertate*, ed. C.L. Kingsford, A.G. Little and F. Tocco, B.S.F.S., 1918, p. 24.
24 Secular Masters of the Sorbonne, e.g. W. of St-Amour, quoted in Thouzellier, op. cit., p. 81.
25 Pierre Dubois, at the Council of Vienne (1311-12), quoted in *De recuperatione Terrae Sanctae*, ed. Langlois, Paris, 1891, qu. in A.G. Little, *Studies in English Franciscan History*, Manchester, 1917, pp. 129-30.
26 W. of St-Amour, quoted in Gerard of Abbéville, op. cit., p. 91; R. FitzRalph, *Defensorium curatorum adversos eos qui privilegiatos se dicunt*, Paris, 1633, pp. 73 and 85.
27 J. Bromyard, *Summa Praedicantium* (*S.P.*), Venice, 1586, 'Paupertas'.
28 Ibid.
29 G.R. Owst, *Preaching in Medieval England*, Cambridge University Press, 1926.
30 H. de Romans, *Treatise on Preaching*, ed. W.M. Conlon O.P., Westminster, Maryland, 1951, p. 70.
31 Ibid., p. 103.
32 A. Franz, *Drei deutsche Minoritenprediger aus dem XIII und XIV Jahrhundert*, Freiburg en Brisgau, 1907, pp. 90, 87, and 61.
33 Bromyard, *S.P.*, 'Accidia'.
34 Ibid.; Bernard of Clairvaux, quoted in Duby, *Les trois ordres*, p. 272.
35 *S.P.*, 'Paupertas'.
36 *S.P.*, 'Divitiae'.

37 M. Mauss, *The Gift; Forms and Functions of Exchange in Archaic Society*, London, Cohen & West, 1969, pp. 54-5.
38 P. Michaud-Quentin, 'Les sermones ad pauperes au XIIIe siècle' in *Cahiers de la Pauvreté*, Paris, Centre de Recherches sur la Pauvreté, 1966-7, p. 42.
39 T. Brinton, in M.A. Devlin, *The Sermons of Robert Brinton, Bishop of Rochester*, Camden Series, vol. 85, 1954, p. 194.
40 *S.P.*, 'Paupertas'.
41 Brinton, op. cit., p. 138.
42 Bossuet, 'Panegyric in honour of St Francis of Assisi', quoted in B. Groethuysen, *The Bourgeois, Catholicism Versus Capitalism in Eighteenth Century France*, London, 1968, p. 140.
43 J. Pecham, *Tractatus tres de paupertate*, p. 26; *S.P.*, 'Labor'.
44 Quoted in G.R. Owst, *Literature and Pulpit*, Cambridge University Press, 1933, p. 556.
45 Franz, op. cit., pp. 88-9.
46 Brinton, op. cit., p. 83; *S.P.*, 'Accidia'.
47 Brinton, op. cit., p. 194.
48 Quoted in G.R. Owst, *Literature and Pulpit*, p. 550.
49 M. Mollat and P. Wolff, *Ongles bleues, Jacques et Ciompi*, Paris, Calman-Levy, 1970, p. 308.
50 M.A. Devlin, *The Sermons of Robert Brinton*, Introduction, p. XXIV.
51 Brinton, op. cit., p. 196.
52 Both Brinton and Bromyard, quoted in G.R. Owst, *Literature and Pulpit*, pp. 365-6; J. Batany, *Approches du Roman de la Rose*, Paris, Bordas, 1973, p. 86.
53 G.R. Owst, *Literature and Pulpit*, p. 367.
54 Ibid.
55 Franz, op. cit., p. 89.
56 Ibid.
57 *S.P.*, 'Operatio'.
58 P. Michaud-Quentin, 'Le vocabulaire...', p. 84.
59 R. Hilton, 'Idéologie et ordre social dans l'Angleterre médiévale', in *L'Arc*, no. 72.
60 W.E. Ross, *Middle English Sermons*, E.E.T.S., no. 209.
61 Ibid., p. 237.
62 Ibid., p. 301.
63 Brinton, op. cit., p. 139; *S.P.*, 'Civitas'.
64 G.R. Owst, *Literature and Pulpit*, p. 565.
65 Ross, op. cit., pp. 310-311.
66 G.R. Owst, *Literature and Pulpit*, p. 295.
67 The greatest fund-collector for FitzRalph's campaign was Thomas de la Mare, abbot of St Albans. *Gesta Abbati Sancti Albani*, II, pp. 404-5, quoted in D. Knowles, *The Religious Orders in England*, vol. II, Cambridge University Press, 1957, p. 43.
68 The battle of 1356-7 in London took place at the invitation of the dean of St Paul's.

69 R. FitzRalph, *Defensorium*, p. 85.
70 'Mendicare malentes in ocio quam per laborem querere victum suum'. B.H. Putnam, *The Enforcement of the Statute of Labourers during the First Decade after the Black Death, 1349-1359*, New York, 1908, Appendix, pp. 8 ff.
71 'Potens in corpore...non vivens de mercatura, nec certum excercens artificium, nec habens de suo proprio unde vivere vel terram propriam circa culturam cuius se poterit occupare...', in ibid.
72 G. of Abbeville, op. cit., p. 186.
73 H. Th. Riley, *Memorials of London and London Life... 1276-1419*, London, 1868, p. 304.
74 R.B. Dobson, *The Peasant Revolt of 1381*, London, Macmillan, 1970, p. 74.
75 G.R. Owst, *Preaching*, ch. 'Bishops and curates'.
76 A. Williams, 'Chaucer and the friars', in *Speculum*, XXVIII (1957) no. 3; Szittya, op. cit.
77 Published in L.L. Hammerich, 'The beginnings of the strife between R. FitzRalph and the Mendicants', in *Historisk Filologiske Meddelelser*, XXVI (1932).
78 *Defensorium*.
79 A. Murray, 'Piety and impiety in thirteenth-century Italy in popular belief and practice', 9th Summer meeting and 10th Winter meeting of the Ecclesiastical History Society, Cambridge University Press, 1972, p. 93.
80 Appropriation of land plot by plot had taken place even in earthly Paradise, according to FitzRalph, in *De Pauperie Salvatoris*, in R.L. Poole, Appendix to Wyclif's *De dominio divino*, Wycliffe Society, pp. 395-400.
81 P. Vilar, 'The age of Don Quixote', in P. Earle (ed.), *Essays in European Economic History*, Oxford University Press, 1974.
82 Lecanuet, op. cit., pp. 452-3.
83 Ibid., p. 429.
84 *Puntos iniciales de la Falange Espanola*, Madrid, 1933.

10 SCIENCE AND MAGIC IN SEVENTEENTH-CENTURY ENGLAND

Christopher Hill*

There are few subjects on which the attitudes of historians have changed more in the last few decades than the origins of modern science in the seventeenth century. We used to think of a conflict between religion and science in that century as in the nineteenth. We then argued about whether Protestantism or Catholicism was the more stimulative/permissive to science. The assumption in most of these discussions was that science and religion were polar opposites; magic hardly came into the picture at all. But recently historians, especially those influenced by anthropological studies, have become increasingly aware of how entangled with magic science still was in the seventeenth century. I am thinking especially of the work of K.V. Thomas, Frances Yates, Charles Webster. In trying to deal with my subject I shall draw very largely on their writings, though confining myself mainly to England.

Part of the problem is to define our terms. Magic today is something that happens in fairy stories, or in Christmas pantomimes; or it is something bogus that people pretending to be witches play about with. It is by definition irrational, anti-scientific. But if we start from Bernal's dictum, 'magic was evolved to fill in the gaps left by the limitations of techniques',[1] then we can see magic in more anthropological terms, as an attempt to control the outer world by methods which modern science would consider irrational, methods which assume the existence of entities and forces in the universe which are neither material nor susceptible of what we would regard as scientific analysis. In these terms there was a great deal of magic about in the seventeenth century, some of it intellectually respectable. Sorcery and witchcraft probably meant as much as Christianity in the lives of most Englishmen. Mr Laslett's notorious statement: 'all our [seventeenth century] ancestors were literal Christian believers, all of the time'[2] is true only if we give a very unfamiliar meaning to the word 'Christian'. Almost every English village had its 'cunning man', its white magician who told those who had been robbed how to recover their property, advised on propitious times and seasons for journeys and foretold the future. Nor were such beliefs limited to ignorant villagers.

---

*Christopher Hill, among many works on seventeenth century England, is the author of *The World Turned Upside Down*, *Puritanism and Revolution*, and *Milton*. A founder-editor of *Past and Present*; former Master of Balliol College, Oxford.

Many eminent seventeenth-century scientists believed in magic in the sense in which I have just defined it. I shall shortly give examples. Belief in witchcraft and the existence of witches was still widespread. It was coming under criticism from the sixteenth century onwards, and by the eighteenth century prosecutions for witchcraft had virtually ceased in the English-speaking world. But witches were still being burned, and defenders of their existence included not merely an amateur theologian like James I but many eminent scientists. Two generations after James's reign Sir Thomas Browne and Fellows of the Royal Society like the Rev. Joseph Glanville still argued that those who denied the existence of witches denied the existence of spirits, and so ultimately of God. They had a point, as I shall suggest later.

Another example concerns what are now regarded as the pseudo-sciences of astrology and alchemy. Most astronomers took astrology seriously - the science which studied the influence of the stars upon events on earth, the belief that the conjunctions of planets under which a man was born would affect his whole future life, and that at certain times and seasons the heavens were propitious for certain types of action. Most royal persons had their court astrologers: the great astronomers Tycho Brahe and Johann Kepler occupied such a post at the court of the Holy Roman Emperor Rudolf. It was primarily for astrological purposes that Tycho Brahe made the vast collection of observations which enabled him to redraw the map of the night sky. Sir Isaac Newton said he first turned to the study of mathematics in order to understand a book of astrology. John Locke and Robert Boyle used astrological reckonings to find a time favourable for planting peonies.[3]

Conversely, professional astrologers were well-versed in up-to-date scientific methods. Simon Forman's astrological studies stimulated a 'constant and conscientious striving after accuracy'. In the 1650s the astrologer Nicholas Culpeper was making use of the recent invention of logarithms to aid his astrological calculations.[4] Come to that, the man who invented logarithms sixty years earlier, John Napier, was said to value them most because they speeded up his calculation of the mystic figure 666, the number of the Beast in *Revelation*. Interpretation of the biblical prophecies was the job of mathematicians, from Napier to Isaac Newton. There was an astrological millenarianism which agreed with the scholarly consensus among protestant theologians in thinking the end of the world was likely to come in the 1650s or perhaps 1666.[5] Fifth Monarchists like John Spittlehouse and Peter Chamberlen accepted astrology.[6] The fiercest opponents of astrology were orthodox theologians, whether popes or Puritans. Pope Sixtus V condemned astrology and magic in 1586; Urban VIII condemned both astrology and Galileo - though he practised astrology himself.[7]

To the defence of astrology came - the scientists: John Dee, Tycho Brahe, Kepler. There was a very respectable academic

Society of Astrologers in London a dozen years before there was a Royal Society. Serious rational characters like Jean Bodin in France, in England John Seldon, Bulstrode Whitelocke, John Lambert, William Rainborough, Mrs John Lilburne, consulted astrologers; important politicians like Elizabeth's Earl of Leicester, the Duke of Buckingham, and Wallenstein, as well as monarchs, kept their own astrologers. The Earl of Clarendon in a speech to Parliament in September 1660 quoted astrologers who prophesied good things for the reign of Charles II.[8] Mr K.V. Thomas has suggested that astrology represents an attempt to explain social and human behaviour in scientific terms, in terms of law as against apparent arbitrariness; in some respects it anticipated sociology, he thinks. There was as yet no recognition that heredity or environment influenced human behaviour: astrology was a serious attempt at scientific explanation - and so ultimately at control. That is why many orthodox theologians opposed it - as a rival system of explanation of events otherwise inexplicable, and a rival system of control.[9] Although the idea of planets influencing human behaviour now seems absurd, it did not in the seventeenth century. And indeed, what was the supreme scientific achievement of that century, Newton's theory of gravitation, but an explanation in terms of a single heavenly force working across vast spaces - in ways that Newton himself had difficulty in explaining?

Similarly with alchemy - serious alchemy, not the mere hunt for quick means of converting base metals into gold satirized by Ben Jonson and many others. Bacon and Boyle thought it a worthwhile subject. Newton was fascinated by it all his life, and left hundreds of pages of unpublished manuscripts on alchemy. Sir Richard Steele believed in it.[10] Chemistry, from Paracelsus in the early sixteenth century to Van Helmont in the mid-seventeenth century, was responsible for many of the main advances in medicine. Paracelsus and the alchemists strongly emphasized the need for experiment, for working in laboratories with one's own hands, trying out new chemical combinations. This led to real discoveries in medicine and distillation.

In addition to astrology and alchemy, there was in the sixteenth and seventeenth centuries a revival - or intensification - of interest in natural magic as a philosophical system; and it is here that our definition of terms becomes crucial. Those serious scholars who worked in this tradition did not regard themselves as conjurors who produced rabbits out of hats or made brazen heads speak (though some of them might enjoy skilful mechanical tricks like the latter). Natural magic was defined as 'the wisdom of nature' by Sir Walter Raleigh, 'that which bringeth to light the inmost virtues and draweth them out of nature's bosom to human use', for 'the help and comfort of mankind'.[11] *Magi* who worked in this tradition - Robert Fludd, for instance[12] - believed that the wisdom which gives control over nature had been known to the ancients - especially to Milton's 'thrice-great Hermes' -

Hermes Trismegistus - whose writings were believed to have been composed in Egypt about the time of Moses. Much of this occult wisdom, it was thought, had been lost, much had been corrupted. The ancient philosophers - Moses in the early books of the Bible, as well as Hermes Trismegistus - expressed themselves in parables, wrapping up truth in mystery for later generations to unravel. But because the Hermeticists believed in ancient knowledge which had been lost, they worked for its recovery by the direct study of nature, by experiment, rather than by the study of books. Francis Bacon's *Wisdom of the Ancients* was in this tradition, an attempt to elucidate the scientific wisdom concealed in classical myths; and Isaac Newton was convinced that he had merely rediscovered the law of gravity, which he believed was hinted at in many ancient texts.

There was then a continuing magical tradition of some intellectual respectability, which flourished down at least to the end of the seventeenth century, though by then it was growing a little shame-faced. Now magic, of course, is as old as human history, as men have attempted by various devices to control the forces of nature. What is new in the fifteenth to sixteenth centuries - or what seems to be new - is the renaissance of a serious intellectual magic, the Hermetic renaissance. I use the word renaissance advisedly. 'The Hermetic texts', writes Dr French, 'encouraged a basic psychological change that released the human spirit and thus prompted *magi* like Dee to experiment with the powers of the universe.'[13] Dee was the greatest sixteenth-century English mathematician, who tried to establish contact with spirits and may well have been the model for Marlowe's Dr Faustus - possibly even for the friendlier portrait of Prospero in *The Tempest*, whose relationship with Ariel was not unlike that to which Dee aspired.

The magical revival was based on rediscovery in the fifteenth century of the texts attributed to Hermes Trismegistus. The spread of these texts and commentaries on them was made possible by the invention of printing. The scholarly Hermetic tradition bears the same sort of relation to popular magical beliefs as protestant theology bears to traditional popular heresy. The secret wisdom of the ancients had had a long life before the invention of printing: manuscripts *necessarily* circulated privately, reading was a skilled art of the clerisy. But printing, combined with a new emphasis on literacy in protestant countries so as to be able to read the Bible, made possible a wider popularization of Hermeticism.

The salient features of the Hermetic tradition are the assumption that the world is a living soul, not a dead machine; that no part of the world is devoid of consciousness. Also assumed is the analogy between the microcosm and the macrocosm, that there are resemblances and parallels between what modern science would regard as different levels of organization of matter. Robert Fludd gave a chemical description of the circulation of the blood which parallels the circular motion of the sun.[14]

Such assumptions draw on age-old popular beliefs, which died hard even among the scientists. Certain herbs - like the mandrake root - cure certain illnesses because they look like the relevant parts of the body. Certain colours repel or attract the influences of particular planets. Just as the seed is buried in the earth, dies and is resurrected as grain: so metals can be transmuted by fire and resurrected in a nobler form. Christianized alchemy is thus an outward symbol of internal regeneration. Pursuing another analogy, heat in chemical experiments is seen as parallel to the action of digestion in the human body. Chemical processes can also be regarded as analogies of sexual intercourse, with a new procreation as the outcome.[15]

The concept of analogy is the basis for belief in sympathetic magic; the idea that an application of medicine to the *weapon* which caused a wound can cure the patient. This belief was held by Francis Bacon, Sir Kenelm Digby and other Fellows of the Royal Society. Digby's importance in the history of biology is rated high by modern scholars; it may be that his sympathetic powder did in fact achieve cures because whilst the power was applied to the weapon, the wound itself was left clean and without the noxious ointments which seventeenth-century doctors favoured. Anyway the poet Thomas Flatman, later Fellow of the Royal Society, was cured of a wound by a plaster applied to the offending knife; the powder of sympathy was administered to the rationalist Earl of Shaftesbury by the rationalist Dr John Locke.[16] Here is a prescription for relieving 'violent nephritical pains' (pains of the kidneys): 'take three stone quart jugs - fill them with the urine of the patient, stop them close, bury them a yard underground and lay a tile over them that the earth fall not close upon them'. The date is 1681: the doctor is John Locke.[17]

This all derives from a traditional animism which also died hard. Giordano Bruno and Campanella believed that the earth and other planets were alive. Kepler said 'once I firmly believed that the motive force of a planet was a soul' and he continued to assume that planets had an inner motive force. The universe above the moon was thought to be composed of a matter different from and superior to that of the sublunary sphere: it was a great shock when Galileo's telescope revealed that the moon was not a perfect sphere, that there were spots on the sun. Kepler believed that the universe was constructed around geometrical forms and musical harmonies.[18] There was a similar belief that minerals grow in the earth, and that every now and then a mine should be left alone to give it time to replenish; or that, as Bacon and others held, worms and other small insects are spontaneously generated in mud and slime - as well they might seem to be before the invention of the microscope. All these beliefs were still perfectly respectable in the seventeenth century, and indeed reasonable in the then state of technical knowledge: spontaneous generation was first clearly challenged by Harvey in 1651. In such a world there was nothing outrageous about alchemy, astrology, witchcraft or magic: they all fitted well into universally held assumptions.

Giordano Bruno in the late sixteenth century fused Copernicus's heliocentric doctrine with the Hermetic tradition. As late as the 1670s and 1680s the Secretary of the Royal Society, Henry Oldenburg, and John Flamsteed, Astronomer-Royal, both regarded the Copernican hypothesis as not yet scientifically established.[19] Recent students of Francis Bacon, the ideological founder of modern science, have stressed the Hermetic and millenarian elements in his thought. Exponents of the Paracelsan and Hermetic traditions in the early seventeenth century were no less critical of the traditional scholastic Aristotelianism of the universities than were the experimental mechanical philosophers. In 1654 John Webster, just as much as his opponents Wilkins and Ward, looked back to Bacon.[20] Indeed, *serious* study of the folk magic practised by cunning men is strictly analogous to the Baconian insistence on scientists learning from the rule-of-thumb techniques practised time out of mind by industrial craftsmen - iron-workers, bakers, brewers. (Cf. popular medicine in China today.) As Dr French put it: 'Only by viewing applied science as 'real artificial magic' can the Renaissance relationship between *magic* and science be fully understood... Practical science can be seen to have developed, at least in part, out of the renewed interest in magic' - and he quotes Dee as the man who most of all bridged this apparent gap, or combined these two roles.[21]

'The magical desire for power', Mr Thomas sums up,[22]

> had created an intellectual environment favourable to experiment and induction; it marked a break with the characteristic mediaeval attitude of contemplative resignation. Neoplatonic and Hermetic ways of thinking had stimulated such crucial discoveries in the history of science as heliocentrism, the infinity of worlds and the circulation of the blood. The mystical conviction that number contained the key to all mysteries had fostered the revival of mathematics. Astrological enquiries had brought new precision to the observation of the heavenly bodies, the calculation of their movements and the measurement of time.

This illustrates Bernal's important point that 'the discovery of problems....is more important than the discovery of solutions'. 'The greatest effort is required not so much in discovering new things as in breaking obsolete ideology sanctified by custom of religion.'[23] The bold speculations of Renaissance magicians, alchemists and astrologers helped to pose new problems, and to thrust aside the obstacles set by conventional ways of thinking.

One of the remarkable features of England in the three generations before the civil war is the number and high quality of popular scientific books published in the vernacular, and the opportunities for education in mathematics and science which existed in London. These scientific books are inextricably entangled with alchemy, astrology and magic, as the names of their leading authors indicate - John Dee, Thomas Digges, William Gilbert. The early acceptance of the Copernican system in England owed much to astrologers and to the writers of popular almanacs preoccupied with astrology as well as astronomy. By 1650 the English had the reputation of being 'great astrologers'.[24] If you asked me - or anyone else- to name the most rational and forward-looking of the Leveller intellectuals, we should think of Richard Overton and John Wildman. Yet the former consulted astrologers for advice on political action in 1648 (of all crucial years); Wildman invoked the aid of devils, spirits and fairies in a search for hidden treasure. John Dryden made an astrological prognosis of one of his son's illnesses. Robert Hooke, reporting on the weather for 19 November 1672, added the words 'conjunction of Saturn and Mars. Fatal day' on which John Wilkins died.[25] Not only Sir Thomas Browne but also John Milton still believed in the existence of guardian angels 'appointed to preside over nations'.

The most interesting problem seems to me to be to account for the change by which, by the end of the seventeenth century, the mechanical philosophy had replaced animism; and the magical/alchemical movement, which in the early years of the century seemed at least as well established and influential as the Baconian movement, lost its intellectual appeal. No doubt the ultimate reasons for this are economic and social; the mechanization of the world picture could only happen in a society in which machines of some complexity, and the principles of mechanical causation, were already familiar. But both Hermeticism and the mechanical philosophy are ideologies, the affair of intellectuals: a change in the 'world picture' is a change in ideas, through which economic changes are mediated.

I see a complex of interlocking and sometimes contradictory causes at work in the century or so which preceded the triumph of the mechanical philosophy. First, there is the point I have already made: the fiercest early opponents of magic were not scientists but theologians, and among theologians especially protestant theologians, among protestant especially Calvinist theologians, starting with Calvin himself. The Laudians in England, including the archbishop himself, were much more interested in astrology. There are perhaps analogies between the Roman Catholic emphasis on unwritten tradition and the Hermetic doctrine of a secret law handed down by the *magi*. What is politely called neo-Platonism was strongest in Roman Catholic countries, notably Italy and Germany - Ficino, Pico della Mirandola, Cornelius Agrippa, Bruno, Campanella. The lone English figure was John Dee - and he went to Prague for his most actively magical period: in England his house was wrecked in a popular demonstration against him as a magician.[26] Syncretism, the ability to absorb into the popular faith elements from pagan and other non-Christian sources, had always been a feature of Roman Catholic thought. Puritan protestantism, with its stark emphasis on the Bible and its monotheism, was less all-embracing.

Protestantism, and especially Calvinism, protested precisely against the magical elements in medieval Catholicism, from the sale of indulgences to buy souls out of Purgatory onwards. Thousands of Protestant preachers in thousands of pulpits denounced the miracle of the mass in terms which were often crudely rationalistic and materialistic. Catholic wonder-working images were exposed to rational criticism, and so were Catholic practices like use of holy water, crossing, exorcism, etc. Saints and the Virgin lost their power to intervene in events on earth. The abolition of Purgatory made belief in ghosts less easy.[27] Protestants tended to push all miracles into the distant past, to the age of Christ and the Apostles; and to assume that events which apparently transcended the normal laws of cause and effect were *either* improperly understood *or* the result of the intervention of the devil and his agents. Mr K.V. Thomas has acutely pointed out that the abolition of mediating saints and of magical practices generally appeared to *enhance* the power of the devil, to leave men and women more naked and exposed to his assaults. 'The Reformation, ... by taking away the protective ritual of Catholicism, made witchcraft appear a serious danger to ordinary people.'[28] Holy water, relics, incantations, crucifixes, exorcisms, no longer protected men as they had done. Yet this did not immediately lead to an internalization of the struggle against the forces of evil. It led rather to a growth in the importance of the cunning man, the lay magician, who filled the place vacated by the priest.

Many things happened in the world of sixteenth-century men and women for which there appeared to be no rational explanation. I quote from an account of Henry Hudson's voyage to find the North-East passage in 1608: 'On the morning of 15th June, in latitude 75 on a clear day, two of the company (their names Thomas Hills and Robert Rayner) saw a mermaid. She came close to the ship's side, looking earnestly on the men. A little after a sea came and overturned her. From the navel upwards her back and breasts were like a woman's; her body as big as ours; her skin very white; and long hair hanging down behind, of colour black. In her going down they saw her tail, which was like the tail of a porpoise and speckled like a mackerel.'[29] Since we often (rightly) emphasize that the cold matter-of-fact reporting of observations made on voyages led men to be sceptical of some old-wives' tales, it is worth remembering that they might also create new ones.

Reverting to belief in the devil, Mr Thomas suggests that a sense of the power and menace of witchcraft *increased* in Britain in the century after the Reformation, not because there were in fact more witches, but because men had lost the traditional magical remedies against the devil and his agents (and also because social tensions were increasing). We can see in some of the investigations of the Calvinist divines - e.g. Perkins, and Increase Mather in New England - a combination of scientific scepticism with a firm belief in the ultimate power of the Evil one. In case after case certain phenomena are dismissed as the result of fraud, hysterical self-deception, malice; until in the end some facts are left for which there appears to be no rational explanation: and these are attributed to the machinations of the devil and to witches who have sold themselves to the devil. Mr Pennington has pointed out that there is better historical evidence for the existence of the devil than for many facts which we should today regard as established.[30] The Bible gives clear and convincing evidence of the existence of witches and of the duty of punishing them.[31] So we get a curious combination of scepticism about magic leading to increased persecution of unpopular old women; and scientific techniques of investigation being used to convict them - though it remains true that witch persecution ended first in protestant countries, starting with the Netherlands.

It was then only a short move forward for the philosopher, in Hobbes's *Dialogue ... of the Common Laws of England*, to say that he could not 'conceive how the devil has power to do many things of which witches (are) accused' - though the divines still continued to say 'Deny spirits and you are an atheist.' Sir Thomas Browne thought scepticism about witchcraft was propagated by the devil himself. Commentators like John Aubrey, again and again, and Sir William Temple, testify that belief in witches, fairies and magic generally took a downward turn with the free discussion and enlightenment of the civil war decades.[32]

There were, of course, other factors. By and large protestantism and especially Calvinism appealed to the urban middle-class and lower-middle-class citizens of Geneva, Amsterdam, La Rochelle and London: by and large witch beliefs were strongest in the countryside. The Puritan attack on witches is part of an attempt to impose new *mores*, new standards, on the traditional paganism of the countryside just as the Puritan (and Shakespearean) ethic of marriage is an attempt to impose new social patterns on the easier-going sexual habits of traditional society.

But for this very social reason, the sects which protestantism so rapidly spawned, and which flourished most among the lower classes of society, were closer to popular beliefs, including belief in magic, than urban Calvinism. And so, as Mr Thomas has abundantly shown, although 'the Reformation took a good deal of the magic out of religion, leaving the astrologers and cunning men to fill much of the vacuum, ... the sectaries brought back much of the magic which their early Tudor predecessors had so energetically cast out'. The radical sects in England and New England retained more magical beliefs and practices than the high Calvinism of the haute bourgeoisie and of the universities: a Familist midwife was accused of being a witch in Massachusetts in the 1640s:[33] the accusation was frequently directed against midwives, and later against Quakers.

The Calvinist theologians' opposition to magical techniques tended to make them suspicious of certain types of experiment: the sects with their very strong emphasis on personal experience as the sole test of the validity of religious experience were far more receptive to the experimental approach. The sects were strongest among craftsmen, many of whose technical processes were drawn upon by the early experimental scientists. However we explain it, there seems to be a clear connection between alchemical beliefs, especially chemical medicine, and religious and political radicalism - from Paracelsus in the early sixteenth century. In Germany, Dr Yates has argued, the alchemical Rosicrucians in the second decade of the seventeenth century were associated with a political radical movement looking to the Elector Palatine, which established links between England, Bohemia and Germany. In France in the 1620s there was a witch-hunt against Rosicrucians, who were alleged to be socially dangerous: this was the intellectual background from which Cartesianism emerged, in which Mersenne attacked the mystical tradition and built up the mechanical philosophy in opposition to it.[34]

In England too there were close links between the Hermetic tradition and politico-religious radicalism. In the revolutionary decades hitherto unpublishable works on astrology and alchemy were printed in profusion: Mr Thomas speaks of an 'unprecedented vogue' for astrology. More Paracelsan and mystical chemical books were published in English translation in the 1650s than during the whole preceding century. In 1646, we are told, 'the Familists are very confident that by knowledge of astrology and the strength of reason they shall be able to conquer the whole world'.[35] The Comenian group, centring on Samuel Hartlib, combined plans for social, economic and educational reform with an interest in chemistry. The group included men like William Petty, Gabriel Plattes, John Hall, Robert Boyle. Nicholas Culpeper, republican and sectary, who was wounded fighting for Parliament at Newbury, was the leading alchemical reformer, the chief enemy of the monopoly of the College of Physicians. He published astrological almanacs and, like William Lilly, used them to make anti-monarchical and anti-clerical propaganda.[36] John Webster, chaplain and surgeon in the Parliamentary army, was associated with the religious radical William Erbery, accused of being a Seeker if not a Ranter. Webster published an attack on Oxford and Cambridge which combined a rational critique of traditional scholasticism and a demand for Baconian reforms with a simultaneous insistence that chemistry, astrology, Hermeticism and natural magic should be taught in the universities. He was denounced as an exemplar of the 'Familistical-Levelling-Magical temper'. When the Ranter Lawrence Clarkson took up physic in the 1640s, its natural accompaniment was astrology, and it led him to aspire to the art of magic.[37] Gerard Winstanley, the Digger, most consistent radical of all, wanted astrology to be taught in his ideal commonwealth. He carried the Hermeticist idea that God equals reason so far as virtually to deny the existence of any personal God.

There is thus a sharp contrast between anti-magical high Calvinism, on the one hand, and the leanings towards astrology, alchemy and magic of many of the political and religious radicals, though both were opposed to the Aristotelian scholasticism of the universities. Calvinism (like Augustinian Jansenism in France) prepared for the reception of the mechanical philosophy. The radicals were closer than the Calvinists to the ideas of ordinary people, among whom magical assumptions were still commonplace. For this very reason their ideas contained - or were thought to contain - a political threat to the men of property in the revolutionary decades. The keynote of the late 1650s and the restoration era in England is opposition to 'fanaticism', 'enthusiasm', whether in religion or in politics, in science or in medicine. The mechanical philosophy, among other things, rejected magic: it was a secularized Calvinism.

The Royal Society, and especially Thomas Sprat in his propagandist *History*, trumpeted their rejection of any belief in portents, prodigies, prophecies - though Sprat in 1659 had not been above citing the 'wonders' and 'miracles' which accompanied Oliver Cromwell all his life. The Society wanted science henceforth to be apolitical - which then as now meant conservative. Some astrologers and alchemists were Fellows of the Royal Society, but they abandoned the democratic associations of their bodies of ideas. With the restoration of the Church of England, many leading scientists became bishops; Charles II, wisely, became patron of the Royal Society as well as head of the church. Thomas Hobbes, who had the reputation of being an atheist, was excluded from the Society; so was the radical Samuel Hartlib. Sprat played down the role of Hartlib's colleague, Theodore Haak, in its pre-history, and historians have perhaps mistakenly followed him. In 1664 Joseph Glanvill was anxious to differentiate the mechanical philosophy of the Royal Society from the mechanic atheism of the radicals. 'The mechanical philosophy yields no security to irreligion,' he proclaimed.[38] Despite the efforts of the Society of Chemical Physicians, alchemy, astrology and magic sank into the intellectual underworld of cranks and charlatans; their rejection was thus self-validating. The Royal Society and the College of Physicians eclectically accepted some of the practical achievements of Paracelsan and Helmontian chemistry: the cosmic speculations and the social-reforming applications of alchemy and natural magic were abandoned. Newton never published his voluminous alchemical writings. Charles II took an alleged astrologer to Newmarket and told him to spot winners. By the end of the century the Archbishop of Canterbury was a Copernican.[39] 'Latitudinarian' is the word used after the restoration to describe conformist Puritans like Wilkins.

It is important to realize in human terms what the triumph of the mechanical philosophy meant. I have known and quoted for more than forty years Pascal's famous remark, 'the eternal silence of those infinite spaces terrifies me', but I think only when I came to prepare this chapter did I feel on my pulses what Pascal meant. We have got used to boundless space; but it is very new in human history. 'The infinite is unthinkable', Kepler said when he heard what had been revealed by Galileo's telescope; yet he and Pascal and all men had to learn to live with the unthinkable. Perhaps it made less of an impact in England, where Thomas Digges's *Parfit Description of the Celestiall Orbes* had envisaged an infinite universe. Between its first publication in 1576 and Galileo's observations it had gone through at least seven editions - in the vernacular.[40]

Pascal's terror came from the transformation of the universe from something relatively cosy, bounded and understood, to a vast blank nothingness. The music of the spheres was silenced; the heavens were no longer populated by hundreds of thousands of spirits, pushing the spheres around, going on divine errands, bearing influences. The universe had become *void*. Moreover, it had suddenly enormously increased in size. Instead of being a series of concentric spheres each neatly enclosing its own bustle of spirits, it was not infinite in extent as well as empty. The Christian pattern of fall and redemption had already been upset by exploration of America, Africa and Asia, which revealed that millions of men and women had no means of knowing the truths of the Gospel, traditionally held to be necessary for salvation. But now even vaster perspectives opened up, of other worlds, possibly inhabited: how could they be fitted into the traditional Christian pattern? This earth was no longer the centre of the universe, the object of God's particular attention: it was difficult to go on thinking of it as created solely for man. Then why did it exist at all, and what was man's place in it? Located by some accident in a corner of an infinite and unfriendly universe - why here rather than elsewhere? 'And yonder all before us lie deserts of vast eternity', stretching out into the past and future as space stretched out until it was lost in infinity.[41] God's purposes suddenly seemed far less clear than they used to do - or at least man's knowledge of these purposes. Copernicus thought of heliocentrism as a mathematical formula, and could live with it on those terms. Galileo glimpsed something of its physical reality; a profoundly religious mathematician like Pascal was struck by the full horror of the empty universe. No wonder he could not swallow, as well, the impersonal God of Cartesianism. For Pascal knew that, in addition to the vacancies of infinite space, on earth truth on one side of the Pyrenees might be a lie on the other: truth was relative, the human mind fallible. Geometry had stripped the universe of all human qualities, depersonalized it. Pascal flung himself on to the bosom of a personal God, the God of Abraham, of Isaac and of Jacob, not of philosophers.[42]

All depends on the telescope now, Henry Oldenburg (future secretary of the Royal Society) wrote in 1659, 'the vulgar opinion of the unity of the world being now exploded, and that doctrine thought absurd which teacheth the sun and all the heavenly host, which are so many times bigger than our earth, to be made only to enlighten and to quicken us'.[43] The sun and the heavenly host - a phrase now used purely as a metaphor - no longer exist for man's sake and for no other purpose. The discovery of the microscope likewise stretched the human imagination, to comprehend the infinitely small as well as the infinitely large. By revealing things invisible to the naked eye, the microscope helped to call in question commonsense reliance on the human senses, and to show that forms of life existed with which it was difficult for men and women to feel affinity. A similar isolation of man resulted from the discrediting of alchemical metaphors. 'When metals no longer "marry", "copulate", "die" and are "resurrected", they appear alien to us. Although we can manipulate them, they remain stubbornly *other*. We dominate them, but we are separated from them by a gulf; they do not share our consciousness or our purposes.'[44]

'The mechanization of the world picture' occurred as men became, if not more mechanized, at least more accustomed to living in a world of machines, a world which was beginning to appear rational and predictable, less at the mercy of forces outside human control, - even before the upsurge of technology which we call the Industrial Revolution. 'The decline of magic', says Mr Thomas, 'coincided with a marked improvement in the extent to which [the] environment became amenable to control'. He lists better communications and fire-fighting devices as well as insurance, technical improvements in agriculture and industry and the concept of statistical probability. We may add the greater political stability, the reduction of arbitrariness at least for the propertied classes, which followed Parliament's victory over personal monarchy, the common law's victory over prerogative. The political activities (and successes) of ordinary people during the interregnum contributed to a greater belief in the possibilities of human action and initiative in controlling society and the universe, linking up here with the triumphs of science itself, with the discovery of the New World and the new heavens. Add too better and more widespread medical knowledge, thanks in part to publication during the revolutionary decades of Nicholas Culpeper's and many other English translations of medical classics. 1665 saw the last great plague in England. Death was beginning to strike with less obvious arbitrariness. All these things conspired to do the cunning men out of a job, for all but the very simple and credulous.[45]

Nor should we forget protestant scepticism of miracles not attested by Scripture, and humanist and protestant canons of textual criticism, which enabled Casaubon to show in 1614 that the allegedly very ancient Hermetic writings dated from the second or third century AD - though this did not stop Newton supposing that they incorporated very ancient traditions. Earlier, men had taken any evidence in print at its face value, without testing it: miraculous stories in a Latin poet were treated no less seriously than the miraculous stories in the Bible.[46] In the 1650s, scepticism even of biblical miracles was expressed in print, and the sanctity of the text of the Bible itself was questioned.

Everything worked against the old ways of thought. The Hermetic doctrine of a primitive wisdom was part of a general assumption that the ancients were wiser than the moderns, that the most we could hope for was to recapture some of their knowledge. Yet in the great ideological battle of the seventeenth century, the moderns inevitably overcame the ancients. The discovery of America and the antipodes proved the ancients to have been wrong; the telescope revealed that they were mistaken in thinking the universe above the moon different in kind from the sublunary world; and so on, and so on. Many of the radical scientists themselves held an optimistic Baconian belief in the power of experiment, the possibilities of using science for the relief of man's estate, and this too cut across the idea of a secret traditional wisdom as well as going counter to the universities' naive belief in the superiority of classical authorities. The experimental philosophy went better with a belief in progress than in decay.

The decline of magic was a surprising outcome, which could not have been predicted at the beginning of the seventeenth century. Down to that period magic and science had advanced hand in hand. But now magical science, by its association with political radicalism, had become - or was thought to have become - socially dangerous. The mechanical philosophy saved experiment from magic, excluded magic from science, as the Calvinists had already excluded it from religion. This is one of the social and ideological reasons for the triumph of the mechanical philosophy (over and above, of course, the technical scientific reasons with which I have neither time nor competence to deal). But there was loss as well as gain. The *magi* had aspired to see the universe as a whole, to have a total grasp of reality. In this sense Newton is rightly described as the last of the magicians. Now specialization set in, with all its limitations. Knowledge was no longer shut up in Latin, to be interpreted for ordinary people by priestly scholars; but it came to be no less securely shut up in the technical vocabulary of the sciences, which the new specialists had to interpret. Newton was as incomprehensible to the common man as Aquinas had been. The wide vision, especially the social vision, of the radical Baconians, was totally lost. Bacon's own millenarianism was hushed up.[47] There was some pure gain - e.g. in technology, in medicine, in the cessation of witch persecutions. But there was also the dehumanization of nature, the alienation of man in an unfriendly universe, once he ceased to be linked to nature by the micro/macrocosm correspondence, once chemical processes ceased to be seen as analogies of sexual reproduction, or of death, burial and resurrection.

Some twentieth-century scientists consider that the mechanical philosophers threw a number of promising babies out with the animistic bathwater. I quote J.Z. Young: 'All of us, animals, plants and bacteria, form one closely interlocked network....It is easy to elevate these facts into a portentous scheme of the whole living world as one "organism". Yet there is a sense in which this is true....The whole mass [of life upon earth] constitutes one single self-maintaining system'. That reminds me of ideas which prevailed before the triumph of the mechanical philosophy. Chemistry and physics, a historian of science tells us, have become united in the present century only after physics renounced the view that matter consists of indivisible and impermeable atoms, and chemistry renounced its doctrine of ultimate immutable elements - a doctrine evolved originally in opposition to the alchemists. Take Newton's problem of the nature of the 'force' of gravity - 'it is inconceivable that mere brute matter should without the mediation of something else, which is not material, operate upon and affect other matter without mutual contact' - but the inconceivable was smuggled in by phrases like 'universal gravity', 'electromagnetic field'. We can see all this in better perspective today, when 'the concepts of matter and causality as understood both by classical physics and by common sense experience have been abandoned by modern physics'.[48] Perhaps even the dualism of mind and matter, which has bedevilled philosophy since Descartes, originated in an obsessive rejection of animism.

Religion changed too.[49]

> The religion which survived the decline of magic was not the religion of Tudor England. When the devil was banished to hell, God himself was confined to working through natural causes, 'Special providences' and private revelations gave way to the notion of a Providence which itself obeyed natural laws accessible to human study....It was a religion with a difference ... At the end of our period we can draw a distinction between religion and magic which would not have been possible at the beginning.

So to summarize:

1 There was a revival of magic in the fifteenth to sixteenth centuries, which acted as a stimulus to experiment, to the scientific imagination.

2 This magical revival was opposed by the Calvinists, but was received more sympathetically by the popular radical sects linked with millenarian revolutionary politics. In the upsurge of 1640-60 both radical sectarian and magical ideas came to the fore. Yet, paradoxically, the events of the Revolution - freedom of publication and discussion, decline of the power of the clergy, led ultimately to a greater rationalism, a greater scepticism about witches, fairies and magic generally; the moderns triumphed over the ancients.

3 The defeat of the radical revolutionaries, plus a lingering fear that their influence might revive, created social conditions

which favoured the victory of the mechanical philosophy - acceptable of course on scientific grounds too.
4 But maybe the circumstances of the acceptance of the mechanical philosophy allowed ideological elements to be incorporated into it from the start, which today have become hindrances to its further advance; total rejection of the ways of thinking of the *magi* may have closed some doors which might with advantage to science have been left open. Science, in Bernal's striking phrase, is not only 'ordered technique'; it is also 'rationalized mythology'.[50]

I end by quoting Mr Thomas again, at his most disturbing:[51]

> The role of magic in modern society may be more extensive than we yet appreciate .... Anthropologists to-day are unsympathetic to the view that magic is simply bad science.... If magic is to be defined as the employment of ineffective techniques to allay anxiety when effective ones are not available, then we must recognise that no society will ever be free from it.

No society ever? Well, not ours anyway.

NOTES

1 J.D. Bernal, *Science in History*, 3rd edn, London, 1965, C.A. Watts, p. 40.
2 P. Laslett, *The World We Have Lost*, London, Methuen, 1965, p. 71.
3 K. Dewhurst, *John Locke (1632-1704), Physician and Philosopher*, London, Wellcome Historical Medical Library, 1963, p. 31.
4 A.L. Rowse, *Simon Forman*, London, Weidenfeld & Nicolson, 1974, p. 8; N. Culpeper, *Works*, 1802, no. 1, pp. 33-9.
5 See my *Antichrist in Seventeenth-Century England*, Oxford University Press, 1971, *passim*; C. Webster, *The Great Instauration: Science, Medicine & Reform, 1626-1660*, London, Duckworth, 1975, p. 549. I have benefited greatly by reading Dr P.A. Trout's unpublished DPhil.thesis, *Magic and the Millennium: Motifs in the Occult Milieu of Puritan England, 1640-1660*, University of British Columbia, 1974.
6 B.S. Capp, *The Fifth Monarchy Men*, London, Faber, 1972, pp. 187-8.
7 D.P.Walker, *Spiritual and Demonic Magic from Ficino to Campanella*, University of Notre Dame, 1958, pp. 204-9; W. Shumaker, *The Occult Sciences in the Renaissance*, University of California Press, 1972, p. 54.
8 Quoted by M. McKeon, *Politics and Poetry in Restoration England*, Harvard University Press, 1975, p. 231.
9 K.V. Thomas, *Religion and the Decline of Magic*, London, Weidenfeld & Nicolson, 1971, pp. 327-35, 361.
10 I. Ehrenpreis, 'Jonathan Swift', *Proceedings of the British*

Academy, 1968, p. 153.
11 Quoted in my *Intellectual Origins of the English Revolution*, Oxford University Press, 1965, p. 147.
12 S. Hutin, *Robert Fludd (1574-1637)*, Paris, 1971, pp. 83-4, 99.
13 P.J. French, *John Dee*, London, Routledge & Kegan Paul, 1972, p. 161.
14 A.G. Debus, 'Robert Fludd and the Circulation of the Blood', *Journal of the History of Medicine*, XVI, 1961, pp. 374-93.
15 Thomas, op. cit., p. 271; Hutin, op. cit., pp. 98, 113, 150; Shumaker, op. cit., pp. 193-8.
16 Ed. G. Saintsbury, *Minor Poets of the Caroline Period*, Oxford University Press, 1905-21, p. 413; R.T. Petersson, *Sir Kenelm Digby*, 1952, pp. 267, 272-4, 278, 342.
17 Dewhurst, op. cit., p. 204.
18 F.A. Yates, *Giordano Bruno and the Hermetic Tradition*, London, Routledge & Kegan Paul, 1964, pp. 244-5, 380-1, 451; A. Koestler, *The Sleepwalkers*, London, Hutchinsons, 1959, pp. 259, 396.
19 Ed. A.R. and M.B. Hall, *The Correspondence of Henry Oldenburg*, X, 1975, p. 555; ed. E.G. Forbes, *The Gresham Lectures of John Flamsteed*, London, Mansell, 1975, p. 322.
20 Debus, *Science and Education in the Seventeenth Century: the Webster-Ward Debate*, New York, Neal Watson, 1970, pp. 24, 28-9, 42-3, 60-3.
21 French, op. cit., p. 109.
22 Thomas, op. cit., pp. 229, 109, 642-4.
23 Bernal, op. cit., pp. 913, 966.
24 My *Intellectual Origins*, pp. 25, 49, 69, 147-9; *Mercurius Politicus*, no. 33, 16-23 January 1651, p. 545.
25 Thomas, op. cit., pp. 236-7, 313; Ehrenpreis, op. cit., p. 152; M. Espinasse, *Robert Hooke*, University of California Press, 1956, p. 113.
26 Thomas, op. cit., pp. 369-70; Yates, op. cit., ch. VII.
27 Ed. A. Peel and L. Carlson, *The Writings of Robert Harrison and Robert Browne*, New York, Fernhill, 1953, p. 9.
28 Thomas, op. cit., pp. 498-503, 543, 638-9.
29 G.B. Harrison, *A Second Jacobean Journal*, London, Routledge & Kegan Paul, 1958, p. 102.
30 D.H. Pennington, *Seventeenth Century Europe*, 1970, p. 126.
31 W. Perkins, *Works*, 1609-13, I, p. 40, II, p. 333, III, pp. 607-46; I. Mather, *Remarkable Providences*, 1890, pp. 189-94.
32 Hobbes, op. cit., ed. J. Cropsey, Chicago University Press, 1971, p. 122; Browne, *Works*, 1852, I, p. 84; my *Intellectual Origins*, p. 118, and references there cited. Cf. Jeremiah Whitaker, *The Christians Hope Triumphing*, 1645, pp. 28-9, a sermon preached before the House of Lords; H. More, *An Antidote to Atheism*, 1653, in *A Collection of Several*

Philosophical Writings, 1712, p. 142.
33 Thomas, op. cit., p. 638; C.M. Andrews, *The Colonial Period of American History*, Yale University Press, 1964, I, p. 469.
34 F.A. Yates, *The Rosicrucian Enlightenment*, London, Routledge & Kegan Paul, 1972, pp. 111-13.
35 Thomas, op. cit., pp. 304, 376; Debus, *Science and Education*, p. 33.
36 See W. Lilly, *The Last of the Astrologers*, ed. K.M. Briggs, Folklore Soc., 1974, pp. 63, 68, 78, for use of astrologers as propagandists by the Parliamentarians.
37 My *The World Turned Upside Down*, Harmondsworth, Penguin, 1975, p. 290; L. Clarkson, *The Lost Sheep Found*, 1660, p. 32.
38 Glanvill, *Scepsis Scientifica*, 1664, Dedication to the Royal Society.
39 My *Intellectual Origins*, p. 126.
40 Ibid., p. 19.
41 B. Pascal, *Pensees*, ed. E. Bourtroux, Collection Gallia, n.d., pp. 85-8, 94.
42 Ibid., p. 232.
43 Ed. A.R. and M.B. Hall, *The Correspondence of Henry Oldenburg*, Wisconsin University Press, 1965, I, p. 277.
44 Shumaker, op. cit., p. 198.
45 Thomas, op. cit., pp. 650-62.
46 F.E. Manuel, *The Religion of Isaac Newton*, Oxford University Press, 1974, p. 44; Shumaker, op. cit., p. 254.
47 Thomas, op. cit., p. 643; my *World Turned Upside Down*, p. 293, 304-5; Webster, op. cit., p. 24.
48 J.Z. Young, *An Introduction to the Study of Man*, Oxford University Press, 1971, pp. 115, 640; Koestler, op. cit., pp. 501, 518, 536.
49 Thomas, op. cit., pp. 639-40.
50 Bernal, op. cit., p. 9.
51 Thomas, op. cit., pp. 667-8.

11 DETERMINISM AND ENVIRONMENTALISM IN SOCIALIST THOUGHT

Logie Barrow*

In this chapter I will argue, firstly, that the strategy of most British socialists and of many other activists until around 1910 must be viewed in a very long chronological focus since it was, in some respects, as old as the eighteenth century Enlightenment. I will argue, secondly, that some of the roots of this persistence lie in what I define as 'plebeian autodidact culture'. Autodidacts are those who make their education their own affair, independent of social betters; autodidact culture involved only a minority of plebeians (i.e. lower- middle- or working-class people): otherwise, we could substitute for 'plebeian' the looser word 'popular'.

'Enlightenment' refers to a number of principles elaborated by various intellectuals in a number of countries during the middle and late eighteenth century. Its central drive was the attempt to evaluate everything according to human reason rather than religious revelation. This had political potential, as well as anti-religious. True, an emphasis on reason did not necessarily involve estimating the intellect of, say, the cobbler as already equal with that of the king, nor excluding an appeal to kings to enforce enlightenment. But any deafness of kings to such appeals was an outrage simultaneously intellectual and political. Kings and priests thus came to be viewed as conspiring together against reason; and the stronger this view, the greater the relative intellectual prestige (actual or potential) of, say, cobblers, particularly among cobblers.

Unfortunately, among poorer people in general, enthusiasts for enlightenment were only a minority. This disappointment required explanation, and one was readily available. Although everyone had equal potential for reason, such potential was fulfilled unequally. This was because, within the existing society, the environment was unequal and, for most people, hostile.

'Character' was 'determined by environment'. This environmentalism was fundamentally important. It also seemed simple: so much so that, as we will see later, its two greatest or most influential enunciators - Robert Owen during the first half of the nineteenth century and (as I will argue) Robert Blatchford around 1900 - both erroneously believed themselves to have discovered it. Its seeming simplicity increased its attractiveness to many people of every degree of prominence in or near the

---

*Logie Barrow is a lecturer in history at Bremen University, and an associate editor of *History Workshop Journal*.

working class. More important, as we will also see, its actual incoherences affected these people's strategy. In particular, it produced a dilemma which surfaced from the early 1890s, in the then newly founded Independent Labour Party (ILP) and eventually split it during 1911. Further, the more one viewed one's contemporaries as stunted by their environment, the greater this dilemma became: should one rely more on changing that environment or on appealing to people's admittedly stunted intellects? One response was to concentrate on education - whether of children or adults. Among this response's many attractions was its simultaneous appeal to intellect and to 'changing the [learner's] environment of ideas'. The latter phrase was a favourite among Owenites. Sadly, as a solution to the dilemma, it was no more than verbal. The question remained.

Such continuity of confusions was assisted by confidence of a peculiarly Enlightenment kind. This confidence flowed from the constant association of reason with the natural sciences. As the latters' 'conclusions' were assumed to be certain, so were those of reason. Much followed from this assumption. In particular, since there could be no competing certainties, so there could be no plurality of reasons. This implied two things: not only should reason bring agreement but also, even more important, each area of rational endeavour assisted all others. This particular confidence made the strategic dilemma seem far smaller than it always proved to be in the political long run.

Thus environmentalism helped produce, not one strategy, but rather a range of them. I will define this range later. But that it existed can be seen at once from both Owen and his followers. Owen, one of Britain's pioneer socialists, can be seen oscillating within it. Till about 1820, he hoped that a lightning conversion of the rulers of Europe would suffice to introduce his socialist 'millennium', and he reverted to this a bit during the 1850s, as a spiritualist, when he sometimes seized the opportunity at seances to probe for inside information as to whether various crowned heads were crypto-socialist.[1] In between, he had to varying degrees emphasised the preaching of determinism and rationalism against religion, the demonstration-effect of ideal communities, of an inter-trade union which would convert the whole working class into its own ideal community, back to demonstration by small communities and, increasingly, to his old rationalist preachings (plus spiritualism). Meanwhile, the main oscillations of his followers included trades unionism, communitarianism, co-operation and self-education.

From the 1850s, most Owenites concentrated on co-operation and/or self-education. Most relevantly here, many of them focused even more than before upon their Enlightenment assumption that intellectual liberation was the precondition to all others. They thus came to call themselves secularists, i.e. militant supporters of Reason against Religion. (A minority of them, including Owen, came also to call themselves spiritualists.)

As Blatchford was to put the matter - with his typically unOwen-like concision, more than a generation later (in the *Clarion*, the socialist weekly whose chief ideologue he was): 'Science, which is the knowledge of facts, will beat superstition.'[2]

This emphasis on reason (rationalism) encouraged - though it did not enforce - the reduction of social change to a series of changes in individuals. The Owenites' Universal Community Society of Rational Religionists, during 1839, after the usual platitudes about man's 'general character' being 'formed for him, not by him', went on, without any transition, to claim that 'through this knowledge, adult man or society may effect the greatest improvement in the character and condition of the human race'. Similarly, Holyoake, who had invented the word 'secularism' during the 1850s and who was now in 1905 contributing to the *Clarion* during the last year of his life, stipulated 'conscience [as] the soul of progress, and conscience is in the individual'.[3] In between, let's quote a republican secularist, arguing during the 1880s against the now revolutionary William Morris, that 'the education of the child ... is a work extending over years of steady and patient application: how, then, can the intellectual development of a nation be accomplished by a Socialistic somersault?'[4] Nor should we forget Blatchford during 1902, at the end of *Britain for British* (one of his major expositions of socialism), after presumably converting his 'Mr. John Smith, a typical British workman', 'a hard-headed, practical man': 'Be you *one* John Smith, be you the first. Then you shall surely win a few, and each of these few shall win a few, and so are multitudes composed.'[5]

Environmentalism did not necessarily presuppose a socialist aim. Rather, it proved an easy conduit, during the years around 1850, mainly from Owenite socialism to individualism and, some decades later, mainly vice versa. It encouraged piecemeal strategies for any aim. Secularism's own origins as part of this atomisation of Owenite strategy affected it in two ways throughout its heyday as a formal movement (i.e. from the late 1850s to the mid 1880s). On the one hand, it reinforced the hegemony of those - like the great secularist Charles Bradlaugh - whose politics were individualist, not socialist. On the other, it allowed old Owenites to accept this leadership. In addition, and even more important, it also allowed both them and young sympathisers an integral place within that movement. In the long term, the plebeian subcultures of environmentalism such as secularism and spiritualism turned out to have been milieux of long-term transmission between the epoch of Owenism and that of the ILP.

These two emphases - on reason and on piecemealness - were deeply incoherent. For, environmentalism could also coexist with almost any view of class. At an extreme of class-reconciliation, we can place Joseph Barker, proclaiming in the opening number of Bradlaugh's *National Reformer*, in 1860, that 'the different classes [were] all improving, and in proportion as they improve, they come nearer to each other, get to know each other better, to respect each other more. As science advances and knowledge spreads, the people of England will become one.'[6] But Reason did not have to be so all-inclusive. It could also go with a no less Enlightenment view, that kings and priests had conspired to twist the people's 'environment of ideas'. 'A very large class', explained one writer in one of Bradlaugh's 1850s papers, 'have a vested interest... [in] the present arrangements of society, and ... are adverse to freethinking lest they ... be swept away in the torrent of new ideas.'[7] It could even follow from this that whole elites were irredeemably evil and should be exterminated. Thus around 1890, one social radical, Dan Chatterton, could warm to his slogan, 'Revolt Workers! Heads Off!'[8]

If Chatterton's position was that of an isolated extremist, it was because for most of his contemporaries, the emphasis on reason magnified a zeal to preach tirelessly, not to exterminate. But this too went with a very crude theory of ideology. Here, whether or not Reason reconciled the classes, and whether or not it was obstructed by ruling-class conspiracy, it was bound to triumph: there could be no conflict of reasons. Holyoake, during the 1850s, saw 'Harmony, the sign of intellectual conquest, ... unfurling its banner' so that the clashing 'deluge of error ... subsided'.[9] 'It is only a question of time and education', another secularist enthused during the 1870s, over a call for 'Labour Representation': 'if the principle is just it must be adopted sooner or later'.[10]

Secularism turned out to be the only movement of plebeian independence to bridge the chronological gap between the middle and late nineteenth century: in the purely political arena there simply was no such bridge. The secularist movement was loosely structured and comprised at most only a few thousand members but, like the Owenites of earlier years, these people were often highly persuasive, even when idiosyncratic. Similarly, too, secularism often formed those who were to become cadres in the wider labour and socialist movement. Not that these people necessarily remained hard atheists. And there were, anyway, far more working-class Nonconformists than atheists. I mean, instead, three things that are cultural, rather than strictly doctrinal.

Firstly, the tension between religion and irreligion allowed the two to live not only off each other, but cheek by jowl. The future TUC president, Ben Turner, learning to read - to the neighbours during his childhood - from, alternatingly, the *National Reformer* and the Rev. Spurgeon's hellfire sermons - sums up the predominant situation.[11] Secondly, this tension persisted after the 1880s when secularism declined as a national organisation. Thus, we should not be surprised that, around 1900, the future communist, Tom Bell, and his fellow apprentices 'read feverishly, discussed fiercely and walked the streets, often after midnight, in an effort to sort out for ourselves the problem of man and the universe;[12] nor that Blatchford, during the 1900s, should have had as vast an impact as an opponent of Christianity as of capitalism; and even less, therefore, that, during the same decade, the *Clarion's* readers should vote Darwin to be 'Britain's Greatest Benefactor', far above any popular heroes or heroines and mainly on educationalistic grounds.[13] I, for one, have been given oral evidence, identical to Bell's memory, from a young communist and railwayman of the early 1920s: identical even down to nocturnal peripatetic discussions.[14] But by then, of course, this intellectual strenuousness had indeed received roughly ten years of renewed institutional reinforcement from the Labour College movement. 'As often happens with young workers who begin to think about political questions', Bell reminisced during the late 1930s, 'we saw religion and the church as the big enemy.'[15] 'After I had read Herbert Spencer's *First Principles*', J.T. Murphy - also an apprentice and future communist - recalls, 'I gave in my resignation as a local preacher.'[16]

Thirdly, the intellectual fare provided by the secularist movement was a good deal broader than mere refutation of the Bible's scientifically sillier episodes, even if such refutation was officially the movement's central purpose. Rather, intellectual liberation and the ability to argue for oneself were inseparable; and the latter, particularly, depended on a wide scientific self-culture. Accordingly, the more than thirty years of the *National Reformer*'s weekly issues bulge not only with verbatim reports of Bradlaugh's legal entanglements and of his multi-evening gladiatorial contests with Christian spokesmen, but also with month-long discussions on developments within science, philosophy and theology.

Nor should we see this as merely a matter of secularist sophistication. For, though secularism saw itself as sole heir to the Enlightenment, it was in fact somewhat burdened with cousins. One such cousin - however surprising at first sight - was mysticism. Many people feverishly strove to rebuild their universe, the moment they had expelled the orthodox God from it; and some of the available building-blocks were spiritual or at least of dubious materiality. Such a recourse even among plebeians (as in Behmenism - the mystical Christianity elaborated, around 1610, by the German cobbler, Jakob Boehme) predated the Enlightenment,[17] but was powerfully reinforced during it.[18] This tendency led to a wide range of positions, among which (as I have argued elsewhere[19]) plebeian spiritualism was one of the most attractive (it attained more members than secularism itself). Thus popular free-thought, although it had boasted 'Halls of Science' long before Bradlaugh's famous citadel of that name,[20] was not the only beneficiary of the propensity, among plebeians, both to read about science and often to do it for oneself.

Worse, 'science' itself involved ambiguities. While much contemporary physical theory allowed secularists and others to believe in a wholly material foundation for everything and thus to be full materialists, materialism was not the only element in the scientific atmosphere. From their side, spiritualists could believe themselves to be part of the 'naturalisation of the supernatural'.[21] The atmosphere was polarised by what can be called the long-term aftershock of electricity. This aftershock was at least coincidental with the reverberations of the Enlightenment. Electrical demonstrations and fads from the late eighteenth century onwards produced or strengthened in many minds a pair of assumptions: firstly that there was one (if not more) imponderable force or forces beneath the ponderable ones and, secondly, that the less ponderable a force, the more fundamental it might perhaps be. Most notoriously, these assumptions had opened the way for Mesmer and his disciples and improvers. Mesmerism is associated with far more than 'the End of the Enlightenment in France' (to quote the title of Dr Darnton's book on that subject).[22] It and its various re-workings and modifications contined to arouse great interest into the late nineteenth century. Their attendant phenomena helped, in turn, to sustain interest in the problematic of imponderables. And the latter encouraged the jumbling of materialism and non-materialism (was the ultimate constituent of matter material or immaterial, and were the ultimate determinants of occult phenomena, if such existed, material or not?) Thus secularists and their journals had to grapple with these problems because they found them in their way: it was not merely a matter of broadening or sharpening their minds or sustaining their readership.

Plebeian interest in doing science for oneself is even more important than secularism's relation to it. For, the nineteenth was a golden century for what we can call 'do-it-yourself' science. To some extent this involved what most of us today would dismiss as mere pseudo-science - such as phrenology (reading people's characters via the bumps of their cranium), physiognomy (via their faces) and mesmerism (which was in the area of present-day hypnotism, but often differently theorised). These pursuits lent themselves easily to public performance and to spare-time apprenticeship (this was their common attraction and, I will soon claim, definition). They were also compatible with the emphasis on reason: secularists were often vocal in their support for both phrenology and mesmerism - Bradlaugh himself for the latter.[23] Secularists' philosophical consistency may not have been at its greatest here - any more than when Owenites had warmed to phrenology: again the metaphor of a range suggests itself.

But other sciences that still enjoy respectability today were also at their most accessible during the nineteenth century: not only was science more widely discussed than ever before,[24] but it was also more widely do-able. Journeymen bakers or colliery storekeepers, grinding their own microscope-lenses, could still hope to become authorities on local geology or botany, and be sought out by leaders in the science, partly because the latter still required information via such routes.[25]

'Do-it-yourself' science overlapped with, and was given added urgency by, 'do-it-yourself' medicine. True, this was very often as much a survival from older traditions as a constellation of nineteenth-century developments. But the urge to control one's own body interacted strongly with that to control one's own intellect. The enemy of both was identified as the meddling bigwigs of church, state and the medical professions.

Orthodox medics had attained their present-day legal position only during the 1850s. For some time thereafter, their legal powers exceeded their curative. Their practices often seemed more lethal than those of *un*orthodox ones, and the latter remained more open to spare-time apprenticeship. Worse, the orthodox went on the offensive in attempting, during the second half of the century, to impose compulsory vaccination. The anti-vaccination movement produced numerous plebeian martyrs and some large demonstrations; as a result, an anti-vaccinationist tradition was to persist within the labour movement in some localities into the inter-war years.

More positively, during at least the third quarter of the century, there were attempts to found a patient-oriented, exoteric and democratic practice of medicine. The main one was based on herbalism: there was more than coincidence in the great Chartist Ernest Jones acting near the end of his life as defence counsel for Josiah Thomas, a Newcastle medical herbalist, and in the latter, on acquittal, being feted by the lion of local - if not British - republicanism, Joseph Cowen.[26]

Herbalism seems to have remained strong - particularly in many Pennine towns as well as in north-east England - into the early twentieth century.[27] True, we may find its opponents' accusations of quackery more worrying when made during the early twentieth century than during the mid-nineteenth. But, in its self-image at least, herbalism was always militantly plebeian, participatory and anti-elitist.

I do not, of course, see the do-it-yourself sciences and medicines as reinforcements of a safely secular reason ('rationalist'). This would indeed be difficult - as the frequent overlap of herbalists with spiritualists and occasionally of herbalism with mediumistic healing should remind us. But as I have argued elsewhere,[28] it would be no less difficult to label spiritualism firmly as *ir*rationalist. Rather, the labels of rationalism and irrationalism are inappropriate for a continuum which comprised interpenetrations of reason with the occult and, in many a plebeian science, of the Enlightenment (with all its ambiguities) with - directly or (as with herbalism) via the American backwoods - older, often rural, techniques and assumptions. John Gast, the great pioneer of nineteenth century artisan trades unionism and free thought, came within this range at the time he was arrested for fortune-telling.[29] This is so, irrespective of whether he had already begun his study of astrology (a sophisticated - or sophistical - determinism), and of whether the episode was at worst, a mere matter of charlatanry brought on by starvation.

Thus the plebeian sciences' key qualities were not scientificity, (however we define this) but accessibility and participatoriness. (Similarly, within medicine, herbalism can be contrasted with homeopathy, many of whose adepts might share herbalism's scorn both of orthodox medicine and of vaccination, but all of whom were legally qualified and to that extent middle-class.) This polarity can often be applied even to the so-called occult sciences: whereas plebeian spiritualists attempted to democratise the occult, their middle-class equivalents tended, during the mid-nineteenth century, towards religious orthodoxy and, occasionally during subsequent decades, towards pseudo-hermetic cults such as Theosophy. (The polarity can often be applied also to religions: most of the seventeenth and eighteenth centuries' open antinomians being plebeian.)[30]

The plebeian emphasis on participatoriness helps dispose of another paradox. One side of the latter is that, within working-class agitation over formal education, 'from the later 1860's, the strategy of substitution - of an alternative [working-class] educational system - was replaced by a demand for more equal access to facilities that were to be provided by the [existing, as yet undemocratised] state'.[31] While I would agree with this historian that 'the consequences of [such an] adaptation' must have been 'immense',[32] the other side of the paradox is that *in*formal plebeian *self*-education remained at least as lively as before into the early twentieth century. Also, while Johnson may be right that such self-education no longer had 'the ambition of being [sic] an alternative system, especially with regard to children',[33] the fact remains that both the Secularist and the succeeding socialist Sunday Schools saw themselves as a direct part of a strategy for bringing a new order of things; so, less consistently or not, did the more numerous spiritualist equivalents, the Lyceums. The solution to the paradox is, of course, that the activity of self-education usually proved more important than its content. This was eventually, as we will see, to help undermine much of this autodidact culture.

My argument so far can be summarised within one sentence. During the rough period from 1850 to 1910, the involvement of many independent-minded plebeians in a culture of self-education reinforced their openness to environmentalist strategies. I will now discuss the chief pair of such strategies among socialists, and will then look at how they influenced the wider labour movement; finally I will sketch out why I believe plebeian autodidact culture withered away during the early twentieth century.

Blatchford based everything on a crudely Enlightenment theory of human nature. In 1889 he had rejected socialism on the ground that 'human nature [was] not sufficiently developed to allow of it'.[34] Within a month he was proclaiming his conversion to socialism. Accordingly, he reversed the terms: 'we Socialists', he boasted four years later in *Merrie England* (his pamphlet which quickly sold nearly a million copies), 'have studied human nature and ... our opponents object to Socialism because they don't understand human nature at all.'[35]

What was this malleable dogma of human nature? It was our old friend, environmentalism. 'Men', Blatchford announced, 'are what circumstances make them.'[36] So, it might seem, in this determinism it was environment that determined character. Yet (just as Owen had, consistently or not, emphasised the importance of character), for Blatchford too, though 'freedom may be won by slaves ... it cannot be kept save by men with free souls'.[37] So, equally, only character could guarantee environment. Altogether, environmentalism was like a wheel, and wheels can go backwards or forwards, other factors remaining equal. 'Julia Dawson' - pen-name of the editor of the *Clarion's* woman's page for many years - exemplifies this dilemma. She felt bound, on the one hand, to warn voluntaristically that 'so long as man denies justice to dumb animals, he is unlikely to give it to those who can speak'. But on the other, to warn fatalistically in the next sentence that 'it [was] not possible to get socialism while overworked men continue to be cruel to overworked animals';[38] or similarly (in words likely to induce self-pity among even middle-class readers) to ask: 'how *can* people grow up beautiful enough to bring about a beautiful scheme like Socialism, when they have to sit on chairs like this?'[39] Even more patronising is one readers's (only at first sight voluntaristic) question: 'if our slum-dweller had the perception of beauty of a William Morris, how would they dwell in the slums?'[40] Environmentalist doctrine put its own advocates into a superior dimension. The historical importance of this is not lessened by its extreme lack of doctrinal originality. I have quoted Dawson's use of the word 'give'. 'I say it is ... wiser,' wrote Blatchford in a paragraph which he printed verbatim during both 1895 and 1911,[41] 'to give freedom by slow degrees. A man will never learn to use his eyes in Stygian darkness.'

I have used the word 'patronising' on the understanding that the patronage by the more enlightened of the less does not necessarily involve differences of class. Rather, the patronage was, as often, part of the morale not only of the enlightened in general, but also, more important, of autodidacts.

Worse still, while environmentalist concepts allowed a rational, if patronising, account of the average person's enlightenment or lack of it, they could give little account of themselves: why had they first been formulated by particular individuals and not by others? Only at first sight is this incoherence unimportant. It was the most doctrinal of the factors behind Owen's patronising behaviour towards his own followers - for example, his status among them as 'Social Father', or again, his blaming of reverses on their lack of enlightenment.[42] The same factor also helps us to recognise certain of Blatchford's proclamations as more than mere megalomania. During the 1900s in particular, he argued that conversion to what he actually called 'determinism' would be the best method of conversion to socialism. This was not the first time he had urged philosophical, as a preliminary to political, change, nor the first time he had taken credit for a philosophy which owed almost everything to Owen, apparently unawares. Rather, the important thing is that Blatchford really does seem to have seen 'his' determinism as 'greater than Buddha, greater than Plato, greater than Christ':[43] 'if my theory were universally accepted, there would be no more wars, ... poverty, ... sweaters, ... slums, ... unemployed ....The churches, the parliaments, the universities, and all the political movements of the whole world are of very little consequence to the human race': 'if I am right, ... all the educational systems of the world must be revised, all systems of politics, economics, sociology must be thrown upon the scrapheap'.[44]

What we must marvel at is the incoherence of this determinism. For, to speak summarily: although environment determined character, the only sure way to change environment and thus to guarantee superior character, was, on the contrary, to guarantee the superior environment by raising peoples' character beforehand - even though, after all, above and against their environment. Such confusions were inherently endless. In other words environmentalism - Owen's, Blatchford's or anyone else's - is a strict non-sequitur: this, irrespective of whether one tries to get from character to environment or vice versa.

These twin absurdities survived or recurred during generations. Indeed, this confusion - so fundamental that it is often passed over as irrelevant - structured the main cleavage within the ILP (Independent Labour Party) from the latter's inauguration in 1893 till its split in 1911.

On the one hand stood Blatchford, who was what I call an educationalist. I add the syllable 'al' since the ready word 'educationist' had come to imply a formal, or at least an institutional definition of education. This is far too one-sided for most plebeian autodidacts such as Blatchford. Educationalists assume that 'education of the people' (however defined) is not merely one necessary precondition for realising an aim (this is so within all strategies save the most spontaneist), but will actually suffice to realise it. As Blatchford never tired of intoning, 'Give us a Socialistic people, and Socialism will accomplish itself.' Officially, the work of his thousands of loosely organised followers - his 'Clarionettes' - was to gather this gift, by 'making Socialists'. Within this framework, while legislation would ultimately ratify the gift, the legislator's main task was to assist the educational process, rather than to try to accumulate reforms - pleasant though these might be in themselves. Premature reforms were any which involved 'compromises', or which confused the process - in other words were what we might call counter-educational. This was the burden of Blatchford's polemics against the leaders of the ILP - Keir Hardie, Ramsay MacDonald and the rest.[45]

The alternative to education, within an environmentalist perspective, was legislation, which from the 1880s onwards was canvassed as the main vehicle towards the socialist goal. With, as I call it, 'legislativistic' logic, socialists did not need to insist that such legislation be enacted by socialists. From the mid 1880s, the pamphleteers of the Fabian Society raised socialism (or reduced it) to a steady stream of detailed reform-proposals. There were thus roots both old and new for MacDonald's statement, in 1909, that socialism 'need not come via a socialist party',[46] or J.R. Clynes's that, in legislation, 'each act [was] contributing to the total of change'.[47] In the legislativistic perspective, even at the early stage where British socialism found itself around 1900, the onus on legislators was not, as with educationalists, to proclaim their principles clearly (i.e. purely) but, rather, to legislate - using compromise where necessary. There was, of course, much room to disagree on how far to compromise, and the ILP leaders sometimes aired such disagreements in public. But it was they, as legislators, who ultimately had to decide. The main task of the party's rank and file was to keep the leaders in the legislature. Thus the logic of legislativism was to raise leaders above led, while the logic of educationalism was - as repeatedly occurred during the ILP's internal debates - for the led to suspect and seek to control all leaders except, potentially, educators. Educationalism involved a convergence, among many ILP members, between two rhetorics: those of educationalism and, secondly, of many trade unionists' suspicions towards anyone definable as a leader.

Historians conventionally describe the ILP's 1911 split - in which a large minority of branches seceded in order to merge, at the 'Socialist Unity' conference, with other socialists (notably the Marxist SDF/SDP) to form the British Socialist Party - in terms of Left splitting from Right. But a reading of the weekly which spent four (indirectly many more) years preparing this explosion - a reading, that is, of the *Clarion* - suggests to me that the main line of polarisation was between educationalistic splitters and legislativistic stayers. And by the time war supervened, many stayers, too, were starting to split along similar lines.

I am not claiming that environmentalism was equally important within every strategy during our period. It was of less importance within most varieties of popular liberalism and Lib-Labism, since these were more modest in aim than those doctrines which owed something, however indirectly, to Owenism. On the other hand, I have already noted examples of how environmentalism could sometimes (via a piecemeal emphasis) lead precisely to a scaling-down of aims: hardly an *un*-Lib-Lab result. Thus Bradlaugh - again, along with many of his followers - functioned through many years as both secularist and active Liberal.

Sometimes an impasse within one area helped reproduce an

impasse within others. Take trades unionism and the SDF. These two may be thought to have very little to do with each other. And this relates precisely to my point. At the national level, the SDF's prickly allegiance to Marxism did not prevent it being, in practice, somewhat educationalistic (however legislativistic it might be at the municipal level). Its Marxism combined the faults of '2nd-International' orthodoxy with others more peculiar. Not only did the inevitabilism, which resulted from the SDF's economic-reductionist approach to almost everything, reduce it in practice to a 'preaching of socialism' that was often, bar the name, educationalistic (thus producing a significant number of working-class socialists, even though most of these quickly left for other political pastures). There was also the SDF's peculiar belief in the 'iron law of wages' - whereby trades unionism was viewed (till the arrival of the unskilled) as anti-socialist and, afterwards, as diversionary. This belief lost it most of the benefits it might have gained from the presence of many of its members and recent ex-members within the founding leaderships of the New Unions. Worse, even so faithful an SDF member as Will Thorne, the leader of the gas workers, seems to have behaved little differently from his non-socialist fellow-members of the TUC Parliamentary Committee.[48]

Admittedly, this must be seen as part of the wider baffling of socialists within the institutions of the trades union movement. True, at TUC conference, socialists raised much steam with collectivist resolutions. But, meanwhile, as an ILP journalist cynically remarked, the leaders of the Old unions stayed in control of the engine and 'determined, if not the direction, the speed': their 'leading idea', this journalist concluded, was 'not to overweight the safety valve'.[49] This was slightly one-sided, for the socialists were to persuade the very next TUC to begin founding what became the Labour Party. None the less, once the turbulence of around 1890 was passed, New unionists, whether socialist or not, polarised in ways rather similar to the Old.

Even more important, though, the SDF, by default, hardly encouraged them to behave very differently. Not only were SDF politics irrelevant to unionism, but the SDF's organs and spokesmen proclaimed this proudly. 'Strikes', its weekly *Justice* pontificated during the 1897-8 engineering struggle, were 'a worn out method of class warfare'. And the paper's solidarity-fund during these weeks was eloquently tiny in comparison with that of Hardie's *Labour Leader*, let alone that of the *Clarion*.[50] Or, as H.M. Hyndman - the SDF's leader and, often, bane - bellowed in 1914, 'there are only two weapons.... Vote straight and shoot straight. Strikes are but the weapon of despair.' He was orating amid a crowd, assembled in support of victimised strike-leaders, which was described by no less an anti-working-class paper than *The Times* as 'one of the largest ... ever seen in London'.[51]

This separation between industrial and political struggles was shared by many socialists, not all of them SDF members. This can be shown clearly at the 1911 'Socialist Unity' conference which chanced to convene only a few weeks after the first and largest wave of the industrial unrest. The most significant thing to be heard during its deliberations was not some ILP members talking like SDF members (i.e. exceptionally reductionist Marxists), nor some SDF members talking like educationalists, nor some Clarionettes sounding like either: this should not surprise any who have read this chapter from the beginning. The important thing, rather, is that, despite the magnitude of the industrial events, the old SDF leadership managed, after one of the lengthiest debates, to obtain a three-fifths majority for reaffirming the traditional separation between industrial and political struggles. Indeed, the industrial unrest, though it was to recur into 1914, seems to have taught no more than a large minority of the new party's membership the need to break down the separation.[52]

Of course, the separation between industrial and political struggles was partly due to the force of very old habit among far more than merely socialists. Liberal and Lib-Lab trades unionists, for example, had always tried to keep the two areas apart. And in the very period of the Socialist Unity conference itself, the doctrine most associated (exaggeratedly or not) with the industrial upheavals of the time, syndicalism, involved the same separation. The strict syndicalist doctrine rejected politics no less emphatically than, as much as nearly a century previously, the strict Owenite.

There were, of course, powerful reasons for the tenacious recurrence of this separation. I am not claiming that strategy develops unbrokenly (though I would argue that the break in 1889 has been fundamentally overestimated); that activists, sympathisers or audiences were constantly agonising over strategy (on the contrary, the latter's very incoherences might encourage a period of under-emphasis followed by devastating re-emergence during splits and other crises); or that those recognised at the time as major ideologues - even Owen or Blatchford - enjoyed obedience as against admiration from a significant proportion of activists. Above all, I am not claiming that strategy develops in isolation from other facets of activity. On the contrary, I have just noted how even something as persistent as separatism began to break up under the impact of the industrial events of the 1910s. What I am saying is that an environmentalist perspective remained a constant, informing doctrinal and political division on the Left. Environmentalism can be seen as one among a number of strategic idioms - radicalism and Lib-Labism would be others - which remained available and relatively unmodified through the nineteenth and early twentieth centuries, partly because they underpinned more than they undermined each other, and partly because they related no less compatibly to habits and institutions recurring within trades unionism and working-class politics.

Thus, the separation between political and industrial arenas was one underlying guarantee of environmentalism's continued currency within the former area. In any case, though, those political strategies which based themselves on reason and on the piecemeal were peculiarly irrelevant to broad industrial struggle, though not to conciliation or to trade sectionalism. And this irrelevance no doubt provided its own minor reinforcement of the separation.

Something else which was both result and (not so minor) reinforcement of this separation was lack of clear correlation between industrial and political views. Any search for examples of confused correlation need go no further than the aftermath of the 1897-8 engineering struggle. Under this impact, individual trade unionists' political allegiance - whether Liberal, ILP or SDF - counted for very little more than jargon amid not so much a confusion as a (for a time) self-multiplying chaos of union strategies.[53]

Compared with such confusions and failures, one is even tempted to underrate the importance of those seemingly clear political strategies that were available. None the less, I see plebeian autodidact culture as one factor behind the political ambiguity of the labour movement during the decades 1850-1910. There were, of course, other factors - such as the involvement of many of this culture's actual and potential participants in 'skilled' trades unionism (which was itself a rich amalgam of democracy and elitism). And, in return, political, union and cultural ambiguities reinforced each other. But these mutual reinforcements precisely helped give the cultural emphasis its *self*-reinforcing character.

And we can enhance their clarity when we relate them to the long disputation - recently revived - as to the existence, nature and role of the 'labour-aristocracy', particularly for the period *c*.1850-1910 in contrast with the periods before and after.

For the decades 1850-1910, I would certainly see skilled workers - a category whose definitional ambiguities are more empirical than those of the labour aristocracy (at least as sometimes theorised) - as relating to my argument in two ways. Economically, the acceleration from around 1910 of their loss of privileges as against the mass of their unskilled fellow workers went with the economic undermining of plebeian autodidact culture which became catastrophically manifest after the 1926 strike. Secondly, while it is true that the skilleds' exclusiveness within the workplace towards the unskilled hardly made for cultural solidarity with them outside it, it is still the case that the skilleds' social ambivalence went with a reliance on ambiguous concepts such as 'respectability' and 'independence' which, unlike the middle-class use of such terms, could have meanings both individualist *and* collectivist.[54] Now, it is again true that the skilled's use of such words was also that of autodidacts;

and this usage relates to what I have already discussed within strategy as a piecemeal approach. But we should not conflate autodidacts with the skilled (though probably many were), nor should we conflate plebeian autodidact culture with the culture of the skilled - though empirical study often discovers that the two overlapped considerably in many towns:[55] overlap is not identity.

It is important to make these discriminations as sensitively as possible. For, during my period, the plebeian autodidact milieu had a particular relationship with working-class politics. This peculiarity contrasts the period with those before and after. During the Chartist years, many could see this milieu - which had existed, if possibly less densely than during my period, for some decades[56] - as potentionally if not actually part of a united working-class movement: thus the 1830s 'War of the Unstamped' could subsequently be seen as contributing to the fight for the Charter. And again, in the 1910s and 1920s, in a period of industrial instability greater than anything since the 1842 general strike, the early Labour College movement brought plebeian autodidact independence back indeed into the mainstream of class struggle.

Why then, did this culture wither from the mid 1920s? True, as Macintyre says, 'it is easy enough to point to indices of change':[57] one could enumerate economic pressures, union defeats, growing right-wing intolerance, demoralisation within the left and the withdrawal of official Communist Party participation. I believe, however, that my contribution points to one aspect that is not so much an index as a culture. I have argued that plebeian autodidact culture was strengthened by a separation between the industrial and political arenas. The scale of events during the 1910s and 1920s lessened this separatism, even before most such events had come to involve working-class defeats.

It also, within the now much widened arena of the Labour Party, appeared to bury the problems of environmentalism by appearing to make one of the latter's poles, legislativism, seem so self-evidently more relevant than the other, educationalism. This relevance was also boosted by the increasingly political involvement of the trade unions in the Labour Party: their political needs had always been legislative.

However, I would only say 'appears to bury' because, even though environmentalist language had ceased to inflect the Labour Party's internal disagreements (a contrast, as we have seen, with around 1900), the effects of this change were very current. For, if legislativism has always predominated among MacDonald and his successors (idealistic rhetoric apart), it has, particularly during the early 1930s and less and less intermittently since the 1950s, produced a feeling among many of this party's activists reminiscent of that among their predecessors around 1910: a sickening feeling of having been outwitted and boxed in by existing institutions. Further, there are some clearly bad effects to be observed from the disappearance of plebeian autodidact culture and Labour's long-term shift ever further from class self-education and ever more thoroughly into a Fabian from-above approach.[58]

Not that educationalistic activities automatically withered everywhere: Their inter-war proliferation under the aegis of the Royal Arsenal Co-operative Society may refute this.[59] I say 'may' partly because of the need for further research into how participatorily intellectual this education was, into the role of the Communist Party within it and into how firmly rooted the whole effort turned out to be.

In general, till around 1910, cultural forms of activity had often (as among many secularists and Clarionettes) substituted for political; subsequently, they tended more and more to unfold within a political, sometimes even a party-political, universe. Here, within and around the smaller world of the Communist Party, the intensely Party culture of the 'Little Moscows' (those few industrial settlements, in various parts of Britain, where the party was at least a major influence in the local labour movement) are the clearest instance.[60] A belief that the old interests had become less important may account for the feeling - perceptible through Communist autobiographies and polemics - of putting away childish things, however long-windedly. Alike, events and Leninist doctrine set new criteria of relevance, which the old culture was not constructed to meet. The clearer the urgency of the new criteria - those established by the October revolution - the wider the long-term defeat of the contemplative, by the activist or Leninist approach to philosophy.

The 'battle of ideas' which took place in the Plebs League in the 1920s, specifically on the place of Dietzgen among the great teachers of socialism, and more generally on the relationship of socialism to 'science' could be seen as a crucial moment, in which T.A. Jackson, as the bearer of a new philosophical militancy, and arguing as the spokesman for Communism, defeated the British working-class followers of the more abstruse (if also more proletarian) philosopher Joseph Dietzgen. Here, the nature of the terrain on which this defeat occurred had, I believe, devastating consequences not only for plebeian autodidact culture but, even more fundamentally, for democratic approaches to science - ultimately, therefore, for definitions of socialism. For, Dietzgenism's continued popularity may possibly have owed much to plebeian confusion over the 'crisis in physics' - the disintegration of the billiardball-materialist atom (a crisis which itself had earlier triggered Lenin's *Materialism and Empirio - Criticism*). From around 1900 till today, the most talked-of developments in science have usually been the most esoteric and sometimes by far the most counter-commonsensical. Nothing would have been more bewildering to old-fashioned plebeian enthusiasts for science. (The great 'materialist', Robert Blatchford, for one, found the atom 'guilty of conduct unbecoming a material entity', and bewildered himself into spiritualism, partly as a result[61].) The Dietzgenite vogue shows plebeian autodidacts responding, within this continuing crisis, with a closing caricature of their traditional yen for all-embracing views of the universe - among which even the materialist versions (as I have instanced elsewhere[62]) turn out to be at least potentially idealist. Again, of course, the most actual refutations were Leninist.

But this brings us back to the political aspect. Here, for generations of plebeian autodidacts - whether influenced by Owen, Bradlaugh or Blatchford - intellectual (and, potentially, other kinds of personal) liberation came strategically prior to political. Thus they often saw their own culture - secularist or, as both earlier and later, socialist - as having greater long-term importance than any political movement, let alone party. The Labour Churches, along with the whole early-1890s 'religion-of-socialism' phase were merely a short-lived extreme of this habit.[63] If I may twist a term which has recently emerged as one of abuse between historians, it was a very *culturalist* culture. Its resulting tendency to introversion - whether of the 'God-is-in-the-Labour-Movement' Labour Churches or of the jokily in-groupy Clarionettes - rivalled the official concepts of the SDF for irrelevance to industrial struggle. Thereby, this culture at least reinforced the tendency - so multiform during the three generations from the 1840s - to separate the industrial and political arenas, just as, in return, it was strengthened by this separation.

Not that we should view this cultural emphasis during 1850-1910 in a wholly negative light. Some of those who do so forget the need to approach sciences without falling into either of the two extremes of elitism and Lysenkoism. The importance of the latter and of its context make it harder for me to condemn plebeian culturalism. For, in the 1930s, the scientific qualities imputed to the Soviet regime, together with the image projected by Soviet science itself, reinforced in Britain amongst progressives of all classes an approach to science which (apart from intermittent enthusiasms for Lysenkoism: that disastrous exception) was elitist - not, certainly, in comparison with the officially approved sciences of the time but, for us more important, with plebeian scientists of an earlier one. The politics of non-plebeian worship of science (here H.G. Wells, despite his class origins, was obviously the longest-lasting representative) might vary from communist to right-wing Labour. But it approached those people who were not full-time scientists, less as immediate fellow-practitioners (potential or actual) of science than as its grateful beneficiaries and, at the highest, its external liberators.

Around the early 1930s, in other words, the remaining bones of plebeian autodidact culture were scavenged by member-species of a new, broader-than-plebeian, genus among which the Left Book Club was the largest. Autodidacts are still, thankfully, with us. An autodidact culture is not.

To sum up: I see the milieu of plebeian autodidact culture and the range of strategies associated with it as two among a number of overlapping factors governing the general nature of the British labour movement during the period *c*. 1850-1910. This is a tentative formulation framed so as to avoid merely inverting the assumption among many labour historians that the relations of production can be made to account constantly for all such factors. Both assumption and inversion[64] remain questionable.

NOTES

I owe many thanks to members of the Cambridge seminar in Social History and of Professor Doctor Bernd Lange's seminar at the Technische Universität Braunschweig, to whom parts of this contribution were read and who commented stimulatingly.

Place of publication is London, unless otherwise stated.

1 Quoted in F. Podmore, *Modern Spiritualism*, London, 1902, vol. 2, p. 22.
2 *Clarion*, 6.12.1912.
3 Ibid., 28.5.1905, 2.6.1905.
4 George Standring (a vice-president of Bradlaugh's National Secular Society from his youth) in his *Radical*, vol. 1, no. 4, September 1886. By far the fullest treatment of this phase of secularism is Edward Royle, *Radicals, Secularists and Republicans*, Manchester, 1980.
5 R. Blatchford, *Britain for the British*, London, 1902 edn, pp. 7, 172.
6 *National Reformer*, opening number (14.4.1860).
7 *The Investigator*, vol. 5, p. 50.
8 For this slogan, see, e.g., *Chatterton's Commune: The Atheistic Communistic Scorcher*, no. 10, 1886. For Chatterton generally, see the same irregular periodical throughout its forty-two issues (ending in 1895); J. Quail, *The Slow Burning Fuse*, London, 1978, pp. 175-7; and Royden Harrison, *Before the Socialists*, London, 1965, pp. 226 f., 242n.
9 G.J. Holyoake, *Principles of Secularism*, 1859, p. 3.
10 C.C. Cattell in *Secular Chronicle*, vol. 7, p. 180f.
11 Sir Ben Turner, *About Myself*, 1930, p. 27.
12 Tom Bell, *Pioneering Days*, 1940, pp. 31, 96.
13 L.J.W. Barrow, 'The Socialism of Robert Blatchford and the *Clarion* Newspaper, 1889-1914', London PhD thesis, 1975, pp. 107-12.
14 Interviews with Mr Harry Wicks, 1975-7.
15 Bell, op. cit., pp. 31, 96.
16 J.T. Murphy, *New Horizons*, 1941, pp. 27f.
17 See G. Rowell, 'The Origins and History of Universalist Societies in Britain, 1750-1850', in *Journal of Ecclesiastical History*, vol. 11, 1971.

18 Same; also R. Darnton: *Mesmerism and the End of the Enlightenment in France*, Harvard University Press, 1971.
19 L. Barrow, 'Socialism in Eternity: Plebeian Spiritualism, 1853-1913', in *History Workshop Journal*, Spring 1980, issue 9.
20 I. Prothero, *Artisans and Politics: John Gast and his Times*, Folkestone, 1979, pp. 253, 297, 308.
21 F. Podmore, *The Naturalisation of the Supernatural*, New York, 1908.
22 Darnton, op. cit.
23 *National Reformer*, 28.7.1860, where he mentioned the famous Drs Elliotson and Ashburner, and the equally famous case of Harriet Martineau - whose mesmerist had been Spencer T. Hall, (father of the 1910s semi-syndicalist, Leonard Hall).
24 More even than in the late-Enlightenment France described by Darnton, op. cit.
25 See Barrow, *Socialism in Eternity*, particularly the text for notes 156 and 157.
26 *Eclectic Journal and Medical Free Press*, April 1867, pp. 242-8; December 1867, p. 378.
27 Despite every bias, obscurity and unevenness, the 1910 *Report as to the Practice of Medicine and Surgery by unqualified persons in the United Kingdom* (HMSO) can suggest this much. I am indebted to Dr R. Cooter for alerting me to the very existence of this tantalising document.
28 Barrow, *Socialism in Eternity*.
29 Prothero, op. cit., pp. 63, 262f.
30 See e.g. C. Hill, *The World Turned Upside Down*, London, 1972, particularly chs 8, 9, 10 and 15; G. Rowell, *The Origins*, same article, p. 55f.
31 R. Johnson, '"Really Useful Knowledge": radical education and working-class culture, 1790-1848', in J. Clark, C. Critcher, R. Johnson (eds), *Working Class Culture: Studies in History and Theory*, London, 1980, p. 94, similarly p. 95.
32 Ibid., p. 95.
33 Ibid., p. 99.
34 *Sunday Chronicle*, 3.2.1889.
35 R. Blatchford, *Merry England*, 1894 edn, ch. 15.
36 *Clarion*, 10.3.1916.
37 *Sunday Chronicle*, 5.10.1890.
38 *Clarion*, 8.11.1910.
39 Ibid., 8.11.1908, her emphasis.
40 Ibid., 2.1.1904.
41 Ibid., 2.11.1895; 22.12.1911.
42 See particularly R.G. Garnett, 'Robert Owen and the Community Experiments', in S. Pollard, J. Salt (eds), *Robert Owen, Prophet of the Poor*, Lewisburg, PA, 1971.
43 *Clarion*, 18.9.1906; 17.12.1911.

44 Ibid., 3.1.1906.
45 Barrow, 'The Socialism of Robert Blatchford', III, 3,a,b, d,e.
46 Quoted in R. Miliband, *Parliamentary Socialism*, London, 1961, p. 17.
47 *Clarion*, 5.3.1909.
48 One clear example was on the question of union federation; TUC PC.MS *Minutes*, particularly those for meetings of 22.3.97; 12.10.97; 7.2.99.
49 Joseph Burgess in the *Manchester Weekly Times*, 9.9.1898.
50 See Barrow, 'The Socialism of Robert Blatchford', pp. 348f.
51 *The Times*, 2.3.1914, p. 5; similar slogan reported in *Daily Herald* same date, p. 7. The strike had occurred in South Africa. Some of its leaders had been deported. On the London working-class reaction, see also Barrow, 'The Socialism of Robert Blatchford', pp. 406f. Hyndman probably had the Ulster Orangemen in mind: see his speech on the South African strikes in ibid., 24.1.1914, p. 7.
52 *Official Report of the Socialist Unity Conference ... September 30th - October 1st, 1911*, particularly p. 10-13, 17ff., *The First Annual Conference of the British Socialist Party ... Official Report*, 1912.
53 See L. Barrow: *Crisis and Federation: Rank and File Confusion*, (forthcoming).
54 G. Crossick, *An Artisan Elite in Victorian Society*, London, 1978, particularly p. 134.
55 See, e.g. R.Q. Gray, *The Labour Aristocracy in Victorian Edinburgh*, Oxford, 1976.
56 See, e.g. P. Hollis, *The Pauper Press*, Oxford, 1970; E. Royle, *Victorian Infidels*, Manchester, 1974; J.H. Wiener, the *War of the Unstamped*, Cornell University Press, 1969; G.A. Williams, *Rowland Detrosier: A Working Class Infidel, 1800-34*, York, 1965; and, above all, Prothero, op. cit.
57 S. Macintyre, *Proletarian Science*, Cambridge, 1980, p. 238.
58 Steve Baron and others, *Unpopular Education*, London, 1981, *passim*.
59 John Attfield, paper to the May 1981 meeting of the Society for the Study of Labour History.
60 S. Macintyre, *Little Moscows*, London, 1980.
61 Robert Blatchford, *My Eighty Years*, 1931, pp. 261-6; also, ibid., *More Things in Heaven and Earth*, 1925, *passim*. But note that the physicist he most quoted - Sir Oliver Lodge - was particularly idealist and outdated.
62 As argued in Barrow, 'The Socialism of Robert Blatchford', pp. 124-39, 210-18, 230-43, 253-65.
63 See S. Yeo, 'A New Life: The Religion of Socialism', in *History Workshop Journal*, issue 4, 1977.
64 The nearest approximation to an inversion is perhaps Stanley Pierson's grandly psychologistic and therefore

inevitabilist *Marxism and the Origins of British Socialism*, Cornell University Press, 1973, and his *British Socialists: The Journey from Fantasy to Politics*, Harvard University Press, 1979. Luckily, the empirical interest of Pierson's ingredients is not lessened by the gothically idealist shape of his cake-mould.

12 THE DIFFUSION OF MARXISM IN ITALY DURING THE LATE NINETEENTH CENTURY

Franco Andreucci*

The history of Marxism in Italy has been very well studied and documented for the period of the Second International. In fact, the work of an entire generation of historians - at least in that phase of their intellectual life corresponding to the 1950s and 1960s - was dedicated to illuminating various aspects of the history of Marxism in Italy, with particular attention to its internal development and to the relationship between it and the workers' movement in general and to the Socialist Party in particular. I am referring here to the work of Raggioneri, Manacorda, Procacci, Santarelli, Cortesi, Bravo, Bosio - to mention just a few - whose results are so well known and accepted that I have no need to go into them here.[1]

What we do not know, however, is still quite a lot. We do not know, for example, how Marxism really spread in Italy. I mean the precise ways, means, and circumstances - I would almost like to say the various occasions - by which Marxism became known by a greater number of persons than Marx's and Engels's correspondents in Italy, the roads Marxism travelled to reach - if indeed it did reach - the workers or, at least, the simple militants. No one up to now has tried to enter the difficult labyrinth of collective Marxism; no one has studied its role in the process of the formation of the party's ideology and its transmission downward, as Steinberg has done for Germany. No one has done it even though, as is easily evident, discovery of the connotations of a Marxism which becomes a party ideology represents a key for throwing into focus from an especially

*Franco Andreucci is director of the Ernesto Raggioneri Institute, Florence, and editor of the *Biographical Dictionary of the Italian Labour Movement*. A founder-editor of the new Italian journal *Passato e Prescute*.

privileged position the bright and dim spots, the rise and decline of the Italian Socialist Party.

As is the case more or less everywhere in the last decades of the nineteenth century, in Italy we find a marked spread of Marxism. As elsewhere, it takes three directions, with three different methods, rhythms, and degrees of intensity: (1) through written criticism, general works on socialism, manuals, journalistic or scholarly books. The authors are sometimes opponents, but more often proponents of socialism; (2) through the party press and literature; (3) through daily propaganda, pamphlets, conversations, debates, lectures, rallies.[2]

The first point poses an important problem which has been neglected up to now and whose premises have been more or less ignored: this is the fate of the enormous amount of information on Marxism which circulated in Europe in the last quarter of the century. Even though the word 'Marxism' was slow in taking hold, as G. Haupt has shown, Marx's name, however, and a summary knowledge of his doctrines were very well-known over a large area. I shall ignore the non-Italian manifestations and illustrate with a few examples the characteristics of the copious literature which in Italy informed readers of every party, and thus a quite broad cross-section of public opinion, about Marx and Marxism. I am thinking above all of that sector of public opinion which carried a decisive weight in the consolidation of the Italian Socialist Party, students and unemployed intellectuals, the *declassés* whom Bakunin described so enthusiastically a number of years before but who were still around in great numbers between the 1880s and 1890s. And so we ask, what could the common readers have known about Marxism?

If we look at the titles listed by Pagliaini in his *Catalogo della libreria italiana*, even without considering the numerous additions and integrations indicated in Michels's bibliography, and group them chronologically, we find that in the decade between 1885 and 1895 the total reaches almost three hundred titles. This is the equivalent of more than two books a month on socialism and Marxism for a decade.[3] These include translations of foreign works of a general nature, such as Rae's famous text, *Contemporary Socialism*,[4] but for the most part we have here an autochthonous literature - it is sufficient to mention Biraghi's book which appeared in the Manuali Hoepli series, the most widespread series of manuals in Italy[5] - expressing the Italian reverberations of the great European literature on socialism and the social question (De Laveleye, Schäffle, G. Adler, Leroy-Beaulieu, Rae, etc.). If we add to this the interest in Marxism expressed in the great Italian magazines - from *Nuova Antologia* to *La Riforma Sociale* - we can easily see the outlines of a panorama that is quantitatively quite rich, representing a conspicuous amount of information. Why this information, these publications have fallen into oblivion is a chapter in the history of Marxism which has never been explored.

But let us try to see what image of Marx and Marxism is reproduced in these texts. (It is certainly not through the mediation of Engels, whose work remains always on the margins of this type of writing, which knows Marx either directly or through the mediation of *Kathedersozialisten* or the literature of other countries. Engels is hardly ever mentioned, except in rare instances where he appears as a minor figure.)

Biraghi's sources are found in the literature of the *Kathedersozialisten*. His authors are the Adler of *Rodbertus, der Begründer des wissenschaftliches Sozialismus*, the Meyer of *Emanzipationskampf des vierten Standes*, Wagner, etc. Marx, then, appears as a continuer of Rodbertus's great work, and his originality stems from the fact that he added to the former's theories 'the revolutionary organization of the party'. Furthermore - and here we have a rather significant cliché with an international circulation - Marx had a 'reserved and contemptuous character, arrogant beyond measure, and was a Communist with no heart and no affections. Absolutely devoid of any ideals, Marx saw the social question only in terms of a material interest, in the interest of his stomach.'[6] And so on, with similar banalities.

Along a slightly different line - nearer to the literature in French by Reybaud, Guyot, D'Eichtal, etc. - we have Scarabelli's text on socialism and the class struggle (*Il Socialismo e la lotta di classe*) which both Engels and Labriola mention in their criticism, according to which Marx's theory of value is the following:[7]

> According to Marx capital is the value which every year, every day, is cheated out of the mass of workers who toil, for example, for twelve hours while their pay is compensation for only six or eight hours, so that the product of six or four hours for each worker is enjoyed by the entrepreneur who gets richer and richer.

This is a literature whose origins are partly academic, partly journalistic, and it would be very interesting to do for Italy what Eric Hobsbawm did concerning the Victorian critics of Marx. It includes histories of socialist doctrines from Plato to the nineteenth century and manuals describing workers' organizations. Marx and Marxism play a leading role, with particular interest shown in the theory of value and historical materialism. Even if these are often works set up along the lines of an ingenuous 'scientific honesty' - it is enough to cite as an example the essay on socialism in Italy by A. Bertolini, an economist who was a student of Ferrara and of Pantaleoni, which serves as an introduction to the Italian translation of Rae's text[8] - socialist public opinion could certainly not hope to be well informed on Marx and Marxism by the Liberal economists, by Gerolamo Boccardo or the *Nuova Antologia*, that is, by texts which appeared outside any socialist tradition.

In the field of academic culture with socialist leanings, one point which we must consider is that of the meeting of Marxism with the positivist culture which in that period dominated many Italian universities. It will be useful to point out immediately, in order to emphasize the difference between the case of France and Germany and that of Italy, that at least as far as the meeting ground between Marxism and positivism is concerned, it was expressed only in a very low-level criminological culture, of which the case of Enrico Ferri is the most significant.

Ferri, who was considered one of the most prestigious authors in socialist culture during the period of the Second International - less, perhaps, in Germany than elsewhere, even if Kautsky's highly critical review of *Socialismo e scienza positiva* in the *Neue Zeit* arose from the fact that in Germany as well the book appeared in a prestigious series published by Otto Wigand[9] - was also one of the highest officials of the Italian Socialist Party, for a long time editor of *Avanti!*, and one of the leading stars in the firmament of Italian socialist culture. Without quite reaching Gramsci's flavourful definition of him, Antonio Labriola wrote to Engels in protest at Ferri's contribution to *Vorwärts*: 'That among German Socialists there are some imbeciles, is quite possible. But that the *organ* of the party should teach such *Marxism* to its readers, is just too indecent.'[10] It was, in fact, Ferri who was at the origin of one of the interpretations of Marxism dominant in the party. His synthesis of Darwinism and Marxism has nothing in common with Kautsky's. Like many of his colleagues, Ferri's knowledge of Marx was rather hit-or-miss; he appears not to have gained a great deal from reading the French edition of *Das Kapital* and one gathers from a number of his observations that he must have just read it a bit here and there and have been put off by the difficulty of the work.[11] This did not however keep him from offering confident and adventurous definitions: Marx 'gave scientific expression to the logical applications of experimentalism'; Marx, had completed the trinity of 'the two theories of telluric determinism (Montesquieu, Buckle and Matschnikoff) and anthropological determinism' with his 'economic determinism'; Marx had expressed the great idea that 'the economic phenomenon is the basis and the condition of every other human and social expression', an idea, Ferri continued, that answered to the biological law 'according to which function is determined by the organ and every man is the result of innate and acquired conditions'.[12]

Reflecting on similar grotesque formulations not only throws into sharp focus the interpretation of Marxism which was given by the man whom many contemporaries considered one of the major exponents of Marxism itself (the definition appears in a great number of the reviews of Ferri's works appearing all over the world); it also serves to give an idea of a climate and a cultural environment of which Ferri was only the tip of the iceberg. And thus we can understand Turati better, since he was breathing in and giving out a similar cultural air, and perhaps we can also give a slightly different meaning to the effort to affirm and spread Marxism that in those same years was being made by the burgeoning Italian Socialist Party.

In the pages of *Critica sociale*, as in *La Lotta di classe* - the periodicals whose characteristics allow us to consider them the two most influential periodicals of the party - we can observe the first conscious and programmed presentation of Marxism as the dominant doctrine of the party and of the party as a Marxist party. The weekly is called 'the class struggle', *La Lotta di classe* (a concept which is itself considered the symbol of Marxism); its sub-title is the *Manifesto*'s motto, 'Workers of the world, unite!'; and it publishes numerous texts by Marx and Engels in its Appendix. The same and more can be said of *Critica sociale*, which did not stop at the publication of classic texts which some might even have considered a bit dated, but went on to publish 'Marxist' contributions of a more political nature, whether by Marx or Engels or by their disciples across the Alps.[13]

But what effect did these publications, these texts, have on the formation of the party's ideology? Were they read and quoted, did they have any weight in the formation of the ideals of Italian socialists? Questions of this sort can be answered satisfactorily only after sufficient research, especially in the bibliographical field, and a close analysis of the party press - as Michelle Perrot did in her review of Willard's book - or in the area of publishing, the local popular libraries (bibliotecha popolari), etc.[14]

On the basis of preliminary surveys, I think I can affirm that the first result of this plan for the dissemination of Marxism was a kind of popular simplification. In the first instance there was a simplification of the doctrine itself - and this not only in Italy - such as that expressed by Stern's little book in the series 'Bibliotechina della Critica Sociale', *Karl Marx's Theory of Value Explained to the People*, about which Croce wrote that it gave a 'macaronic' version of Marx's theory - and he was right.[15] But along with these we should mention the reduced versions of *Das Kapital* which appeared in the press and which take their place alongside the by now classic books by Cafiero and Deville as well as those, lesser known, by Ettore Fabietti.[16] In a second stage there was a further, even poorer and more barbaric elaboration of the Darwinist-Marxist theme.

Examples of third- and fourth-hand expositions of the fusion between Marxism and Darwinism are so numerous and so completely at the heart of Italian socialist culture at the beginning of the 1890s, that we can limit ourselves here to a simple mention of them.

According to Carlo Monticelli, who is one of the principal popularizers of eclectic socialism with a pronounced sentimental accent - he, in fact wrote, 'social' poems such as the following: 'You who refuse bread to the hungry/ And spend a thousand lire for a jewel/ You who lend a featherbed to a dog/ And don't give a glance to the poor man' - according to Monticelli, as I was saying, the interpretation of bourgeois society and the class struggle from the point of view of Darwinist Socialism was well represented by this fable used by Colajanni:[17]

> Two individuals are running a race. One has strong legs, but must go by foot. The other is lame and crippled, but goes by carriage. Who wins? The one who has the stronger and sinewy heels? No: the other, who is helped by his comfortable carriage and nimble steed. And thus it is in life.

The results of these processes of simplification, that one could say concerned the social sciences as a whole, did not certainly remain limited to the field of intellectual debate. This Marxism *sui generis* was projected directly on to the field of the analysis of contemporary society, into the area - which concerned the Socialist Party - of political and historical forecasting.

Anyone, for example, who wished to pass the time analysing the concept of revolution as it is expressed in the party's publications from the mid-1890s, would easily discover the number and type of deterministic layers which enveloped it. In a significant discussion in the pages of *Critica sociale* in 1894 - and Kautsky in the *Neue Zeit* was treating the same theme in quite a different tone and accent - Turati is opposed to a Tuscan comrade on the problem of the relationship between 'revolt' and 'revolution'.[18] Turati's revolution is nothing more nor less than a natural event: he speaks of it invariably in naturalistic metaphors. The character of the revolution is like that of a fruit, prepared by the long process of ripening; the time required for its development is similar to that of human procreation, etc.; and the same can be said for the class struggle, which comes about - we read in *Lotta di classe* in March 1893 - even though it is not predicted and desired by the theorists, like the rain, fair weather, eclipses, and the phases of the moon.[19]

But we should also say that the constellation of socialist ideologies or, to put it more clearly, perhaps, the components of eclectic socialism with which Marxism meets, are extraordinarily more complex and rich than is commonly thought: there is not only Darwinism, or Mazzinianism, or Benoit Malon, or anarchism. There are other components as well which enjoyed a rapid and easy spread, perhaps also because of the forms in which they are expressed. It should be enough to think of the weight wielded by Tolstoyism, which carried over well into the twentieth century, or of Bellamy's book which, as elsewhere in the world, had enormous influence in Italy,[20] to the point of being mentioned in the party press: 'What strange luck small things have!' wrote C. Treves in November 1892.[21]

> First Bellamy's Socialist novel *Looking Backward*, and now an antisocialist one by E. Ritter, *After the Victory of Socialism*, have hundreds of thousands of copies circulating throughout the world; and they are certainly both read and discussed and reviewed and criticized more than happened

with Spencer's *Principles of Sociology* or even Marx's *Capital*.

And in the same Appendix to *Lotta di classe* which had published Marx and Engels there now appeared with a great fanfare William Morris's *News from Nowhere* and *The Third Defeat of the French Proletariat* by B. Malon.

Michels, in a page from his *Critical History* which, despite its anti-socialist orientation which makes it suspicious, is still worthy of note, gives a rich image of the 'great theoretical impurity' of Italian Marxism in the 1890s, its many unnatural matings 'with an infinitude of other systems, widely disparate, often at opposite poles from its method and results'.[22] Even Gnocchi-Viani - who was, in fact, known as one of the principal supporters of the Marxist school - 'quite happily represented', Michels observes, 'modern socialism as a synthesis of the theories of Fourier, Mazzini and Bastiat with those of Marx, who in turn was presented as a follower of the experimental method of our own great Galileo'.[23]

We must also add that in Italy, but not only in Italy, Marxism does not mean only, or above all, Marx and Engels. It means, in order, Lafargue, Deville, Liebknecht, some Kautsky, and Bebel. It means, therefore, in the best of cases, a third-hand popularization, and in the worst of cases a rough approximation of the overheard and the not read. Antonio Labriola was right when he complained about those whom he called the 'novices' who 'took as good coin the Marxism which was more or less invented by its adversaries'. 'The greatest paradox lies in this,' he added, 'the fact that many believe that the theory of value and surplus-value, as it is usually presented in easy explanations, contains, *hic et nunc*, the practical canon, the driving force, one might say the moral and juridical legitimacy of all the proletariat's claims.'[24] There still remains the fact, however, that despite the prevailing fashion, the texts by Marx or Marxists which were published in this period by the Socialist Party as independent volumes do not seem very numerous.

An examination of the catalogues of the leading publishing companies, which is a preliminary task for attaining to a knowledge of socialist culture, has not even been attempted. The Nerbini catalogue, which is the most important of these publishers, will be published soon, but we know absolutely nothing about Mongini or the *Avanti!* books, and the list could grow. Certainly, we can see from the little that it is possible to discern from publishers' advertisements appearing in the press that furthering the spread of Marxism was a task that socialist editors were not eager to assume. Of the approximately seventy volumes published in the *Critica sociale* and *Lotta di classe* series in the mid-1890s, the texts by Marx and Engels number only five. Some texts by Marxists do appear - but we should remember that Kautsky had minimal luck in this first phase of the socialist movement's existence in Italy - but for the most part the publications are low level propaganda pamphlets and works by people such as Loria, Bellamy, and Nordau.[25]

The Marxism manifested in these party publications was in essence an adulterated version of the Second International Marxism that characterized particularly German Social Democracy.

This Marxism, at any rate, was still at the origins of the party and of the political organization of the proletariat, as has been demonstrated by all the studies done of the origins of the Italian Socialist Party. Thus at this point, among many problems, there is posed the general problem of the meaning of this type of ideology in the history of the Italian workers' movement and the role it played - if indeed it played one - in the process of the emancipation of the proletariat from the hegemony of the dominating class.

There is a well-known passage in Gramsci that seems worth reproducing on this question:[26]

> The intellectual and moral (that is, religious) reform which in the modern age has touched the masses took place in two stages: in the first stage with the spread of the principles of the French Revolution, in the second stage with the spread of a series of concepts taken from philosophy of praxis and often contaminated by the philosophy of the Enlightenment and later of scientific evolutionism. The fact that such a 'reform' was spread in fairly haphazard forms and in the form of pamphlets is not a valid objection to its historical significance; it is not believable that the masses, under the influence of Calvinism, could absorb concepts which were even relatively more elaborate and sophisticated than those offered by this pamphlet literature. We are therefore faced with the problem of the directors of this reform, with their inconsistency and lack of a strong and energetic character.

The elements on which we must reflect seem to me to be two: the problem of the directors of the intellectual reform - to whom I have tried to devote the observations in the preceding pages - and that of the character of such a 'reform' among the masses. Let us try to put into focus this second aspect.

As we all know, it is not possible for us to get a satisfactory idea of what the workers and peasants were thinking as they were approached by the ideas of socialism in the years of the founding and earliest expansion of the Socialist Party. Certainly, their world, which was a world of poverty, sickness, and illiteracy, still heavily under the sway of the enormous weight of the Catholic Church and more generally of the ruling classes, is not likely to be able to offer us a direct witness to ideological or political tendencies. It is worthy of note, among other things, that the fact itself that some of the liveliest documents of the existence of the subordinate classes are those originating in the parishes gives the sense of a form of control which is both solid and efficient.[27]

Thus, as always happens, with very rare exceptions, we must be content with a few meetings between disparate pieces of information. Let us try to put a few problems into focus, such as: the forms and contents of everyday propaganda, the dialogues and debates, the socialist sermons which were often delivered to the faithful as they left the church after Mass and which confirm the idea of the weight exercised by the Church; and then the lectures, the socialist schools for the people, the solidarity campaigns; the daily local correspondence. From all this - and here I am anticipating a point to which I shall return later - we gather the image of a profound change in the life and collective mentality of the subordinate classes; it is the process accompanying the formation of the Socialist Party. Let us try to give a few examples.

The name and symbol of Karl Marx - aside from the 47 cm high bust publicized by the press or the hundreds of lithographs decorating Socialist clubs - begins to etch itself into the memory of the masses in a way that justifies our attention. In March 1893 a very large number of workers' clubs commemorated at the same time the twelfth anniversary of the Paris Commune and the tenth anniversary of Marx's death, and a consciousness of the process by which political autonomy is won from the bourgeoisie is expressed through the deliberate construction of new symbols, in which Marx takes the post of honour, while some protest that Mazzini is left aside. Something takes place that was not, nor could ever be an easy process in the mentality of the subordinate classes: the symbols and the traditions of the bourgeoisie are refused, the mythology of the Risorgimento and patriotism. *Lotta di classe* wrote on 12 March 1893, concerning the commemorations of Marx and the Commune: 'Little by little the conscience of the masses, which is being penetrated by the new truths, detaches itself from the old patriotic holidays and celebrations, whose falsity becomes ever more apparent and which can no longer be anything but the celebrations of the bourgeoisie and its victories.'[28]

In the area of lectures, lessons, rallies, and the education of the workers, finally, absolutely nothing is known. Certainly, there never existed in Italy party schools like those of German Social Democracy or the Centre d'Education Ouvrière which De Man created in Belgium. On the other hand, there did exist the Societa umanitaria di Milano, the Humanitarian Society of Milan, and the group of Popular Universities (Universita popolari) which are the subject of M.G. Rosada's very interesting book.[29]

But, for the most part, these are later initiatives. In the period we are studying - between the 1880s and mid-1890s - the only initiatives of any import in this area of the spread of socialism are the lectures held in the workers' club headquarters or short-lived initiatives such as the school of propaganda which held two lessons weekly on socialism, created in Milan in the headquarters of the Unione Democratica Socialista (Democratic

Socialist Union) in Via S. Piero all'Orto.[30]

Research into the ideological and cultural contents of such activity would be extremely interesting, even if, as I believe, it would substantially confirm the image given by the propaganda pamphlets, manuals, and periodical press. But I feel that a problem of this nature should be faced from another point of view as well: what did these lectures mean in the context of the workers' history? We must repeat that they were a great novelty in the collective life of thousands of workers. Twenty chairs gathered around a tavern table, as we sometimes read in the local reports in the workers' newspapers, guaranteed at least a minimum of 'socialization' and an inversion of the tendency towards isolation of the family nucleus especially in the country-side, and the same can be said with even more reason about the Socialist clubs, which were the fundamental structure of the party organization. The themes were almost always the general ones of socialism and workers' politics: What is socialism? How can it be attained? etc. But it is interesting as well to see how everything changes at the end of the century and how the themes move to parliamentary struggles and most specifically to the reforms for which the Italian Socialist Party was fighting. Some basic surveys of police records have convinced me that such research is feasible.[31]

But, and this is another important point which we must remember, the proletariat was not obliged only to listen. It spoke out as well, and became in its turn agitators and propagandists. Oddino Morgari, in a little book appearing in 1896 which was a sort of statute of the party, a behaviour manual for the socialist militant, gives workers the following advice:[32]

> They should count over the reasons which to them were most convincing; reread them; recite them as they walk down the street, as with school lessons; copy them, if necessary, into a notebook; and ask friends for any necessary explanations. A few months of such intellectual exercise will be enough to make them familiar with all the subjects which appear most frequently in discussion and debate; what is more, they will learn to know the party's tactics, its strengths, its men, its history. They should also study some of the less expensive pamphlets, which contain a summary of the Socialist idea, and as they go they should practice repeating mentally its contents. In fact, they should take long walks with just this purpose. These valiant workers must not be discouraged; they should read, read diligently. In a short time they too will be able to communicate with others, and compared to the haughty fops of the bourgeoisie, even if these latter do have university degrees, the workers with calloused hands will seem knowledgeable.

Karl Marx was a frequent companion on these walks, even if in general it is difficult to say what he actually represented. The very fact that in order to describe his characteristics comparisons were made with other great thinkers gives an idea of the veil which continued to cover him; in economics, or in social questions, he was from time to time Darwin, Spencer, Moses. Nor was the propagandist's life an easy one, as Morgari intimates to us when he speaks of the debates. Gramsci, in a text that I want especially to remember here, gives a beautiful image of the condition of the man of the masses: a man who does not know how to argue with the supporter of a point of view with which he does not agree but who is none the less his intellectual superior, and who takes refuge in a sort of class faith, a faith in arguments that he is not able to repeat but that he feels belong to his social group.[33]

Socialist propaganda is full of this Marxism which is learned 'by ear' and whose substance its proponents no longer know how to argue. Often, for example, we find expressed in propaganda pamphlets or in newspaper articles the concept that Marx's theories, resisted and refuted by academic critics which one does not know how to fight, will, however, be valid and true in a more or less distant future. This is the case with the curious affirmation by Romeo Candelari who, intending to answer De Laveleye's confutation of the theory of value, affirms that Marx's theory would be valid only after the socialist revolution and that therefore every attempt to refute it was useless.[34] It is difficult, faced with this and similar widespread affirmations and formulas, not to recall another passage from Gramsci's prison notebooks in which mechanical determinism is assumed as 'a formidable force of moral resistance, cohesion, obstinate and patient perseverance. "I am momentarily defeated, but the force of things is working for me in the long run, etc." One's actual desire is transmuted into an act of faith, into a certain rationality of history...'[35]

What should I say to conclude this chapter? That research of this sort, interested above all in the mechanisms of the spread of Marxism, and thus in the road that Marxism followed in its movement towards the simple militants, presents a problem which is difficult to solve: on one hand, a Marxism which has been impoverished and reduced to an outline, a simple summary, or dismembered into various parts which take on a life of their own (historical materialism, theory of value, class struggle, etc.); on the other, the fact that this ideology, this component of the collective mentality lives on and brings about processes of emancipation and liberation that are at the heart itself of the history of the workers' movement.

One could wish that Marxism were 'pure' and that the organized workers' movement were a sort of cloak over the revolutionary spirit of the masses. But, until the contrary is proven, exactly the opposite is true, and because of just this fact the contradiction lives on undaunted before our eyes and in the face of our research

Translated by Susan Scott Cesaritti

NOTES

1 See E. Santarelli, *La revisione del marxismo in Italia. Studi di critica storica*, revised and enlarged edition, Milan, 1977, which contains a useful bibliography.

2 For a general analysis of these problems, see F. Andreucci, *La diffusione e la volgarizzazione del marxismo*, in *Storia del Marxismo*, II, *Il marxismo nell'eta della Seconda Internazionale*, Turin, 1979, pp. 5-58.

3 A. Pagliaini, *Catalogo generale della libreria italiana dall'anno 1847 a tutto il 1899*, 3 vols, Milan, 1901-1905; R. Michels, *Storia del marxismo in Italia. Compendio critico con annessa bibliografia*, Rome, 1909.

4 *Il socialismo contemporaneo di Giovanni Rae, prima traduzione italiana autorizzata dall'autore*. With a note on socialism in Italy by Angelo Bertolini, Firenze, 1889.

5 G. Biraghi, *Socialismo*, Milan, 1896.

6 Ibid., pp. 94-102.

7 I. Scarabelli, *Il socialismo e la lotta di classe*, Ferrara, 1894. For a note on Labriola, cf. *La corrispondenza di Marx ed Engels con italiani 1848-1895*, ed., G. Del Bo, Milan, 1964, p. 595.

8 *Il socialismo contemporaneo di G. Rae*.

9 See Kautsky's book, *Darwinismus und Marxismus*, which takes up the thread of his review of Ferri's book in *Die Neue Zeit*, XIII (1894-5), vol. 1, pp. 709-16.

10 See *La corrispondenza di Marx ed Engels con italiani*, p.612.

11 For a confirmation of my views, see 'Enrico Ferri', in F. Andreucci and T. Detti, *Il movimento operaio italiano. Dizionario Biografico 1853-1943*, vol. II(Cec-J), Rome, 1976, pp. 342-8.

12 E. Ferri, *Socialismo e scienza positiva (Darwin Spencer Marx)*, Rome, 1894, p. 156. But see, in general, the whole of chapter XIV, with the significant title, 'Marx completa Darwin e Spencer'.

13 Particularly in the first years of its existence, *Critica sociale* published numerous writings as well as those of Marx and Engels by Lafargue, Plekanov, Bebel, Liebknecht, etc. Cf. the useful indices of the review edited by M.T. Lanza in *Critica sociale*, by M. Spinella, A. Caracciolo, P. Amaduzzi and G. Petronio, vol. III, Milan, 1959.

14 Cf. M. Perrot, 'Les guesdistes: controverse sur l'introduction du marxisme en France, in *Annales*, XXII (1967), pp. 701-10, the important volume by C. Willard, *Le mouvement socialiste en France (1893-1905): les guesdistes*, Paris, 1965. See also M.G. Rosada, 'Biblioteche popolari e politica culturale del PSI tra Ottocento e Novecento', in *Movimento operaio e socialista*, 1977, no. 2-3.

15 G. Stern, *La teoria del valore di Carlo Marx spiegata al popolo*, trans. G. Montalto, Milan, 1892; B. Croce,

Materialismo storico ed economia marxistica, Bari, 1961, p. 144.

16 *Il Capitale riassunto e volgarizzato da Ettore Fabietti*, Florence, 1902.

17 C. Monticelli, *Canti sociali*, Venice, 1896, p. 18; id., *Socialismo popolare*, Venice, 1897, pp. 81-2.

18 F. Turati and Un. Gregario, 'Rivolta e rivoluzione', in *Critica sociale*, III (1893), p. 182 *et seq*.

19 'La nostra intransigenza', in *Lotta di classe*, 18-19 March 1893.

20 G. Fink, *The Italian Controversy*, in *Edward Bellamy Abroad. An American Prophet's Influence*, ed. Sylvia E. Bowman, New York, 1962, pp. 324-51.

21 C. Treves, 'Strologia sociale', in *Lotta di classe*, 5-6 November 1892.

22 R. Michels, *Storia critica del movimento socialista italiano. Dagli inizi al 1911*, Florence, 1921, p. 135.

23 Michels, *Storia del marxismo in Italia*, p. 74.

24 A. Labriola, *La concezione materialistica della storia*, edited with an introduction by E. Garin, Bari, 1965, p. 200 (letter to Sorel, 10 May 1897).

25 Important notes on the Italian fortune of M. Nordau in E. Ragionieri, 'Un Max Nordau del nostri tempi', in *Il nuovo corriere*, 22 July 1951.

26 A. Gramsci, *Quaderni del carcere*, 'Edizione critica dell'-Istitute Gramsci', ed. Gerrantana, vol. III, Turin, 1975, pp. 1985-6.

27 A. Gambasin, *Parroci e contadini nel Veneto alla fine dell'Ottocento*, Rome, 1973. Deals with the subject of the transformation of peasant life in connection with the workers' movement and with socialism, E. Weber, *Peasants into Frenchmen. The modernisation of Rural France 1870-1914*, Stanford University Press, 1977, which was fully reviewed by R. Vivarelli, 'I contadini francesi tra il 1870 e il 1914 e il problema della trasformazione culturale delle campagne', in *Rivista Storica Italiana*, XCI (1979), pp. 52-70. See particularly at the end of this chapter, the timely consideration of the terms 'popular culture' and 'repression'.

28 *Lotta di classe*, 11-12 March 1893.

29 M.G. Rosada, *Le Universita popolari in Italia 1900-1918*, Rome, 1975.

30 On this question, there is much information in the columns of *Milano operaia*, on *Lotta di classe*.

31 Conference and committee reports can often be found in the personal files of socialist spokesmen, in *Archivio Centrale dello Stato, Ministero dell'Interno, Direzione generale di Pubblica sicurezza, Affari Generali e Riservati, Casellario Politico centrale*.

32 O. Morgari, *L'arte della propaganda socialista. Parte prima*, Milan, 1896, pp. 15-16.

33 A. Gramsci, *Quaderni del carcere*, pp. 1390-1.

34 Cf. the introduction by A. Bertolini to *Il socialismo contemporaneo di G. Rae*, p. VIII, commenting on the episode.
35 A. Gramsci, *Quaderni del carcere*, p. 1388.

13 THE PEASANT DREAM: RUSSIA 1905-7*

Teodor Shanin**

Умному ребенку

Dreams matter. Collective dreams matter politically. That is a major reason why no direct or simple link relates political economy to political action. In between stand meanings, concepts and dreams with internal consistencies and a momentum of their own. To be sure, their structure bears testimony to the relations of power and production they are embedded in and shaped by. However, such interdependencies are never one-sided. Patterns of thought, once established, acquire a causal power of their own to shape, often decisively, economy and politics: that is true particularly of the political impact of ideology, understood here as the dream of an ideal society in relation to which goals are set and the existing reality judged.

Doubts have often been expressed about the very possibility of studying peasant ideology or thought. Such an analysis can never be undertaken, so the argument runs, for lack of convincing evidence. Peasants differ between regions and between villages as well as within every village: the rich and the poor, the farmer and the part-craftsman, the man and the woman, the old and the young - how can one generalise about 'the peasant mind?' To make things worse, most of the peasant lore is oral, while most of those who write of the peasantry are outsiders to it - how can one trust such testimony? Anyway, collective thought is notoriously difficult to express, to record and to divine. Nor does it quantify easily and relevantly - a major sin to those to whom mathematics is synonymous with true scholarship.

Yet, on the other hand, a prudent refusal to generalise about peasant thought would also mean giving up the full analysis of

*This chapter forms part of a larger study devoted to the peasants and state in Russia at the turn of the century.
**Teodor Shanin is Professor of Sociology at Manchester University and author, among other books, of *The Awkward Class*, a study of the Russian peasantry 1910-25.

peasant political action, for there can be none without considering peasant goals. Nor would the problem be resolved by narrowing the analysis to a specific peasant stratum or to a single village. The same argument applies to each such subdivision, until one is left with many single, different and unrelated personas - a caricature of social reality if ever there was one. That is why the alternative often adopted was simply to deduce patterns of consciousness from the interest of classes, groups or societies. Such a short-cut, a substitution for actual consciousness of its presumed causes, is tautological and resolves little. The causes and context of consciousness must be explored, not postulated.

Can one provide any meaningful and significant generalisation about the collective thought of the Russian peasants. If so, is there sufficient evidence to study the peasant political ideology?

A major case in point may help us answer the first of those questions. The rules of inheritance within the Russian peasantry from 1861 to 1911, were never legislated by the state but explicitly left, at Emancipation, to the 'local custom' as understood by the peasant magistrates of *every community*. Our knowledge of the procedures which actually resulted is fairly good. Several intensive studies of the decisions made by peasant magistrates were undertaken by the Russian court of appeal. These studies concerned the decisions of peasant courts in many thousands of villages, differing as regards their history, climate, riches and type of agriculture as well as their interaction with the nobility, the towns and the broader economy. Besides the diversities, the studies reveal a repetition of the basic principles of inheritance and property relations throughout the Russian peasantry. This evidence is all the more striking in that these principles differed consistently from the corresponding relations operating within the other social classes of Russia as well as from the 'national', i.e. non-peasant, official legislation.[1] We are talking here of family property (as against both private and collective ownership), the non-admissibility of the will, the equal division of land between all resident sons and sons-in-law, the specific female property and so on. It goes without saying that these generic characteristics of the norms, views and actual procedures concerning property were closely linked with the nature of the peasant economy and the structure of the peasant households and villages. However, this was a link of mutual interdependence and not a simple reflection of the one in the other (whichever the 'one' and whichever the 'other'). The Russian peasant common law is central to any consideration of the peasant economy and its dynamics. To conclude, generalisations about the Russian peasant mind find justification in a major piece of evidence. This massive and strategic example should suffice to show that such generalisations are possible and, when justified, provide considerable illumination.

Despite the fact that a major part of the Russian peasants were illiterate, extensive evidence relevant to the study of peasant collective thought in Russia is available, representing in particular the political views of the peasantry during the period 1905-7, when thousands of petitions, resolutions of communal assemblies (*prigovory*) and instructions to delegates (*nakazy*) were recorded. They were addressed to the Tsar, to the government (especially after the Decree of 17 February 1905 which actually called for their submission), to the deputies of the Duma and to the All-Russian Peasant Union. The Peasant Union congresses also passed a number of major resolutions. Later, the peasant deputies addressed the Duma, putting the case of their electorate. A number of relevant reports by observers as well as by police and army chiefs and by state administrators about the peasant's views and moods are also available[2] and so are some memoirs of officials, nobles and 'intelligentsia'. The evidence is rich, if uneven, and within the heterogeneity of expressions shows considerable consistency of content.

One may begin the review of the peasants' views about the type of society they wished to see, from the debates and the decisions of the two 1905 congresses of the All-Russian Peasant Union of which the protocols were published.[3] A broad consensus was clearly established at both. While well aware of the limitations of their capacity to impose their wish fully on the Tsarist state, the peasant delegates showed considerable unanimity in their preferences. The ideal Russia of their choice was one in which all the land was to belong to the peasants, to be held according to a roughly egalitarian division and worked by family labour only, without the use of wage-workers. A pool of all Russian farming lands was to be established and the land-holdings equalised in accordance with the size of the family and/or a 'labour norm' i.e. the amount of labour of which the family was capable. Trading in land was to be abolished and the actual control of land placed in local hands. The local authorities, elected to represent equally the entire population, were to be invested with considerable powers, to oversee land-holding and redivide the land in case of need, as well as to run the public services, among which free education for all was particularly emphasised. At the state level, a parliamentary monarchy was somewhat more vaguely envisaged, with civic equality, freedom of speech and assembly, and 'compassion' as a major principle to guide the state policies - a semi-religious formulation of an idea not unlike that of a 'welfare state'. The officials were to be elected. Women were to be granted an equal vote ('which may help to fight against drunkenness'). Solidarity was strongly expressed with all those engaged in the confrontation with the government: the workers, the soldiers, the 'intelligentsia' and the 'ethnic peripheries'.

There was also a fair consensus at the congresses of the All-Russian Peasant Union as to the delineation of the evil forces which had stopped peasant dreams from coming true. Those were first and foremost the state officials (*chinovniki*), described succinctly as 'malevolent to the people' (*narodu vredny*). The squires, the Kulaks and the local Black Hundreds[4] were also named as enemies (in that order) but ran a clear second to the 'apparatus of the state'. In the major transformation aimed at, the squires were to lose their land, the Kulaks their ability to exploit the neighbours and threaten village unity, the Black Hundreds their capacity to perpetuate terror in conjunction with the local police. Some of the decisions voiced a moral-political consensus, relevant once more to the peasant ideal of society: rejection of the death penalty, a demand for general political amnesty, a denunciation of drunkenness and condemnation of the anti-Jewish *pogroms* as 'shameful and sinful'. Much of the debate was couched in moral, often biblical terms of the fundamental rights and wrongs, assumed to be as evident to all good men as the difference between day and night. An endlessly repeated statement 'Land is God's' is an example and a central case in point - a *Weltanschauung*, a moral judgment, a political stand, and a strategic demand, all in one.

The many disagreements within the All-Russian Peasant Union congresses mainly concerned the road towards realisation of these goals and not their nature. They were related principally to the issues of land redemption and the form that the struggle should take, i.e. how far it would be accomplished by revolutionary violence. To begin with the first issue, everybody agreed that the land of the state should enter the redistributional pool free of charge. A majority preferred the peasant control of Russia's land to include also the 'buying-off' of private owners, financed by the state, while a substantial minority objected to any such payments, for 'land was created by the holy spirit' and not being man-made should not carry a price-tag. An image of a peaceful and orderly transformation of land and power with a new consensus safeguarding the stability of that change was often referred to and was clearly at the root of the tactical preferences of the majority of the delegates. The issue of tactics was central to the Peasant Union's debate. The awareness of confrontation with the combined weight of the state machinery and the landed nobility, a confrontation which would grow harsher, was strong in the minds of the peasant delegates. The methods of struggle agreed on were the boycott of state officials and their appointees, the removal of 'loyalist' elders by holding new elections, the setting up of Peasant Unions' committees called upon to take over local affairs and the passing of resolutions formulating demands (*prigovory*) by the assemblies of peasant communes and *volost*'s. The very spread of the Peasant Union branches, district organisations and conferences, both legal and illegal, was also a direct challenge to and pressure upon the authorities. The November 1905 Congress extended the above measures by banning the sale or rent of lands, and by declaring that any increase in police pressure on the union activists would be countered by refusal to pay taxes and draft recruits. In line with the position taken by all the revolutionary parties and the Petersburg Soviet of Workers' Deputies, the November Congress decided to boycott the Duma - the Parliament granted - until a fully democratic electoral law was accepted by the government. At the same time, the All-Russian Peasant Union dissociated itself from the 'taking apart' of the manors (which was declared counterproductive but explicable in terms of the peasant grievances, bitterness and disorganisation).[5] Further progress in peasant organisation and an amnesty were to take care of that. The next step in the escalation of the struggle was to be a 'general peasant strike' (doubtless with the example of the success of the urban strike in October 1905 in mind). The general peasant strike would mean the withdrawal of peasant labour from the manors and the refusal to pay rent and taxes. Many of the speakers called for resistance by force (*dat' otpor*) as a way of keeping the 'forces of order' under some constraint. The possibility of a massive invasion and *de facto* take-over of the manorial and state lands 'in the Spring' was seriously discussed. A call for an armed uprising was considered but refused.

The attitudes to the Tsar were one of the major issues over which the particular mixture of peasant radicalism and peasant conservatism (or caution) found its expression. The state and its officialdom were rebuked and abused constantly, yet the Tsar was usually 'left out of it'. To some of the delegates, doubtless representative of a sizeable part of the peasantry, it was still the belief that the Tsar must be misled by some wicked ministers not to understand what was so self-evident to them. An increasing number of the peasant activists clearly knew better but voiced suggestions (especially at the November Congress) to continue 'not to touch him' as their villagers might not be ready for such a challenge and a split over monarchist loyalties might be disastrous. To nearly all the delegates, while struggle for the peasant control of all lands and a change in the local power were central, the attitude to the state, the capitals, and the national centres was more distant. A peasant delegate expressed this in a half-jocular, half-serious report to the November Congress. He proudly recounted his *volost'* assembly's reply to an official who, after listening to their debates about the future, demanded to know 'where did you place the Tsar in all that?' The peasants' answer was 'of him we did not speak at all'.[6] Schweikian wit and tactics of avoidance were still the old and tested peasant weapons, a fine way to face a puffed-up outsider and to draw a quiet grin of appreciation from one's neighbours.

The intellectuals watching peasant congresses often expressed surprise or dismay at discrepancy between the powerful rhetorics and the actual decisions. Members of the revolutionary parties craved revolutionary action. Peasant violence was reported all through Russia. At their congresses of 1905 peasant delegates spoke sharply of grievances and demands but did not endorse violent action (without actually ever refusing it either.)

Yet, that contradiction lay mostly in the eyes of intellectuals; every peasant assemblyman knew the difference between a true wish (carefully hidden from the 'outside', yet forcefully expressed to unite the assembly round him) and the recognition of the realities one had to live with. Every peasant also understood the simple tactics of any peasant market: to bluster, then try to settle by a compromise which secures the concession and is 'right' within the peasant code of propriety (*po chesnomu*). There was in such attempts neither surrender nor despair. The delegates of the mostly unarmed and land-bound villages called for an attack but were not ready (yet?) to adopt the tactics of armed struggle.

Peasants also knew the limitations of their own political organisation. To unite localised peasant power nationally and to do it effectively, one needed either a base outside, i.e. a revolutionary army or an established guerrilla force ready to march against the peasant enemies, or else some measure of legality which makes communication and unification possible. With the first not in evidence, peasant activists tried to make use of the second, while building up their power. They brushed aside advice to the contrary offered by the revolutionary parties, both the Social Democrat (SD) representative's proposal of a republic and the Socialist Revolutionary (SR) delegate's call for an armed uprising. The majority of the peasants, in the eyes of whom power (and particularly local power) was central, clearly strove to minimise violence, that is, to use it limitedly, selectively and on the whole defensively. These were not, however, the decisions of some distant opportunist leadership playing parliamentary games of respectability. The local reports showed the consistency of the opposition to the destruction of manors by the 'conscious' peasants on the spot, even though they did not usually break ranks when their villages went on the attack. Nor was there lack of courage in it all, for the extent of calm bravery shown by many of the peasant activists in the face of the pacification squads, prisons and trials was impressive and these were the very villages from which the Russian infantrymen who fought in the wars and the civil wars were to come. The sober realism of recognising the superiority of strength of the regular army in any face-to-face engagement was proven well enough by the entire experience of 1905-7. That is also why, all in all, the delegates of the peasant union seem to have represented the 'conscious' peasants' grasp of their own interests well. It was characteristic that the great realist, Lenin, admitted to just that.[7]

The representative nature of the Union's view of the Russian peasantry at large, was challenged at once by its contemporary critics. The popular press supporting the government and usually financed from its 'secret funds' ('loyalist' in government designation, 'reptile' to its enemies), promptly denounced the All-Russian Peasant Union as an organisation of arsonists and its congresses a conclave of the intelligentsia dressed up as peasants. At the other end of the political scale, an SR delegate to the November Congress (Studentsov) claimed that the congress was dominated by its presidium, representing intelligentsia and/or rich peasant delegates. That was how he explained the November Congress's refusal of the SR delegate's call for an armed uprising.[8] Shestakov, an SD Bolshevik representative at the July session, felt similar dismay at the peasant congress's moderation,[9] and subsequently explained, in a fairly similar way to the SR delegate, the refusal of the first congress to declare for a republic, its decision to give partial compensation to private landowners, and the November Congress's refusal to give the SD workers' delegates the privilege of addressing it and so of allowing the peasants to learn from the workers' superior revolutionary experience. Maslov, the major Menshevik theorist of rural society eventually accepted, like Lenin, the assumption that the peasant congresses of 1905 did represent peasant political thought, but claimed that they were socially an exclusive expression of the remainders of the peasant repartitional commune and geographically restricted to the areas where those existed.[10]

It so happened that these doubts and comments of contemporaries concerning the impact of the liberal or populist 'intelligentsia' on the Peasant Union came speedily to an acid and spectacular test. As already mentioned, the Peasant Union's decision to boycott elections and the mass arrests meant a veritable purge of Peasant Union activists from the first Duma. With the call for a boycott universally rejected by rural Russia, the peasant deputies were also mostly unattached to any political party. During the election campaign, the arrests and deportations of the rural radicals produced as pure a case as can ever be of peasants' choice uninterfered with by the political organisers of the day - in the language of a 1906 report about the pre-election atmosphere 'all of the political life in the villages seemed dormant'.[11] The impact of the authorities was mainly exercised through pressures against candidates deemed unreliable rather than through organising a faction of their own. The liberals of the KD, the only party which proceeded with a systematic electoral campaign, did little in the countryside and gained the support of less than one-sixth of the peasant-elected deputies.

The resulting first Duma with its massive 'non-party' peasant representation, produced a sigh of relief in the Establishment: the Duma's conservatism seemed assured. The parties of the Left agreed with this expectation, and so did the liberals. What actually followed sent a shock of surprise through the Russian political scene for a moment, drawing attention from the triumphant reaction following the defeat of the revolutionaries in November/December 1905. The largest group of the 'non-party' peasant deputies promptly banded together into a Labour Faction (*Trudoviki*), incorporating representatives from all over Russia, inclusive of a number of delegates from the Western provinces where the repartitional commune did not exist. Within a month the Labourites produced demands, both 'agrarian' and more general, which were practically indistinguishable from those of the All-Russian Peasant Union.[12] Any idea that some hidden agents of the Left or of the All-Russian Peasant Union had hijacked the peasant vote was dispelled by the political position of the peasant deputies who stayed outside the Labour Faction. To the further shock of the authorities, the KD majority of the Duma and their Marxist critics alike, the peasant deputies spoke what was described by a Soviet scholar of our own generation as 'the language of Socialist Revolutionaries',[13] one must add, in all but the desire for a revolution. Even the self-declared peasant conservatives and monarchists among the peasant deputies supported the agrarian programme tabled by the Labour Faction. Some of the peasant deputies from the ethnically non-Russian areas joined national factions ('the autonomists') which stressed the demand for self-rule along ethnic lines. They consequently objected to the national 'pool of land' demanded by the Labour Faction, but once again agreed with the rest of its programme. The peasant deputies who joined the KD faction supported, unlike the Labourites, redemption payments for *all* private lands but wanted them requisitioned in full and turned over to the landless and smallholding peasants. Cross-cutting boundaries of party allegiances, regions and ethnicity, the peasant land demands were well put in the words of the somewhat later instructions (*nakaz*) given by the otherwise highly conservative and monarchist Krasnichinsk Orthodox Parish of Lublin gub. to its deputy to the second Duma: 'You can compromise on all other issues but in the question of land you should join the extreme tendency, that is, without fail demand the transfer to peasants [*nadelenie*] of lands and forests.'[14] Not land alone was at issue. To a major part of the peasantry, the resolution (*prigovor*) of the assembly of the village Shnyak in Kazan gub. was clearly as relevant: 'Worse than poverty, more bitter than hunger is the suppression of the people by absolute arbitrariness/powerlessness [*bezprav'e*]. Without a permit, you cannot take a step, say a word or else it is a fine, prison or exile to Siberia....Instead of the courts it is the local police which passes all sentences.'[15]

The homogeneity of the positions taken by the present communities and the peasant deputies in fact increased even further after the government's 'declaration of intent', in the first Duma by which any takeover of privately owned land was flatly rejected. As the work of the Duma proceeded, the opposition of the peasant deputies to the government solidified while outside its walls the peasants' direct attack against the landowners reached a new peak in 1906.

The next stage, and one more test of peasant consistency of

beliefs and demands, came when the government banned the majority of the deputies to the first Duma from re-election. The second Duma, which met in 1907, therefore carried a new slate of deputies. Despite the heavy government pressures on the electorate, the second Duma proved more radical in membership than its predecessor. A quarter of the deputies of the new Duma were by now self-described revolutionary socialists of the SD and SR, another quarter belonged to the Labour Faction which increased considerably, a quarter went to the KD - a formidable opposition line-up against the government. The Labour Faction, nearly totally new in its membership and without any proper extra-parliamentary organisation to secure its consistency, promptly repeated all its initial 'Labourist' demands (i.e. the project of the '104'). Meeting directly after the enactment of the so-called Stolypin Reform, a government decree promoting the privatisation of communal land, it also showed unqualified hostility to this. An equal hostility was expressed in the instructions to the Duma deputies voted by villages all through Russia.

In the second Duma, a number of other substantially peasant factions (e.g. that of the Cossacks) once again came out in full support of the land demands of the Labour Faction. Significantly, even the deputies of Volyn' - the one place where the Black Hundreds swept the peasant vote - presented agrarian demands not unlike those of the peasant radicals elsewhere. In the ethnic context of Volyn' such demands were directed against the Polish nobles and Jewish merchants, which secured a victory for the Black Hundreds' xenophobic appeal.

Even the elections to the third Duma in 1907 still produced a massive peasant vote for the opposition. The new electoral laws had now stopped most of the Labourists from reaching the Duma, but those few who succeeded came to state once more similar demands and preferences. A major proof of both the substance of the peasant demands and the surprise and fury they caused was offered by a sequence of vitriolic attacks by government supporters and the right-wing parties on the Labour Faction. To give an example, one such publication described the Labour Faction collectively as a group consisting of people with[16]

> (1) half-way arrested natural abilities resulting from incapacity as much as from lack of a consistency which can be acquired only by good education, (2) incredible self-esteem resulting from supremacy over one's own ant-hill, i.e. an environment which is lacking in any culture, (3) untrammeled utopianism determined by a mixture of half-education and insolence, (4) a hate of everything which is cleaner, whiter, more sophisticated, - a type of hate without which the impudence and the utopianism would lose any meaning or justification.

The author clearly knew all one could know about class hate and about the depths of the deepest class gulf in Russia. His own emotions centred, typically, on the plebeian elite representing the mainstream of the Russian peasant movement and supported by considerable groups of workers, intelligentsia and some of the ethnic minorities.

While the deputies and delegates to the peasant congresses and to the Dumas argued out the demands and dreams of the Russian peasantry *in toto*, every village proceeded with its own never-ceasing debate throughout 1905-7. Scraps of news were endlessly re-told, discussed and embellished, printed sheets were read and read out, the thirst for knowledge seemed infinite. A rumour that a meeting was to be held or that a 'knowledgeable man' was visiting a village brought neighbours on foot, in carts, and on horseback from many miles away. The villagers also sent out delegates 'to find things out' and to invite 'an orator' from the local towns or neighbourhoods. A village in the south specified such a request, ordering its messengers 'to bring over a student or a Jew to tell of the news' while another village voted to offer payment of an 'orator's' wages from the communal purse. At the centre of this immense process of communication was not outside propaganda, but rather a grandiose and spontaneous effort at political self-understanding by millions of illiterate and half-literate villagers. In an endless, slow, often clumsy and ill-informed and over-heated debate, masses of peasants looked at their life and environment anew and critically. They conceived and expressed what was often unthinkable until then: an image of a new world, a dream of justice, a demand for land and liberty. For, once again, it was not only land which was in question.

It is usually the local evidence which is the most difficult to come by where peasant movements are concerned. However, for once, in Russia 1905-7, much of the peasant thought was expressed publicly, formulated and written up. An Anglo-Saxon parliament in which its members are free to act as they deem fit, would have struck the Russian peasants as distinctly odd. The experience of communal self-management taught them otherwise. A deputy was to be told specifically what he was sent to say - hence the *nakaz*, somewhat along the lines of the *Cahiers de doleances* of the French Estates General in 1789, but more direct as regards the legislation demanded. The authorities and especially the Duma were to be told of the peasants' hardships and needs - hence the communal decision (*prigovor*) and the petitions. Major waves of these documents corresponded to (i) the government's official call for legislative suggestions in early 1905, (ii) the peak of the All-Russian Union activities in November 1905 and (iii) the first and (iv) the second Duma in summer 1906 and spring 1907 respectively. The revolutionary parties, especially the Social Democrats, opposed the petitions to the government and Duma as Utopian and reformist, but failed to make any headway with that position.[17] The communal and *volost'* assembly offered a ready-made machinery for such actions, while, for once, the newspapers and the analysts publicised them broadly.

The direct and representative nature of the peasant petitions and instructions was manifest. The documents themselves declared time and time again 'we wrote it ourselves' (*sami sochinili*), to which the language used readily testified. So did the signatures, which usually began with that of the village elder (the document 'certified true' by his stamp) and continued with those of all the village literates. Then followed a long line of crosses made by the illiterates, declaring not only the support of a view formulated by somebody else, but direct participation in the wording of the letter or the decisions. The sophistication of some of these tracts, especially in areas from which every active member of the intelligentsia had by then been removed by arrest or exile, showed to what extent knowledge of politics is not chiefly a matter of books or of universities.

A collection of documents addressed to the first Duma from the villages of Sumara gub. offers a fair example of the species.[18] Of the seventy-eight items, thirty-eight were addressed to individual deputies, thirty-one to the Duma *in toto*, and nine to its Labour Faction collectively. They asked for land, for lower rents, for agricultural credits and for progressive taxation of incomes. They asked also for 'liberty', amnesty of political prisoners, free election of officials, free education for all, state salaries for the clergy (which would free the peasants from the necessity to pay their keep) and, for courts whose proceedings would be 'equal, prompt, just and merciful'. The leading complaint in its frequency, next to that of shortage of land, was that concerning *proizvol*, i.e. official lawlessness and the arbitrary nature of the local authorities' rule - the peasant's main antonym to liberty, self-management, and good order. One village told the Duma deputies that it did not take over the land of the local manors by force 'which could easily be accomplished' because 'a law is needed'. Many others called on the deputies to stand fast and not to yield over the basic demands. The villagers clearly appreciated, more realistically than the Russian liberals, what might happen to the peasant delegates who did just that: the deputies were told 'to bear their cross for they are the last hope' and 'God and their people will stand by them'. Last, a village assembly announced to the deputies its decision to close the local church 'for if there were a God, he would not permit such injustices to continue'.

A single letter to the Duma may be of particular interest here, representing as it did a deep stirring of the most neglected half of the peasant population. It came from the peasant women of three villages in the Tver' gub. who met in secret. Once again, no 'rural intelligentsia' was involved - the text was written down by a young pupil of the local primary school. The letter addressed to the members of Duma protested against the fact that while 'our men are quite ready to entertain themselves with us (*gulat' s nami rady*) they refuse to talk to us about the land and the new laws....Before now, they admittedly beat us at times, but serious matters were decided together. Now they say that we are not partners any more, for only they elect the Duma.' The women asked for an equal vote which is necessary 'to handle matters in a godly manner'. The Duma 'must offer expression to all: the rich as well as poor, the women as well as men, for otherwise there will be no truth on earth and no peace in the families either'.[19]

Soviet historians have attempted to analyse quantitatively the large numbers of peasant petitions and instructions available in the archives. Such a content analysis was performed on the above documents from Samara gub., on the 146 instructions from branches of the Peasant Union, on 458 instructions to the first Duma, on some 600 village petitions to the second Duma and so on.[20] Once again, the fundamental homogeneity of the results, concerning documents originating from different peasant communes and groups, over a huge country is the most striking. A comparison of the petitions and instructions of villages in the poorer (northern) part of Samara gub. as against those of its richer region in the south showed a more intensive participation of the relatively richer areas in the 'petitions campaign', these areas also laying more stress on the political demands. In general, in terms of the socio-economic indices, the participants in the 'petition movement' were said to be mostly 'middle peasants', i.e. both the poor (but neither landless nor the destitute *golytba*) and the better-off (but not the richest) within the rural population. The inhabitants of the larger villages were shown to be more active than those of the smaller ones. Overwhelmingly, any comparison of local evidence leaves the impression of mainstream similarities - a unified ideology, a dream remarkable in its consistency, overriding the socio-economic, regional and local differences.

The terminology of peasant political thought is itself of interest. Some of it has been referred to already. Words to express the new experiences and demands were sought and found in tradition or in legend as much as in the new vocabulary of the newspapers and towns. Some of it was produced by the intelligentsia, other terms came from the peasants themselves and entered the language of the educated. The 'golden manifesto' and the 'second freedom' expressed the hope in a decision by the Tsar to follow up the emancipation of serfs in 1861 by dividing the rest of the nobles' land between the peasants. The concepts of 'equalisation' (*uravnitel 'nost'*) and of the 'labour principle' (*trudovoe nachalo*) - i.e. the adjustment of the land grant to the extent of the family labour of each unit - were used by peasants and the intelligentsia alike. The Black Repartition (*Chernyi peredel*) and the global all-embracing commune (*Vselenskii mir*) embodied the most radical designation of change - world of peasant righteousness, of total and equal redivision of all land and of Russia as a commune of communes, with very little social space left to the non-peasants. There were some words which declined in usage signalling the new times.

The word 'humbleness' (*smirenie*), so often used in the descriptions and self-definitions of the Russian peasants of old, was fading away. The term 'strike' came to symbolise a class attack and a challenge - 'we have struck (*zabastovali*) the grazing lands' the peasants said of the land seizures in the south of Russia. The word 'student' became synonymous with 'revolutionary', and so on. The government press referred to all this as the infestation of the peasant mind by the 'rural intelligentsia' or else a proof of illiteracy or miscomprehension on the part of the peasant mass. Yet these were the new dreams which found expression in new words. One could not make them up synthetically any more than one could produce by stealth the political dreams which came to move masses of Russian peasants in those days.

The nature of the peasant dream of a good society which surfaced in 1905-7 was interlinked with and generated by the way of life we refer to as peasanthood: the specific economy, policy and communal life as well as the cognitions involved. This was what had underlain the stubborn consistency and generality of peasant 'dreaming'. Both comparison with other peasant societies of the day and consideration of Russia's past made it clear. The slogan 'land and liberty' expressed those dreams remarkably well as slogans do, i.e. it pinpointed the essentials without quite exhausting their full content. Production on the land, usually operating within a three-field system, with family labour as its main output, related directly to the demand: the land to those who till it and to them only. The idiom of survival was characteristic of and necessary to a way of living in which survival had been the essential goal for millennia. It meant also the deep suspicion of all other land-holders in the area and both the considerable tensions and the overwhelming unity when facing outsiders within every rural commune. Liberty was envisaged mainly as the freedom from external restraints. It was to a decisive degree the image of self-management known to all of the peasant communities, writ large and idealised. Education was mainly the access to literacy and to the skill of a village scribe - a badge of equality with the non-peasants as much as a way to new non-farming jobs for the 'surplus' son or daughter, who could be 'educated out' in that way. It was therefore definitely a 'good thing' and to be open to all of the peasant youth. The demands for charitable government 'fair and merciful courts', the election of the officials and popular control came as much from legends as from the rural life experience, mostly negative. Past traditions mixed with new characteristics of the peasantry in crisis - the type of crisis referred today as that of the so-called 'developing societies'.[21] The forms in which it was expressed have shown it clearly: cognition and terminology of conservatism, conventionality, patriarchalism, and semi-magical beliefs injected with new words, views and experiences and put to use to grasp and shape a rapidly transforming society and to understand a revolution in which the peasantry was massively involved.

The Russian peasant rebellion also prefigured some features of contemporary peasant unrest and revolt: (a) the 'crisis of authority' linked to the ecological and demographic crises as much as to the impact of markets and 'monetisation' associated with socio-economic polarisation and pauperisation; (b) the 'opportunities' granted by extra-rural confrontations which weakened, split and immobilised the powers-that-be; (c) the socio-political points of strength and weakness of the major peasant populations - their size, spread and monopoly of food production as well as segmentation, backwardness and low 'classness'.[22] Also the peasant demands were often legitimised by reference to the good old times i.e. the past rights lost unjustly - 'das alte Recht' for which the German peasants fought in the Peasant Wars of the 1520s, before and after. The non-economic aspects of peasant struggle must be seen also to understand its characteristics, stages and connotations. The Russian peasant struggle of 1905-7 has shown what was called in a different time and place the peasant 'moral economy' - a peasant ideology of righteousness - at the root of their revolt. That is where the patterns of cognition and dreams link directly into political confrontation and peasant war.[23] That is also why the ideas, words and symbols of the Russian peasants during the revolutionary epoch would have been more easily understood by peasants from far off, than by most of the well-educated Russians of their own generation. A few Russian poets like Klynev offered an exception but paid the price of being treated rather as a curiosity, tolerated for a while. The basic disunity between the *literati* and the ethnically 'their own' peasants often hid, at least for a time, the consistency and the rationale of peasant demands and dreams from the Russian officialdom and intelligentsia. In that, once more, the Russian peasantry was not exceptional.

Issues of consciousness and struggle cannot be disconnected from the Russian peasantry's past. In the most direct sense, its older generation still remembered the emancipation from serfdom in 1861, both the dramatic change and the many disappointments. However, one can and should go further back historically. There is enough evidence to show that well hidden from 'official Russia', the memory of great peasant rebellions of the sixteenth and seventeenth centuries was never quite extinguished in some areas of Russia, especially in the mid-Volga (to recall an area particularly active in the 1905-7 peasant rebellions, e.g. Saratov gub.) For centuries the state meted out punishment even for remembering Ryazin and Pugachev, the church anathemised them, yet legends were told, ballads sung and millennial dreams woven - well described by a writer as a veritable 'samizdat of those illiterate'. Those songs and legends carried the message of peasant defiance, but also some basic ideas round which new ideology could take shape. The idea of turning all the peasants of Russia into Cossacks, i.e. independent, free, armed and self-ruling peasant communities - was remembered: the model used by Ryazin and Pugachev alike was that of the Cossack *Krug*. The call for land for all and war on the landowners, on officials and on corrupt clergy and even the tale of the 'just Tsar' whose 'golden manifesto' was hidden by evil advisors, were all still in use in 1905-7. Some of it was carried through centuries by the Old Believers' sects who added to it a specially xenophobic dimension - to them Tsar Peter was the symbol and root of oppression as well as of devilry - an anti-Christ invented by the Germans.

This historical consistency of the political ideas of the Russian peasants was expressed in relation not only to the past but also to the future. 1907 and the end of the revolution left the Russian peasant with more tangible results than any other social group which rebelled. Those who fought for a republic seemed utterly defeated, the main organisations of the intelligentsia and workers suppressed, the liberals' parliamentary dream caricatured and rendered powerless in the third Duma. Russian peasants did not receive all the Russian land they fought for and the 'liberty' they demanded. However, a considerable amount of land was now rapidly being transferred into peasant hands, admittedly benefiting more the better-off, but not exclusively. The sales of lands of the nobility to peasantry and the Peasant Bank activities peaked dramatically from 1906 onwards. Also, most of the peasant debt was cancelled by the state. More generally, the authorities were taught a major lesson with regard to the peasants' anger, of their potential strength and something of the limitations of their patience, a lesson which nobody was likely to forget for a while. Yet, the majority of the Russian peasants were neither mollified nor ready to retreat from their basic demands.[24] The *prigovory, nakazy*, the reports and the election results and the reports of the police show that while the mass of the peasants was silenced by 1907, they remained dissatisfied, they knew it clearly and more than ever before were conscious of the class divisions, the political camps and the possible alternatives they faced. Not only land and abject poverty remained at issue, but also the societal division, fundamental and sharp, into the peasant 'us' and the variety of 'them': the state, the nobility and the 'clean quarters' of the city, the uniforms, the fur coats and the golden spectacles, or even the elegantly rolling phrase. Within a decade this peasant awareness and self-awareness as well as the political dreams deeply rooted within peasant practice and crystallised by the 1905-7 experience, came to play a decisive role in a new revolution and a revolutionary war which ended differently from 1905-7 and made Russia, for a while, more peasant than ever before or ever after.

NOTES

1 See chapter 2 which used in particular the codification of peasant common law by V. Mykhin, *Obychnyi poryadok nasledovaniya u krest'yan*, St Petersburg, 1888.
2 E.g. the reports of the governors of the provinces and of the officers in charge of pacification and of the punishment expeditions collected in *Revolyutsiya 1905 goda i samoderzhavie*, Moscow, 1928.
3 *Uchreditel'nyi s'ezd vserossiiskogo krest'yanskogo soyuza*, (Protokol), Moscow, 1906; *Protokoly delegatskogo soveshchania vserossiiskogo krest'yanskogo soyuza*, Moscow, 1909.
4 A xenophobic monarchist organisation known for its physical attacks and intimidation aimed at the radicals, the non-Russians (especially Jews) and others suspected of liberalism.
5 'When strong we got our way by peaceful means, when split we turned to arson and similar means. As long as we are not organised, arson and bloody means will continue.' Report of a delegate from Minsk guberniya, *Protokoly etc.*, p. 61.
6 Ibid., p. 8.
7 'It was truly popular mass organisation, which has shared, of course, many of peasant prejudices... but definitely "of the soil" real organisation of masses, definitely revolutionary in its essence... extending the framework of the peasant political creativity.' V.I. Lenin, *Sobrannye sochineniya*, vol. 10, pp. 232-3.
8 A. Studentsov, *Saratovskoe krest'yanskoe vosstanie 1905 goda*, Penza, 1926, pp. 42, 46.
9 A.V. Shestakov, *Krest'yanskaya revolyutsiya 1905-1907gg v Rossii*, Moscow, 1926; V. Groman, *Materialy po krest'yanskomu voprosu*, Rostov, 1905.
10 T. Maslov, *Agrarnyi vopros v Rossii*, St Petersburg, 1908, pp. 277-81.
11 B. Veselovskii, *Krest'yanskii vopros i krest'yanskoe dvizhenie v Rossii*, St Petersburg, 1907, p. 138.
12 The 'Project of the 104', for the text of which see *Agrarnyi vopros v pervoi gosudarstvennoi dume*, Kiev, 1906, pp. 5-9.
13 M. Gefter in *Istoricheskaya nauka i nekotorye voprosy sovremennosti*, Moscow, 1969, pp. 22-3.
14 The archives of the Second Duma quoted after E. Vasilevskii, *Sotsial'no-ekonomicheskoe soderzhanie krest'yanskikh prigovorov i nakazov*, Vestnik MGU, 1956, no. 179, p. 132.
15 Ibid., p. 130.
16 Quoted from N. Vasil'ev, *Chto takoe trudoviki*, St Petersburg, 1971, p. 4.
17 Maslov, op. cit., p. 214; Shestakov, op. cit., p. 59;

Lenin, op. cit., vol. 13, p. 121; To quote chapter and verse, the whole petitions movement was described as 'the fruit of the governmental demagogery and of the political underdevelopment of the peasants' by the future president of the USSR, Kalinin, in the 9.8.1905 issue of the main Bolshevik newspaper *Proletarii*.

18 *Krest'yanskie nakazy samarskoi gubernii*, Samara, 1906, pp. 6-80. See p. 40 for a petition which carries forty signatures and 280 crosses to represent all of its households - a literacy index of 12.5 per cent for the heads of households.

19 Quoted after Maslov, op. cit., p. 308.

20 See O. Bukovec, 'K metodike izucheniya "prigovotnogo dvizheniya"', *Istoriya SSSR*, 1979, part 3. For the Peasant Union Dubrovskii, op. cit., pp. 111-13. Also for the first Duma sources see V. Mikhailova, 'Sovetskaya istoricheskaya literatura of krest'yanskikh nakazakh i prigovorakh', *Nekotorie problemy otechestvennoi istoriografii i istochnikovedeniya*, Dnepropetrovsk, 1972. The Second Duma found a much better coverage, especially in the works of Maslov, op. cit., pp. 282-8, E. Vasilevskii, op. cit., and A. Nilve, *Razvitie V.I. Leninym agrarnogo voprosa v teorii nauchnogo komunizma 1893-1916*, Moscow, 1974.

21 For particularly important work on the Russian peasant ideology and its early semantic expressions see Wada H. 'The Inner World of Russian Peasants', *Annals of the Institution of Social Science*, (no. 20), Tokyo, 1979, and his not yet translated book 'The World of Peasant Revolution' (in Japanese). His article has drawn in part on the recent works published in USSR by A. Klibanov, V. Kristov and N. Gromyko.

22 For discussion see E.R. Wolf, *Peasants*, Englewood Cliffs, 1966, part 4; T. Shanin, *Peasants and Peasant Societies*, Harmondsworth, 1971, part 4; G.M. Foster, 'The Peasants and the Image of Limited Good', *American Anthropologist*, 1965, vol. 62, no. 2; J. Berger, *Pig Earth*, London, 1979, etc.

23 For the major attempt to consider these matters see E. Wolf, *Peasant Wars of the Twentieth Century*, New York, 1969; Also J.C. Scott, *Moral Economy of the Peasant*, London, 1976; T. Shanin, op. cit., part 3; E.J. Hobsbawm, *Primitive Rebels*, London, 1963.

24 For evidence, see the investigation by I. Chernyshev, *Obshchina posle 9 noyabrya 1906 g.*, Petrograd, 1917. Also N. Perris, 'The Russian Peasantry in 1917', *Historical Workshop*, 1977, no. 4.

Politics

14 DRUIDS AND DEMOCRATS: ORGANIC INTELLECTUALS AND THE FIRST WELSH RADICALISM

Gwyn A. Williams

'I am giving you the Patriarchal religion and theology, the Divine Revelation given to Mankind, and these have been retained in Wales until our own day': it was Iolo Morganwg speaking in 1792, a stonemason Bard of Liberty from the Vale of Glamorgan and a leading figure, along with the vivacious societies of the London-Welsh, in a Welsh literary-historical revival. He was announcing to the Welsh the rediscovery of their ancient Druidic tradition; he was giving them, for the first time in centuries, a coherent vision of their own past, to inform and direct the re-creation of their Nation. He was offering them in his newly minted *Gorsedd,* or Order of Bards of the Island of Britain, a democratic organisation of their intelligentsia, a cadre of People's Remembrancers, as its instrument.[1]

A few months earlier, at one of the eisteddfodau[2] which the London-Welsh had revived in order to re-engage an interrupted tradition, in Llanrwst, a north Wales market centre of the remarkable stocking trade of an intensely poor and intensely Welsh mountain people, William Jones, a follower of Voltaire who lived in the village of Llangadfan as a teacher and country healer among the Welsh and Independent weavers of Montgomeryshire, circulated a dramatic Address. It announced that the Lost Brothers, the Welsh Indians descended from that brave and peace-loving Prince Madoc who had discovered America three hundred years before Columbus, had been found on the far Missouri . . . 'a free and distinct people . . . who . . . have preserved their liberty, language and some trace of their religion to this very day'. William Jones read the whole history of the Welsh as one long struggle against English oppression. He was composing a Welsh National Anthem, *Toriad y Dydd, Daybreak,* as a counter to *The Roast Beef of Old England* and he called on the Welsh to quit their Egyptian slave-masters and join their Lost Brothers to re-create Wales in the new Land of Liberty.[3]

A few months later, in 1793, Morgan John Rhys, a Baptist minister of Pontypool in the industrialising south, who published the French freethinker Volney in Welsh translation and would have published Voltaire had not his printers taken fright, brought

*Gwyn Williams is Professor of History at the University College of South Wales, Cardiff. Author, among other books, of *The Commune of Medieval London, Artisans and Sans Culottes*, and *Madoc, the Making of a Welsh Legend.*

out the first political periodical in the Welsh language: *Y Cylchgrawn Cymraeg, The Welsh Journal.* Morgan John had launched a crusade for Protestant liberty in the revolutionary Paris of 1792. As the self-appointed Moses of the Welsh Nation, he was to ride the entire length of the new American Republic in 1794-5, to fight for a black church in Savannah, Georgia and for Indian identity at the peace talks at Greenville, Ohio which expelled the Iroquois from history. In 1795, he was to stand on 'the unbroken grass' west of that Ohio and, on Bastille Day, claim the American Frontier as a National Home for the Welsh People, a *Gwladfa.* In his *Journal,* he printed an Exhortation from a newly resurrected and Jacobin Madoc to the renaissant Welsh: *'Dyma ni yn awr ar daith ein gobaith',* 'Here we are now on the journey of our hope.'[4]

In the 1790s, a handful of intellectuals in Wales, in common with men like them from other 'non-historic' peoples in Europe, those antiquarians, historians, poets, of the Czechs, the Catalans, Serbs, Croats, who were stamping nations out of the ground and weaving new tricolours out of old legends, summoned the Welsh to the re-creation of a Nation they had rediscovered. When they encountered indifference, hostility and repression in the Great Britain of the age of Atlantic revolution, they tried to transport that nation across the Atlantic.

This Welsh Nation of the intellectuals was born of an alternative society which had been slowly forming in Wales under the carapace of the gentry-parson squirearchy and which, no less than that ancien régime, was a product of Great Britain with its Atlantic dimension.

WELSH IN A GREAT BRITAIN

Great Britain took shape around the union of England and Scotland in 1707 and was built on merchant capitalism, imperialism, naval power and liberal oligarchy. In its sweep to maritime supremacy, its hegemony over the Atlantic trade with its slave economies, its agrarian modernisation with its unparalleled productivity, in its monstrously dominant capital of London, it evolved a highly unusual, indeed probably unique structure, in which what was in fact a multi-national state achieved a British uniformity and created a British nation, sanctified during the traumatic experience of the generation-long war against revolutionary and Napoleonic France, when Wellington and Nelson were erected into *British* heroes and 'God Save Great George Our King' into a *British* national anthem.

The battles of the seventeenth century had destroyed absolutism and demystified monarchy, had established a Bank of England, religious toleration, a governing aristocracy which directed the state to mercantile and increasingly bourgeois objectives. They had created a powerful civil society and a parliament which could hire kings from the Dutch and the

Germans. When the partisan conflicts of the later Stuarts were over, this polity, after disarming the English provinces and putting through a prudent restriction of the franchise, was able to ride commercial and agrarian growth into an extraordinarily relaxed and informal pattern of government.

It had to tolerate a licensed area of popular anarchy in times of dearth. It erected a law in defence of property and oligarchy which was terrifying in its severity but, except at moments of crisis, tolerant in its application.[5] It won a 'moment of consent' which lasted over a century and which acquired popular depth and resonance during the wars against revolutionary France. The government of this Great Britain reduced politics to the play of predatory faction around a Whig core under a broad, flexible, ruthless, semi-capitalist and innovatory oligarchy which, in its hustings, its licensed mobs, its flexible web of libertarian traditions and its Freeborn Englishman mentality (systematised into an ideology in confrontation with the American and French Revolutions) permitted the commons a voice.

This remarkable state, out of which a British *nation* emerged into historic existence, seems to be taken for granted by English historians. Frustrated and aspirant Europeans of the eighteenth century certainly perceived it as extraordinary; many took this modern 'Republic of Venice' as their model. Within it, the Welsh, like the Slovaks during the Austro-Hungarian empire, had 'disappeared' into the dominant partner. Their pattern of response, in both assimilation and resistance, was not un-Slovak either, though the organic intelligentsia which the growth of this Great Britain created in its Welsh province at the end of the eighteenth century behaved more like Czechs. For the effects of this almost insensible growth of Great Britain and its Atlantic dependency on Wales were far more serious than those of the seventeenth-century struggles, for all the latter's drama.

The economy of Wales, essentially a Tudor creation, experienced subtle but significant change. Poor and marginal in general terms, it may have been one of the few regions of Britain which still had 'peasants' (though this is becoming increasingly doubtful). What has been overlooked, however, is the extent to which it had already been penetrated, and was increasingly being directed, by merchant capitalism of an imperial character, with its attendant rural proto-industrialisation. Even the tiny and scattered charcoal furnaces of south Wales were producing a sixth of British pig iron in 1720. The Shropshire iron industry, going over to coal, pulled well ahead and by 1788 was producing twice as much. In that year, however, south Wales, still accounting for a sixth of British output, had seen the first giant and integrated plants raised by London and Bristol capital, derived essentially from the Atlantic slave trade and the Indian empire, and by Midlands technology, on its hill-country coalfield; it was beginning to use coal and, in the puddling process, the 'Welsh method', had just acquired the key to its meteoric expansion in the 1790s, when it established, and maintained for two generations, a 40 per cent grip on the pig iron production of Britain. In the mid-eighteenth century it was in no sense the virginal land which the celebrated iron-master dynasties of Crawshay and Guest allegedly deflowered.

Far more striking were copper, tinplate and their related industries. British production centred almost wholly on the Swansea-Neath area in the south, which was in turn linked to the mines of northern Anglesey, where Thomas Williams had established virtually a world monopoly. Copper, brass, tinplate (with a base in south-eastern Monmouthshire and its Pontypool japanning plants as well) were directed almost wholly to Atlantic export, particularly to the West Indies and the world the slave empires fed. The ultimate destination of south Wales iron is less visible, with Ireland looming large as an early customer, but this whole sector of the economy was essentially mercantile-imperialist in character.[6]

This was no less true, however, of more traditional, less organised and less capitalised trades which were turning whole tracts of rural Wales into networks of 'factory parishes'.[7] The cloth trade had migrated to mid and north Wales since Tudor times and was subjected to the Shrewsbury Drapers. Its farm-based production was turning the country people of a great tranche of Wales, running from Machynlleth on the west coast, in a broad arc through Merioneth and Montgomeryshire in north and north-centre to Denbighshire and the English borderlands, into a population of rural industrial workers with demographic and life-chance rhythms radically different from those of 'traditional peasants'. Most of that production went out through Blackwell Hall to Europe and the Americas. Even the poorer quality cloth of rock-ribbed Merioneth, and above all its intense stocking trade which could produce sales of £18,000 at markets in Bala and Llanrwst, went through the busy little port of Barmouth to Charleston and the Gulf of Mexico, to serve British soldiers, poor whites and American slaves.

Shropshire, whose technicians were revolutionising iron production in Glamorgan and Monmouth, was also stimulating growth on the north-eastern coalfield which, while ultimately abortive, was at first of a southern intensity and turned Denbigh and Flint into potent centres of innovation. In the late eighteenth century, in fact, the largest concentration of people in Wales was in the parishes of Wrexham in the north-east around the biggest fair in the Principality; 8,000 lived there. There were only 6,000 in Swansea which had developed, however, into a fully articulated if miniature, mercantile, social and intellectual capital. The whole south, like Denbighshire had a scatter of industry and improving landlords; the Vale of Glamorgan and south Pembrokeshire were the nearest approach to the champion farming country of southern England. There was a cluster of lively little towns, over-supplied with artisan crafts, professional men and printers, in Carmarthen, Brecon, Haverfordwest,

Neath, Denbigh, Caernarfon, and a brisk if forgotten fraternity of seamen, particularly numerous on the western coasts facing Ireland and the Atlantic. Even the 'peasant' society of allegedly self-subsistent hill-farmers had developed a major drovers' trade in store cattle which sent great herds into England, Wales's 'Spanish silver fleet', bringing back currency, breeding banks and its own peculiar guild of organic intellectuals, who were to prove of some cultural significance.

This lively if porous mercantile capitalism was transforming much of rural Wales, had created pockets of modernisation and reservoirs of technical skills and had turned the economy of a country measuring scarcely 200 miles from end to end into a plurality of modes of production. Major work has still to be done in this field, but it would appear at present that merchant capitalism had not effected any profound structural change before the explosive impact of industrial capitalism in the 1790s. To the human beings subjected to it, it appeared to operate on the margins and in the interstices of a population of about half a million who were still penned to the mountain core of Wales's hollow heart. The stockings which went out to the Gulf of Mexico from Merioneth were knitted by a poverty-stricken people who used to gather *en masse* over the winter in chosen farmhouses to save money on candles; entertained by harpists and singers, they turned the area into a legendary stronghold of Welsh vernacular culture, as it was later to be of Dissenting ministers and craggy polemicists over Biblical texts in the Sunday Schools. There was a very similar stocking trade concentration in the south-west around Llandovery and Tregaron in that land no less legendary in the history and mythology of Welsh-language popular culture and Dissent, the land which lived by seasonal migration to the lowlands and England, the Galicia of Wales and the district in closest human contact with the America of the Nonconformists. North Wales was passing from the control of Shrewsbury to that of Liverpool; Bristol enmeshed the south; the London-Welsh were still the main source of native funds and enterprise. Many of the Welsh, on their upland farms and at their treadmill of loom and spinning wheel, were trapped in a back-breaking poverty and an economy of unremitting colonial dependence, its most vivid symptoms the great droves of skinny cattle and skinny people seasonally tramping into England to be fattened.

Nevertheless, there was a panic over American Independence in Dolgellau in 1775 and it was when Barmouth was closed during the French wars that Merioneth, like Montgomeryshire and Denbighshire, lurched into its *Jacobin* crisis of proletarianisation, pauperisation, radicalisation and millennial emigration. Merchant capitalism, with its multiplying rural dependents, its small concentrations of urban industry, its colonies of skilled workers, its little shipping fleets, its merchants, salesmen and hucksters and above all, perhaps, in the crafts and professions it called into existence or nurtured to service it, was sending ripples of insistent change through slow-moving parishes. Throughout the eighteenth century there is a shuffling but visible rise in the numbers of artisans, craftsmen, professional agents of the service sectors, many of them 'on tramp', a notable increase in the strength of the professions, lawyers, teachers, doctors, a surprising number of them of relatively humble origin.

This steady rise of what later generations would call a 'lower middle class', moreover, accompanied a dramatic fall in the status of that numerically strong lesser gentry of Wales, a product of its old kindred social structure and a characteristic feature of its distinct identity. From the late seventeenth century, land-holding became once more an aristocratic and thrusting business. Under the spur of agricultural change and commercial growth, the great estate made the running. The lesser gentry of Wales could not stand the pace. They lost their traditional anchorage in the universities and the Inns of Court, in politics and parliament; they lost their toe-hold in the dominant culture. They shrank back into a merely local and precarious prestige and even there, they were challenged by the multiplying 'middle orders'. The consequences were serious for Wales's political structure and its sense of identity.[8]

By the eighteenth century, some thirty to forty parliamentary families, worth perhaps £3,000-£5,000 a year, monopolised Commons seats and the patronage which went with them.[9] Beneath them, the local gentry, the £500 a year men, perhaps twenty-five to fifty families a county, served as JPs with their parsons and ran the place through their country club of a Quarter Sessions. In some relatively affluent counties like Glamorgan and Denbigh, as many as 1,500 men could vote and the forty-shilling freeholder was a force. The tiny boroughs, forty villages in the squires' pockets, were well under control; voters could be created virtually at will to ward off local mal-contents or some new rich 'nabob' horning in. Before the constitutional conflicts of the late eighteenth century, genuinely political issues were largely absent and rarely disturbed the even tenor of traditional practice among the 20,000-25,000 Welshmen who possessed the franchise, though a challenge could turn elections into Eatanswill orgies and precipitate bankruptcies. Encrusted with its dependent interest groups, buttressed by its myriad hungry servitors and lubricated by deferential but robust Church-and-King ideologies which could find room for Welsh sentiment or sentimentality if safely antiquarian or anodyne in cultural content, the system worked well enough for its purposes and was to prove durable.

During the eighteenth century, however, there was a visible constriction in this system which opened up a kind of vacuum in Welsh society. A handful of great families came to exercise a virtual monopoly: dukes of Beaufort in Monmouthshire, the earl of Pembroke in Glamorgan, the marquis of Powys in mid-Wales. A profusion of Welsh heiresses, traditionally marketed during the Bath season, led to the installation of a striking number of Anglo-Scottish houses, Butes, Campbells and their kin. Together with the greater Welsh clans, Morgans in the south, Vaughans and Pryses in mid-Wales, Middletons in the north-east, Wynns and Bulkeleys in the north-west, they established in the early eighteenth century a political monopoly which lasted nearly two hundred years.

This process, coupled with the drop-out of the lesser gentry from serious political life, emptied that political life of any recognisably Welsh content. In 1830, Wales's own judicial system, the Great Sessions, could be abolished with scarcely an eye-brow raised. Within the church the situation was, from this point of view, probably even worse. The church was a broad-bottomed and Whig corporation; one of its bishops was accused of atheism by his clergy. The poor Welsh dioceses, treated as stations of the cross in a clerical progress towards cross-border redemption, saw absenteeism and pluralism spectacular even for this century. Clergy in the lower and middle ranges and the occasional bishop were in no way as indifferent to the Welsh as the Nonconformist nineteenth century was to claim, but much of the ecclesiastical establishment became marginal to its flock. Lesser clergy followed lesser gentry into a kind of limbo within their own country.

Several historians have suggested that there is a connection between this driving back of lesser gentry and clergy into a provincial obscurity and the growth of Dissent, the acceleration of the Methodist movement and the upsurge of interest in Welsh antiquities, language and history, all of which become visible by mid-century and intensify rapidly from the 1780s. Men of short purse, long pedigree and diminished status cherished local roots and developed an alternative system of values.

But an alternative system of values, alternative local leaderships, alternative ideologies, alternative societies in embryo, already existed in the quite literally trans-Atlantic world of Dissent and its fellow-travellers, in the strengthening communities of artisans, tramping craftsmen, local professional groupings, commercialised farming families with cultural aspirations. The peculiar development of Great Britain in this, one of its marginal yet mercantile and Atlantic-oriented provinces, was slowly but remorselessly prising its society apart, opening a gulf between classes and social groups depersonalising it and creating social and intellectual space for alternatives. In the late eighteenth century, this Great Britain, with the loss of its American colonies, suffered its first post-colonial crisis which was also in some respects a British civil war of the mind and heart, at the very moment when economic growth accelerated, industrial capitalism massively penetrated Wales and quantitative change became qualitative.

At that moment, a freemasonry of organic intellectuals from the excluded classes equally abruptly proclaimed the rebirth of a Welsh nation. They were unconscious heralds of a generation of explosive change which actually created one.

AN ALTERNATIVE SOCIETY

One major source for an alternative society lay in the scattered groups of chapels, societies and schools of Dissent, those inheritors of the Puritan Revolution of the seventeenth century who rejected the State Church.[10] Originally Calvinist, they had been granted limited toleration after the Glorious Revolution, but were denied full citizenship. The major affiliations had formed an effective pressure group, with a London committee directed at the Whigs and parliament, around the 'Three Denominations' of Independents (Congregationalists), Baptists and Presbyterians. In Wales, they were a small minority but an influential one, rooted in people of the humbler classes who were of some substance and independence.

Those 'common people' of Wales, the *gwerin* (folk) as they were later to be called in idealistic salute after their conversion to Nonconformist radicalism, were largely monoglot Welsh, though an instrumental knowledge of English, spreading from the borders and the market towns, was more widespread than has been assumed. They lived a Welshness in which the old language was dissociating into local patois, but in which survivals of the traditional skills of the highly-trained and exclusive guild of poets continued to exist among local groups and in local prestige, in country poets as the Welsh call them *(beirdd cefn gwlad)* and in which popular practice enshrined traditions, Catholic and pagan in origin, now shaping into a way-of-life strongly 'folkloric' in character: muscular games and sports, ballads, story-tellings, wordplay, complex contrapuntal harp-song, the *penillion,* distinctive communal and marriage customs of informal vigour, popular and generally picaresque festivals, erratically punctuated by beery and incoherent 'eisteddfodau' and penetrating a literature marginal to polite discourse through almanacs and 'interlude' popular drama.

Out of this world grew artisan crafts and some of the new professional groups and inter-penetrating with it was Dissent, cultivating an ambiguous, occasionally sympathetic but generally patronising attitude towards it. If Dissent were to grow, it needed to colonise and ultimately to control these people, but it was conscious of what it considered superior intellect (a consciousness which strengthened as it absorbed eighteenth-century science) and to a lesser extent (at least before its explosive expansion from the 1790s) its character as Calvinist Elect. To join Dissent was to distance oneself.

From the early eighteenth century, a time of relative agrarian prosperity which touched those service sectors of the 'middle orders' from which the sects drew some sustenance, Dissent turned in on its own intense intellectual life. This was in fact an immersion in the European Enlightenment which was to produce startling results when its evangelical passion was renewed in the challenge presented by Methodism and abrupt social change, which made the 1790s into an intellectual cauldron of competing ideologies in Wales.

Such proselytising energies as it possessed went into education and this carried it into the developing world of the Anglo-American polity. The Puritan regime had created the first state schools in Wales; out of their ruins and motivated by much the same impulses, handfuls of Dissenters and Anglicans of evangelical temper resumed the campaign, even under repression. In 1678 such people sponsored a new Welsh translation of the Bible which was distributed free in its thousands. Individual Dissenters like Samuel Jones in Glamorgan launched those Academies which during the eighteenth century grew into distinguished educational institutions, running behind the universities of Scotland.

From the early eighteenth century, these efforts meshed into a major evangelical drive for literacy in the service of saving souls which was strictly an Anglo-American phenomenon in a human Atlantic being created by British commercial and naval power and the transplantation of British communities. The Society for the Propagation of the Gospel and the Society for the Promotion of Christian Knowledge, together with societies for the 'improvement of manners' embraced Wales within their missionary and Atlantic compass. They achieved some success, but were limited in their effect because of their use of the English language as the vehicle of enlightenment.

It was from these endeavours, however, that a remarkable circulating school movement emerged, so striking in character that it caught the attention of Catherine the Great of Russia. Griffith Jones, an Anglican clergyman of Carmarthenshire, grounded his schools in the Welsh language; with a minimal reading and Biblical curriculum and the use of mobile teacher-apprentices, he geared his schools effectively to the rhythms of living and working of hill communities of the poor. By 1761, his people claimed to have taught nearly 160,000 children and anything from 300,000 to 450,000 adults over fourteen, when the population of Wales could hardly have exceeded 500,000. However inflated these claims, the movement clearly scored a success comparable to some of the more spectacular literacy drives of our own day. A supporter, Madame Bevan, maintained the schools after Jones's death, but on her death in 1779, her will was challenged and the system collapsed, to be replaced by the sporadic, if intense, work of the Sunday Schools of both Methodism and Dissent.

There were to be major losses in the first manic sweep of industrial capitalism, but a central fact of the eighteenth century is that by its final quarter, a majority of the adult population had become technically literate in Welsh. It was in that century that the Welsh learned to read. From the same period dates the real emergence of the Welsh press, that no less remarkable phenomenon which left Wales 'over-producing' printers, as it was later to 'over-produce' ministers and school-teachers, which equipped almost every little country town in

Wales with its press, to bombard the Welsh with a myriad journals, 'over-produced' in total sectarian dedication, to make the Welsh a People of the Book.

The Book, of course, was Holy. The Welsh learned to read in an almost totally religious context; they learned to express themselves in the language and imagery and concepts of the Bible and of Protestant sectarianism. And they learned to read during the Atlantic Revolution, that great tide of revolutionary aspiration and ambition which swept the entire Atlantic basin, from the Thirteen Colonies to France, the Rhineland, the Low Countries, Spain, Ireland and the Americas north and south.

This was one, though not the only or a major root of the Calvinistic Methodist movement in Wales. Its origins in the 1730s, though located in the same stir of 'moral improvement', were independent of those in England. The instincts it shared with such movements everywhere and not least in the American colonies - where the revival led by Jonathan Edwards in 1739 occurred at much the same time and inter-penetrated with it - were the more powerful in a Wales whose established church seemed remote and cool and whose people were robustly indifferent or hostile. The movement began within the Anglican church and for long remained within it, distancing itself from the older, and somewhat disconcerted, Dissent.

Young Anglicans, whether ordained or not, started to stand up in the open air and to bear witness, to ram home awareness of sin and, employing every device known to reach the senses as well as the intellect, to achieve that cataclysmic conversion, which had men and women 'born again'. Howell Harris, an outstanding preacher and organiser and a towering personality of somewhat psychopathic temper, started in Breconshire; Daniel Rowland, who could throw thousands into those public ecstasies which earned them the nickname of Holy Rollers, in Cardiganshire; William Williams, Pantycelyn, probably Wales's finest lyric poet, found his outlet in hymns which have become irredeemably central to a 'Welsh way of life'.

They did not become a way of life, however, until several generations later. The movement's growth was slow and molecular, though highly organised from the start, through its local *seiat* (society) and its *sasiwn* (session) into a federal structure, a church within the Church, plagued by repeated heresy and secession, but firmly controlled from the centre (they were, after all, 'precisians' as well as 'jumpers'). Methodists remained resolutely within the Church of England, despite growing strain and despite the hostility they encountered, especially in north and west, where the gentry could organise mobs against them. Their Calvinism was largely accidental, stemming from Harris's service as deputy to George Whitefield during the latter's American missions, but it hardened into a tribal identity, with orthodoxies, witch-hunts and sectarian fragmentation. When the Arminian (Wesleyan) Methodists penetrated the Calvinist fief of Wales early in the nineteenth century, the theological thunder deafened Welsh ears; the myriad documentary relics have since populated the dusty shelves of Welsh second-hand book shops.

As Methodism gradually accumulated a people devoted to 'vital religion', Dissent drifted in the opposite direction. As late as the early 1800s, a Baptist minister in the mushrooming industrial town of Merthyr Tydfil was hooted in the streets for trying to *introduce* hymns into chapel. Dissent's academies were open to the trade winds and the currents of Enlightenment, to Newtonian science and political theory. Their founding fathers had cut a king's head off, on principle; legally they were second-rate citizens. However respectable they became, their stance had necessarily to be somewhat political; their London committees were the first organised extra-parliamentary pressure groups.

The Carmarthen academy of the Welsh Independents succumbed early to heresies, to Arminianism with its relative autonomy for the human will, to Arianism, a partial denial of the divinity of Christ, to Socinianism, a total denial. Its controllers moved the academy about Wales in an effort to stamp them out; in 1743 it split again and in 1755 the Congregational Board in London temporarily excommunicated it. It was in 1726 that Jenkin Jones from Carmarthen took over a church in south-east Cardiganshire and began the process that was to turn a particular south-western district on the river Teifi into a persistent seedbed of rationalist heresy, the *Black Spot* of Calvinist demonology.

The schoolmaster-ministers of this tendency, which tended to breed or to appeal to mathematicians and scientists, exercised an influence out of all proportion to the group's tiny number. It carried the small Presbyterian denomination, whose name came simply to signify liberalism in theology (and politics). A particular conquest were the Independent communities (total in their congregational autonomy) of fairly affluent and literate Glamorgan and Gwent, with their comfortable Vale causes and their craggier hill-country chapels being taken over by workers from the new iron industry. Over a single generation, the *Presbyterian* families of the south-east, largely commercial and artisan in character, with a flow of recruits from the south-west, clustered so strongly around the new iron town of Merthyr Tydfil that they made it the base for the launching of a new Unitarian denomination in 1802. Out of the Unitarianism and the 'unitarian' impulses in other denominations, which developed considerable power through the industrialisation of south-east Wales and the central textile districts, emerged a new political tradition. In 1831, Unitarian democrats captured local control in Merthyr, Wales's first industrial town; they were to be central to the first phase of the Chartist leadership. It was two Unitarians who published Wales's first working-class journal in 1834.

Most of the people in Merthyr, however, came from south-west Wales and while Methodism was a minority creed in south and east, these people came in hot for 'vital religion'. As Methodism grew, particularly in the last years of the eighteenth century, its modes and practices penetrated a resurgent Dissent. Within the Old Dissent, the 'methodised' current ran harder than the 'unitarian' and in the opposite direction, away from science and politics, towards passionate, proselytising and systematically censorious personal reformation. Blank if not hostile to popular politics, its leadership, particularly among the Methodists themselves, could become a bilious form of intransigent Toryism. In the last quarter of the century, the older sects went into crisis. The Baptists, in particular, who in their upsurge rivalled Methodists as missionaries among the poor, entered a prolonged crisis from 1779 which twenty years later ended in schism.

The crisis was a crisis of growth. From the third quarter of the century, the pace of growth within Methodism accelerates; from the 1780s or so, Old Dissent follows. During the 1790s there were campaigns which resembled mass mission drives and in the first years of the nineteenth century, growth was torrential. When the Methodists were driven out of the Church by persecution in 1811, Nonconformists old and new may have accounted for perhaps 15-20 per cent of the population. By the first religious census of 1851, they outnumbered Anglicans on average by five to one; in many places the ratio was seven and even ten to one. In the early nineteenth century, the sects of Dissent threatened to become as much of a 'national church' for the Welsh as Catholicism had become for the Irish; their breakneck advance seemed to be turning the Church of England in Wales into a sick historic joke.

This is one of the most remarkable cultural transformations in the history of any people. A people which around 1790 was still officially overwhelmingly Anglican and Tory, over little more than a generation, became a Nonconformist people of radical temper. A major irony is that, in the process, an old frontier, that between the March and Welsh Wales, for five hundred years the frontier between innovation and conservatism, re-appeared in Wales. For the victory of Nonconformity was the product of a crusade from the south and east into the north and west. In the early eighteenth century, there were some seventy Dissenting congregations on record; only ten were in the north and those mainly in the north-east. The Methodist leader Thomas Charles who rooted his sect in north Wales and gave the Welsh Sunday Schools their characteristic form (a species of directed democracy of exacting catechismic self-education) made Bala in Merioneth the capital of the creed, but he had come up from southern Carmarthenshire. At the great Bapitst *gymanfa* or preaching festival in Nefyn in the northern Llyn peninsula in 1792, a climax of the crusade, seven of the nine preachers were from the south. The greatest Baptist preacher of his day, Christmas Evans, another southerner, made hitherto infidel Anglesey his fief. In the Dissenter breakthrough, it was Methodists who made the running in north and west, outstripping Baptists and Independents. The consequences were striking.

In 1823 Thomas Clarkson, the anti-slavery crusader, went on tour in Wales. As soon as he crosses from south-east Wales (where Independents, Baptists and Unitarians were legion) into Cardiganshire, the tone of his journal abruptly alters. Dissenters, now mostly Methodists, were much more under the shadow of an oppressive and aggressive Establishment; the gentry would not sit with them on committees. The social strain grew worse as he moved north. In Caernarfonshire, John Elias, a Methodist leader who towered over many Welsh minds like a Pope, with his Bulls of Bala, dared not meet Clarkson at home; they had to meet in secret in Chester. Not until he reached northeast Wales could Clarkson relax. He was shattered by the experience. Eastern Wales, he claimed, was fifty years behind England in its politics; western Wales fifty years behind the east.[11]

What does this mean, this re-emergence of an old frontier? It means that Methodist advance, with Dissent following up, visible from the 1790s, synchronises with the advent of rapid economic change in general and with the advent of industrial capitalism in particular.[12]

By 1796, the iron industry of Glamorgan and Gwent, with its mushrooming coal dependency, had outstripped Shropshire and Staffordshire, to produce 40 per cent of British pig iron. Some of the largest and most advanced plants in the world ran in a clamorous belt along the northern rim of the south-eastern valleys. The 1790s saw a canal mania in both counties, ribbed them with tramways. Along one of the latter Trevithicks steam locomotive, first in the world, made its run in 1804. Exemptions granted the port of Newport spawned a sale-coal industry run by Welsh entrepreneurs on a shoestring. Entirely novel communities sprouted on the coalfield, sucking in population from the rest of Wales and starting the process which was to wrench its centre of gravity into the south-east. Monmouthshire's population increased at a rate faster than that of any other county in England and Wales; Glamorgan came third on the list. Already the dissident south-west, with its riotous little capital of Carmarthen was being transformed into the human matrix and the service centre of a new industrial society in the south-east. At this stage, the transformation of the north-eastern coalfield was scarcely less decisive, with Denbighshire and Flintshire moving rapidly into industrial capitalism.

The most unhinging impact, however, was on rural west and north. The acceleration of industrial growth in England brought factors from Liverpool and Lancashire into the cloth country, to break the hold of the Shrewsbury Drapers. The consequences were complex: the emergence of petty local entrepreneurs, a sharp increase in pauperisation during the French war, a fairly rapid proletarianisation. 'Machines are eating people' shouted old William Jones in Llangadfan; Voltaire's prophecy was coming true, soon there would be nothing but tyrants and slaves. The first cloth factories rose along the Severn, at Newtown, Llanidloes, Welshpool, even in Dolgellau. Rural centres of

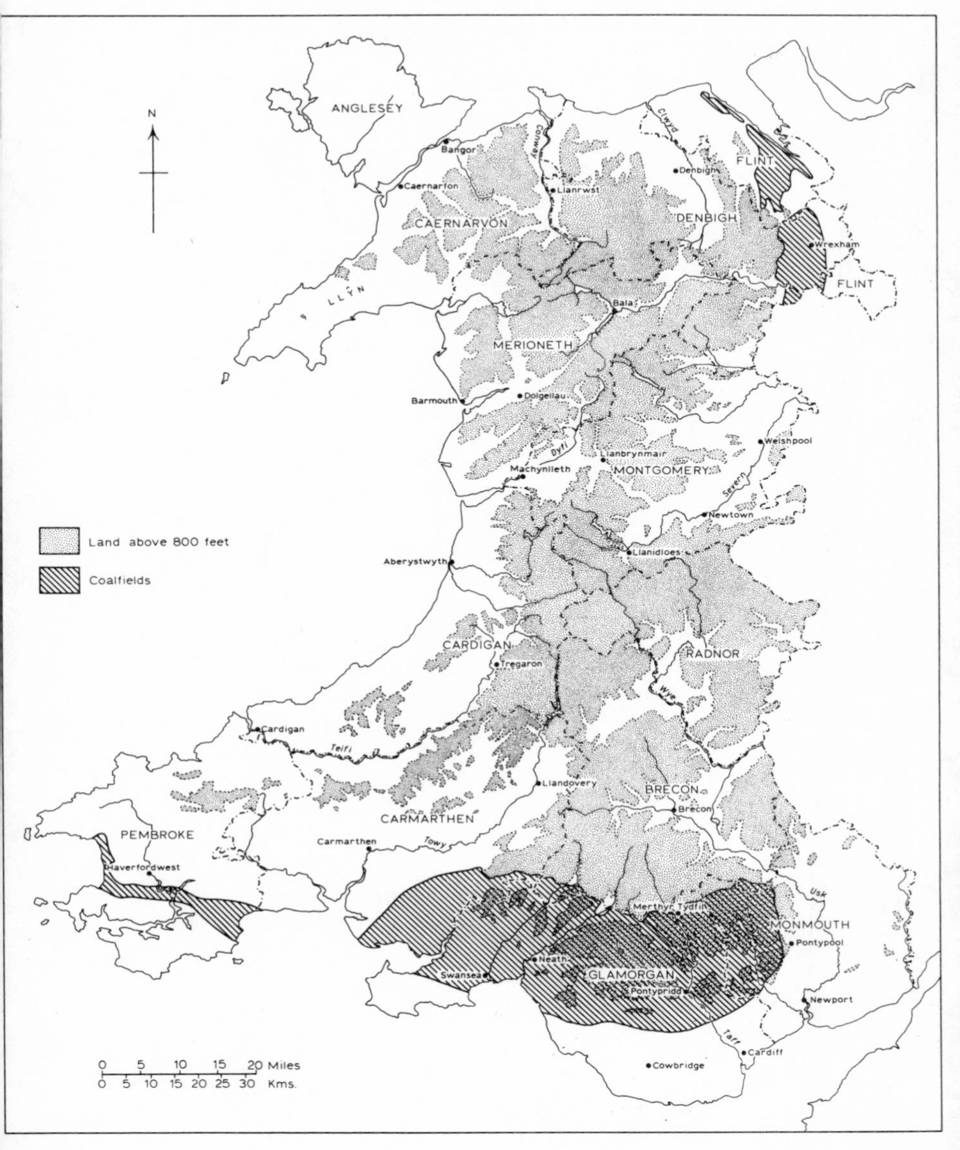
N
ANGLESEY
Bangor
Caernarfon
CAERNARVON
LLŶN
Conwy
Llanrwst
Clwyd
Denbigh
FLINT
DENBIGH
Wrexham
FLINT
Bala
MERIONETH
Barmouth
Dolgellau
Dyfi
Llanbrynmair
Welshpool
Machynlleth
MONTGOMERY
Severn
Newtown
Land above 800 feet
Coalfields
Aberystwyth
Llanidloes
CARDIGAN
Tregaron
RADNOR
Wye
Cardigan
Teifi
Llandovery
BRECON
Brecon
PEMBROKE
CARMARTHEN
Carmarthen
Towy
Haverfordwest
Usk
Merthyr Tydfil
MONMOUTH
Pontypool
Neath
Swansea
GLAMORGAN
Pontypridd
Newport
Taff
Cardiff
Cowbridge
0 5 10 15 20 Miles
0 5 10 15 20 25 30 Kms.

production, like the Llanbrynmair which was a stronghold of Independency, went into prolonged crisis.

The crisis was immeasurably intensified by the War of 1793 with its taxes, levies, press gangs and militia lists; its merciless inflation the closure of Barmouth. Capitalist rationality moved in massively on even this marginal agriculture. During the long wars, cultivation marched higher up the hillsides in Wales than it did during even Hitler's War. Modernisation meant enclosures, the annual lease, rack-renting, the disruption of traditional community. The 1790s were a decade of virtually continuous disturbance in the Wales which lay outside the coalfields, building up to dramatic peaks during the terrible years of famine prices in 1795-6 and 1799-1801. Waves of revolt broke across rural west and north in an arc of tension which follows the curve of the cloth country; Macynlleth, Denbigh, Llanbrynmair saw large scale civil disobedience. Troops were repeatedly marching and counter-marching through Bala, the tiny Mecca of Calvinistic Methodism and there were Jacobin toasts in its pubs.[13]

The crisis of the south-west was more occult, a surface deference and quietism in matters political masking a society riddled with tension, secret societies and the growing alienation of an increasingly Nonconformist people from all establishments. Cardiganshire was hit harder by the population explosion than any county in Wales. With its smallholders, hill farmers, frustrated artisans, lead miners and squatters encroaching without cease on the two-thirds of its stubborn soil owned by the Crown, it became a community of land-hunger and inching self-improvement, as were its sister societies in upland Carmarthenshire and northern Pembrokeshire. In the post-war period, this region was to be the most disturbed in Wales; this was the homeland of the later Rebecca Riots, the celebrated guerrilla struggle of small farmers, the 'Mau Mau of West Wales'. And this, too, was the prime recruitment zone for workers in the new industries on the coalfield to the east. It was the secret societies of the south-west, organised around the *ceffyl pren* - the wooden horse marched around villages to the accompaniment of 'rough music' in enforcement of communal and extralegal discipline - which helped to shape the equally celebrated and notorious guerrilla movement of the Scotch Cattle, the 'industrial Rebecca' of the colliers of Monmouthshire.[14]

This was, above all, a region of strong and living American connection. It became a major source of that distinctive migration movement which was one highly visible symptom of the crisis. From that sweep of rural and semi-industrial Wales they went, the curve of social tension from Cardigan and Carmarthen up through William Jones's country into Denbighshire, with the farmers and fishermen of the northern Llyn peninsula in revolt against enclosures decimating the population of their community in an independent movement into upstate New York, as their compatriots drove for the new Welsh liberty settlements struggling into life in Pennsylvania and Ohio. From 1793, there was a small-scale but steady flow, led essentially by artisans, rural industrial workers and above all, Dissenters, swelling into major movements during the crisis of 1795-6 and 1800-1. It was men of some small substance who went, while behind them thousands trapped in poverty clamoured to get away. The first native-born Governor of the state of Ohio in the USA was the son of a man from the rebellious Independents of Llanbrynmair.[15]

Millenarian in tone, this migration was peculiarly Dissenter in spirit, leadership and substantially in personnel. This may have been a contributory factor to the marked regional differentiation between the sects of Nonconformity which becomes a factor of major significance from this period. While the denominations were competitively present everywhere in Wales, it was the richly productive hinterland of Carmarthen in the county of the Rebecca Roots, the textile districts around Llanidloes and Newton (birth place of Robert Owen) and, above all the south-eastern coalfield, which emerged as the centres of the more liberal, more combative, more rationalist and more radical doctrines - Unitarians, quasi-Unitarian chapels among the traditional denominations, radical Baptists, Welsh revivalists, a fringe of Deists. In Merthyr Tydfil, in its Unitarian Association of 1802, its Cyfarthfa Philosophical Society of 1807 and its burgeoning world of *patriot* eisteddfodau and chapel verse and musical festivals, such people were establishing some kind of institutional base.[16]

To north and west, however, it was Methodism and its kin which won a local and popular hegemony. This defined a distinct people no less, but defined it in a kind of defensive withdrawal. It tended to lock its people away in a bunker. Not until it was forced to by the repression of 1811 did Methodism leave the Church; for long it remained respectful. The consequences were long-lasting. It was the Old Dissent which was to produce Wales's first serious Welsh-language journals, to turn Carmarthen-Merthyr-Llanidloes into a permanent radical triangle in the frontier years of the nineteenth century. Not until 1843 did the Dissent of rural Wales acquire a questioning and radical press; not until then, in response to an Anglican counter-offensive, did it move to the attack, in its turn to create a new and different Welsh 'nation' which formed along a religious line which was also a language and a class line. Frequently in the nineteenth century, the line ran between brothers. To put it crudely, among a people whose mind was being formed by preacher-journalists, the Methodist was a-political and quietist, the Independent or Baptist a 'politician'. This is why the complex phenomenon embraced in the catchphrase 'the radicalising of the Methodists' was so central to nineteenth-century Welsh politics.

One would hardly think so, however, from the correspondence of the gentry of north Wales during the 1790s when the process of differentiation began. According to one distraught curate in

Anglesey, whose report was passed to the king, 'hordes of Methodists' were 'overrunning north Wales' and 'descanting on the Rights of Man' (indeed some of them, in that place at that time, might well have been).[17] For what both Methodists and Dissenters offered, in the vacuum which had opened in Welsh life, was an alternative local leadership in a time of economic change widely experienced as human cataclysm.

What made this particular dislocation potentially the more serious was that this embryonic alternative society was being offered a new Welsh national ideology of radical temper together with some new Welsh institutions to serve it.

A JACOBIN INTELLIGENTSIA

The new Welsh nation was manufactured in London.[18] The first *Gorsedd* (order) of Iolo's directive elite of people's remembrancers was held on Primrose Hill; Jac Glan y Gors, Wales's Thomas Paine, kept the *King's Head*, Ludgate.

Since the carpet-bagger Tudor migrations, the London-Welsh had become central to the economic and the cultural life of Wales, a surrogate capital for their invertebrate homeland. Waves of seasonal migrants, drovers, tramping hosiers, even poorer weeders and transient labourers, were accompanied by more permanent residents. Out of them had emerged the premier London-Welsh society dedicated to a revival and purification of Welsh life and letters, the *Cymmrodorion*.

An interest in Welsh history, language and antiquities had been growing, even as their practice shrivelled back home (a recurrent feature of Welsh life). Edward Lhuyd, second keeper of the Ashmolean Museum in Oxford, had established a Welsh classical scholarship in the early eighteenth century, to be followed by individuals in colleges and gentry houses, patrons like the Pennants and the Williamses of Aberpergwm, Henry Rowland who resurrected the Druids. It became something of a cultivated hobby for enthusiastic if ignorant gentlemen, parsons and, increasingly, artisans, professional men and small merchants of lively if sometimes quirky minds.

It was Welsh London (a minority, of course, among London Welshmen) which powered such interests with money, commitment and the skills which found a natural focus in the capital. The celebrated Morris brothers of Anglesey, particularly Lewis, together with the poet Goronwy Owen, who characteristically found his way to America, established an Augustan school of poets, antiquarians and writers. They used the Cymmrodorion to rescue, edit and publish forgotten texts and to re-establish a literary and historical tradition.

The Cymmrodorion were in reality a bunch of commercially successful and frequently wall-eyed philistines afflicted with the Welsh *pietas* of self-satisfied expatriates and adorned by a few aristocratic drones. In the 1780s they yielded, with some abruptness, to the *Gwyneddigion*. These were much more active and populist. They drew their recruits in particular from Denbighshire, in its throes of capitalist modernisation. A crowd of bright young men came bustling through from Denbigh and elsewhere to people London's merchant houses, literary societies, intellectual taverns. A surprising number found a niche in the printing trade.

They reflect in a little Welsh mirror what was happening all over the Atlantic world, in the shift from academies to *sociétiés de pensée* in France, the *amigos del pais* of the Spanish empire, the literary societies and debating clubs of the Anglo-American polity. Central was Owen Jones, *The Scholar* (Owain Myfyr) born in Denbighshire in 1741, who laboured for years as a currier in the fur trade and ended owning a business and a wealthy man. That wealth he poured out in the service of Welsh literature and history. He spent £180 on the society's edition of the medieval poems of Dafydd ap Gwilym, over £1,000 on its massive collection *The Myvyrian Archaiology*. He helped send the brilliant Walter Davies, *Gwallter Mechain*, to Oxford, subsidised Iolo Morganwg and a host of others. The hardest worker was William Owen, *Gwilym Dawel,* Will Friendly, a Merioneth man educated at Manchester, a freelance writer and something of a minor polymath in eighteenth-century style. An FSA, he edited the early poems *Llywarch Hen* in 1792, produced a Welsh dictionary between 1793 and 1803, published a *Cambrian Register* and *Cambrian Biography,* translated *Paradise Lost* and was a pillar of the *Archaiology*.

Around such men gathered an extraordinarily lively coterie of antiquarians, poets, intellectuals: John Edwards, *Sion Ceiriog,* musician, astronomer, wit and professional gadfly; David Samwell, *Dafydd Ddu Meddyg,* surgeon to Captain James Cook on the *Resolution* and the *Discovery*, accomplished botanist, amateur anthropologist and professional womaniser, who had made the first written record of the Maori language at Queen Charlotte Sound; Jac Glan y Gors, John Jones, who brought out pamphlets in 1795 and 1797 which were Thomas Paine in Welsh and who coined the celebrated expression *Dic Sion Dafydd* to describe that familiar type of Welshman who, on crossing Severn, becomes so English he makes the English feel foreign.

This extraordinarily congenial crew hits the historian like a sunburst. Meeting constantly in pubs, often riotous, sometimes raucous, always felicitous, their discourse at its best had something of the flavour of the correspondence between John Adams and Thomas Jefferson. They were the last, warm, freethinking, sometimes pagan glow from an old but awakening Wales before the Calvinist curtain came down.

And while Edward Jones, harper to the Prince of Wales, informer to Pitt's anti-Jacobin Privy Council and 'silly young man' according to Fanny Burney, was a Tory, most of them were radical. Swept into a millenarian politics by the French Revolution following so hard on the American, they had the engraver to the French National Assembly strike their competition medals when they revived the eisteddfod as an embryonic Welsh academy in 1789. At a time among 'non-historic' peoples when to publish a dictionary could be a revolutionary act, they poured out dictionaries, registers, biographies, translations and established Welsh scholarship on a new (if distinctly shaky) basis. Credulous, pre-scientific and unscholarly by twentieth century standards they undoubtedly were, but on their massive tomes, now safely embalmed in the British Museum, a new Welsh nation was built. And a radical one: when the Gwyneddigion set up a political club during the euphoric early 1790s, Jac Glan y Gors wrote its initiation song; it was a hymn to Madoc who had taken his people out of an old, brutal and corrupt world into a spring-fresh land of liberty, to find a new start in freedom for an old people.

It was precisely here that the Gwyneddigion's collaboration with Iolo Morganwg was so crucial. 'Why take needless alarms?' Iolo once asked his long-suffering wife Peggy, who used to comment on his vagaries in pungent verse, 'I do not intend to publish my petition for the Abolition of Christianity until long after I have finished with the work in hand'.[19] The stonemason from Glamorgan's Vale, who went on incredible tramping journeys all over southern England, stands out now as one of Wales's most fecund if maimed geniuses. His family would have interested the early D.H. Lawrence. His father, intelligent and literate, was a working stone-mason, his mother, frail, aloof and a dreamer, was the poor kinswoman of a distinguished gentry family and a descendant of one of Glamorgan's ancient dynasties of Welsh poets. She never let Iolo forget his twin cultural inheritance. Taught lexicographical and antiquarian skills by local gentlemen, Iolo plundered libraries and collections wholesale and built himself into the most learned man of his day on Welsh literature and history. He was much cherished by Southey and the English Romantics who saw in him an Original Bard out of the Celtic Twilight, an image he unscrupulously cultivated. His imagination was no less unscrupulous. A romantic and a forger in an age of iconoclastic poets and high-minded forgers in a good cause, the age of Wordsworth, the Noble Savage, the Druid, the Bard and William Blake, Iolo wove fabrications without number into his genuine discoveries; he invented Welsh traditions the world had never seen. It has taken the heroic work of a dedicated Welsh scholar of this century to cut him free from his fantasies.[20]

In that process, however, Iolo is not seriously diminished. His very forgeries embody a certain logic, convey a vision of which no one else would have been capable. He called for a Welsh national library, a national museum, a national eisteddfod; he was one of the first serious folklorists in Wales. He had an intuitive grasp of the *historical* function of Welsh traditions and of their functional utility to the starved, neglected and often self-despising Welsh of his own day. Welsh poets, he observed, had not been poets as the English used the term; they had been the rib-cage of the body politic, remembrancers, a collective memory honed for historic action. So he invented a *Gorsedd*, a guild of those 'Bards' who would be so much more than mere poets, antiquarians or historians, a directive and democratic elite of a new and democratic Welsh nation, conceived in liberty, deploying a usable past in order to build an attainable future.[21]

Many of the Londoners had the same instinct. The foremost Orientalist of the time, Sir William Jones, was a Welshman; his researches seemed to suggest that the Celtic tongues were related to Sanskrit. Was Welsh the degenerate descendant of Earth's Mother Tongue? William Owen, who became a close confidant of the millenarian Joanna Southcott, joined with his friends to purify the language of centuries of servitude and corruption, to invent a new orthography (in which he did not differ much, after all, from those typical new Americans, Noah Webster who wanted to turn old Gothic English into the Esperanto of Liberty or Dr Benjamin Rush who wanted to make New World medicine into a new world medicine.).[22]

These obsessions ran into confluence with many of the bohemian fashions of the time. The ghost of their distant compatriot, that Dr John Dee the Elizabethan polymath and magus who had created the historical Madoc, returned to his homeland.[23] His vast and cosmic scheme for sixteenth-century regeneration, defeated in the Counter-Reformation, had gone underground to live an increasingly weird life as Rosicrucianism. In the eighteenth century, a version of it re-surfaced on the fringes of Freemasonry and those societies of *Illuminati* which the Counter-Revolution, the Abbé Barruel, Robinson, Edmund Burke, were to identify as the generator of the French and the world revolution. The London Swedenborgians made contact with the *Illuminés* of Avignon in the late 1780s and these Welsh Londoners moved on the fringes of the circle of William Blake and the radical artisanry of the capital.

A whole new dimension was added to the misty perception of the past which Iolo and the Gwyneddigion were cultivating. Iolo came to see Druids as Patriarchal figures of vast Celtic lands, charged with the Jewish Cabala, key to the language which God gave to Moses, antecedent to both Christianity and Hebraism. Theirs was a version of Rousseau's natural religion, purged of superstition and priestcraft, unitarian in its belief in a single God, Masonic in its descent through secret societies of Enlightenment to the present. The medieval guilds of Welsh poets thus became the last living representatives in Europe of that libertarian Druidism. Their descendants, the Jacobin Bards of the Welsh, must resume the march towards freedom and justice.

This millenarianism ran in harmony with the more measured, scholarly millenarianism which was coursing through orthodox religion, notably Dissent and of which Dr Joseph Priestley himself, philosopher and martyr to democracy, was such an exemplar.

Morgan John Rhys, an original and imaginative Baptist in Glamorgan and Gwent, was possessed by it. A committed American in spirit, active in the campaign against the slave trade and in all manner of reform causes, he like many others saw the French Revolution coming hard on the heels of the American as the precursor of the Last Days. Liberation had become an urgent necessity. He crossed to France to preach it. Driven home by the outbreak of European War, he mobilised the Baptist Association of south-west Wales in a project to translate the old Puritan and unorthodox Bible of John Canne into French and *en masse*.

Inevitably, the Gwyneddigion, launching its freedom eisteddfodau from 1789, its first *Gorsedd* in 1792, supporting Morgan John Rhys's *Journal* in 1793, shuffled into loose alliance with men like Rhys and a scatter of individuals across the brittle and bitter parishes of Wales. An unstructured but active collective intelligentsia began to form, spiritual Americans to a man, and were swept into millenarianism by the new dawn of 1789. For the London-Welsh were up to their eyes in the radical London of the Corresponding Societies, of Blake, of that John Thelwall who used to preach democracy to a hostile world in fire, fury and a cudgel-proof hat. Their millenarian vision could act as a unifying factor; Unitarianism and Freemasonry run as underground currents through this first phase of Welsh re-creation. It was a new and possessed nation which reached out to its half-aware adherents back home.

Heavy weather they made of it. Hardly had their eisteddfodau and their *Gorsedd* got off the ground when Britain went to war with the Revolution and drowned them in successive waves of repression and John Bull jingoism. It was precisely at that point, however, that they found a new focus. The Nootka Sound crisis between Spain and Britain over legal title to North America in 1790 had sparked off, as such crises invariably did, a revival of the old myth of Madoc the Welsh prince who was said to have discovered America three hundred years before Columbus. In 1791, Dr John Williams, a learned Welsh divine of Sydenham, published a scholarly study of the claim. Within a year he had to bring out a new edition. For the consequences were startling. All the interests of this heterogeneous but dedicated fistful of organic intellectuals of the Welsh and of their growing band of followers, came to a sudden focus on the Ohio and the Missouri. Over there, after all, a free and liberal Dissenter Wales already existed.

AN AMERICAN DIMENSION

Welshmen were everywhere in the New World, from the West Indies to furthest Canada and had been since John Dee's Madoc.[24] During the eighteenth century, a number made for Spanish North America. There were a handful of Welsh merchants in New

Orleans and a Rees family were prominent in New Madrid. The most amazing of them made St Louis his base. This was Charles Morgan, a Welsh West Indian known as Jacques Clamorgan, who was the driving force in Spain's last great enterprise in North America, the Missouri Company thrusting up the unexplored Missouri to win control of the fur trade, break through to the Pacific and pre-empt the oncoming British and Americans.[25]

Most Welsh migrations, however, went into the British colonies in denominational groups. The first serious migrations had followed the Restoration, when John Miles, founder of the Welsh Baptists, took his people to Swanzey (Swansea) in New England. Such movements tended to be Puritan, millenarian in temper, with a vision of a *gwladfa,* a national home for the Welsh. Pennsylvania rapidly became a focus. The Quaker *gwladfa* in Penn's promised Welsh Barony never materialised, but Welshmen were very prominent in the colony, Thomas Lloyd of Dolobran, Montgomeryshire, serving as Penn's deputy. Compatriots overflowed into the Welsh Tract in Delaware and there was a cluster of settlements bearing Welsh names and served by Welsh churches in an arc from Meirion to Pencader. Arminian Baptists from mid-Wales moved to the colony and around 1700-1 were followed by an important influx from south-west Wales where the mother church of Rhydwilym had its roots. Calvinistic Baptists, they quit the Arminians to people the Welsh Tract and Pencader. From these nuclei the Welsh grew in considerable strength, planting offshoots in the Carolinas, particularly at the Welsh Neck on the Peedee river.

Pennsylvania remained the Welsh heartland. A St David's Society was launched in Philadelphia as early as 1729; Welsh books were published there, including the first Welsh Biblical concordance. The only English translation of a Welsh classic, Theophilus Evans's *Drych y Prif Oesoedd (Mirror of the Early Ages),* appeared in Ebensburg, Pennsylvania, itself the product of the Madoc fever of the 1790s and was made by George Roberts, a Llanbrynmair Independent. For although migration faded out in the mid-eighteenth century, the Welsh-American population grew substantial. American Baptists in particular were for long notably Welsh in character. Their oldest church, Pennepek near Philadelphia, was served by a succession of Welshmen, having been founded by one; Jenkin Jones opened Philadelphia First Baptist as its daughter. Many churches in the Great Valley and Pencader were Welsh in spirit and served by ministers from Cardiganshire; Abel Morgan ran their celebrated academy and from the middle of the century, the Baptists entered another cycle of growth. A prime mover was Morgan Edwards, a Monmouthshire man who rode thousands of miles on circuit and wrote their history.

From 1762 Edwards was central to the creation of the Baptists' own college, Rhode Island College, later Brown University. One core of the college's library were books bequeathed to it by William Richards of Lynn, a Baptist from south-west Wales who was an ardent partisan of America and published a defence of the atheism of the French Revolution. Edwards's colleague in the launching of Rhode Island College was an even more remarkable Welsh-American, Dr Samuel Jones, a Glamorgan man in origin, who served Pennepek from 1762 to 1814. The real author of the College's charter, Samuel Jones came to rank as 'a sort of bishop among the Baptists.' In 1770 there were said to be 300 Baptist churches in America; by 1786 Samuel Jones was claiming that numbers had tripled, with the south and newly settled Kentucky as particular conquests. The mother organisation in Philadelphia embraced 50 churches and there were twelve other Associations, with Welshmen and Welsh-Americans prominent in the leadership.

Moreover, the Baptists remained in close contact with the homeland. Morgan Edwards returned to Wales to solicit funds for the College and established links with Joshua Thomas, a fellow-historian. Americans frequently demanded Welsh preachers During the late 1780s Samuel Jones opened a correspondence with leading Welsh Baptists at home which brings to light a remarkably intense trans-Atlantic world. There was a constant two-way traffic in books, letters, information and ultimately people. This Baptist International had its own ships, four or five favoured vessels, notably the *Pigou* and the *Benjamin Franklin* of the Loxley family, pillars of Philadelphia First Baptist, intermarried with the Welsh and London-Welsh Baptists at home and headed by Captain Benjamin Loxley, who had run the Continental Arms Laboratory during the War of Independence and had been Benjamin Franklin's technician.[26]

It was during the 1790s that Samuel Jones's correspondence suddenly turns into the chronicle of a diaspora; it abruptly fills with letters of dismission and warnings of the arrival of 'another seven score' from Pontypool, Newcastle Emlyn or Llanbrynmair. George Lewis from Caernarfon proposes to transplant the Independents of north Wales as a body to the Ohio. Jedidiah Morse, the famous American geographer starts to send massive information on immigration prospects to Wales, listing the places which needed ministers. It was the Philadelphia Baptist Association which revived the Welsh Society of the city (embracing most of its elite as honorary Welshmen) in 1795 precisely to deal with the sudden inflow from Wales. During the 1790s Samuel Jones found himself acting virtually as an unofficial Welsh consul in the USA as the Baptist network was mobilised and as it began to look in the middle of that revolutionary decade as if half the Welsh nation was ready to transplant itself.

For it was at that critical moment, with Welsh people particularly in the north and west, going under the harrow of industrial capitalism and the little Jacobin 'nation' of the Welsh butting head-on into the first storms of counter-revolution in Britain, that Dr John Williams's learned book restored Prince Madoc, mythical Welsh discoverer of America and founder of a Welsh nation in the New World, to his people.

The story of Madoc, rooted in Welsh seafarers and European romances of the twelfth century, had been promoted as a discovery of America, essentially by Dr. John Dee, in the first Elizabethan imperialism. It had been transmuted into a myth of Welsh Indians in the seventeenth century. Madoc was reborn in another conflict of imperialisms, this time the rivalry over the lucrative fur trade of the Far West between Americans, Spaniards and British out of Canada.[27]

In 1792 a French trader from Spanish St Louis came across a tribe on the Upper Missouri, key to the vital Pacific route, the Mandans, and pronounced them 'white like Europeans'. The Welsh West Indian Jacques Clamorgan organised St Louis to despatch expedition after expedition up the difficult river to secure this miraculous tribe and get to the Pacific ahead of Spain's enemies. For years there had been rumours of such a tribe, the White Padoucas. Filtering back into the settled areas of the east, they fused with a revival of the old yarns of Welsh Indians in the Carolinas, given 'warrant' by the Madoc myth lodged in such official and semi-official Elizabethan texts as Hakluyt's authoritative *Principall Navigations . . . of the English Nation*. By the 1780s a tidal wave of Welsh Indian stories was breaking on English-speaking America and in the last years of the century, there was a minor outbreak of Madoc fever there.

The fever hit Wales after 1791 and at a singularly appropriate moment. Overnight the legendary prince became the most miraculous hero of them all, a Jacobin Madoc. There was an outbreak of Madoc and America fever, particularly in Dissenter and liberal circles. Christmas Evans raised his organ voice in protest against the Two Clever Talkers who were unhinging the Godly in Wales, even some of the Methodists - *'Mr Gwladaethwr a Mr Mynd i America'*, Mr Politician and Mr Go-to-America. Iolo appointed himself missionary to the Welsh Indians, reconstructed their 'history', presented a paper to the Royal Society in British imperial terms and to his Jacobin friends in terms of a Welsh Republic in the New World. Young John Evans, a Methodist from Waunfawr near Caernarfon, threw up career and family, moved to a circle of Welsh Jacobins in London, crossed to America in the steerage along the Baptist network and entered the service of Spain and Jacques Clamorgan. He set off alone up the Missouri, with one dollar and seventy-five cents in his pocket, on an abortive mission. Driven back, he enrolled as second-in-command to the Scottish explorer James McKay in the greatest expedition Spain ever sent up the river, to win the Mandans for Spain and to find the Welsh Indians. He did indeed reach the Mandans, he lived through one of the worst winters on earth; he did hold those Mandans for Spain against the Canadian fur companies, helping indirectly to fix the future Canada-USA border; he drew excellent maps which Lewis and Clark were to use on their classic first land crossing to the Pacific only nine years later. Madoc and Jacobinism turned this Welsh Methodist (who duly defected to the Baptists and the Freemasons) into a pioneer of American exploration and the last of the Spanish conquistadors in the north. A disillusioned hero, he died of drink in New Orleans at the age of twenty-nine and was forgotten for a century and a half.[28]

After him, two years later, went Morgan John Rhys the Jacobin Baptist, giving up the unequal struggle at home as his *Journal* succumbed to the reaction. After a horseback grand tour of the American Republic, he launched the Welsh national home, the *gwladfa,* at Beula in western Pennsylvania.[29] And after both of them, particularly during the desperate years, 1795-6 and 1800-1, years of famine prices, mass riots, political witch-hunts and redcoats marching and counter-marching across north and west Wales, went Welsh families by the hundred, braving hideous sea-crossings with their 50 per cent casualties, Algerian corsairs and hostile British warships.[30]

They went, as many of them told the clerk in Philadelphia as they took out their American citizenship papers, to found *The Kingdom of Wales.*[31]

BIRTH AND DEATH OF A NATION

For politics in Wales begin with the American Revolution. The first purely political publication in the Welsh language was a translation of an English pamphlet on the dispute with the American colonies. For a few years even the homespun ballad-mongers were disturbed. Temporarily unhinged by what they saw as a civil war, they were able to relapse with relief into their customary John Bull jingoism only with the entry of France and Spain into the conflict. So visible were Welsh-Americans in the struggle that the people at home firmly believed that most of the signatures to the Declaration of Independence were Welsh. Five certainly were; David Jones, minister of Great Valley Baptist, had a price put on his head by the British. John Rice Jones of Merioneth migrated to fight alongside the Americans in 1776 itself.

The war turned most Welsh Dissenters and whole ranges of people who espoused the liberties being fought for into spiritual Americans within British society. From that point, politics thrust its enquiring snout into the book production of the Welsh-speaking Welsh. In the 1760s, there were some 230 publications in Welsh; by the 1790s the total had climbed to nearly 500 and among them the number of political texts multiplied six-fold. Over a hundred appeared, mostly in the 1790s, and their message echoed through the larger numbers of historical studies, biographies, verse, left its impress even on the serried ranks of volumes (600 and more out of the total of 1,300 printed between 1760 and 1799) devoted to theology, sermons and hymns.[32] David Williams, a celebrated Welsh Deist, dated the birth of Jacobinism from 1782 and located that birth not in France but in Britain. It was certainly during the 1780s that the

Gwyneddigion in London acquired their distinctive character.

Out of that post-colonial crisis grew the first serious reform movements in Britain, calling for the political emancipation of Dissent, the end of British slavery, the creation of a representative parliament, finally for political democracy, a thrust which, after the French Revolution, debouched into the first systematic popular politics. Welshmen, mostly Dissenters, who were enmeshed in this movement were relatively few in number but strategically placed. One striking centre was Glamorgan, which emerges as a nursery of the democratic intellect.[33]

One of the wealthiest and most literate of the Welsh counties, its Vale nurtured not the customary scattered Welsh hamlets, but nucleated villages, which could cultivate urban graces. Bristol, an intellectually lively and politically alert city, was the region's capital. Swansea was itself a cultivated little town, Cowbridge Book Society could disseminate seminal works and the new town of Merthyr Tydfil, nearly 8,000 strong and growing at breakneck speed, could boast a bookseller taking weekly consignments from London. The Vale, anglicised in early modern times, was experiencing a Welsh-language revival. Perhaps it was the very interaction and friction between Wales's two cultures which made it so open and lively a place. It has the feel of that Philadelphia which was the spiritual capital of so many of its village intellectuals. This society with its creative bilingual artisanry and its aspiring lower middle class, could produce men like John Bradford, a Deist dyer at ease in the literatures of France and England and passionate in the cause of Welsh revival, William Edward who built the lovely single-span bridge at Pontypridd, Lewis Hopkin a multi-purpose craftsman after Ben Franklin's heart who trained a coterie of Welsh poets, Edward Ifan, a poet who became the first Unitarian minister in the hill country. This was the society which produced not only Iolo Morganwg, but two of the best-known trans-Atlantic radicals of the age of revolution: Dr. Richard Price, celebrated as a political Dissenter, alleged author of the Sinking Fund, defender of the American and French Revolutions and the occasion for Edmund Burke's *Reflections*, a man formally invited by Congress to serve as financial adviser to the American Republic; David Williams, author of a Deist religion which won praise from Voltaire, Rousseau and Frederick the Great, friend of Condorcet and the Girondins, a man formally invited over to France to advise on its new constitution. From the scarp edge of Vale and hill-country came Morgan John Rhys, mentor and Moses to the Welsh on their journey of hope.

There were pockets elsewhere, in Denbighshire where Jac Glan y Gors was born, among Independents in north Wales and the concentrations around Llanbrynmair; Merthyr village was said to be full of 'sturdy old Republicans'; Iolo Morganwg spent much time there, his son opened a school in the heart of its radical, Unitarian, Masonic, eisteddfodic quarter (later its Chartist heartland). There were contagious individuals like

William Jones Llangadfan. A small and scattered minority at home, they were much more visible in the trans-Atlantic perspective proper to British Jacobinism.

Their journey of hope was brief. Their campaigns mounted to a climax in the celebration of the centenary of the Revolution of 1688 just at the point when Washington took the presidency of the new U.S. Republic and the Bastille fell in France. There was a brief but brilliant explosion of Welsh Jacobinism, in the eisteddfodau, the *Gorsedd*, Morgan John Rhys's *Journal*, Jac Glan y Gors's pamphlets. Official Britain reacted violently from as early as 1791; its magistrates hounded Jacobins, its mob wrecked their houses. In 1793 Britain went to war with France, in 1794 the leading English radicals were tried for treason, in 1795 English liberties were suspended for the duration. These, too, were the years of the first implantation of modern industry in south-east and north-east, the years of the first cloth factories on the Severn, the closure of Barmouth, the crisis running through rural Wales. They were years, no less, of a surging growth of Methodism, which turned a face of brass to this new Welsh 'nation', to be copied by the more conservative leaders of Dissent. Morgan Rhys's journal was snuffed out after five issues; two attempts to restart it failed. Jacobinism shrank from public view into private correspondence; men like William Jones Llangadfan were leaned on; his mail was opened, he was threatened by shadowy figures. In this corner of a Britain disciplined by the suspensions of Habeas Corpus, patrolled by the Volunteers, deafened by 'God Save Great George Our King' sung five times over in the playhouses to drown 'God Save The Rights Of Man', where could Welsh patriots turn but to the Land of Liberty where kindred spirits were waiting and where the Lost Brothers were even now ranging the Missouri?

These were the years in which minority radical Britain succumbed to what Mrs Lindsay called 'the rage to go to America'; the emigrants' handbooks came pouring from the presses; during the treason trials of 1794 there was a minor stampede for the America boats. In Wales the migration assumed Utopian and dramatic forms as Madoc suddenly returned, to give struggling Jacobins a point of contact with a people in travail.

Their frontier proved a frontier of illusion. The liberty settlement, Beula, after a heroic struggle, was cracked by the simultaneous opening of the easier Ohio lands and the abrupt acceleration of emigration in 1801. The people dispersed to found Welsh communities in Ohio at Paddy's Run and Welsh Hills, at Utica in New York State, but they shed their Cymric ambition. Back home, the Jacobin nation was extinguished as the wars of the French Revolution became the Napoleonic Wars. A new Wales being shaped by industry, Methodism and a measured Dissent had no place for such as Iolo and William Owen. By the first years of the new century, they were already beginning to look like creatures from another time. It was a hundred years before the new and reconstructed Welsh recaptured their memory by an act of will.

And yet, if political economy, evangelical religion, Methodism and a methodised Dissent, a novel form of respectability, were colonising many of the Welsh, the year before the 'sturdy old Republicans' of Merthyr formed their Unitarian Association, colliers and ironworkers of the town, after a massive grain action in 1800-1801, made contact with insurrectionary and republican movements in England which debouched into the abortive Despard Conspiracy. The first trade unions in Wales came hard on the heels of the Cyfarthfa Philosophical Society. Jacobinism, however brief and illusory its moment of truth and fantasy, left a living and constantly renewed tradition which interacted with the new world of industry and so inter-acted in increasing and intensifying power.[34]

The ideology of democracy is pre-industrial; witness America, Britain, France, western Europe, even Russia. It was the new Welsh democracy of an old regime which came to inform and ultimately to shape an even newer Welsh working class.

There were two strongholds of radicalism in Wales during the 1790s, Merioneth-Montgomeryshire (with the south-west slithering into social malaise) and Merthyr-Monmouthshire. In the former, Jacobinism took wing towards the Ohio, in the latter, it could find a home at home.

The history of the first Welsh working class, in the industrial valleys of Gwent and Glamorgan, around the textile townships of mid-Wales, in the smouldering hinterland of sans-culotte Carmarthen, is largely the history of the interplay between Unitarian and Infidel heirs of the Jacobin tradition and the leaders and organic intellectuals of the newer plebeian and proletarian people.

When Wales produced its first working-class journal in the service of Owenite socialism, the *Gweithiwr/Workman* of 1834, its editors were two Unitarians straight out of the Jacobin tradition: John Thomas, *Ieuan Ddu,* from Carmarthen town, the finest Welsh music scholar of his day, the man who introduced Handel's *Messiah* to Welsh choirs, a man of freethinking sympathy who started eisteddfodau of Free Enquirers (the Zetetics of Richard Carlile's *Republican*) in the Merthyr of the Reform crisis, and Morgan Williams, master-weaver, son of one of the 'sturdy old Republicans' of the Merthyr of the 1790s, mathematician star of a family of harpists and destined to become the foremost Chartist leader in Wales. It was Taliesin Williams, schoolmaster of Merthyr and the son of Iolo Morganwg, who gave them a motto which in time became the motto of the town itself, a motto which Iolo had wished on a sixth-century Glamorgan saint and which appeared in the *Myvyrian Archaiology* of the London-Welsh: *nid cadarn and brodyrdde,* no strength but brotherhood.[35]

The leadership of the first working-class movements in Wales represents a posthumous triumph for the European Enlightenment in its particular Welsh translation.

NOTES

1 A *gorsedd*, originally meaning a mound, was a term applied to an open-air tribunal. Iolo Morganwg extended the term to embrace a guild of poets who were 'bards' because they exercised social functions (*beirdd* in Welsh, the root of 'bards', simply means 'poets'). Iolo charged this guild with mythical Druidic properties and located its origin in remote Celtic Britain (hence the 'Island of Britain'); he invented robes, ceremonies and ritual for it. A version of his *gorsedd* ultimately lodged in the National Eisteddfod of Wales (below) to entertain and bewilder TV audiences.

Basic sources on Iolo are his manuscripts in the National Library of Wales, Aberystwyth (henceforth NLW), G.J. Williams, *Iolo Morganwg* (University of Wales, Cardiff, 1956: in Welsh), his broadcast essay in English, *Iolo Morganwg* (BBC, Cardiff, 1963) and Prys Morgan, *Iolo Morganwg* (Welsh Arts Council and University of Wales, Cardiff, 1975: in English).

I provide a fuller portrait of Iolo and his work in my *Madoc: the making of a myth* (Eyre Methuen, London, 1980) and, in context, in my *The Search for Beulah Land: the Welsh and the Atlantic Revolution* (Croom Helm, London, 1980).

2 An eisteddfod is a competitive cultural festival, with poetry in the strict classical metres as the premier mystery, free poetry, prose and music as secondary themes. In modern times, it has acquired a strongly folkloric and quasi-nationalist character. Institutions of this type existed in the middle ages; those of the guild of poets were strict and exclusive and imposed rigorous standards in the manner of an academy; they can probably be traced back to the shadowy guilds of lawmen, remembrancers and poets of Celtic Britain; early Ireland provides the most developed models.

3 The address: 13 June 1791 in W. Jones-W. Owen, 6-7 August 1791, NLW 13221, fo.341-342-339, 340-343; on William Jones, voluminous correspondence in William Owen papers particularly NLW 13221 and a schizophrenic obituary by Walter Davies, *Cambrian Register 1796*, ii, 1799, pp. 37-51; I provide a fuller portrait of this remarkable man in my *Madoc: the making of a myth*.

4 My *The Search for Beulah Land* focuses on Rhys and is based on American as well as Welsh material; see the references there. There is a memoir, J.T. Griffith, *Morgan John Rhys*, Philadelphia 1899 and W.M. Evans, Carmarthen, 1910, and a life and times in Welsh, J.J. Evans, *Morgan John Rhys a'i Amserau*, Cardiff, University of Wales, 1935.

5 *Albion's Fatal Tree*, London, Allen Lane, 1975, especially Douglas Hay, 'Property, Authority and the Criminal Law', and E.P. Thompson, *Whigs and Hunters*, London, Allen Lane, 1975.

6 B.R. Mitchell and Phyllis Deane, *Abstract of British Historical Statistics*, Cambridge University Press, 1962, inadequate on iron, where I have been helped by my friend Brian Davies; S. Drescher, *Econocide*, Pittsburgh, 1977, a study of the abolition of the slave trade, very revealing on copper; A.H. John, *The Industrial Development of South Wales*, Cardiff, University of Wales, 1950; W. Minchinton (ed.), *Industrial South Wales* (Cass, London, 1969) and a host of local studies too numerous to mention.

7 A mass of material summarised in my *The Search for Beulah Land;* key texts: R.T. Jenkins, *Hanes Cymru yn y Ddeunawfed Ganrif*, Cardiff, University of Wales reprint 1972, a short and brilliant essay on 18th-century Wales; D.J.V. Jones, *Before Rebecca: popular protest in Wales 1793–1835*, London, Allen Lane, 1973; Geraint Jenkins, *The Welsh Woollen Industry*, National Museum of Wales, Cardiff, 1969; A.H. Dodd, *The Industrial Revolution in North Wales*, Cardiff, University of Wales, 3rd ed, 1971.

8 My *The Search for Beulah Land* and *Madoc: the making of a myth.*

9 A very useful summary of his own comprehensive work in Peter D.G. Thomas, 'Society, Government and Politics', in Donald Moore (ed.), *Wales in the Eighteenth Century*, Swansea, Christopher Davies, 1976.

10 This section of the essay represents a reworking of material from multiple sources which I have deployed in several books, notably *The Search for Beulah Land, Madoc,* and 'Locating a Welsh working class: the frontier years', in David Smith (ed) *A People and a Proletariat: essays in the history of Wales 1780–1980*, London, Pluto Press and *Llafur*, Society for the Study of Welsh Labour History, 1980.

11 The Clarkson Diaries are in NLW.

12 A more detailed picture of the crisis and the migration movements in my *The Search for Beulah Land, Madoc*, and *The Merthyr Rising*, London, Croom Helm, 1979. Critical sources: papers of Dr Samuel Jones, Pennepek in Mrs Irving H. McKesson Collection (Jones section) Historical Society of Pennsylvania (Philadelphia); the work of David Williams, see bibliography in special number of *Welsh History Review* (1967) in his honour and especially his *The Rebecca Riots*, Cardiff, University of Wales, 1955; D.J.V. Jones, *Before Rebecca;* D. Thomas, *Agriculture in Wales during the Napoleonic Wars*, Cardiff, University of Wales, 1963. A good general survey of Welsh migration to the USA is E.G. Hartmann, *Americans from Wales*, Boston, Christopher, 1967.

13 A vivid source are the letters of William Jones Llangadfan in William Owen collection, especially NLW 13221.

14 Essential here is D.J.V. Jones, *Before Rebecca*, with its brilliant essay on the Scotch Cattle.

15 I have covered this remarkable migration, made in the teeth

of appalling difficulties, in *The Search for Beulah Land.*

16 My *The Merthyr Rising* and an essay in the twenty-first celebration number of the *Welsh History Review* in June 1981, 'The Merthyr Election of 1835'.

17 My *Artisans and Sans-culottes*, Edward Arnold, reprint, London, 1973, pp. 74-6.

18 On the London-Welsh, R.T. Jenkins and Helen T. Ramage, *A History of the Honourable Society of Cymmrodorion and of the Gwyneddigion and Cynreigyddion Societies*, London, Cymmrodorion, 1951; I present a picture of them in *Madoc.*

19 E. Williams-M. Williams, n.d. Iolo 822(NLW); I try to cope with this wizard in *Madoc.*

20 G.J. Williams, *Iolo Morganwg* (in Welsh); unfortunately the incomparable Griffith John Williams, professor of Welsh in un-Welsh Cardiff, died before he could finish his second volume. The loss seems irreparable.

21 A version of the *gorsedd* was associated with the eisteddfod from the early nineteenth century; a version of it is today an integral part of the ritual of the National Eisteddfod of Wales (which has also become Royal). I doubt whether Iolo would have recognised it, until 1974 that is, when the late Dai Francis, Communist Secretary of the NUM South Wales Area and founder of the South Wales Miners' Eisteddfod (bilingual, in sharp contrast to the monoglot Welsh National) and a leading member of *Llafur*, the Welsh Labour History Society, was admitted under the bardic title of *Dai o'r Onllwyn* (Onllwyn is a mining village in the anthracite).

22 Benjamin Rush, mercilessly pilloried by William Cobbett, then a bilious Tory in Philadelphia, became a friend of M.J. Rhys and supplied the land for the Welsh liberty settlement, as he did that for the New Caledonia attempted by the son of the Scottish social philosopher John Millar.

23 I deal with John Dee in a Welsh context in *Welsh Wizard and British Empire: Dr. John Dee and a Welsh identity*, Gwyn Jones Lecture, University College Cardiff and Welsh Arts Council, 1980, and in *Madoc.* Central is the remarkable scholarship of Dame Frances A. Yates in many hypnotic volumes, notably perhaps *The Occult Philosophy in the Elizabethan Age*, London, Routledge & Kegan Paul, 1979. See also, in the same stimulating tradition, Peter French, *John Dee: the world of an Elizabethan Magus* London, Routledge & Kegan Paul, 1972.

24 I detail the Welsh-American connection, the migrations and Morgan John Rhys's epic journey in *The Search for Beulah Land.*

25 I deal with Jacques Clamorgan and his enterprises in *Madoc.*

26 To supplement the Samuel Jones Pennepek papers, the Loxley Papers, Uselma Clark Smith Collection, Historical Society of Pennsylvania. M.J. Rhys married a daughter of Ben Loxley, a very striking figure of a revolutionary artisan, originally from Yorkshire. He, and all the others, put flesh

on the notion of an 'Atlantic Revolution' in the late eighteenth century; I discuss him in *The Search for Beulah Land*.

27 I have discussed the Madoc myth at length, tried to locate its various forms in social and political context, and concentrated on the 1790s in my *Madoc*.

28 I have treated John Evans's remarkable career at length not only in *Madoc* but, with the precise references denied me in the book, in 'John Evans's mission to the Madogwys 1792-1799', *Bulletin of the Board of Celtic Studies*, xxvii, 1978.

29 My *The Search for Beulah Land* comes to a focus on the Rhys mission.

30 For some hair-raising accounts - Rees Lloyd-Jonah Lloyd, 4 September 1837, Cambria Historical Society, Ebensburg, Pennsylvania; George Roberts-Samuel Roberts, 1 March 1850, *Y Cronicl*, printed in Alan Conway (ed.), *The Welsh in America: letters from the immigrants*, trans. Judith Lewis, University of Wales, Cardiff, 1961, and George Roberts-his parents, 13 October 1801, NLW 14094 and others, reprinted in A.H. Dodd, 'Letters from Cambria County 1800-1823', *Pennsylvania History*, xxii, 1955.

31 Based on the naturalisation records of the federal district court, the county court of Philadelphia and of fifteen Pennsylvania counties: Veterans' Building Federal Record Centre and City Hall Philadelphia and local courthouses in the state.

32 Listed in J.J. Evans, *Morgan John Rhys a'i Amserau*, pp. 121-2, but no source given.

33 I derive my picture of Glamorgan and its organic intellectuals from G.J. Williams, *Traddodiad Llenyddol Morgannwg*, University of Wales, Cardiff, 1948: on Glamorgan's literary tradition), Ceri W. Lewis, 'The literary history of Glamorgan from 1550 to 1770', in Glanmor Williams (ed.), *Glamorgan County History*, iv, Cardiff, 1974, and from my own work.

34 On the Jacobin tradition and the Welsh working class, my *The Merthyr Rising*, 'Locating a Welsh working class: the frontier years', in *People and Proletariat*, 'The Merthyr Election of 1835' and 'South Wales radicalism: the first phase', in Steward Williams (ed.), *Glamorgan Historian*, ii, 1965.

35 My 'Dic Penderyn, the making of a Welsh working-class martyr', *Llafur*, 2, 1978.

15 STATE FORMATION, NATIONALISM AND POLITICAL CULTURE IN NINETEENTH-CENTURY GERMANY

Geoff Eley*

'Families barely know what holds them to this state of which they are a part, . . . They regard the exercise of authority in the collection of taxes, which serve to maintain order, as the law of the strongest, seeing no reason to yield to it other than their powerlessness to resist, and they believe in avoiding them whenever they can. There is no public spirit, because there is no common, known, visible interest.'

Anne-Robert-Jacques Turgot, cited by T. Zeldin, *France 1848-1945*. vol. II: *Intellect Taste and Anxiety*, Oxford, 1977, p. 5.

'While the period of reaction has made Germany an economic totality, while every day general law-making encroaches by means of treaties farther on the independence of the individual state, while extensions of authority by the federal diet and "internal constitutional developments" make this people every day more accustomed to a central administration, the petty, vulgar, self-centred, and greedy behaviour of the small states disgusts everybody more and more, the "hereditary" princely house becomes every day more burdensome, and the realization penetrates every cottage "that we must begin to clean up, first at home and then in Frankfurt".'

Johannes Miquel in 1857, cited by T. Hamerow, *The Social Foundations of German Unification 1858-1871*. vol. I: *Ideas and Institutions*, Princeton, N.J. 1969, p. 145.

'self-help and self-responsibility, the two pillars of German nationality.'

Max Wirth, *Die deutsche Nationaleinheit in ihrer volkswirtschaftlichen, geistigen und politischen Entwicklung an der Hand der Geschichte beleuchtet*, Frankfurt am Main, 1859, p. 454.

Hurrah Germania! The *Reich* is complete, the Ultramontanes and their adherents are defeated, the black night of spiritual brutalization is beginning to disperse and the dawn of German unity and freedom begins to gleam on the horizon of the Fatherland'

Wochenschrift der Fortschrittspartei in Bayern, 5, 1871, p.57.

*Geoffrey Eley is a professor of history at the University of Ann Arbor, Michigan. Editorial board member, *Social History*.

'the masses have come of age (through elementary education, mass conscription, universal suffrage, and the cheap oil lamp).'
Hermann Rassow, in a letter to Admiral Alfred von Tirpitz, 12 April 1898, Bundesarchiv-Militärarchiv Freiburg, 2223, 94943.

I

The most satisfying accounts of nationalism have related it to the uneven development of European capitalism, or (in an alternative notation) to problems of 'modernization'. Much of the impetus for this perspective comes from work on the third world, and the union of older approaches from intellectual and political history (which earlier tended to dominate the field) with different types of developmental sociology has produced some interesting results.[1] Of course, the formal ideology of nationalism has its own history, which seems to originate with the French Revolution.[2] But to explain the nature of the ideology's appeal, the changing content of nationalist ideas, and the vitality of the nationalist tradition over the subsequent century, something more than a straightforward history of ideas is clearly needed. The European diffusion of nationalist ideology could not proceed by the intrinsic attractions of the ideas alone, and required a definite set of historical circumstances to become possible, whether we think of crude economic development, a distinctive social structure, and a strong sense of cultural (ethnic, religious, linguistic) identity, or developed communications, improved literacy, and the spread of new levels of socio-political organization into previously isolated rural areas. It is here that developmental or sociological perspectives have shown their usefulness. The incidence of 'patriotic' activity in a society, first amongst the intelligentsia and then amongst the masses, can be convincingly related to some complex combination of the above conditions.[3]

Returning to the ideology as such, we might see nationalism at least in part as a conscious reflection on this developmental syndrome. In the concrete circumstances of the nineteenth century, in a world marked by the domination of French arms and English manufactures, it was the classic ideology of 'underdevelopment' for societies seeking to overcome their political and economic backwardness and constitute themselves as unified territorial states. Originating in the democratic ambience of the French Revolution, nationalist ideas migrated eastwards in the first half of the nineteenth century, borne initially by the revolutionary armies, but accumulating contradiction as they went. East of the Rhine, nationalist commitments could be motivated as much by fear as veneration of Jacobin radicalism, and when lacking the sustenance of a democratically defined popular constituency, such nationalisms might fall easy prey to romantic populism, stressing the organic community of the uncorrupted folk rather than a political ideal of citizenship. Of course, the metropolitan ideal of progress remained the ultimate goal, and in its British and French guise exercised a vital influence throughout the nineteenth century. But at the same time the nationalities of Central and Eastern Europe (or more accurately, some of their representatives) craved the legitimacy of the past, grounding their claims for self-determination in mystical notions of cultural continuity and the invariable myth of origins. This simultaneous celebration of future and past, progress and authenticity, became a hallmark of nationalist ideology.[4]

Clearly, all the implications of these assertions cannot be pursued here.[5] My aim is more modestly concerned with certain questions of German nationality in the last third of the nineteenth century and its forms of political definition. But for working purposes we might consider a three-way conceptual distinction centred on the experience of the French Revolution. First, there are definite processes of institutional growth within territorial states which allow specifically patriotic (as against parochial or cosmopolitan) loyalties to take shape. Secondly, there is a special type of ideological commitment (nationalism) which seeks to rationalize (or initiate) these processes in a particularly pointed way, normally through some democratic or populist conception of social and political order. Thirdly, there are further processes of cultural unification, normally but not necessarily consciously directed, which presupposes the nation's established existence as a territorial, linguistic, religious or other type of community. These three phenomena - underlying processes of state formation, the elaboration of nationalist ideology, the drive for cultural conformity - are clearly not cleanly separated in time. They certainly may follow one another in a rough chronological sequence (France would be the strongest case). But things are usually more confused. Political independence can be either a condition or a consequence of the ideological and cultural activity, and the growth of nationalism can just as easily follow as precede the formation of territorial units of the 'nation-state' type.

II

The relevance of these assertions may be clarified once we turn specifically to Germany. The Second Reich was a new state, of finite duration: though a 'united Germany' had some sort of continuity between 1870 and 1945, this was a remarkably short time by most standards, and in any case the imperial state differed markedly from the republican one between 1918 and 1933, and from the Nazi one that began to take shape in the later 1930s. As for the period before 1870, it cannot be said too strongly that the foundation of the empire was a radical, even a revolutionary departure, with no convincing precedent in the political history of Central Europe. Indeed, it is doubtful whether 'Germany' ever corresponded to the nationalist *desideratum* of the 'nation-state'. At most times its boundaries have included large 'non-German' and excluded equally significant 'German' populations, and in the most recent period (1945-81), when the great post-war migrations have permitted an unprecedented degree of ethnic homogeneity, the 'German' region of Central Europe has been securely divided into three distinct territorial states. Not surprisingly, the most consistent German nationalists have been perpetually dissatisfied with the established political arrangements, which have only ever approximated to the postulated unity of territory, language, political institutions, and wider culture. To this actual disharmony between state organization and cultural formation (as nationalists see it), we might add a diversity of constitutional forms, which have run the full course between federalism and centralism, dictatorship, monarchy, and republic.

In this case 'German history' becomes something of a problematic concept, reproducing the contradictions of the nineteenth-century political discourse itself. Is it to include or exclude Austria? Is it to follow the shifting and often arbitrarily drawn political boundaries of states, or the linguistic frontiers of a cultural region? How are the national minorities to be dealt with, or for that matter the more dispersed German populations of Eastern Europe and the Baltic? Can 'German history' in the conventional political sense be written at all without replicating the cultural preconceptions of the German nationalist tradition, or should the territorial state be exchanged for the region (either the larger cultural area cutting across political frontiers, or the smaller locality within a state), as the unit of analysis most suited for dealing with these complexities? This indeterminacy has been noted by a number of recent authors, who point to the enduring effects of the *kleindeutsch* perspective bequeathed by the Bismarckian unification and rapidly institutionalized into German historiography. In a valuable exercise in sustained scepticism, for example, James Sheehan identifies its residual primacy in the implicit assumptions of most German historians, and suggests that it needlessly limits the kind of questions that tend to be asked. Carefully distinguishing the outcome of unification from the diversity it subsumed - the aggrandizement of Prussia from the regional bases of political culture, the political foundations of the national market from alternative patterns of regional and international trade, the growth of a national public from widespread parochial isolation, the polite from the popular culture - Sheehan stresses the *artifical* and *provisional* nature of the Bismarckian settlement, rather than its 'pre-determined' character or rootedness in any deeper cultural or historic unity. As he says, 'as a singular process', German history had only really begun.[6]

This both emphasizes and qualifies the importance of political, as opposed to social, economic or cultural determinations. On the one hand, for instance, it reminds us that German unification resulted from specific political decisions and a specific combination of political events in the 1860s, which were very far from being a logical correlate of the wider nationalist movement, let alone of any operative cultural solidarity amongst German-speaking people. As Robert Berdahl puts it: 'The Bismarckian state was not "pre-determined", it was "self-determined", not by popular sovereignty or the *Volk*, but by its leading statesmen.'[7] Without falling into the naive voluntarism of a dogmatic anti-determinism, this should re-direct us to the relative 'openness' of succeeding historical situations. The Bismarckian 'small-German' solution was the largely unanticipated success of only one amongst a number of national programmes, which included not only the 'small-German'/'greater-German' option, but also the full spectrum of possible constitutions, in various permutations. At the same time, on the other hand, we may note the relative narrowness of the political nation in the 1860s, and the possibly limited resonance of unification beyond the small circles of the politically initiate. It is unclear how far the political manoeuvres of the 1860s entered the consciousness of most ordinary German-speakers, especially in the countryside, and in the future the new state faced a long-term problem of establishing its popular legitimacy. To this extent unification entailed a subsequent process of cultural coalescence which in theory it had already presupposed. In this fundamental sense the creation of the empire was the *beginning* rather than the end of unification.

The process had gone furthest by the early 1870s in the most basic area of all, the capitalist economy and its conditions of existence. Of course, German historians have hotly denied the bourgeois (let alone the liberal) character of the imperial state, pointing to the limited powers of the Reichstag under the 1871 constitution, the executive authority of the monarchy, and the Prusso-German dualism that guaranteed the special position of the Junkers. But whatever else it was, as Perry Anderson affirms, 'the fundamental structure of the new state was unmistakably *capitalist*'.[8] Between 1867 and 1873 liberal demands for national economic integration became the centrepiece of the constitutional settlement, which consummated the process begun by the Customs Union earlier in the century: freedom of movement for goods, capital, and labour; freedom of enterprise from guild regulation; emancipation of credit; favourable conditions for company formation; the metric system of weights and measures, a single currency, and unified laws of exchange; a federal consular service and a standardized postal and telegraph system; patent laws; and the general codification of commercial law. Central financial institutions soon followed. As industrialization proceeded, the state did much else to organize the environment for capital - by regulating rail and water transportation, by managing external relations through commercial treaties and tariffs, by colonies and the protection of markets, by contracts for army and navy, and by a host of social interventions (in welfare, education, labour legislation, and so on).[9] To this we might add the codification of criminal law, the standardization of judicial procedure, and the eventual adoption of a new Civil Law Code (in 1896). All of this presupposed the achievements of unification. Disgruntled opponents of Bismarck's settlement might speak disparagingly of 'a customs parliament, a postal parliament, and a telegraph parliament',[10] but in precisely these respects (and the others mentioned above) the new Reichstag had helped reconstitute the legal basis of Germany's social order.[11]

Within limits these are functions common to any capitalist state, in the sense that the accumulation and centralization of capital within nation-states structurally requires a certain range of state interventions. As well as those already mentioned (the basic guaranteeing of property rights, liberalization of the economy, standardization, management of external relations, and so on), we might also include taxation, the development of technology, and the general problem of legitimation.[12] Of course, the danger of this line of thought is an over-facile functionalism, where the activity of government is made to correspond to a series of structural imperatives, based on the 'needs of the economy' or the 'logic of capital'. Shifting focus, there is a similar tendency in much of sociology, stressing the moral solidarities essential to a society's effective functioning or sense of stability. This is especially marked in the case of nationalism, which Ralph Miliband calls 'the "functional" creed *par excellence*', perfect for ensuring the overall cohesion of the social formation.[13] These are seductive, ideas, as the functionalist argument appears to explain so much. German historians have certainly found it hard to resist the temptations. Recent work has combined nationalism's explanatory potential (in these functionalist senses) with the imperial state's prevailing authoritarianism, to suggest that nationalist ideology was essentially *conservative*, *stabilizing*, and *integrative* in its social effects.

As such, nationalism is thought to have been generally available for manipulation by the state. By stressing what united rather than what divided the citizenry, nationalist ideology placed a powerful weapon in the hands of a centralizing government, which could then de-legitimize and marginalize certain kinds of opposition or dissent. This was most easily accomplished (as 1914 was to confirm) in times of war, but a comparable sense of national solidarity might also arise in peace-time, by artfully manufacturing a 'moral equivalent of war'.[14] This might be done in a number of ways, from the use of war scares, diplomatic successes, and aggressive foreign adventures, to the uncovering of domestic subversion (by isolating ethnic and religious minorities, immigrants, revolutionaries, and anyone 'soft' on patriotic priorities), and the political exploitation of cultural achievements (in science, technology, the arts, and sport). By careful ideological labour (through state apparatuses like schools or a conscript army, or through manipulating public employment), the nation might be solidified into a powerful ideological community, fortified by symbolism and ritual.[15] This could never eliminate political conflict, let alone social contradiction. But the tangible reality of 'the nation' gave appeals to the 'national interest' a seductive credibility. They could be skilfully used to moderate and even to suspend certain kinds of disagreement.

German historians have developed a particularly strong version of this argument. In the first place the new German state badly needed to consolidate its superior legitimacy over older regional, confessional, and dynastic particularisms, whose disruptive potential was all the greater for coinciding in the south of the country. The *Mainlinie* amounted to a serious fracture in the nation's cultural unity. In the 1870s, moreover, the situation was quickly complicated by the rise of the SPD, with its radical challenge to the empire's undemocratic constitution. According to most German historians, the resolution of these problems was hampered by the narrowness of the *Kaiserreich's* social base, which heavily privileged the Junkers and precluded the reformist option of limited democratic concessions and a pluralist political system. Consequently, to achieve an adequate consensus of defensive interests and maintain the stability of the status quo, Germany's rulers were forced into elaborate techniques of 'secondary integration', for which nationalist ideology provided the ideal materials. This was already anticipated in the *Kulturkampf* of the 1870s, but the possibilities only came to full fruition in the colonial agitation of the 1880s, which has been called 'the diversion outwards of internal tensions and forces of change in order to preserve the social and political status quo'.[16] This 'Machiavellian technique of rule' rapidly became institutionalized in the state's political, administrative, and ideological practice. It was massively extended in the imperialist agitation of the 1890s. It was applied to the treatment of national minorities (especially the Poles), to the overall conduct of foreign policy, to the demands for greater military and naval armaments, and to the political isolation of the labour movement. All in all, this amounted to 'the manipulative application of nationalism for the purpose of stabilizing the social power structures and of thereby internalizing the sublimated power relations' which were characteristic of imperial Germany.[17]

There is much to be said for this 'integrationist' approach. There can be little doubt that German governments tried to undertake this kind of ideological offensive, and this can be clearly shown for the army and the schools (the obvious cases), where elaborate measures were taken for the inculcation of patriotic values in the interests of political conformity.[18] Whether they were successful or not is another matter. We know a great deal about the anti-socialist directives of the educational bureaucracy, for example, but far less about the daily practice of schools and teachers, not to speak of the real effects on children. There is no reason why the findings of much educational sociology, with their stress on the limited impact of schooling and the countervailing importance of family, neighbourhood and peers in the socialization of the young, should be inapplicable to this earlier society, particularly one which seemed to be as segmented along ethnic, religious, and class-cultural lines as imperial Germany. In some ways, given the relative sparseness of public education and the incompleteness of the educational apparatus before 1914, we should expect them to be more pertinent rather than less: in 1882 the average class size in Prussian elementary schools was 66, and by 1911 it had only been reduced to 51.[19] Besides, attempts to expand educational provision and increase its efficiency could easily meet with opposition. The Polish resistance to Germanization is perhaps an extreme example. But the peasantry, particularly in the Catholic south, put up determined opposition to the extension of schooling (enforcement of attendance, raising the school leaving age, reforming the curriculum, and so on), which seemed to threaten the patriarchal authority of the peasant family and undermine the system of child labour.[20] At a time of growing secularization the clergy had an obvious interest in sustaining this kind of resistance. Moreover, not only the Catholic Centre Party, but also the Social Democrats maintained impressive cultural organizations of their own, with high levels of educational activity. Each of these factors qualified the effectiveness of state educational interventions.[21]

None of this is to dispute the importance of public education (or conscription, and other areas of state intervention) for the general dissemination of patriotic values. But the formation of nationalist consciousness in school students (or military recruits) could only result from very complicated processes of ideological negotiation, through which nationalist commitments (whether formal or unspoken) acquired a variable specific content. We can see this by looking at the example of the *Kulturkampf*. Without entering the discussion of Bismarck's motivation, which remains obscure, it is clear that for the German liberals this was a logical accompaniment of unification. The attack on the Catholic religion *per se* was less important than a positive ideal of how the future German society was to be constituted. In the abstract this amounted to a centralist drive for the primacy of the citizen-state relation in the organization of public life, with radical implications for both traditional ideas of social order and the Prusso-centric version of federalism. As such it was both inimical to Prussian Conservatives and a dangerous game for Bismarck to play, with potential consequences going far beyond the disastrous countermobilization of Catholics in the Centre Party. For liberals, the *Kulturkampf* meant exactly that the term said, a struggle to unlock the potential for social progress, freeing the dynamism of German society from the 'dead hand' of archaic institutions. This was clearest in the localities, where clerical control of charities, poor-houses, and schools tied up capital resources, kept the poor in dependent ignorance, and shackled the chances for social and economic development.[22]

In other words, the unification of Germany had a specific social logic, which partially determined the character of the new state, and infused German nationalism in the 1860s and 1870s with a particular content. The *Kulturkampf* articulated this specificity perfectly. At one level, of course, it was a natural extension of the Bismarckian (Prussian, small-German) solution to the German question, by emphasizing the North German, Prussian, and Protestant bias of the new state. It also had positive functions for state formation, by cutting back the independent public authority of the church and strengthening government control of education. But in other respects it strengthened the momentum of exactly those forces in civil society - the liberal movement for German unity - that in the 1860s Bismarck had sought to control. After the liberalization of the economy the *Kulturkampf* was the object of the greatest liberal effort in the 1870s, and also saw the liberals' maximum penetration into the state apparatus (under Adalbert Falk at the Prussian Ministry of Culture and his counterparts in the other states). In this sense it threatened to upset the uneasy compromise on which the empire had been founded. Liberals were engaged in a secular crusade against the very values, institutions, and vested interests that Bismarck's constitution was meant to defend. 'Junkers and priests together/Put townsmen and peasants in tether', ran one liberal slogan, and having done with the one, they might well turn to the other.[23] The ideal of German-national citizenship disclosed by liberal campaigning implied both an attack on corporate particularism and a strengthening of local self-government, and neither were possible in the terms of the Bismarckian constitution. Consequently, liberals found themselves pitted against a growing constellation of conservative social forces.

This was nothing new. Liberals came to power in most German states at the end of the 1860s through broad regional coalitions against aristocracy, particularism, and reaction. This was especially true in the South - in Baden, Württemberg, the Grand Duchy of Hesse, and more uncertainly Bavaria - but also applied to many parts of Prussia, particularly those annexed in 1866 (Hanover, Nassau, and the Electorate of Hesse).[24] The liberal cause suffered momentary setbacks after 1866, but the events of 1870-1 rebounded massively to its advantage. In the Grand Duchy of Hesse, to give an example, unification swept the Progressives into office in 1872 with 41 of the 50 seats in the Landtag. Moreover, this political hegemony presupposed much deeper processes of institutional growth and cultural formation going right back to the start of the century, by which liberals staked out their claims to social leadership. Here the forms of associational life were crucial, providing the practical environment in which a self-conscious bourgeois public could gradually take shape. Normally centred on an exclusive social club, where the town's notables would consort for a mixture of business, relaxation, and political discussion, this new public domain was textured by a rich variety of charitable, educational, cultural, and economic activities, from fire service and rifle club, to choir, theatre, and commercial society. Linked to press, petition, and public meeting, it opened new possibilities for political mobilization which were a key feature of the unification years. The emergence of a public sphere in this sense - as 'a sphere which mediates between society and state, in which the public organizes itself as the bearer of public opinion'[25] - was the essential foundation of liberal politics. The movement for national unification (which for liberals was a vital condition of 'progress') originated in the same coalescence of political culture.[26]

This emerges clearly from the character of the opposition. The critics of the new nation-state were often acutely uncomfortable with the new public opinion, its ideology of citizenship, and demand for civil freedoms. There were naturally elements to whom this does not apply - the democrats of central and south-west Germany, or a variety of special interests (like the financial oligarchy in Frankfurt) which benefited directly from the prevailing conditions of decentralization and political fragmentation - who opposed the 'Prussian solution' from the same cultural and institutional resources of a flourishing civil society. But the conservative opponents of the Bismarckian settlement, the supporters of Austria and upholders of particularism, inhabited a much older institutional world, one dominated by courts, the church, and aristocratic society. In opposing unification, they opposed the forces of change and reform.[27] The main supporters of the Guelph cause in Hanover, for instance, were noble landowners, the Lutheran clergy, sections of the Hanoverian administration and officer corps, and all those whose livelihood was linked to the royal household and the court. Of course, their resentment was directed as much at the particular form of unification - Prussian annexation - as the general principle. But the supporters of annexation (a majority of the Hanoverians who went to the polls for the North German Confederation in 1867) were probably no less conscious of Hanoverian traditions. They simply had a different conception of where they were to be found and of which institutions were to be preserved. In transferring their formal allegiance to the Prussian monarchy, for example, the citizens of Hanover were mainly concerned to maintain the levels of civic achievement - 'the rich installations, collections, and institutions for art and science, for the education and the instruction of youth, and training for trade and technology'. Hanoverian liberals pushed for greater self-government in precisely the same areas, meaning principally public works and social welfare. It was no accident that the Guelph Fund was used for much the same purpose after 1869, to subsidize road-building, railway construction, educational installations like the Hanover Polytechnic, public monuments, cultural institutions like museums, the Natural History Society, and the Hanover Botanical Gardens, and the royal resort at Nordeney. This was a shrewd use of resources, emphasizing the Hanoverian contribution to German culture and pandering to civic pride, to build the cultural no less than the economic infra-structure of the new nation-state.[28]

Where does this leave us? Basically it returns us to the three-way distinction suggested above, between processes of state formation, the emergence of nationalist ideology, and processes of cultural unification. It would clearly make little sense to discuss German nationalism without recognizing the important contribution of the Prussian state to the incremental definition of German nationality during the nineteenth century, particularly in the period of Bismarck after 1862. In this first sense, therefore, German nationalism was a complex effect of unification from above, beginning with the Napoleonic occupation, continuing through the Austrian-Prussian condominium, and finishing in the successive realignments of the 1860s, during which the German governments generated a new institutional framework for the formation of public consciousness. Within limits, as we saw, nationalist ideology could then function within the institutions of the *Kaiserreich* to solidify the new social and political status quo. But at the same time, German governments (and certainly not Bismarck) seldom acted with specifically nationalist intentions, rationalized by a coherent ideological commitment to the overriding legitimacy of national sovereignty. In this second sense - the formation of nationalist ideology - the German nation was conceived in the minds of intellectuals and realized in a political movement. That movement was principally liberal, though it contained a democratic left wing, and defined itself through opposition to the already constituted governments.

The contradiction between state and civil society ran through the centre of the national question in Germany. By contrast with the 'core' states of Western Europe, nationalities East of the Rhine lacked the advantage of an early acquired statehood. Of necessity the real labour of constituting the 'nation' had to be conducted by private rather than public bodies, by individual intellectuals and voluntary associations rather than governments, though the latter could seriously affect the terms under which it was done. Accordingly, the process of 'proposing and elaborating the category of the nation' (W.J. Argyle) was to a great extent identical with the growth of a public sphere, with the 'nation' conceived simultaneously as a political community of citizens.[29] The inter-penetration of these two terms - nation and citizenry - in the discourse of both liberals and democrats in the mid-nineteenth century was extremely close and complex. Thus when it came to defining the obligations of national citizenship, the boundaries of the private and the public, and the distribution of sovereignty in the new German state, divisions quickly opened between the state authorities and the various political tendencies, especially given the absence of direct parliamentary government. The labour movement and the left liberals pushed the disagreements furthest. But National Liberals (as most German nationalists became after 1867) also had their positive objectives. Essentially this was what the *Kulturkampf* was about.

This brings us to the third facet of definition, concerning processes of cultural unification and the 'nationalization of consciousness' in society. Here the transition to statehood - in Germany between 1864 and 1871 - is crucial. As the realization of nationality in its strongest political form, this transforms the conditions of existence for nationalist movements and their ideas. It immeasurably simplifies the process of manufacturing, strengthening, or imposing a set of shared political loyalties on the putative national population. Moreover, once political independence has been attained, the nation comes to represent an ideological and institutional structure of immense power, which begins to set limits on the possible forms of political action and belief. Almost imperceptibly nationalism loses its character as a sectional creed articulating the aspirations of liberal and other tendencies within the bourgeoisie, and passes into the common heritage of a political culture - becoming, as Tom Nairn puts it, 'a name for the general condition of the modern body politic, more like the climate of political and social thought than just another doctrine'.[30] The process of national integration simultaneously, gradually, and subtly transforms the content of the national idea, universalizing its legitimacy, while endowing it with a vital plasticity. Thus, though drives for cultural uniformity within nations (Germanization, Russification, the imposition of Parisian culture on provincial France, and so on) may be vigorously state-directed, they are also subject to private initiative and political contestation, involving protracted struggles for leadership and control. Though open to functionalist interpretation, therefore, stressing the need for social solidarity, the initiating role of the state, and the conservative or stabilizing effects of nationalist propaganda, this can only be a part of the picture.

III

If we problematize the concept of the German nation, therefore, by converting unspoken assumptions into a very basic question (i.e. what *was* the German nation, and how did the answer vary?), some fundamental issues come into view. Overall, these concern what we might call the definition of an individual's political identity (or in a current idiom the constitution of political subjects), for if *national* consciousness was very low in the 1860s, other kinds of allegiance clearly functioned in its stead (e.g. family, kin, village, locality, region, state, church, religion), and any attempt to strengthen loyalty to the nation almost certainly implied moderation, subordination, or active suppression of its rivals: how exactly individuals came to think of themselves primarily as citizens of Germany (or Britain, France, Italy, and so on), as opposed to the members of some smaller community, or the participants in some larger cultural enterprise like the Catholic Church, is a very under-researched problem. Moreover, as this chapter has begun to suggest, it is a mistake to assume that in pursuing the goal of national solidarity the state had things all its own way - or even that the state was the most active agent in the process. So far from simply imposing its own definitions of the national interest, in fact, government entered some bitterly contested terrain, on which socialists and catholics, liberals and democrats, radical agrarians, anti-semites, and Pan-Germans, had all entered their claims. In this sense the 'national interest' was open to widely conflicting interpretations, amongst which the official view of the Prusso-German state was just one example. Once this is grasped, an excessively functionalist account of nationalism's place in the maintenance of an authoritarian dominant culture (the most influential analysis of German nationalism under the *Kaiserreich*) is more easily avoided.

This is a salutary observation. Mere control of the socializing institutions (the schools system, the church, the conscript army, the organs of opinion, and so on) cannot guarantee ideological conformity or national integration, however authoritarian the political system. Efforts at ideological incorporation can always be contested, from a wide variety of positions. As Hobsbawm notes, the insight was grasped by the French philosopher Ernest Renan, in his classic lecture in 1882 *What is a Nation?*.[31] Voicing an extreme scepticism regarding objective criteria for the existence of nations, Renan emphasized the elements of cultural invention and historical process. Nations were 'the result of a long history of effort, sacrifice and devotion', requiring both 'a rich legacy of memories from the past and consent in the present'. They stood for 'a great solidarity', but one in constant need of creative renewal. Once created, a sense of national identity had to be continuously reaffirmed, by a difficult, unpredictable, and time-consuming labour of ideological reproduction. This is what, in a striking phrase, Renan called a silent 'daily plebiscite'. But it proceeded not simply by an unmediated interaction between governments and subject populations. By the state/civil society couplet we postulate a field of ideological negotiation, in which organized agencies of one kind or another (political, religious, cultural, economic) are necessarily present. That being the case, the content of nationalist ideology, the meaning of national loyalty, and the very category of the nation itself, were all open to alternative definitions.

This was becoming clear by the end of the 1870s. As suggested, the basic work of constituting the nation (by proposing a German nationality, and propagating a German-national view) originated in the growth of civil society as a public arena of freely associating citizens, distinct from the state and beyond its arbitrary supervision. In Germany, as elsewhere in the nineteenth century, this process had a self-consciously liberal colouration, and the buoyancy of the liberal movement formed the context in which the demand for nation-states became a realistic proposition. After unification - a political act, which necessarily left the nation's social and cultural consolidation incomplete - liberals continued to press for the same ideals of progress and unity, initially with the state's resources behind them. The *Kulturkampf* dramatized their commitment, and in this respect resembled the drive for republican consolidation in France in the 1870s and 1880s.[32] But the brief period of liberal dominance only really lasted from the early 1860s to the end of the 1870s, with a further decade or so in many of the regions. By the end of the empire's first decade the liberals were just one sectional tendency amongst others, no longer hegemonic in the political culture, without privileged access to government, and (ironically for the party of national unification) potentially factionalized on a wide variety of issues on an increasingly regional basis.

From this point on it becomes impossible to speak of a single national movement. If National Liberals still claimed the leading voice over specifically national questions, this was no longer undisputed. Moreover, liberal nationalism became less and less of a dynamic social force, taking more and more of a refuge in older ideological themes like the *Kulturkampf,* which spluttered on in the liberal heartlands of the Rhineland and the south-west as an impoverished and more straightforward anti-clericalism, a German version of waving the bloody shirt. Otherwise, apart from the passage of the Civil Law Code and an amended law of association between 1896 and 1900, which in liberal minds belatedly completed the legal side of unification, National Liberals put most of their energies into foreign policy, on matters like colonies, the navy, and the promotion of foreign trade. Even here they were outflanked in innovative thinking, because between 1892 and 1907 left liberals readdressed the same questions and emerged with a more challenging programme of imperialism and social reform. More seriously, the Catholic Centre Party began affirming its own nationalist credentials in the 1890s, as a new generation of bourgeois catholics displaced the clerics and aristocrats from the leadership and demanded civic equality within the German nation rather than simply defence of the Church. It was no accident that the national achievements most prized by National Liberals in the 1890s - the Code of Civil Law and the two Navy Laws - were realized through parliamentary coalitions with the Centre. Over to the right, Prussian Conservatives were also discovering the virtues of nationalist argumentation in their campaigns for agricultural protection.[33]

In other words, nationalism had ceased to be the prerogative of a particular group in German society and had entered the universal currency of political debate. The parties increasingly clothed themselves in the modern legitimacy of the 'national interest'. In effect they vied for the general will, claiming for their primary constituency (whether bourgeois, peasant, *mittelständisch*, or working-class) the real embodiment of national virtue. Even the Social Democrats had their conception of the German nation, drawn from the experience of 1848, the democratic patriotism of the 1860s, and the popular democratic vision of a socialist electoral majority, against which the emotional resonances of the Second International proved to be no impediment.[34] This multiplicity of nationalist conceptions - which was virtually inevitable given the structured ideological context of the nation, and the territorial boundedness of the nation-state and its institutions - made nationalist appeals as much a source of conflict as unity. Despite its own elevated sense of classless cultural solidarity, nationalist ideology could never escape the contradictions of German society before the First World War.

This is the central paradox of the post-unification period, namely the indisputable suffusion of national values in a society where the exact *content* of the national tradition and its future direction were a matter of bitter dispute. This divisiveness - the fissiparity of the national idea - was highlighted in the 1890s by the rather turbulent popular mobilizations of that decade, which collectively redrew the boundaries of the political nation. Not only the working class in the towns, but also the *Mittelstand* and smallholding peasantry in the countryside showed new levels of political interest, activating themselves through new types of economic and political organization, and generally invading the public sphere. But this was not some unproblematic process of national integration, as the state and its metropolitan culture penetrated more deeply into the recesses of rural society, obliterating difference and homogenizing political identity. On the contrary, the Catholic farmers and small tradesmen of South-West Germany, their anti-semitic counterparts in Hesse, and the radical *Bauernbündler* of Bavaria, all bitterly resented the processes of national penetration, which seemed to further progress and integration mainly at their own expense (e.g. through the new economic and fiscal legislation, the unfavourable siting of railway branch lines, the extension and reform of schooling, the imposition of conscription, and so on).[35] Yet nor, in most cases, did these mobilizations take place under narrowly particularist or localist auspices, which dealt with the new national context by refusing its legitimacy altogether. At the grass roots there was much sentiment of this kind, but most of the discontent (certainly over the longer term) was articulated through organizations with an aggressively national presence (the Centre Party, the Anti-Semites, the Agrarian League). From this point of view the modalities of mobilization (the different ways in which people became inducted into the political system) could have a crucial effect on the form and the content of the nationalist orientation.

In this respect the contradiction between centre and periphery resembles the conflicts between dominant and small nationalities, particularly in regions with a distinctive culture, institutional history or social structure (like the backward Catholic parts of Germany, or the areas annexed by Prussia in 1866). Indeed, the 'progressive' case for the assimilation of small 'backward' peoples by large 'developed' or 'advanced' nations was simultaneously an argument for metropolitan over provincial or local cultures, and this 'was directed as much against the regional languages and cultures of the nation itself as against outsiders'.[36] As Eugen Weber has reminded us, the impact of a dominant metropolitan culture on a parochial village world could be just as traumatic and alienating *within* a particular nation as any encounter between separate nationalities.[37] At the same time, the penetration of a centralizing nationalism into the countryside was neither always nor simply a process of destructive repression. Induction into the dominant culture was also a potential passport to mobility, new experiences, and self-improvement. When things went well (e.g. at times of general prosperity and expanding employment, without blatant national discrimination or dramatic inequalities between the economies of region and metropolis), assimilation could easily work. At all events, a particularist sense of regional identity, cultural nationalism or ethnicity is not *by definition* incompatible with willing participation in a larger nation and its state. In fact, the twentieth-century ideology of 'americanism' in the United States is predicated on precisely this type of contention.[38]

The point of these observations is to stress the different effects of being socialized or educated into a sense of national awareness. We can see this very clearly if we consider the attempts for the imperial state to equip itself with a patriotic public tradition which was distinct from the existing paraphernalia of princely ceremonial, and which could foster a form of patriotism specific to itself. Commemoration of unification was the obvious form for this to take, and while celebration of Sedan Day began immediately in the 1870s, the most concentrated period of innovation seems to have begun with the later 1890s.[39] Its principal form was the building of the great national monuments (the ones on the Kyffhäuser mountain and the *Deutsches Eck*, both finished in 1897, and the *Siegesallee* built in Berlin between 1898 and 1901), which were carefully laden 'with specific ideological-historical associations'. As well as the major public festivals like Sedan Day and the Kaiser's birthday, we should also mention the extended repertoire of ceremonial and ritual observed in public institutions like the army and the schools. Superficially this confirms the functionalist account of nationalism, with its stress on the latter's unifying potential, as a force for cohesion and solidarity in an otherwise divided society. As Hobsbawm says, 'these systematically planned ceremonial campaigns' promulgated not only 'a particular version of German history' for use in the schools, but also 'the ritual practices, badges and symbols through which identification with the new

Germany (as distinct from any other kind of Germany or any other German state) was internalized'.[40]

Yet this can be easily exaggerated. The imperial cult competed with the older pageantry of the individual states, which kept a vigorous existence down to the turn of the century and derived much legitimacy from the federal nature of the Constitution.[41] Similarly, the agrarian mobilizations of the 1890s made great play of local political traditions, often with a particularist and heavily anti-Prussian emphasis (again particularly in the annexed territories of Hanover and Hesse), appropriating the forms of popular Lutheranism and the iconography of 1848.[42] More seriously in the longer term, the SPD made a systematic attempt to challenge the hegemony of the official nationalism, counterposing its own carefully articulated version of the national tradition, with a rich variety of symbolism and ritual expression. May Day and other political festivals, the commemoration of dead leaders and great events, and a rich texture of symbolic forms (banners, portraits, badges, *tableaux vivants*, radical iconography, and other emblematic devices), all helped cement the cohesion of the SPD's subculture. A counter-mythology of the past was an important aspect of this activity, stressing the European revolutionary tradition, German popular resistance, and the SPD's inheritance of the democratic past. A populist view of 1848 as the thwarted uprising of the democratic nation was a central feature of this historical imagery, whether in the successful popular history of Wilhelm Blos, or the public discussion accompanying the Revolution's fiftieth anniversary in 1898.[43]

Moreover, not all the patriotic inventiveness stemmed from the state. To a great extent the commemoration of German unity (no less than the process of unification itself) originated in civil society. The *Hermannsdenkmal* (1841-75), the *Niederwalddenkmal* (1874-85), the Kyffhäuser Memorial (1896-7), and the *Völkerschlachtdenkmal* (1894-1913) were all launched by private initiative and kept alive by various kinds of voluntary effort and public subscription, with a minimum of direct subsidy from the state. On a smaller scale but a similar basis, some 500 of Wilhelm Kreis's Bismarck towers were built between 1900 and 1910, normally with some sort of civic support, but owing little to the initiative of the state as such. Most of the impetus for the holding of patriotic festivals came originally from non-official sources. To promote the general idea a National Festival Society was formed in 1897, growing out of the earlier Central Commission for People's and Youth Sports set up in 1889, and closely linked locally to the choral and gymnastic movements. Though the actual occasions of patriotic celebration were inevitably dominated by dignitaries and officialdom, therefore, much of the drive and imagination came from private individuals or associations. Furthermore, at a certain point this meshed with the activities of the nationalist pressure groups (Pan-Germans, Navy League, Colonial Society, Eastern Marches Society, Defence League, Society for Germandom Abroad, and a number of lesser organizations), which often formed themselves into local patriotic coalitions, and had their own strong views about how nationalist propaganda should be conducted.[44]

This revealed the contradictory, centrifugal effects of nationalist ideology most pointedly of all. In certain respects the activity of such nationalist associations was obviously conjoint with that of the government - e.g. the general propaganda for colonies, navy, and military spending, the anti-Polish activities in the East, or the promotion of patriotic values through the schools (as in the rewriting of text-books, or the organization of school trips to colonial and naval exhibitions). Moreover, at the local level they busied themselves with much the sort of patriotic manifestations which the imperial state desired, as with the patriotic evenings which formed the high point in the Navy League branches' annual calender, or the organization of film shows which exposed the importance of the navy to the maximum possible audience.[45] But while sharing the same general aims, the *nationale Verbände* also diverged sharply from the government on a number of issues. This was partly because their demands were more extreme (for more ships, faster development of the colonies, harsher treatment of the Poles, a much more 'German' foreign policy). But they also developed searching criticisms of the government's general political practice, demanding an end to parliamentary conciliation (particularly of the Centre Party), a fullscale assault on particularism, and a patriotic mobilization of the people against the Reichstag. Most fundamentally of all, they questioned the government's own patriotic credentials (and by extension those of the right-wing party establishments), accusing it of neglecting Germany's interests in the world, surrendering to the pressures of special interests in the Reichstag, and ignoring the threat from the left. In 1907-8, during a crisis in the Navy League and the *Daily Telegraph* affair, this broadened into an attack on the monarchy itself. Though these tendencies towards 'national opposition' were only partly realized before the First World War, a radical nationalist politics to the right of the government had definitely taken shape.[46]

This, perhaps better than anything else, demonstrates the complexity of the national question in imperial Germany and the dangers of an overly functionalist account. National integration was certainly an urgent priority for the imperial government, given the difficulties of constructing a stable governing consensus while basic questions of national identity remained unresolved. The new government had to deal with strong particularisms in eastern Prussia, Bavaria, and elsewhere, a potential liberal-democratic opposition, religious divisions, and a rising labour movement, without the benefit of a centralized state apparatus (given the entrenched federalism of the constitution) or national cultural institutions. In the circumstances a strong emphasis on national unity was clearly some sort of 'functional' necessity. But in the event the strengthening of the national framework did little to solve the problems of integration in anything but a formal and very general sense: by universalizing the legitimacy of the 'nation' or national values, it simply transferred the contradictions from the margins to the very centre of the national idea. Though the contextual reality of the nation-state and its institutions increasingly structured the possible limits of dissent, conflicts now took place over how the nation was to be represented. Moreover, not only did Catholics, radical agrarians, Junkers, and even Socialist Democrats add their own national conceptions to the older one of the liberals. Radical nationalists also entered the fray (Pan-Germans, anti-semites, Navy Leaguers, and all sorts of independent patriots), attacking the government's official nationalism with a new populism of the right.

Nowhere was this clearer than in the centenary celebrations of 1913, organized to commemorate Germany's war of liberation against Napoleon. In conjunction with Wilhelm II's silver jubilee, this seemed to afford a golden opportunity to enhance the prestige of the empire and to tighten the moral bonds of public solidarity and identification. Events proceeded throughout the year, centring on the double climax of civic festivities in March and the opening of the *Völkerschlachtdenkmal* in Lepizig in November. Yet the national consensus revealed itself fractured by disagreements. Not only were the official celebrations attacked by the SPD, who reminded the enthusiasts of Germany's 'national liberation' that the Prussian people were still awaiting their civic and political emancipation. The transmutation of the history of 1813 into a glorification of dynastic traditions was attacked from many other quarters too: the left liberal press, sections of the cultural intelligentsia, parts of the youth movement, but most importantly of all, the Pan-German right, who charged the government with falsifying the popular nature of the struggle against Napoleon.[47]

IV

There are many aspects of German nationalism which this essay has not discussed. Several of the problems raised during the previous section might have received more extensive treatment - e.g. the process of popular mobilization in the 1890s and its reconstitution of the political nation; the nature of radical agrarianism; the complex interactions between rural society, particularism, and political catholicism in the formation of the Centre Party's secular patriotism; the Social Democratic conception of the German nation; the radical nationalist critique of official patriotism and conventional conservative politics; or the role of symbolism, ritual, and invented tradition. Other questions have not been mentioned - e.g. the treatment of the national minorities, racialist and social-Darwinist definitions of the nation, anti-semitism, the impact of colonialism and the idea of a big navy, the new economic nationalism of the protectionist period after 1879, or the forms of anti-socialism. By concentrating on the period of unification and the problems of national integration I have said nothing about two later conjunctures - the imperialist upturn after the end of the depression in 1895-6, and the vital climacteric of the Great War - which profoundly affected the terms of the national question and the place of nationalist ideology. This is partly because I have discussed these matters elsewhere.[48] But my object in this essay has been more modest. It has been to abstract some general points of definition from Eric Hobsbawm's writings on nationalism, to deploy their insights in the context of pre-1914 German history, and to suggest some new lines of discussion for the future.

To conclude we can do far worse than quote Eric Hobsbawm. In his most concise statement he has called nationalism[49]

> a dual phenomenon, or rather an interaction of two phenomena, each of which help to give shape to the other. It consists of a 'civic religion' for the modern territorial-centralized state, and of a mode of confronting social changes which appear to threaten and disrupt certain aspects of the complex of social relationships. The former reflects a specific historic situation, characteristic of Europe since the French Revolution, and of most of the non-European world in the twentieth century: the combination of economic development . . . with the mass participation in politics of a mobilized population. . . . The latter is in principle not confined to any particular historic period of society, though it only acquired the full features of 'nationalism' as we know it in the specific historical era since 1789, and would probably not have done so in another setting.

Arguably, this is precisely the point, between the formation and impact of states and the social determination of political culture, where the most interesting questions of nineteenth-century European history begin.

NOTES

1 See in particular the following: A.D. Smith, *Theories of Nationalism*, London, 1971; M. Hechter, *Internal Colonialism. The Celtic Fringe in British National Development, 1536-1966*, London, 1975; C. Tilly (ed.), *The Formation of National States in Western Europe*, Princeton, N.J., 1975; T. Nairn, *The Break-Up of Britain. Crisis and Neo-Nationalism*, London, 1977. See also the following works by Eric Hobsbawm: *The Age of Revolution*, New York, 1962, pp. 163-77; 'The attitude of popular classes towards national movements for independence', *Mouvements nationaux d'indépendance et classes populaires aux XIXe et XXe siecles en occident et en orient*, Paris, 1971, pp. 34-44; 'Some reflections on nationalism', T.J. Nossiter, S. Rokkan, A.H. Hanson (eds),

Imagination and Precision in the Social Sciences, London, 1972, pp. 385-406; *The Age of Capital*, London, 1975, pp. 82-97; 'Inventing traditions in 19th century Europe', Past & Present Society (ed.), *The Invention of Tradition*, London, 1977, pp. 1-24; 'Some reflections on "The Break-Up of Britain"', *New Left Review*, 105, 1977, pp. 3-24.

2 See J. Godechot, 'Nation, patrie, nationalisme et patriotisme en France au XVIIIe siècle', *Annales historiques de la Revolution Francaise*, 206, 1971, pp. 481-501.

3 The most important analysis of this kind is M. Hroch, *Die Vorkämpfer der nationalen Bewegung bei den kleinen Völkern Europas*, Prague, 1968. Unfortunately, due to the limited currency of German and East-European languages in the English-speaking world and the general ignorance about historical work in the socialist countries, Hroch's work is badly neglected. Eric Hobsbawm, who has introduced the latter into English-language discussion, is an important exception. Otherwise see J.-P. Himka, 'Polish and Ukrainian Socialism: Austria, 1867-1890', University of Michigan PhD. thesis, Ann Arbor, 1977 (shortly to be published), and J. Chlebowczyk, *Procesy narodotwórcze we wschodniej Europie środkowej w dobie kapitalizmu: Od schylku XVIII do poczatków XX w.*, Warsaw, 1975. Mention should also be made of a seminal work of sociology, K. Deutsch, *Nationalism and Social Communication*, Cambridge, Mass., 1966.

4 See Nairn, op. cit., pp. 92ff., 329ff., for the most eloquent defence of this view.

5 I have tried to discuss them in a recent essay, G. Eley, 'Nationalism and social history', *Social History*, 6, 1981, pp. 83-107.

6 J.J. Sheehan, 'What is German history? Reflections on the role of the *nation* in German history and historiography', *Journal of Modern History*, 53, 1981, p. 10. See also the following: R.M. Berdahl, 'New thoughts on German nationalism', *American Historical Review*, 77, 1972, pp. 65-80; W. Real, 'Die Ereignisse von 1866-67 im Lichte unserer Zeit', *Historisches Jahrbuch*, 95, 1975, pp. 342-73; N.M. Hope, *The Alternative to German Unification. The Anti-Prussian Party: Frankfurt, Nassau, and the Two Hessen 1859-1867*, Wiesbaden, 1973; R. Austensen, 'Austria and the struggle for supremacy in Germany, 1848-1864', *Journal of Modern History*, 52, 1980, pp. 195-225.

7 Berdahl, op. cit., p. 70.

8 P. Anderson, *Lineages of the Absolutist State*, London, 1974, p. 276.

9 See here H.-U. Wehler, 'Der Aufstieg des Organiserten Kapitalismus und Interventionsstaates in Deutschland', H.A. Winkler (ed.), *Organisierter Kapitalismus*, Göttingen, 1974, pp. 36-57.

10 Benedikt Waldeck of the Progressive Party, cited by T.S. Hamerow, *The Social Foundations of German Unification*

1858-1871. Struggles and Accomplishments, Princeton, N.J., 1972, p. 330.

11 Ibid., pp. 337ff., for the best brief description of the specific changes brought by unification in this respect.

12 See R. Murray, 'The internationalization of capital and the nation-state', *New Left Review*, 67, 1971, pp. 84-109.

13 R. Miliband, *The State in Capitalist Society*, London, 1969, p. 185.

14 The phrase 'moral equivalent of war' comes from William James's essay of the same name, *Memories and Studies*, New York, 1917, pp. 267-306.

15 Hobsbawm has discussed these processes directly in 'Inventing traditions in 19th century Europe'.

16 H.-U. Wehler, *Bismarck und der Imperialismus*, Cologne, 1969, p. 115.

17 Wehler, *Das Deutsche Käiserreich, 1871-1918*, Göttingen, 1973, p. 126.

18 For an introduction to these problems: M. Kitchen, *The German Officer Corps 1890-1914*, Oxford, 1968, pp. 143-86; W.C. Langsam, 'Nationalism and history in the Prussian elementary schools under William II', E.M. Earle (ed.), *Nationalism and Internationalism. Essays inscribed to Carlton J.H. Hayes*, New York, 1950, pp. 241-61; F. Wenzel, 'Sicherung von Massenloylität und Qualifikation der Arbeitskraft als Aufgabe der Volksschule', K. Hartmann, F. Nyssen, H. Waldeyer (eds), *Schule und Staat im 18. und 19. Jahrhundert*, Frankfurt, 1974, pp. 323-86; H.-J. Heydorn, G. Koneffke, *Studien zur Sozialgeschichte und Philosophie der Bildung. II. Aspekte des 19. Jahrhunderts in Deutschland*, Munich, 1973, pp. 179-238.

19 G. Hohorst, J. Kocka, G.A. Ritter, *Sozialgeschichtliches Arbeitsbuch. Materialien zur Statistik des Kaiserreichs 1870-1914*, Munich, 1975, p. 157.

20 In 1904 in Wurttemberg something like a fifth of all school-age children worked in some kind of paid employment, nearly half of them as domestic servants, not to speak of the still larger numbers whose unpaid family labour was crucial to the viability of small-holdings. See D.G. Blackbourn, *Class, Religion and Local Politics in Wilhelmine Germany. The Centre Party in Württemberg before 1914*, New Haven and London, 1980, p. 139.

21 For an exemplary discussion, ibid., pp. 136-40; for the Polish school strikes, R. Korth, *Die preußische Schulpolitik und die polnischen Schulstreiks. Ein Beitrag zur preußischen Polenpolitik der Ära Bülow*, Würzburg, 1963.

22 See the splendid analyses in G. Zang (ed.), *Provinzialisierung einer Region. Zur Entstehung der bürgerlichen Gesellschaft in der Provinz*, Frankfurt, 1978, especially those by D. Bellmann, 'Der Liberalismus im Seekreis (1860-1870)', pp. 183-264; W. Trapp, 'Volksschulreform und liberales Bürgertum in Konstanz. Die Durchsetzung des Schulzwangs

als Voraussetzung der Massendisziplinierung und -qualifikation', pp. 375-434; and Zang himself, 'Die Bedeutung der Auseinandersetzung um die Stiftungsverwaltung in Konstanz (1830-1870) für die ökonomische und gesellscahftliche Entwicklung der lokalen Gesellschaft. Ein Beitrag zur Analyse der materiellen Hintergründe des Kulturkampfes', pp. 307-74.

23 The slogan comes from a Progressive election leaflet in Hanau-Gelnhausen-Bockenhiem (Hesse) in 1881, cited by D.S. White, *The Splintered Party. National Liberalism in Hessen and the Reich, 1867-1918,* Cambridge, Mass., 1976, p. 100.

24 To be more exact we are dealing here with the National Liberals and their different regional equivalents - viz. that majority tendency of German liberalism which accepted the Bismarckian solution in 1866-7. The best introduction to German liberalism is now J.J. Sheehan, *German Liberalism in the Nineteenth Century,* Chicago, 1978, but there is little detail on regional politics in the 1860s.

25 J. Habermas, 'The public sphere', *New German Critique,* 3, 1974, p. 49. Habermas developed the idea in full in *Strukturwandel der Öffentlichkeit,* Neuwied, 1962.

26 For the importance of voluntary association: T. Nipperdey, 'Verein als soziale Struktur in Deutschland im späten 18. und frühen 19. Jahrhundert', *Gesellschaft, Kultur, Theorie. Gesammelte Aufsätze zur neueren Geschichte,* Göttingen, 1976, pp. 176-205; O. Dann, 'Die Anfänge politischer Vereinsbildung in Deutschland', U. Engelhardt, V. Sellin, H. Stuke (eds), *Soziale Bewegung und politische Verfassung* Stuttgart, 1976, pp. 297-343. I have tried to explore the process in G. Eley, *Reshaping the German Right. Radical Nationalism and Political Change after Bismarck,* New Haven and London, 1980, pp. 30ff., 150ff., and Eley, 'Re-thinking the political: social history and political culture in 18th and 19th century Britain', *Archiv für Sozialgeschichte,* XX, 1981 (forthcoming).

27 See especially Hope's fine monograph, *Alternative to German Unification.*

28 See S.A. Stechlin, *Bismarck and the Guelph Problem 1866-1890. A Study in Particularist Opposition to National Unity,* Hague, 1973, pp. 159-93. The Guelph Fund was created from the sequestrated possessions of the Hanoverian royal family.

29 W.J. Argyle, 'Size and scale as factors in the development of nationalist movements', A.D. Smith (ed.) *Nationalist Movements,* London, 1976, pp. 31-53.

30 Nairn, op. cit., p. 94.

31 E. Renan, 'What is a nation', A. Zimmern (ed.), *Modern Political Doctrines,* Oxford, 1939, pp. 190ff.

32 See S. Elwitt, *The Making of the Third Republic. Class and Politics in France, 1868-1884,* Baton Rouge, 1975.

33 See D.G. Blackbourn, 'The problem of democratization:

German catholics and the role of the Centre Party', R.J. Evans (ed.), *Society and Politics in Wilhelmine Germany*, London, 1978, pp. 160-85, and *Class, Religion and Local Politics*, pp. 23-60; H.-J. Puhle, *Agrarische Interessenpolitik und preußischer Konservatismus im wilhelminischen Reich 1893-1914*, Hanover, 1966.

34 See especially: H.-U. Wehler, *Sozialdemokratie und National staat. Nationalitätenfragen in Deutschland 1840-1914*, Göttingen, 1971; W. Conze, D. Groh, *Die Arbeiterbewegung in der nationalen Bewegung*, Stuttgart, 1966.

35 Blackbourn, *Class, Religion and Local Politics*, pp. 141-64; I. Farr, 'Populism in the countryside: the Peasant Leagues in Bavaria in the 1890s', Evans (ed.), *Society and Politics*, pp. 136-59.

36 Hobsbawm, *Age of Capital*, p. 87.

37 E. Weber, *Peasants into Frenchmen. The Modernization of Rural France 1870-1914*, London, 1977.

38 Hobsbawm's discussion of Welsh and Scottish nationalism provides a good example to this effect. Until recently the successful articulation of popular aspirations into British national parties since the 1860s (first the Liberals and then Labour) effectively pre-empted the emergence of Scottish or Welsh separatism as a serious political force. At the same time 'Scottishness' and 'Welshness' were far from negligible factors in the constitution of popular political identity. For example, since the 1920s the militants of the South Wales Miners Federation have been at once a mainstay of the *British* labour movement, fervently *internationlist*, and proudly *Welsh*. There is no reason for any one to preclude the others. See Hobsbawm, 'The attitude of popular classes'. See also H. Francis, D. Smith, *The Fed. A History of the South Wales Miners in the Twentieth Century*, London, 1980.

39 The reasons for the timing are complex. For a general discussion, see Eley, *Reshaping the German Right*, pp. 41ff.

40 Hobsbawm, 'Inventing traditions in 19th century Europe', p. 5f. See also: G.L. Mosse, *The Nationalization of the Masses. Political Symbolism and Mass Movements in Germany from the Napoleonic Wars through the Third Reich*, New York, 1975; T. Nipperdey, 'Nationalidee und Nationaldenkmal in Deutschland im 19. Jahrhundert', *Historische Zeitschrift*, 206, 1968, pp. 529-85; E. Fehrenbach, *Wandlungen des deutschen Kaisergedankens 1871-1918*, Munich, 1969, and 'Uber die Bedeutung der politischen Symbole im Nationalstaat', *Historische Zeitschirft*, 213, 1971, pp. 296-357; W.K. Blessing, 'The cult of monarchy, political loyalty and the workers' movement in Imperial Germany', *Journal of Contemporary History*, 13, 1978, pp. 357-76. Hobsbawm cites the example of the *Prinz-Heinrichs-Gymnasium* in Schöneberg, where ten substantial ceremonies were held between August 1895 and March 1896, 'including ample commemorations of battles in the war, celebrations of the Emperor's birthday,

the official handing-over of the portrait of an imperial Prince, illuminations and public addresses on the war of 1870-1, on the development of the imperial idea (Kaiseridee) during the war, the character of the Hohenzollern dynasty, etc.'.

41 See Blessing's valuable article on Bavaria, 'The cult of monarchy'. The late-1890s again seem to have been some sort of watershed. Blessing notes that the 25th anniversary of the Franco-Prussian War and Wilhelm I's centenary in 1897 saw a progressive displacement of Bavarian by Imperial symbolism. By 1912-13, with the centenary of 1813, Wilhelm II's silver jubilee, and (ironically) the Prince Regent's funeral, the imperial motifs were clearly on top.

42 For a general discussion: Eley, *Reshaping the German Right*, pp. 19ff.

43 Hobsbawm, 'Inventing traditions in 19th century Europe', pp. 7-9; W. Blos, *Die Deutsche Revolution' Geschichte der deutschen Bewegung von 1848 und 1849*, Bonn, 1978; H. Hartwig, K. Riha, *Politische Ästhetik und Öffentlichkeit. 1848 im Spaltungsprozeß des historischen Bewußtseins*, Giessen, 1974, especially pp. 23-32, 141-71.

44 For the building of monuments, see Mosse, op. cit., pp. 36-8, 58-67, 93-7. For the character of the nationalist pressure groups, see Eley, *Reshaping the German Right*, pp. 41-98, 147-60, 160-235. I have tried to summarize the argument in Eley, 'Some thoughts on the nationalist pressure groups in Imperial Germany', in A.J. Nicholls (ed.), *Nationalist and Racialist Movements in Britain and Germany before 1914*, London, 1981.

45 Eley, *Reshaping the German Right*, pp. 133-9, 206-35.

46 Ibid., pp. 239-90.

47 See K. Stenkewitz, *Gegen Bajonett und Dividende, Die politische Krise in Deutschland am Vorabend des ersten Weltkrieges*, Berlin, 1960, pp. 77-95.

48 Apart from *Reshaping the German Right*, and 'Some thoughts on the nationalist pressure groups', see the following: 'Defining social imperialism: use and abuse of an idea', *Social History*, 1, 1976, pp. 265-90; 'Social imperialism in Germany: reformist synthesis or reactionary sleight of hand?', in J. Radkau, I. Geiss (eds), *Imperialismus im 20. Jahrhundert. Gedenkschrift für G.W.F. Hallgarten*, Munich, 1976, pp. 71-86.

49 Hobsbawm, 'Some reflections on nationalism', p. 404.

16 THE ROOTS OF CZECH STALINISM

Jacques Rupnik*

Among the countries of East-Central Europe incorporated in the Soviet sphere of influence in the aftermath of the Second World War Czechoslovakia undoubtedly went furthest, in 1945-8 and again in 1968, in attempting to reconcile a socialist system with political democracy. However, and this has been a more neglected subject, Czechoslovakia has also produced both in the 1950s and in the 1970s, the most entrenched and lasting brand of Stalinism in East-Central Europe. Paradoxically, both these contrasting features of post-war Czechoslovakia have usually been explained by a reference to the endurance of the country's democratic tradition.[1] Indeed, the roots of the Prague Spring of 1968 can (as we shall argue) be traced back to the profoundly democratic character of Czechoslovak political culture which has shaped not only the political life of the country before the war but also left its imprint on the labour movement, including the Communist Party (KSČ). Conversely, it has sometimes been suggested that the scope of the Stalinist phenomenon has, in a way, been proportional to the vitality of the 'bourgeois' or 'social' democratic legacy it tried to 'overcome' or rather eradicate. However, a closer examination of the origins and development of communist rule in Czechoslovakia suggests that the latter proposition could be a rather misleading oversimplification.

How can we account for the fact that an advanced industrial country among the strongest inter-war democracies in Eastern Europe and with a labour movement (social democratic and at the beginning, communist) characterised by a strong democratic tradition moved after the Second World War towards a Stalinist brand of communism, without the presence of Soviet troops in the country at the time of the February 1948 takeover and without encountering any serious resistance in the political nation? To what extent does this 'double nature' of Czech communism help to shed new light on the Prague Spring of 1968 and its subsequent 'normalisation'? These questions point to the more general issue - the formation of what could be described as 'indigenous' Stalinism. To be sure, external or geopolitical factors have always, in the last instance 'over-determined' the internal forces in Czechoslovak politics whether at the time of the formation of the state in 1918, its destruction at Munich 1938,

*Jacques Rupnik was brought up in Czechoslovakia. Since leaving the country in 1965 he has worked mainly in Paris and he is now researching at the École des Hautes Études. His doctoral thesis has recently been published as Histoire du Parti Communiste Tchecoslovaque, Paris, 1981.

at the beginning of the Cold War between 1945 and 1948 or at the time of the Soviet invasion in 1968. We shall argue however, that these external factors have not operated in Czechoslovakia in the same way as in the rest of Eastern Europe and that: firstly, the roots and the mechanisms of the post-1948 Stalinisation can be traced to the 'bolshevisation' of the KSČ of the late 1920s which profoundly altered the nature of the party and that secondly, the receptivity of Czechoslovak society to that process in the immediate aftermath of the Second World War had its origin in the traumas of the 1938-45 period - the deepest breach in the Czech political tradition - rather than in 1948 itself.

I DEMOCRATIC SOCIALISM AND THE THEORY OF THE 'DETOUR'

It has become an almost ritualistic precaution for historians dealing with Czechoslovak communism to stress 'specific conditions'. Of all the countries where what is now known as 'Realsocialismus' has been introduced in the aftermath of the Second World War, Czechoslovakia was the only advanced industrial country with a large working class which had experienced half a century of political participation in a parliamentary democracy. It was also the only country in the region where the Communist Party had a strong indigenous base with one and a half million members and some 40 per cent of the vote in democratic elections in 1946. In contrast, the communist takeover of 1948 opened a period of the homogenisation of the socio-economic systems and of the political regimes in Eastern Europe through a rigid imitation of the Soviet model which was forcefully rejected in 1968.

In terms of Parliamentary practice, the roots of the democratic and pluralistic character of the Czechoslovak political tradition go back at least to the 1870s when Czech deputies entered the Viennese Reichsraat. By the time direct universal suffrage was introduced, for the elections in 1907, Czech social democrats polled some 40 per cent of the vote in the Czech lands, proportionally more than their Austrian counterparts. Already the pre-1914 Czech political context was marked by competing ideologies and political parties in which the social democrats campaigned with other forces for a greater degree of self-government (though not full independence) as well as the extension of democratic and civil rights. From this perspective the creation of a Czechoslovak state in 1918, supported by the entire socialist movement, can be seen as the culmination of the nineteenth-century striving for national independence and democracy which in the inter-war period produced a 'completely formed pluralist system'.[2] This pattern did not quite apply in Slovakia, where, due to a more archaic socio-economic structure and the legacy of an intensive policy of Magyarisation, political life, in the modern sense of the word, developed only at the turn of the century. However, it could be argued that at least in the first third of this century the Slovaks shared with the Czechs, if only in a weaker form, some of the democratic elements of Czech political culture.

The democratic experience of the First Republic (1918-38) is associated with the name of Thomas Masaryk - whose influence on the country's politics as president has sometimes overshadowed his decisive influence on Czechoslovak socialism.[3] There were two main trends in pre-1918 Czech socialism associated with the Kautsky/Bernstein divide in the social democratic movement. The first trend, represented by Bohumír Šmeral, was Marxist, internationalist and 'statist' and identified with the Austrian state. The second, best represented by František Modráček, was 'revisionist', favoured decentralisation and self management, and was strongly autonomist as far as the national question was concerned.[4] In 1918 Šmeral's pro-Austrian policy collapsed and the whole socialist movement identified with the new state and its president, T.G. Masaryk. It was only two years later, after the nationalist euphoria of 1918 had faded away, that a new wave of social unrest resuscitated the Marxist Left within the social democracy which, led by Šmeral, was to form the Communist Party in 1921. Thus the decentralised, 'self-management' current became after 1918 a 'State' party while the centralist Marxists joined the Comintern and opposed the new state as a tool of social and national oppression. The important point here is that 'statism' had triumphed in the Czech socialist movement whether communist or social democratic. It accounts, at least in part, for the lack of an alternative concept of society on the Left to the state socialism of the Communist Party after 1945.

Whereas Masaryk's critique of marxism was an open one, his rejection of bolshevism was uncompromising.[5] It was based on the recognition of a fundamental gulf that exists between Russian political culture (Byzantium, cezaro-papism, bureaucracy) of which bolshevism was, Masaryk argued, the product, and that of Europe. Given Russia's socio-economic and cultural backwardness, the bolsheviks were, according to Masaryk, bound to reproduce some of the authoritarian features of the regime they had just abolished. In Europe socialism should be the natural extension, not the negation, of political democracy. In other words, Masaryk was not only a symbol of national independence but also the 'ideologue' of a Czech brand of social democracy. And it is not difficult to detect the relationship between some of the Masarykian themes and the 1960s 'humanist' Marxist critique of Stalinism which prepared the ideological background for the 1968 experiment of 'socialism with a human face'.

As for the Communist Party of Czechoslovakia (KSČ), at least two things should be mentioned here about its relationship with that tradition; the party was formed as the result of an organic mutation of the majority of the labour movement from social democracy to communism. As such, the party did not think of itself as a radical break with the past, but to some extent represented continuity with the pre-war Czech socialist movement of which the party leader Bohumír Šmeral was the most illustrious representative.[6] Šmeral himself, unquestionably the most significant figure of the Czech labour movement in the first third of this century, was very much the product of the Austro-Marxist tradition and his conversion to Leninism was by all accounts unenthusiastic. Secondly, the party operated legally, within the framework of parliamentary democracy which, at least until the so-called 'third period' of the Comintern (and again after 1935) it tacitly accepted. Hence also the quip attributed to Otto Bauer: 'I know of only two outstanding social-democratic parties. The first, is of course, the Austrian Party; the second is the Communist Party of Czechoslovakia'. Not surprisingly, 'Šmeralism' became the prime target of the Comintern's bolshevisation campaign launched in the late 1920s against the so-called social democratic 'vestiges' in the Czechoslovak party.

Of all the famous 'eights' which provide standard periodisation of Czechoslovak history (1918, 1938, 1948, 1968) there remains one which is often ignored, but central to our subject: 1928 - the year of the bolshevisation of the KSČ. Its two chief aims, completed at the Vth Congress in February 1929 were:[7] firstly, the total subordination of the KSČ to the Comintern (which by the late 1920s was transformed primarily into an instrument of the foreign policy of the Soviet state); secondly, the ideological and organisational reshaping of the party along bolshevik lines in order to eradicate the 'social democratic' (i.e. indigenous - the two became indistinguishable) characteristics of the party. This was achieved through the systematic elimination of all those who actually or supposedly represented this continuity with the mainstream of the history of the Czech labour movement and their substitution by a new group of younger party officials led by Klement Gottwald without any base outside the party apparatus. Regardless of what one may think of this replacement of an experienced (if perhaps too pragmatic) leadership by a group of apparatchiki characterised with rare exceptions (Šverma, Guttmann) by their intellectual mediocrity and total subservience to Moscow, the important point was that this group was to remain in charge until the party came to power in 1948. Thus, an understanding of the implications of Gottwald's 'seizure of power' inside the party is central to our interpretation of his party's takeover of the state in 1948. The prime aim of the 'bolshevisation' was to build a bureaucratic structure (the apparat) which would 'protect' the party from its environment which, especially in a parliamentary democracy, meant essentially the ever-present 'threat' of the reformist temptation. In this the Czech party had a 'twin' in Western Europe: the French Communist Party. It is because they both operated in an open or pluralistic environment that they could become mass parties. But it is the same environment which also allowed them patiently to build the bureaucratic shield which eventually turned them into two of the most archaically Stalinist parties. In contrast, the Italian or, for instance, the Yugoslav Party were paradoxically 'protected' from such a form of Stalinisation by the extremely unfavourable conditions in which they had to operate in the inter-war period. However, despite the thoroughness of the 'bolshevisation' of the late 1920s, the problems it was meant to have dealt with once and for all periodically resurfaced in each crisis period, always bringing out the tension within the party between its insertion in the national community and in the international communist movement which after 1948 meant essentially the imposition by force of the Soviet model.

That system eventually collapsed in 1968 under the combined effects of an economic and political crisis. The reforms of the Prague Spring, though initiated from above, soon set into motion forces in the society which in turn speeded up the erosion of this apparatus and the resurfacing of the strong democratic components of Czech socialism. Let us simply recall that, as the Spring went on, the debate about the economic reform brought with it workers' pressure for independent trade unions and the first measures concerning self-management; that the abolition of censorship also helped the articulation of social groups and interests as well as the beginning of the institutionalisation of political groupings outside the Communist Party such as KAN (Club of engagés non-party members) K231 (the club of former political prisoners) not to speak about the embryonic social democratic party which was never actually allowed to get off the ground. This limited revival of political pluralism went even further than what existed under the First Republic in the national sphere with the adoption of a plan for the federalisation of the state, granting autonomy to Slovakia.[8]

If it had not been stopped by outside military intervention, what was emerging in Czechoslovakia was, therefore, a new pluralistic concept of socialist democracy. After twenty years of authoritarian Stalinist rule, values that could be, for the sake of convenience, broadly described as social democratic (or democratic-socialist) resurfaced within Czechoslovak society and even in the Communist Party.

These developments have led some Czech and Slovak historians in 1968 to suggest that the Communist Party was then resuming its 'natural course' from which it had been diverted in 1928. In the words of Ján Mlynárik, a leading labour historian: 'According to our historical scholarship [the 5th Congress of the KSČ in February 1929] was the beginning of a forty year lasting detour, a deviation from the natural development started by the Šmeral leadership, and returned back to its original track only after January 1968.'[9] Another historian, Zdeněk Kárník, put the return of the democratic component within Czechoslovak communism in the following perspective:[10]

> Šmeralism or democratic communism was, at the time of its inception, condemned to disappear. But its components and its

> tradition could not die because they represent one of the axes around which is centered the development of modern society. This is also the only explanation for the renewed interest in it precisely at a time when our society went through a short but intense period of destalinisation and socialist renewal.

Mlynárik saw Novotný as the true disciple of Gottwald in that both came to power in the aftermath of a major crisis/purge associated with the enforcement of Stalinist supremacy. Similarly, Kárník saw Dubček as continuing in the footsteps of Šmeral, the first communist leader to have formulated already in 1920 the basic outlines of what is now known as the theory of the 'specific or national road to socialism'.[11] And it is not altogether surprising that the Eurocommunists drew in turn their inspiration from the Prague Spring of 1968.[12]

Thus the theory of the 'detour' is also related to the complex issue of the continuity of the democratic component in the Czech socialist tradition which could be revived within the Party forty years later. That was possible only thanks to a 'missing link' in the theory of the 'detour' namely the democratic interlude or the 'transition to socialism' between 1945 and 1948. Indeed, while Soviet-type regimes were being promptly introduced in the Balkans and the more gradual 'salami tactic' was implemented in Poland and Hungary, Czechoslovakia enjoyed free elections, a multi-party system, a free press, etc. Even the commitment to an essentially socialist economic programme was based in 1945 on a broad consensus of all political forces and was not perceived as undermining political pluralism, but rather as an essential social dimension of political democracy. The Communist Party, which polled some 40 per cent of the vote - the highest score ever reached by any Communist Party in a democratic election - claimed allegiance to the heritage of T.G. Masaryk and to gradual change through the democratic process while the other political parties (including President Beneš) accepted the Soviet concept of 'people's democracy' as an adequate form of transition to socialism. Many of the 40 per cent of Communist voters in 1946 rejected pre-war policies but shared at a deeper level some of the basic values associated with the pre-war political culture. Socialised under the First Republic, they identified with the communist cause during the resistance or immediately after the war when the party advocated the policy of so-called 'national roads to socialism'. Bitterly disappointed by the results of the revolution 'from above' which they had helped to bring about, they were determined in the 1960s to compensate for their co-responsibility for Stalinist crimes by investing all their energies into a rejuvenation of the party and the society 'from below' in the name of the democratic and socialist ideals that had initially brought them into politics.

If the history of Czechoslovak socialism was to be written from the point of view of generations the '1945 generation' would undoubtedly have to be seen as a crucial link in the continuity of its democratic component.[13] But does not continuity thus somewhat artificially reconstructed obscure deeper structural changes taking place within the political culture of the country? The theory of continuity might be a source of 'optimism' about the resilience of a democratic political culture in the face of the communist structure. But it also, in our opinion, tends to underestimate the deeper discontinuity in the modern Czechoslovak political tradition which for its socialist components goes back to the 1928 bolshevisation and for the dominant democratic ethos of the country stems from the post-Munich breach; both these alterations within the Czechoslovak political culture are essential for the understanding of what we can call the indigenous roots of Stalinism in Czechoslovakia.

II THE INDIGENOUS ROOTS OF STALINISM IN CZECHOSLOVAKIA

The 'theory of continuity', or the primacy and persistance of the pre-war democratic and pluralistic political culture in Czechoslovakia is, as we have indicated, essential in assessing the deeper undercurrents behind the 1945-8 and 1968 experiments in democratic socialism. But it can hardly account for the formation in Czechoslovakia of one of the most brutal, entrenched and lasting brands of Stalinism after 1948 and again after 1968. The political trials of the Stalinist era caused more deaths in Czechoslovakia, according to the Czech historian Karel Kaplan (who served on the rehabilitation commission in 1968), than all the East European countries put together during that period.[14] Even the trial in 1952 of the party leadership which itself had earlier set in motion the terrifying machinery of the show trials, the famous Slánský trial, went beyond anything seen in the trials of Rajk in Hungary, Kostov in Bulgaria, not to mention Gomulka in Poland, both in the scope and vigour of its anti-semitic hysteria. Stalinism, it has sometimes been argued, was totally alien to Czechoslovakia's political culture and its brutality in the 1950s was due precisely to the difficulty of imposing from outside a system produced by the Russian experience. The Czechoslovak Communist Party was seen, in this perspective, merely in the role of a 'transmission belt' of the Soviet party.

Though no doubt crucial in the late 1940s and early 1950s, when developments in Prague were a direct by-product of Stalin's internal and external policy course (the split with Tito's Yugoslavia and the more general 'Cold War' context were used to justify domestic repression), the argument seems today insufficient. It does not explain why Stalinism continued in Czechoslovakia only in a slightly modified form throughout the Khrushchevian 'de-Stalinisation' era, especially between the XXth (1956) and the XXIInd Congresses, which also brought with it a move towards 'peaceful co-existence' in foreign policy. Secondly, while in Hungary, five years after 1956 Kadar was able to declare 'he who is not against us is with us', proclaim an amnesty and seek a new compromise between society and the party/state, Czechoslovakia has still not yet shown the slightest sign of moving in that direction - indeed, since 1968, it has undergone the longest period of uninterrupted repression in the last hundred years. As a sustained cultural assault, it is much worse than the 1950s. According to the writer Milan Kundera, this has no equivalent in the country's history since the 'age of darkness' - the period of enforced catholicisation and Germanisation which followed the Battle of the White Mountain in 1620.[15]

In other words, even if Stalinism was initially a 'foreign import' extended from the Party to the society, through coercion, its scope and endurance, even at times when the external factor was no longer decisive, point to the essential role of the domestic factors. These as, we have already suggested, are rooted in the bolshevisation of the Communist Party in the late 1920s and in the breach of 1938-45.

The bolshevisation transformed the nature of the KSČ in two respects: the end of internal democracy and dependence upon Moscow. To the extent that every Communist Party functions as a 'counter-society' and a 'counter-culture' it also represents the microcosm of the society it strives to bring about. Whether the German Democratic Republic actually represents the embodiment of what the Weimar period KPD set out to achieve is a matter of debate; but there can be little doubt that the bolshevisation of the Czechoslovak CP in the late 1920s established the foundations for the Stalinisation of the whole society some twenty years later.

A key factor in this process was the KSČ's relationship with the working class during these two periods. The Czechoslovak CP, which was with the German KPD the largest section of the Comintern, was, in many ways, its opposite: the KPD, formed in the aftermath of a genuine - if unsuccessful - revolution in 1919, had within its membership a strong proportion of the young and unemployed who rejected the system *en bloc*, remained 'prisoner' of its 'revolutionary temptation' until the defeat of 1933. In contrast, the Czechoslovak Communist Party - a split from social democracy - was sociologically as well as in its policies relatively much better adapted to what was then described as the 'temporary stabilisation of capitalism'. Bolshevisation forced a breach with these working-class roots of the KSČ. It was implemented through a massive purge of the cadres as well as of the membership which dropped dramatically from 150,000 in the spring of 1928 to a mere 25,000 just two years later.[16] A split was provoked in the Party-controlled 'Red' Trade Union' simultaneously, with the majority of the communist rank-and-file members and trade unionists eventually 'returning' to the Social Democratic Party. In short, the bolshevik model of the Party and the 'transmission belt' approach to the trade unions were successfully imposed only at the cost of cutting the Party from its roots in the mainstream of the Czechoslovak working class. Thus, during the so-called 'third period' the KSČ shifted its social base from the 'centre' of the working class to the 'periphery' and became, until the mid-1930s, the ultra-radical spokesman of a disaffected lumpenproletariat. The party which a decade earlier under Šmeral's leadership had the support of the bulk of the politically organised workers looked, on the eve of the great depression of the 1930s, to be a rapidly declining political sect. However, the economic crisis was soon to transform the marginalised 'periphery' of the working class into a considerable social force with the unemployed, of which the KSČ became the most articulate spokesman, representing by 1932-3 between a third and a half of the working population. Thus, it could be argued that it was paradoxically thanks to the economic crisis of the 1930s that Stalinism acquired indigenous roots in the Czechoslovak working class.

Although the 1948 seizure of power by the KSČ was a 'revolution from above', the working class was unquestionably a willing 'accomplice'. Indeed, one of the keys to the smooth success of the party in February 1948 was its ability to channel the largely spontaneous explosion of working-class radicalism in 1945. Perhaps the best example of this was the capacity of the KSČ to 'absorb' the works' councils movement within six months of the end of the war. Initially there were two competing tendencies concerning the role of workers in the management of factories and in society at large. The 'syndicalist' current, dominant in the immediate post-liberation period, saw the works' councils both as organs of self-management and as the basis of a new type of trade union movement representing in its diversity the working class and its aspiration for social change independently of the political parties.[17] ('The works' councils shall be the power on which the whole economic structure rests,' declared the Central Trade Union Council on 16 May 1945.) The communists, on the other hand, advocated restricting the councils' powers and launched simultaneously alternative (rival) trade union structures. However as happened in other post-war revolutionary crises coinciding with the reformation of the state, the intensity of the political mobilisation of the workers in the first weeks and months after the Liberation steadily diminished as the new state institutions were being established. As the revolutionary élan of the works' councils (which were by no means popular with other political parties) waned, the KSČ soon managed to take over the leadership of the unified trade union movement (Zápotocký) and altered the initial syndicalist meaning of that unification by introducing 'democratic centralism' as the *modus operandi* of the unions. Then, within a matter of months, the councils were neutralised and transformed into one of the Communist Party-controlled mass organisations. This was possible because no section of the Czech socialist movement was willing, or able, to act as the political spokesman for working-class autonomy embodied in the councils movement and because the emergence of a Right versus Left polarisation within the National Front coalition rallied a substantial part of the working class behind the socio-economic programme of the KSČ. The 'radical-democratic' movement had been defeated and was not revived until the workers' councils movement of 1968-9. But, by the time the famous Works' Council Congress was convened by the KSČ during the political crisis of February 1948 (described then by Gottwald as the real people's parliament, in contrast to the actual elected one), the movement was merely an institutionalised working-class pressure group on the political system. As soon as President Beneš had complied with KSČ demands for the resignation of 'bourgeois' ministers Gottwald rushed to announce the party's victory to several thousand workers at a rally and spelled out the new meaning that workers' mobilisation was now to have: 'We return again to our work, to our construction work for the completion of the Two-Year-Plan'. The 'passive revolution', as J. Bloomfield called it, was over.[18]

Underlying this political process during the period 1945-53, which can be described as the formation of the Stalinist system in Czechoslovakia, were both the most radical socio-economic transformations (nationalisation of industry and banking, etc.) and rapid social mobility. This can be illustrated by looking at the comparative figures of passage from manual to non-manual occupations particularly among skilled and semi-skilled workers over the whole period which goes from the bolshevisation of the party to the Prague Spring of 1968.[19] A threefold policy of the KSČ provides an insight into the new social foundations of the Stalinist system.

Firstly, the evolution of the social composition of the party. At the VIII Congress in March 1946 the KSČ appeared essentially as a working-class party: 58 per cent workers, 13 per cent peasants, 4 per cent artisans and traders, 9 per cent intelligentsia and 16 per cent various others. A series of purges implemented after the Congress was not actually aimed at the so-called petty bourgeois elements, often with a dubious wartime record, who were drawn to the party. A year after the Congress the working-class proportion of the membership had dropped to 45 per cent; peasants from 13 per cent to 8 per cent. Meanwhile, new categories appeared in the Party statistics: employees 6 per cent, civil servants 10 per cent, and the spectacular increase of 'various others' from 16 per cent to 25 per cent.[20] Thus, the absorption of the works' councils was accompanied by the regression of the working-class base of the KSČ and the simultaneous, irresistible rise of the new bureaucracy of the state apparatus which was replacing the old bourgeoisie. The changes in the social composition of the Party in fact reflect the process of osmosis between Party and state begun in 1945, but not completed until after 1948.

Secondly, it would be a mistake to see the rising bureaucracy as in an open conflict with the working class; indeed, as suggested above, it opposed any autonomous social movement (such as the works' councils), but at the same time relied on the tacit support of the working class from which it co-opted large sections into its own ranks after securing a monopoly of political power. Between 1948 and 1953 an estimated 200,000 to 400,000 workers were promoted from the shopfloor into state administration: in the economy, but more particularly in the army and the police.[21]

Lastly, a substantial part of the intelligentsia was simultaneously 'demoted' into the working class. Indeed, the downward mobility of the intelligentsia was much higher in Czechoslovakia after 1948 than in any other country of East-Central Europe. As an example, official statistics indicate that in 1951 alone the authorities fired some 77,000 intellectuals who were 'recycled' into the industrial sector. Despite a system of accelerated professional training for the new cadres, the lasting legacy of the social policy of the Stalinist era explains why in 1962 - the year of the great economic collapse - there were nearly half a million people in decision-making positions for which they were not qualified. The social policy of the Stalinist period accounts, at least in part, for the passivity of the working class during that period; but it also accounts for the scope of the economic disaster which eventually undermined the system and prepared the ground for the changes of the late 1960s.

A process in many ways similar was repeated at the turn of the 1970s when about half a million party members associated with the reforms of the Dubček era were expelled from the party during a purge that has no equivalent in post-war communism, except perhaps the Chinese cultural revolution.[22] This was followed by re-'proletarianisation' of the membership which by the end of the 1970s has recovered its pre-1968 level. A large part of the intellectuals of the 1960s were transformed into construction workers, night watchmen or cab drivers, while new cadres were promoted who were 'working-class' only by origin.

Thus there are clear parallels between the bolshevisation of the late 1920s, the Stalinisation of society in the late 1940s and early 1950s and the 'normalisation' of the 1970s with strict subordination to the Soviet model and the eradication of domestic democratic-socialist forces in the party and society at large, carried out by a purge of both the leadership and the membership of the party. The important difference between the bolshevisation of the party and the Stalinisation of society being that the former concerned just the party; the latter affected society as a whole.

Though it is fairly clear that Stalinism, whether in its post-1948 or post-1968 version, meant cultural *Gleichschaltung* and conflict with at least a part of the country's creative intellectuals, its relationship with the working class is more complex. There is a pattern of working-class accommodation with Stalinism in Czechoslovakia which can, to some extent, be explained by the relative economic privileges obtained (be it the rapid social mobility of the 1940s and 50s or the consumerism of the 1970s). But one cannot help also asking questions concerning the role of deeper psycho-social pre-dispositions which would account for the lack of working-class resistance to Stalinism in Czechoslovakia.

This was the important question which Erich Fromm and his associates had asked themselves at the end of the 1920s in a study for Horkheimer's Institute for Social Research concerning the mentality of the left-wing workers.[23] The result was so disturbing that they decided not to publish it. Contrary to what Fromm had expected, he discovered that a very large section of the left wing, particularly the communist workers had an 'authoritarian personality' which, as he understood, made them vulnerable to the appeal of nazism. The fact that the political radicalism of the KPD was compatible with this authoritarianism accounts to some extent for the switch by a number of communist workers from the KPD to nazism, or, at least, the relative lack of resistance to it. Our intention here is not to draw facile parallels between totalitarian regimes, but simply to ask questions about working class attitudes to state socialism in Czechoslovakia (which contrast with those of workers in Poland: a first generation working class, no indigenous roots of communism, etc.).

III THE FORCES OF APPEASEMENT

Munich and the Nazi occupation represent the deepest breach in modern Czech political history. 'The years 1938-45', writes a Czech historian in a recent essay circulating in *samizdat* (i.e. illegal), 'were a test - and the nation failed it'. 'How could a nation, and its political leadership,' he asks, 'which had striven for decades for an independent statehood and a democratic political system abandon them without even putting up a fight'.[24] To be sure, perfectly rational explanations were made for the capitulation, namely the hopelessness of military resistance after Czechoslovakia had been abandoned by her Western allies on whose support her existence had depended since its very inception. But neither this, nor the attempt to confine the blame to the weakness of political leadership seems sufficient to explain not only the capitulation, but also the degree of collaboration that followed. Wartime resistance was limited primarily to the intelligentsia (which was decimated by the Germans) and its scope cannot be compared either to that of the Polish nationalists or that of the Yugoslav communists.[25] 'The Nazi occupation', says Příbram, 'which the nation allowed without resistance in order to preserve itself deprived it of its identity'. Though the case of Slovakia was different, the support for the pro-Nazi Tiso regime was only partially counterbalanced by the uprising in August 1944; thus the years 1938-45 had a major impact on the political culture for both Czechs and Slovaks.

But it should be added that it was only after the occupation in 1968 that Czech historians attempted to do for their nation what the film *The Sorrow and the Pity* did at about the same time for the French. The essence of their enquiry could be summed up in the words of one of the most courageous of them, Dr Jan Tesař, active during the Prague Spring, who then served seven years in jail during the 1970s precisely for refusing to collaborate with another occupation regime: 'the spiritual content of the period lies in the conflict between subservience to oppressors and the emerging subservience to the future liberators'.[26]

Indeed, in 1945 in Czechoslovakia, not unlike France after the fall of Vichy, the post-Munich capitulation/collaboration complex was over-compensated by a radicalism which combined quasi-xenophobic nationalism with a socialism identified with Stalin's Russia.[27] Under the façade of a continuity restored with the Masarykian heritage and in the name of a slogan shared by all 'Munich must never repeat itself', a radical break with pre-war political tradition took place in 1945 in at least four respects.

Firstly, despite all Beneš's talk about Czechoslovakia being a bridge between East and West, we know today that Beneš himself - and with the support of all the main political forces - had not just accepted, but voluntarily encouraged a complete integration of Czechoslovakia into the Soviet sphere of influence between 1943 and 1945.[28]

Secondly, in the name of eliminating political forces compromised by Munich and what followed the two largest, pre-war political parties, the Czech Agrarian party and the Slovak People's party, were banned. More importantly, the National Front, in which the KSČ played a leading role, was conceived and operated as a coalition of democratically elected parties, but without the right to go into opposition.[29] By shrinking the size of the political spectrum and curtailing its *modus operandi* Beneš and the communists had also reduced the scope for political democracy.

Thirdly, pluralism was simultaneously curtailed within the socialist labour movement: the neutralisation of the works' council movement and the formation of a single trade union operating on the principle of 'democratic centralism'. There was also the plan to merge all the three socialist parties: the KSČ, the social democrats and the Czech socialist party (Beneš).[30]

The dividing line between Stalinism and democratic socialism was blurred, with the former eventually paying only lip-service to the latter, and the latter capitulating to the former.

Fourthly, the 'transfer' of some three million Sudeten Germans out of Czechoslovakia became in 1945 the cement in the Beneš-Gottwald-Stalin alliance. Though understandably perceived at that time as the logical response to centuries of German oppression which had finally destroyed the Czechoslovak state with the active help of the Sudeten German minority, today, dissident historians raise the question of the deeper significance of this historical break with a conflictual Czech-German coexistence in Bohemia that goes back to the thirteenth century.[31] In the twentieth century, population transfers were associated with the emergence of Hitler's Germany and Stalin's Russia; was not Czechoslovakia's restored democracy in 1945 in fact submitting at a deeper level to the terrifying logic set into motion by her two neighbours? By depriving all the non-Slavic citizens of Czechoslovakia (Germans, Hungarians, etc.) of their basic civil rights (including the right to vote) in the name of the theory of 'collective guilt' were not Beneš and the Communist Party setting a dangerous precedent? The same principle of exclusion was to be applied after 1948 to other sections of the population on economic, religious and political grounds thus paving the way for the Stalinism of the 1950s.

The February 1948 seizure by the party of monopoly political power was neither a revolution, as the victors claimed, nor actually a coup d'état, as the vanquished politicians argued in exile. It was, rather, a constitutional solution to a government crisis which *de facto* also entailed a revolutionary solution to the crisis of a regime torn between its democratic and authoritarian components which was brought into the open both by the start of the 'Cold War' and at a deeper level by an internal process in which the Munich *caesura* has been decisive. It is in this broader sense that Beneš's submission to Gottwald's ultimatum in February 1948 was a follow up to his capitulation of 1938. Thus the KSČ conquest of monopoly political power took place in a country without Soviet troops on its territory with substantial popular backing and without encountering any serious resistance. These were tamed revolutionaries and reactionaries without reaction. If there is such a thing as a Czechoslovak 'model' then it must surely be the national and peaceful round to Stalinism.

If we look at 1968, as we did for 1945-8, from the point of view of limits imposed on the democratic process we have to qualify what we have outlined earlier by stressing that the KSČ programme under Dubček insisted on the preservation of the 'leading role' of the party: it encouraged the revival of 'dormant' components of the National Front but opposed the spillover of that process outside; it favoured the democratisation of the trade unions but was reluctant to sanction workers' councils. In this sense, there was a clear element of continuity with the 'democracy without opposition' of the 1945-8 period; The whole 'revisionist' strategy (as it has since been inadequately labelled) remained based on political change through the Communist Party and within its ideological framework. Given the strong indigenous roots of the KSČ, this process went further in Czechoslovakia than anywhere else, but it was the reality of the popular movement gradually set into motion by a party-led reform 'from above' which eventually confronted the party with the taboo question: socialist democracy or merely democratisation of 'actually existing socialism'?

The answer to this question eventually came from Moscow which leads us to the second point: the Soviet constraint on the emergence of democratic socialism. In short: Dubček's ties with Soviet communism were, of course, a departure from the subservience of Gottwald and Novotný era but remain central to the understanding of his refusal to envisage that the Czechoslovak experiment could come into fundamental conflict with Soviet-style communism. Even during the night of the Warsaw Pact invasion, Dubček and his colleagues decided not to resist by force and, almost symbolically, waited in the Party headquarters only to be arrested by the Russians and taken to Moscow as prisoners where they signed the capitulation of their country and of socialism with 'human face'. By refusing to cut the 'umbilical cord' with Moscow and thus make a clear choice between democracy and the 'democratisation' of the system, the Party's 'subconscious' inclination was to let Moscow decide instead.[32] This symbolic 'suicide' of the reformist leadership of the Communist Party of Czechoslovakia was at the same time also an act of self-preservation of the party bureacracy as a privileged caste and a demonstration of the impossibility of transforming the system through a process however well-intentioned, of reconciliation of the Communist Party-state with the democratic components of the political culture in civil society.

IV THE FINAL RUPTURE

There are three points to be made finally concerning this duality that characterises the sixty years long history of Czechoslovak communism. The first and most obvious one is that the conflict between democratic socialism and Stalinism has always been ultimately over-determined by external factors. The second concerns the inter-connection and indeed the overlap after the Second World War between democratic and authoritarian components of the dominant political culture in the country which was brought about by the breach of the years 1938-45 as well as deeper subsequent socio-economic changes at the centre of which there was the relationship between the working class, the largest social force in the country, and the emerging Party-state bureaucracy. Finally, some of the same features of the political culture of the Czech nation, and in particular of its labour movement, which created favourable conditions for attempts to combine socialism and democracy, also account for the weakness of the resistance to Stalinism. It is the indigenous strength (almost the dominance) of the CP after the war which in a way accounts for the relative lack of resistance to Stalinisation. In contrast to Poland, where dominant nationalism was identified with Catholicism and where the main pre-war socialist tradition, which was strongly anti-Russian, formed a political culture strongly resistant to Stalinism, the social democratism as well as the traditionally pro-Russian predispositions of the Czechs and Slovaks have helped to shape a political culture highly 'vulnerable' to Stalinism.

From this point of view, the Soviet invasion of 1968 and the 'normalisation' that followed represent another caesura. Whatever was left of pro-Russian sympathies after the Stalinist era of the 1950s, and the strength of the Marxist tradition in the name of which the Prague Spring was carried out, have vanished in the night of 21 August of 1968. The uninterrupted repression of the 1970s has created an entirely new political environment characterised by an irreparable gap between the State and society and even between what was the Communist Party of the Dubček era and that of Gustáv Husák.

The purge of half a million communists from the Party in the aftermath of the invasion had *de facto* created the base for a potential 'Eurocommunist' opposition which never materialised both because it had no strategy to offer after the defeat of 1968 and mainly because the neo-Stalinist restoration not only eliminated the supporters of the Prague Spring from positions of influence but in fact liquidated political life as such.[33] In this new context the only major challenge to the general 'anesthesia' produced by the 'normalisation' has been the Charter 77 human rights movement. Though rooted in 1968, it is not an attempt to reform the Communist Party-state but rather strives to stimulate independent activity in the civil society, in defence of both democratic rights and cultural freedom.[34] It represents a great diversity of political outlooks, including all brands of socialism but also liberalism and Christian democratic views. All social groups are represented among the 1100 Charter 77 signatories who, contrary to what is often believed in the West, include well over 40 per cent of workers. As such, the movement demonstrates, under extremely adverse conditions, a conscious identification with the country's democratic tradition which no longer tries to assert itself from within the system, not even strictly speaking against it, but simply as a resistance from outside. In this it illustrates the final historical break between Stalinism and democratic socialism in Czechoslovakia.

NOTES

1 See H.G. Skilling, *Czechoslovakia's Interrupted Revolution*, Princeton University Press, 1976, ch. 1.; A. Brown and G. Wightman's chapter in A. Brown and J. Gray (eds), *Political Culture and Political change in Communist States*, London, Macmillan, 1977, p. 159-96.

2 V. Precan's analysis of the breakdown of the multi-party system in Czechoslovakia at the Collegiunm Carilinum conference, *Die Erste Tschechoslowakische Republik als multinationaler Parteienstaat*, Oldenburg Verlag, 1979, pp. 529-52; for a Marxist assessment of the social and political system of the First Republic see V. Olivova, *The Doomed Democracy*, London Sidgwick & Jackson, 1972.

3 Cf. J. Rupnik 'Le socialisme tchéque et la pensée politique de T.G. Masaryk', published in the proceedings of the conference on Masaryk by the Institut National d'Études Slaves in Paris, 1982.
4 Šmeral, *Historické práce*, Prague 1961; F. Modracek, *Samospráva práce*, Prague, 1918.
5 An abridged version is available in translation by E. Kohak (ed.), *Masaryk on Marx*, University of Lewisburg, Pa. 1972; Masaryk's other major work *Russia and Europe* published first in 1913 and translated into English under the title *The Spirit of Russia*, London, Allen & Unwin, 3 vols, 1967. A thousand-page volume devoted to the Masaryk legacy was produced in *samizdat* in Prague, 1980.
6 At the founding congress of the Communist Party, Šmeral explained this success by having resisted the temptation of some others to create the Party already in 1919; an evolutionary rather than a radical break was for Šmeral the prerequisite of a mass party; cf. *Ustavující a slučovací sjezd KSČ r 1921*, Prague, SNPL, 1958, p. 110.
7 For the details on the bolshevisation of the KSČ see J. Rupnik, *Histoire du Parti communiste tchecoslovaque*, Paris, Fondation Nationale des Sciences Politiques, 1981, ch. III.
8 Besides the works mentioned in note 1 see also V. Kusin, *Political groupings in the Czechoslovak reform movement*, London, Macmillan, 1972.
9 J. Mlynárik, 'Kdo má pravdu?' ('Who is right?'), *Literárni Listy*, 15.8.81.
10 Z. Karnik, in *Revue Dejin socialismu*, 1969, no. 2.
11 Šmeral said: 'When I went to Russia in the Spring of 1920, I explained to Lenin that we ardently pursued revolutionary aims but that we could not follow a tactic derived from a Russian theory' c.f. Rupnik, op. cit. p. 69.
12 A.J. Liehm, 'The Prague Spring and Eurocommunism', *International Journal*, 1978, no. 4 p. 804-9.
13 A.J. Liehm, *Trois Generations*, Paris, Gallimard, 1970 (in English under the title *The politics of culture*, New York, Grove Press, 1972).
14 K. Kaplan, *Les procès de Prague*, Brussels, Ed. Complexe, 1981.
15 M. Kundera in *Le Monde*, 19.1.79.
16 Piatnitski in *Inprecorr*, 1931, no. 36 p. 684.
17 K. Kovanda, 'Works councils in Czechoslovakia 1945-47', *Soviet Studies*, 1977, no. 2, pp. 255-69.
18 J. Bloomfield, *The Passive Revolution*, London, Allison & Busby, 1979.
19 J. Rupnik, "La classe ouvrière tchecoslovaque" in J. Rupnik - G. Mink (eds.) *Transformation de la classe ouvrière en Europe de l'Est*, Paris, La Documentation Francaise, 1979, p. 177.
20 G. Wightman -A. H. Brown 'Changes in the levels of membership and the social composition of the Communist

Party of Czechoslovakia, 1945-73, *Soviet Studies* July 1975, pp. 399-401.

21 Z. Strmiska and B. Vaváková, 'La mobilité sociale dans une societé socialiste: l'expérience tchécoslovaque', *Revue d'études comparative Est-Ouest*, 1976, no. 1, p. 129-83.

22 V. Kusin, *From Dubček to Charter 77*, Edinburgh, Q Press, 1978, p. 187.

23 We unfortunately lack the kind of evidence accumulated by E. Fromm fifty years ago for his study of the German working class on the eve of the Nazi Reich. But we cannot help asking some of the similar questions to those raised by his only now published study concerning workers' response to totalitarian regimes. Erich Fromm, *Arbeiter und Angestellte am Vorabend des Dritten Reiches*, Stuttgart, Verlags-Anstalt, 1980.

24 J. Přibram, 'Přiběh s nedobrým koncem', in *Svědectvi*, 1978, no. 55, p. 383.

25 V. Mastny, *Czechs under Nazi Rule*, New York, Columbia University Press, 1971; V. Černý, *Pláč Koruny České*, Toronto, 68 Publishers, 1977; J. Tesař, 'Vlastenci a Bojovnici', in *Listy*, 1969, no. 11.

26 J. Tesař, quoted by J. Sladéček, *Osmašedesátý*, Köln, Index, 1980, p. 151.

27 For an illustration of this see Kopecky's speech at the VIII Congress of the KSČ Sučm Budovateli, Prague, 1946, pp. 114-17.

28 The best evidence of this is the transcript of Beneš's meetings in Moscow, V. Mastný (ed.), 'The Benes-Stalin-Molotov conversations in December 1943: new documents, in *Jahrbücher für Geschichte Osteuropas* (Munich), 1972, no. 3, pp. 367-402.

29 K. Kaplan 'Národni Fronta 1945-48', *Studie* (Rome), 1978, no. 56, p. 81 -114.

30 J. Rupnik, *Histoire du PCT*, pp. 168-70. Entering parliament for the first time in 1929 Gottwald declared in his very first speech: 'We are the party of the Czechoslovak proletariat and our headquarters are in Moscow. We go to Moscow to learn from the Russian bolsheviks how to twist your throats. And as you know, the Russian bolsheviks are masters at that.' In May 1945 the Czech socialist M.P.F. Zeminova, to whom these threats had been personally addressed in 1929, went to see the leadership of the KSČ to offer the merger, of her party with the Communist Party. A similar offer was made on behalf of the social democratic party by B. Laušman. (In Slovakia the merger had already taken place during the uprising of August 1944). The communists politely refused, saying that the time was not yet ripe for such a merger. A few years later F. Zeminová was asked to serve as a witness in the first show trial with her own party leader, Milada Horáková and the dissident Marxist historian, Záviš Kalandra, who were both executed in 1950. As for Laušman, who had escaped to Austria after 1948, he was kidnapped in Vienna

in 1953 and brought back to Prague where he died in jail. Beyond the Kafkaesque absurdity of these itineraries, the important point they reveal is that the non-communist Left had no alternative, independent, political concept of socialism to that of the Communist Party.

31 Danubius, 'Tézy o vysídlení ceskoslovenských Nemcov', *Svědectví*, 1978, n.57, pp. 105-22; for the historical background see J.W. Bruegel, *Tschechen und Deutsche, 1939-46,* Munich, Nymphenburger Verlagshandlung, 1971.

32 A daring psychoanalytical interpretation of the party's behaviour in 1968 is outlined by J. Sladeček in his remarkable study of the Prague Spring, *Osmašedesaty*, p. 283-7.

33 The 'party of the expelled' is by far the largest in the country; if one adds up the expellees from previous purges (about 600,000 between 1946 and 50) and those who left because of political pressures during the purges of the early 1950s one must conclude that a significant proportion of the adult population (perhaps as much as a quarter) had, at one point or another, been a member of the party.

34 For the first comprehensive study of the Charter 77 movement, see Gordon Skilling, *Charter 77 and Human Rights in Czechoslovakia,* London, Allen & Unwin, 1981.

17 THE LABOUR PARTY AND SOCIAL DEMOCRACY

Raphael Samuel and Gareth Stedman Jones*

One difficulty in thinking about the Labour Party in a historically informed way is that beyond clichéd generalities - such as that the Labour Party is 'the party of the working class' - there is so little work to build on, whether as history, theory or politics. Both Marxists and social democrats tend to deal in timeless and unspecific categories - reformism, parliamentarism, leadership, rank-and-file. Little attention is paid either to the major transformations which have taken place within the Labour Party and the trade union movement in various epochs and crises; or at the way in which these might relate, positively or negatively to changing class formation and party affiliation, changes in the

*Raphael Samuel is tutor in social history at Ruskin College, Oxford and an editor of *History Workshop Journal*. Gareth Stedman Jones is fellow of King's College, Cambridge, university lecturer in history, and an editor of *History Workshop Journal*.

character of central and local government and changes in the place of Britain in the global economy.

The first reason for this absence of work is perhaps political - the fact that within the Labour Party divisions do not cluster around historically defined positions, but are determined by the particular configuration of political choice at a given moment in time. The contrast with communism, Trotskyism and anarchism, in which political currents often take their very definition from historically derived divisions, is very striking; nothing is easier than to set a roomful of Marxists by the ears with a reference to, say Kronstadt, the Popular Front or the Spanish Civil War. In the Labour Party, on the other hand, only perhaps in the late 1950s division on 'Clause Four', could it be said that the ghosts of the past had actually determined the course of inner-party controversy. For the rest, even when history is in some sense in play, it is often invisible to the combatants.

This comparative lack of passion or curiosity about the Party's past - even when directly relevent to problems of present strategy - is, if anything, reinforced by the most widely available and generally somewhat colourless accounts of Party history. There has never been an officially commissioned history of the Party, nor in consequence a heterodox and subterranean alternative line of interpretation. The overpowering sense among the Party faithful is that the Labour Party from the moment of its foundation has always been roughly the same - the same sort of people, the same sort of struggles, the same geography of power, the same range of organisations; at most, such a history has consisted of a small number of permutations on a limited set of variables. In standard accounts of the Party, like those of Cole and Pelling, outside social and political forces - the growth of larger units of production, competitive difficulties in the British economy, extensions of the suffrage, the emergence of unskilled unionism, the uncertainties of the late-Victorian professional classes and the hostility of employers to organised labour at the time of Taff Vale - are assigned a prominent place in the advent of the Labour Party. But thereafter external forces are given little space. Once in place, the three aboriginal participants - the Fabians (or professional middle class), the trade unions (or practically minded working class) and the ILP (or romantic socialists, later the Labour left) locked as if in some windowless room, appear to circle around each other in perpetual fugal movement. The growth of the working-class labour vote is treated as a virtually automatic sociological reflex, and it is liberal rather than labour historians who have raised the most interesting speculations upon the impact of the First World War upon political loyalties. The 1918 Constitution and the re-foundation of the Labour Party on an individual membership basis is primarily treated as a chapter in organisational growth. The political and cultural/ideological changes of which they were a product get short shrift, and what the change meant in particular localities is left in obscurity. Attention switches rather to such impoverished and contextless questions as: was Labour fit for government (1924)? and was MacDonald or Henderson the real architect of Labour advance? Textbook histories focus almost exclusively upon electoral growth, institutional machinery, the composition of the Parliamentary Party, Conference decisions, policy-making and quality of (parliamentary) leadership. The interplay of institutional forces - trades unions, ILP, Parliamentary Party, NEC, women's organisations, Fabians, co-ops - is narrated. But the broader social and political constellations which accounted for the shifts within and between these institutions, are treated cursorily, if at all. Histories of the Labour Party are markedly internalist in character, as if changes in the place and stance of the Party could be explained in terms of the conflicts of power and personality within an organisation. In general, such histories depict the view from Westminster writ large.

Within the Labour Party, the only serious attempts to introduce a historical dimension into political debate have come from the right (Crosland, *The Future of Socialism* and the *New Fabian Essays* in the 1950s). Characteristic of this kind of writing - as indeed of the original Fabian 'inevitability of gradualness' - is the sense of cosmic social and economic forces which of themselves determine the course of politics. The moral is that the Labour Party should swim with the tide and discard the outmoded 'fundamentalism' which still dominates party thinking. In the 1890s the moving historical force was conceptualised as 'collectivism' (i.e. the extension of state intervention and municipal enterprise). In recent years it has taken the form of sociological reductionism encapsulating a simple binary opposition between past and present: once there was poverty and unemployment, a simple two-class model of society and traditional working-class communities which provided the fulcrum of Labour Party support. Now there is affluence and an instrumental working class (Lockwood, early 1960s); once the Labour Party was a trade union party, now there has been the growth of a salaried middle class, of white collar rather than blue collar - so the Party must adapt its stance to attract the support of this group; in the dark Victorian years, capitalism was composed of small family firms ruthlessly pursuing profit irrespective of social cost; now firms are larger, ownership has been divorced from control and managers like their workers are interested in growth and a buoyant domestic market - the party should therefore appeal to industry as a whole, and not merely wage workers.

If the Labour right has possessed a simple and rather gross model of historical change of this kind, including strong teleological assumptions about secular movement towards mixed economy and the welfare state, the Labour left possesses no view at all which can properly be described as historical. While the Labour right tends towards economic or sociological reductionism, the Labour left inclines towards moralism and legalism. Its discussions are full of appeals to rights and the letter of the constitution, and since actual Labour Party history can rarely be accounted for in terms of conference decisions or the constitution, such a history is therefore portrayed in demonological terms as the recurrent nemesis of those guilty of deviating from them (MacDonald, Gaitskell). The recurrent imagery is that of betrayal - of rank-and-file by leadership, of conference by NEC, of NEC by PLP, of both by the Cabinet and of Cabinet by leader. Such discussion generally takes place in abstraction from wider social and political change and thus gives the impression of the issues always being the same and the villains playing stock parts in a morality play, whose message is that power corrupts. The roots of this moralism can be traced back to old dissenting modes of perception, or to political nonconformity in the Gladstonian era, which ranged principle against power. But to varying degrees since the 1920s a more specifically Marxist moralism has also been added, in which the Labour Party betrayed the revolution.

This lack of curiosity of the Labour left about history and even fear of it - fear during the post-war boom that historical research might prove the right correct - has been reinforced by the absence of serious socialist historians interested in the recent past and able to push a Labour left critique beyond moralism. Labour history in the twenty years of its existence, both in the *Society of Labour History* and in formations such as the *History Workshop*, has done very little to intervene in the course of current controversy, or to challenge its terms. Some of the reasons for this may be technical - the fact that historical research is apt to be more strongly organised around the remoter past; that papers become available only with a lapse of time - the contrast here with the instant history produced by Harold Wilson or David Owen is striking. But there may also be deeper and less acknowledged motives at work. The inspiration for labour history, ever since it began to take off as a movement, has been the search for an *alternative* non-social democratic tradition. E.P. Thompson's *Making of the English Working Class* (1963) has evidently been one major point of departure, but this book itself was appropriated by a powerful political or sub-political current which has meant that subsequent work has by and large reproduced its biases. Subjects have been chosen for the *dissimilarity* which they offered to the present - heroic periods of struggle, for instance, conceived not so much as forerunners of the present, but rather as examples of what has been lost. This could be said to be true not only of the study of eighteenth-century popular and local insurrections, but also of the work done by labour historians in much more recent times - for instance, the recovery of 'Little Moscows' in 1920s or community-based publications which focus on vanished solidarities.

Another way of looking at it would be to say that there has been a *de facto* division of labour within labour history. The more socialist-minded, including the majority of younger recruits have concentrated largely on alternative history and, in chronological period, eighteenth and nineteenth centuries rather than the twentieth. The more bureaucratic and social democratic have preferred to write biographies of labour leaders, or to chronicle twentieth-century parliamentary politics. Thus the split within labour history has also tended to present itself as a division between politics and society. On the one side, that of Philip Williams' *Gaitskell*, Alan Bullock's *Bevin*, David Marquand's *MacDonald* or Bernard Donoghue and George Jones's *Morrison*, there is an attention to policy-making and the small print of conference resolutions (this is also true of some recent trade union history). There is no sense at all of an underlying historical reality of which the participants at the time were not fully aware. On the other side, there is a culturalist attention to values, such as solidarity, which are treated as a continuous historical subject, permanently and in some sense unproblematically embedded in communities, and existing more or less independently of the course of politics or of any but the most large scale economic changes. The lines of this split are, of course, not wholly symmetrical. There are political biographies of the left like Michael Foot's *Bevan*, just as there are social analyses from the right - say the references to 'traditional' working-class values on which Goldthorpe and Lockwood's *Affluent Worker* depends. But the tendency towards congruence between defeated positions and social explanation and on the other hand between dominant lines of development and due political process, has been unmistakable.

This social and cultural approach of left historians has been characterised by a generous definition of history, an adventurous use of sources and both political and moral passion - a 'history from below' which challenges the complacencies of British politics. We do not want to question its worth, but we do want to point to its costs: the fact that no historical attention has been given to the main political tradition in twentieth-century working-class and left-wing politics, that represented by the Labour Party. The 'history from below' approach to the Labour Party - represented by such fine work as E.P. Thompson's 'Homage to Tom Maguire' or Stephen Yeo's 'Socialism and the new life' is apt to stop short at the point at which the Labour Party becomes institutionalised. It is as if history from below and the epoch of the Labour Party were incompatible - an unwarranted assumption which a few pioneer studies of local labour politics between the wars are already demonstrating to be palpably untrue.

Moreover, if, since 1960, left historiography has generally been characterised by the avoidance of direct contact with the mainstream of twentieth-century social democratic politics, this fear of contamination has found ample apparent legitimation at a theoretical level in the unflinching dissection of something called 'labourism' in the writings of New Left critics like Ralph Miliband and Michael Barratt Brown and in particular the theoretical studies of Perry Anderson and Tom Nairn. In the history of left vocabulary, 'labourism' is a more ambitious epithet than its predecessors. 'Labour fakirs' - the term current among the left before 1914 - suggested little more profound than fairground charlatanism. 'Reformism' - the Leninist term current particularly between the wars - implied a predictable global and non-culturally specific deviation characteristic of the petite bourgeoisie. 'Labourism', on the other hand, - a term scarcely current before the late 1950s - symbolised the lethal disease of a whole culture: an odorous and plague-ridden organism, fit only for the surgeon's knife and not to be handled in safety except with mask and gloves. What the New Left analysis offered was not a complex location of the history of the Labour Party in specific political contexts, but rather an eloquent and polemically brilliant phenomenology of a set of 'enduring reflexes', partially embodied in a set of institutions but mainly hovering like a dense mental fog over the low-lying ideological terrain on which the Labour Party operated. Empiricism, protestant moralism, philistine utilitarianism, reverential parliamentarism and intellectual nullity - these are the symptoms of 'labourism' as a disease. And at each turning point in the history of the Labour Party, it has not been hard to detect the tell-tale signs. But since the complexity of any specific political and historical conjuncture is never evoked with more than a few bold brush strokes, it is hard to assess the real significance of this ailment. As a savage and innovatory indictment of the malaise of the Labour Party and the labour movement in the late 1950s and 1960s, the New Left critique is justly famous. But as a stand-in for the history of the Labour Party, it will not do. Methodologically, its mode of construction resembles that of an ideal-type. A range of suggestive examples taken from widely differing historical contexts are fused into an analytical concentrate - 'labourism'. Then the procedure is reversed. 'Labourism', now allegedly an explanatory concept, is used in turn to decode the latent meaning of a series of prominent episodes in the history of the Labour Party. The procedure is brilliant but circular. To be more precise, however - and this is why it has found so much resonance among a wider left constituency in the 1960s and 1970s - 'Labourism' is thought of as, not so much as an ideal type as a deformed variant of an ideal type - that of the revolutionary party of the working class; and thus, the terms of its depiction constantly gravitate towards the vocabulary of clinical pathology.

If it is now urgent to change the focus of Labour Party history, it is because what seemed to analysts of the early 1960s - both on the right and on the left - to be the apparently unalterable contours of 'labourism', have revealed themselves in practice to be the products of a fragile political conjuncture not a secular stasis. It is thus necessary to move away from a depiction in which the realities of power are encountered in terms of gross abstractions and changeless categories - the trade unions, the leadership, the intelligentsia - and in which battles were fought by unreal historical combatants. We think that a critical history of the Labour Party ought to be able to engage with the minutiae of actual historical choices and to explain the course of politics at particular moments of time. If it is to do so, however, 'labourism' is a category which we must now decently lay to rest.

One of the problems is that both the left critique of 'labourism' and the right critique of 'fundamentalism' are both dependent upon the same standard secondary sources of party history. In this literature, as we have seen, the Labour Party is treated as a continuous and quasi-autonomous historical subject - its character, for good or ill, realised from its point of inception and its subsequent development little more than the realisation or frustration of possibilities always there from the start. Since the histories tend to represent the Labour Party in terms of the growth of something which is always fundamentally the same, interpreters, theorists and even subsequent historians conceive it to be their task to explain this sameness.

The first task of new historical work on the Labour Party must be to escape these tramlines. It was not only at the moment of its foundation that the Labour Party represented a conjunction of diverse and heterogeneous sources. The same has been true at every moment of its history. The continuity of Labour Party history is largely an optical illusion produced by an over-reliance upon certain sources - most notably those of Parliament and Party headquarters - and by the exclusive focus upon certain structural features - most notably, the special relationship between trade unions and the parliamentary party. Such an approach produces an impression of impulses of movement and activity radiating outwards from a parliamentary and TUC centre. It is however, more likely that the process operated mainly in the reverse direction: that successive and heterogeneous movements for change, generated in the first instance outside both party and formal trade union structure, eventually and with very varying degrees of success, impinged upon the character of the party, initially at a local level and ultimately at the centre. 'Bennism', for example, is unthinkable as a development generated by the internal logic of Labour Party growth. Nor can it simply be explained - as the mass media would have it - as the result of the rise of the militant tendency and the impact of polytechnics. The origins of the present inner party struggle between left and right would have to be traced back, among other things, to the student struggles and new cultural forms of the 1960s, to the Vietnam Solidarity Movement, to the growth of the women's movement and its redefinition of feminism and to the novel character of industrial militancy between 1966 and 1974 - all phenomena which arose in the first instance outside the Labour Party and only belatedly began to inflect it at the end of a long period of declining individual party membership. Contrary pressures, particularly upon Labour governments, not only from the City and the international balance of power, but also in ways both more mandarin or more demotic, from social groups outside the ambit of the party, from specialised inteligentsias, from progressive liberalism or from Toryism would also need to be registered. Wilson's defence of the pound and his worries about Rhodesian 'kith and kin', Callaghan's concessions to the right offensive on education are recent examples. One might also note, despite the wartime radicalisation of public opinion, how many of the formative influences upon the 1945 Labour government were non-socialist and non-labour in inspiration - the impact of liberals like Keynes and Beveridge, the adoption of rationalisation or efficiency as criteria of nationalisation, the acceptance of intelligence testing and the Butler Act in education, the espousal of modernism in architecture and natalist policies on the family. Thus, the history of Labour Party politics might be looked at, not as that of a self-sufficient organisational or ideological entity, but rather of a perpetually shifting fulcrum between contending and initially extra-party pressures from left and right.

Much has been gained by interpreting the transformation of the nineteenth-century Liberal Party in this fashion. It is by no means clear why the process in the twentieth-century Labour Party has been markedly different. The objections usually raised against this approach, so far as it has been considered, rest upon the contrast between a party premised upon a set of principles and a party defined by a collection of defensive working-class institutions uneasily meshed together under the aegis of an unchanging set of socialist aims. But the contrast is overplayed. Certain functions of trade unions may be relatively constant (though not as many as is often thought), but the aspirations of trade unionists are not unchanging. Furthermore, the relationship between trade unions and the Parliamentary Party and between trade union leaderships and trade unionists at the base has been anything but constant.

Similarly, the imaginative parameters, the preferred means of realisation and even the definition of socialism itself have assumed markedly different colourations in different phases of Labour Party history. To take but one example, the character of Labour socialism and its array of interlinked associations in the 1920s would be unrecognisable today. At a local level, for instance, if we leave aside trade unions, perhaps the most striking difference would have been the importance attached to Co-operation. In most general histories of the Labour Party, Co-operation merits no more than a cursory mention. It is usually treated as a nineteenth-century remnant harking back to the remote days of Robert Owen and the Rochdale pioneers and this picture is reinforced by its nineteenth-century historians who conceive its evolution to be that from community-building to shopkeeping. But in fact the greatest period of the growth of co-operation was the first thirty years of this century, not only as a form of retailing, but also as a social and political movement. The Utopia of most Labour Party activists at least until the Second World War was entitled the 'Co-operative

Commonwealth'. Nearly all Labour families were convinced co-operators. Thus co-ops were represented on the National Executive Committee, not out of deference to the pre-history of the Labour Party, but because they represented a crucial component of Labour's inter-war strength. The largest women's organisation in the Labour Party was the Co-operative Women's Guild. Meetings of local Labour Parties often took place in recently-built Co-op halls.

The place of Co-operation in the history of the Labour Party after 1918 is only one indication of the extent to which the Party at that time - or more accurately its affiliated institutions - aspired to organise the total environment of its active members in a way reminiscent of the pre-1914 German Social Democratic Party and it is a clue to why so many active supporters thought in terms of a labour movement, rather than just a Labour Party. Not only were there Labour Party theatre groups and a Labour Party symphony orchestra, but Labour Party sunday schools, Labour nursery groups, and Labour alternative to the scouts - Juvenile Co-operators and the Woodcraft Folk. In addition, the Labour Party possessed a strong daily and weekly press - older readers will recall that the direct ancestor of the *Sun* was the *Daily Herald* - while the political education offered by the Plebs League (again like the Co-ops independent, but in this case also unaffiliated) provided a socialist - and predominantly Marxist - alternative to conventional economics, philosophy and history to a generation of working-class Labour Party activists (including several who later became members of the 1945 Labour cabinet). Such a labour culture was quite different from that before 1914 in which an early survey revealed that the formative reading of the first generation of Labour MPs had been Ruskin and Carlyle. Given the paucity of primary research upon the local culture of Labour between the wars (we know more about the culture of Chartism), it is impossible to say how extensive this Labour culture was, or in what way it inflected political behaviour and political expectations. But it is quite clear that we shall not be able to understand the precise significance and the full impact, for better or for worse, of the two MacDonald governments and the depths of the trauma of 1931 until we are able to place them within the context of the Labour Socialism of the period. Questions posed by the available historiography, whether conservative or Marxist (class party or national party?) miss the achievement or failure of Labour judged in its own terms. Similarly, a historically more appropriate criterion of international comparison would be the social democratic parties of the Scandinavian countries or Austria, rather than the Communist Party of the Soviet Union.

This chapter has suggested no more than speculative questions and hypothetical alternatives, based upon fragmentary pieces of evidence and scepticism about what has until very recently been prevalent modes of approach. The urgent topical importance of new forms of understanding of the character of the Labour Party and its history needs no arguing. These are not academic questions, because unless we ask them we shall be the slaves of competing mythologies.

Bibliography

18 BIBLIOGRAPHY OF THE WRITINGS OF ERIC HOBSBAWM

Keith McClelland*

This is not the place to assess the writings of Eric Hobsbawm: one can simply note the sheer volume and range of them and the number of countries in which he has published. For Eric Hobsbawm must be known internationally to a greater extent than almost any other post-war British intellectual. If, in Britain, he is probably best known as an historian of industrial capitalism and the working class, in southern Italy or Peru he is read as the historian of 'primitive rebels', while, to some others, he is not Eric Hobsbawm at all, but remembered as Francis Newton, jazz critic. And as can be seen from the following bibliography, there are many other subjects with which he is associated.

The bibliography includes everything published up to April 1982 known to me save for (a) the numerous reprints of articles or extracts from books, except where the reprint will be more accessible than the original and (b) letters to the press. I have divided it into twenty-seven sections, arranged thematically and, within each section, chronologically. Obviously there are items which could have been listed under more than one section; but the reader should be able to find a title without difficulty.

In compiling the bibliography I received much help and hospitality from Eric and Marlene Hobsbawm: my warmest thanks to them both, for without them it really would have been an impossible task. Any errors or omissions are, of course, entirely my fault.

The bibliography is divided into the following sections:

*Keith McClelland is an itinerant lecturer in history, engaged in research on the nineteenth-century working class, especially on Tyneside.

ABBREVIATIONS

Rev.	Review
Repr.	Reprinted
LM	*Labouring Men. Studies in the history of labour*, (London: Weidenfeld and Nicolson, 1964)
Revs.	*Revolutionaries. Contemporary Essays*, (London, Weidenfeld & Nicolson, 1973)

Journals

BSSLH	*Bulletin of the Society for the Study of Labour History*
Ec.H.R.	*Economic History Review* (All references are to the second series)
Econ. J.	*Economic Journal*
MT	*Marxism Today*
NLR	*New Left Review*
N. Soc.	*New Society*
NS	*New Statesman*
NYRB	*New York Review of Books*
P & P	*Past & Present*
S & S	*Science & Society*
TLS	*Times Literary Supplement*

ELEMENTS OF AUTOBIOGRAPHY

'South American Journey', *Labour Monthly*, XLV, 7, 1963, pp. 329-32.
'In Defence of the 'Thirties', *Granta,* 15 November 1952. Repr. in *The Best of Granta 1889-1966,* ed. J. Philip *et al.*, London, Secker & Warburg, 1967, pp. 111-19.
'As usual during World Crises, a superb day', *Granta,* 2 November 1964.
'Interview with E.J. Hobsbawm' (conducted by Pat Thane and Liz Lunbeck), *Radical History Review*, 19, 1978-9, pp. 111-31.
Interview in *Élet és Irodalom* (Budapest), 28 July 1979.
'La unidad de la historia humana sólo se ha producido en este siglo', *El Pais* (Spain), 2 November 1979. Interview.

CAMBRIDGE

'Cambridge Balance Sheet', *Cambridge Left*, Lent 1954.
'"Cambridge Left"', *Granta,* 27 November 1954.
'Tinker, Tailor, Soldier, Don', *Observer,* 21 October 1979.
'Cambridge spy story - or the politics of treason', *N. Soc.*, 8 November 1979. Rev. of Andrew Boyle, *The Climate of Treason.*

A WRITER'S APPRENTICESHIP

'The Battle', *Punch,* 1 February 1939. Published anon. but attributed in the *Punch* index to 'E.J. Hobsbourn'. Short story.
'Dopey Willy', *Outlook* (Cambridge), (c. 1939).
Contributions to *Granta,* (Cambridge). Between 1936 and 1939 E.J.H. wrote regularly for *Granta,* including film reviews, book reviews, general pieces - e.g. under the title 'E.J.H. Observes' - and, in the spring and summer of 1939, edited the paper.
'Battle Prospects', *Lilliput,* January 1942. Short story.
'It Never Comes Off', *Lilliput,* March 1942. Short story.
'John Share' (pseud.), 'What will they read in defeat?', *World Review,* October 1943. On Karl May, a German boys' writer.
'Centurio' (pseud.), 'Aux Armes, Citoyens!', *University Forward,* October 1943.
'No future for heroes', *University Forward,* May 1944. On film heroes.
'Portrait of a Neighbourhood', *Lilliput,* April 1947. Commentary accompanying four paintings by James Boswell of Camden Town.
'Dumb Friend's Friend', *Lilliput,* May 1948. On 'Humanity' Martin, (1754-1834), chief founder of the RSPCA.

PORTRAITS OF OTHERS

'Sir John Clapham 1873-1946', *Sborník Pro Hospodářská a Sociální Dějiny*, II, 3/4, 1948. (Czech journal)
'G.D.H. Cole (1889-1959)', *Rivista Storica Del Socialismo*, II, 6, 1959, pp. 295-300.
Contribution to 'Paul Baran. A Collective Portrait', *Monthly Review*, XVI, 11, 1965, pp. 108-10.
'Delio Cantimori 1904-1966', *P & P*, 35, 1966, pp. 157-58.
'Maurice Dobb', *Socialism, Capitalism and Economic Growth. Essays presented to Maurice Dobb*, ed. C.H. Feinstein, Cambridge University Press, 1967, pp. 1-9. See also unsigned obit. of Dobb, *The Times*, 19 August 1976.
'George Lichtheim' (obit.) *NS*, 27 April 1973.
'Franz Marek', *Wiener Tagebuch*, September 1979. See also shorter obit. in *MT*, XXIII, 11, 1979, p. 31.

KNOWLEDGE AND THE PAST: PROBLEMS OF METHOD AND HISTORIOGRAPHY

'The Hero in History', *Modern Quarterly* (new series), II, 2, 1947, pp. 185-9. A comment on Sidney Hook, *The Hero in History*.
'History in Soviet Schools', *Times Educational Supplement*, 22 February 1952.
'Where are British historians going?', *Marxist Quarterly*, II, 1, 1955, 14-26.
'The Language of Scholarship', *TLS*, 17 August 1956.
Rev. of J.W. Godfrey and G. Parr, *The Technical Writer*, *The Author*, LXIX, 4, 1959, p. 97.
'Progress in History', *MT*, VI, 2, 1962, pp. 44-8. Occasioned by the publication of E.H. Carr's *What is History?*.
With J.E.C. Hill and Joan Thirsk, 'Anglo-Russian Historical Conference 1963', *P & P*, 26 1963, p. 4. (Note of complaint about the Conference - a model of how not to run such an event.)
'What history is about', *TLS*, 4 June 1964. Rev. of Irene Collins, *The Age of Progress*; V.H. Green, *Renaissance and Reformation;* Hugh Kearney, *Origins of the Scientific Revolution;* Martin Gilbert, *Britain and Germany Between the Wars*.
Rev. of G. Barraclough, *As Introduction to Contemporary History* and *Essays in British History*, ed. H.R. Trevor-Roper, *NS*, 30 October 1964.
'New ways in history: growth of an audience', *TLS*, 7 April 1966.
'Difficoltà dello storico di sinistra', *Libri Nuovi (Einaudi)*, I, 2, 1968.
Rev. of Charles Wilson, *Economic History and the Historian*, *N. Soc.*, 20 February 1969.
'Global Villages', *N. Soc.*, 19 June 1969.

Rev. of R. Nisbet, *Social Change and History* and Gordon Leff, *History and Social Theory, Guardian,* 11 September 1969.
'From Social History to the History of Society', *Daedalus,* 100, 1971, pp. 20-45.
'Class consciousness in history', *Aspects of History and Class Consciousness,* ed. I. Meszaros, London, Routledge & Kegan Paul, 1971, pp. 5-21.
'The Social Function of the Past: Some questions', *P & P,* 55, 1972, pp. 3-17.
'View from below', *N. Soc.,* 5 October 1972.
Rev. of A.R. Bridbury, *Historians and the Open Society, Ec.H.R.,* XXVI, 1973, pp. 721-2.
'Economic and social history divided', *N. Soc.,* 11 July 1974.
Rev. of R.W. Fogel and S. Engermann, *Time on the Cross, Guardian,* 10 October 1974.
'L'umanità e la scienza: Il nostro mondo vulnerable', *Paese Sera,* 17 October 1974.
'Comments' on Peter Burke, 'Reflections on the Historical Revolution in France: The *Annales* School and British Social History', *Review,* I, 3-4, 1978, 157-62.
'An Historian's Comments', *Space, Hierarchy and Society. Interdisciplinary Studies in Social Area Analysis,* ed. Barry C. Burnham and John Kingsbury, B.A.R. International Series, 59, 1979, pp. 247-52.
'"Partisanship" and the sciences', *Culture, science et développement. Contribution à une historie de l'homme. Mélanges en l'honneur de Charles Morazé,* Toulouse: Privat, 1979, pp. 267-79.
'L'état présent de l'historiographie anglaise', *Y a-t-il une nouvelle histoire? (Actes du colloque de juillet 1980),* ed. E. Le Roy Ladurie et G. Gadoffre, *Institut Collégial Européen, Bulletin 1980,* pp. 86-90, with discussion on pp. 92-4.
Contribution to 'Table Ronde Sur les Orientations de l'Historiographie Allemande', *ibid.,* pp. 95-6.
'The Revival of Narrative: Some Comments', *P & P,* 86, 1980, pp. 3-8. Comments on Lawrence Stone, 'The Revival of Narrative: Reflections on a New Old History', *ibid.,* 85, 1979, pp. 3-24.
'In Search of People's History', *London Review of Books,* 10 March - 1 April 1981. Rev. of *People's History and Socialist Theory,* ed. R. Samuel and E.H. Hunt, *British Labour History.*
'Looking Forward: History and the Future', *NLR,* 125, 1981, pp. 3-19.
'Address to the Anglo-American Conference of Historians', *TLS,* 24 July 1981.
'The contribution of history to social science', *International Social Science Journal,* XXXIII, 4, 1981, pp. 624-640.

PRIMITIVE REBELS AND AGRARIAN SOCIETIES

(a) General Studies

Primitive Rebels, Studies in archaic forms of social movement in the 19th and 20th centuries. Manchester University Press, 1959.

The book has nine chapters and an Appendix:

1 Introduction
2 The Social Bandit
3 Maffia
4 Millenarianism I: Lazzaretti
5 Millenarianism II: The Andalusian Anarchists
6 Millenarianism III: The Sicilian Fasci and Peasant Communism
7 The City Mob
8 The Labour Sects
9 Ritual in Social Movements

Appendix: 'In their own voices'

The 3rd edition, (1971), includes minor amendments to the text together with a new Preface.

The Spanish edition, (Barcelona: Ediciones Ariel, 1968), includes the following in addition to those chs of the English edn:
La anatomía de la violencia: "La Violencia" en Colombia, a translation of 'The anatomy of violence', *N. Soc.*, 11 April 1963.
Un movimiento campesino en el Péru
Epílogo a la edición española

The German edition, (1979), contains a new Foreword.

'Per lo studio delle classi subalterne', *Società*, XVI, 1960, pp. 436-49.

Rev. of George Rudé, *The Crowd in History, NYRB*, 22 April 1965.

Rev. of David Jones, *Before Rebecca. Popular Protests in Wales, 1793-1835, Welsh History Review*, VIII, 1976, pp. 110-11.

'Pre-political movements in modern politics', *Powers, Possessions and Freedom, Essays in honour of C.B. Macpherson*, University of Toronto Press, 1979, pp. 89-106.

'Historien des révoltes "primitives" en Europe', *Liberation*, 27-28 September 1980. Interview.

(b) Peasants and peasant societies

'Voices of the South', *TLS*, 21 October 1955. Rev. of G. Russo, *Baroni e Contadini*, R. Scotellaro, *Contadini del Sud*, and F. Cagnetta, *Inchiesta su Orgoloso*.

Rev. of Carlo Levi, *Words are Stones*, *TLS*, 21 August 1959.

'Sicilians speaking', *TLS*, 9 October 1959. Rev. of D. Dolci, *To Feed the Hungry* and Gavin Maxwell, *The Ten Pains of Death*.

Rev. of Margaret Carlyle, *The Awakening of Southern Italy*, *TLS*, 20 July 1962.

'South of Eboli', *TLS*, 29 March 1963. Rev. of D. Dolci, *Waste* and *Conversazioni* and Don Borrelli, *A Street Lamp and the Stars*.

'The anatomy of violence', *N.Soc.*, 11 April 1963.
'Peasants and rural migrants in politics', *The Politics of Conformity in Latin America*, ed. Claudio Veliz, London, Oxford University Press for the Royal Institute of International Affairs, 1967, pp. 43-65.
Rev. of D. Mack Smith, *A History of Sicily*, *N. Soc.*, 18 July 1968.
Review of Sartone Kartodirdjo, *The peasants' revolt of Banten in 1888*, *Bulletin of the School of Oriental and African Studies*, XXXI, 1968, pp. 428-29.
Rev. of Jagdish Chandra Jha, *The Bhumij Revolt, 1832-33*, *Bulletin of the School of Oriental and African Studies*, XXXII, 1969, pp. 182-3.
'Peasants and Politics', *Journal of Peasant Studies*, I, 1, 1973, pp. 1-22. See also: Philip Corrigan, 'On the politics of production: a comment on "Peasants and Politics" . . .', *ibid.*, II, 3, 1975, pp. 341-9 and 'Reply' by E.J.H., *ibid.*, pp. 349-51.
'Peasant land occupations', *P & P*, 62, 1974, pp. 120-52.
Rev. of *Peasants in Cities, Readings in the Anthropology of Urbanization*, ed. William Mangin, *Urban History Yearbook 1975*, pp. 51-2.
'Peasant Movements in Colombia', Commission Internationale d'Histoire des Mouvements Sociaux et des Structures Sociales, *Les Mouvements Paysans dans le Monde Contemporain*, 3 vols, Napoli, ISMOS, 1976, vol. III, pp. 166-86. Also in *International Journal of Economic and Social History*, VIII, 1976, pp. 166-86.
Rev. of J.S. Migdal, *Peasants, Politics and Revolution*, *Journal of Peasant Studies*, V, 1978, 254-6.
Rev. of Mikiso Hane, *Peasants, Rebels, and Outcastes: The Underside of Modern Japan*, *NYRB*, 15 April 1982.

(c) Feudalism and the development of agrarian capitalism
Rev. of J.D. Chambers and G.E. Mingay, *The Agricultural Revolution 1750-1880*, David Grigg, *The Agricultural Revolution in South Lincolnshire* and E. Royston Pike, *Human Documents of the Industrial Revolution*, *NS*, 5 August 1966.
'Problèmes agraires à la Convención', *Les Problèmes agraires des Amériques Latines*, Paris, Éditions du CNRS 1967, pp. 385-93, with discussion, pp. 395-407.
'A case of neo-feudalism: La Convención, Peru', *Journal of Latin American Studies*, I, 1969, pp. 31-50. This paper was given to a conference in Rome, April 1968; see, 'Un esempio di neofeudalesimo: La Convención (Perú)' in *Agricultura e sviluppo del capitalismo. Atti del convegno organizzato dall'-Istituto Gramsci. Roma, 20-22 aprile 1968*, Rome, Editori Riuniti/Istituto Gramsci, Imola, Galeati, 1970, pp. 269-91. See also, in that volume, pp. 565-7, 597-9 and 663-8 for contributions to discussion.
'Feudal Elements in the Development of Latin America', *Między Feudalizmem a Kapitalizmem. Studia z dziejów, gospodarczych i*

społecznych. Prace ofiarowane Witoldowi Kuli, Wroçlaw, Zazład Narodowy Imienia Ossolínskich - Wydawnictwo, 1976, pp. 57-74.

'Ideology and social change in Colombia', in *Ideology and Social Change in Latin America*, ed. June Nash, Juan Corradi and Hobart Spalding, New York, Gordon & Breach, 1977, pp. 185-99.

'Scottish Reformers of the Eighteenth Century and Capitalist Agriculture', *Peasants in History, Essays in honour of Daniel Thorner*, ed. E.J. Hobsbawm, W. Kula, A. Mitra, K.N. Raj and I. Sachs, Calcutta, Delhi, Bombay, Madras, Oxford University Press for the Sameeksha Trust, 1980, pp. 3-29. Note: though first written for this volume, the paper first appeared in French as 'Capitalisme et Agriculture: Les Réformateurs Écossais au XVIIIe Siècle', *Annales E.S.C.*, XXXIII, 1978, pp. 580-601.

(d) Banditry, crime and the outlawed

Rev. of Maurice Keen, *The Outlaws of Medieval Legend, NS*, 23 June 1961.

Rev. of *Secret Societies*, ed. Norman MacKenzie, *Book World*, 17 March 1968.

Bandits, London, Weidenfeld & Nicolson, 1969. 2nd edition, Harmondsworth, Penguin, 1972. This edition contains slight amplifications and changes to the text together with a new Preface and an Appendix on 'Women and Banditry'. The new paperback edition in the USA, New York, Pantheon, 1981, is the same as the Penguin edition save for the addition of a new Introduction and Postscript.

'Social criminality' (abstract of paper), *BSSLH*, 25, 1972, pp. 5-6.

'Social Bandits: Reply', *Comparative Studies in Society and History*, XIV, 1972, pp.503-5. Reply to Anton Blok, 'The Peasant and the Brigand: Social Banditry Reconsidered', *ibid.*, pp. 494-503.

Rev. of J.M. Roberts, *The Mythology of the Secret Societies*, *Guardian*, 3 August 1972.

'Social Banditry', *Rural Protest: Peasant Movements and Social Change*, ed. Henry A. Landsberger, London, Macmillan for the International Institute for Labour Studies, 1974, pp. 142-57,

'Shadow of the gallows', *N. Soc.*, 2 October 1975. Rev. of E.P. Thompson, *Whigs and Hunters* and Douglas Hay *et al.*, *Albion's Fatal Tree*.

(e) Millenarianism and religion

Rev. of Vittorio Lanternari, *Movimenti religiosi di libertà e di salvezza dei popoli oppressi*, *TLS*, 29 September 1961. See also: *American Sociological Review*, XXIX, 1964, pp. 290-91 for rev. of the English translation.

'Early Lives of Saints', *P & P*, 26, 1963, pp. 4-5.

A brief note of Fr Graus, 'Die Gewalt bei den Anfaengen des

Feudalismus und die "Gefangenenbefreiung" der merowingischen Hagiographie', *Jahrbuch für Wirtschaftsgeschichte*, 1961 (i).
Rev. of 'Millenial Dreams in Action', *Comparative Studies in Society and History, Supplement II, English Historical Review*, LXXX, 316, 1965, pp. 627-8.

(f) Urban riots
Rev. of George Rudé, *Wilkes and Liberty*, *NS*, 16 February 1962.

(g) Labour and agrarian capitalism
Rev. of R.C. Russell, *The 'Revolt of the Field' in Lincolnshire*, *Ec.H.R.*, X, 1957-8, p. 494.
'Le agitazioni rurali in Inghilterra nel primo Ottocento', *Studi Storici*, VIII, 1967, pp. 257-81. Note: This was written for simultaneous publication in French as 'Les soulèvements de la campagne anglaise 1795-1850', *Annales E.S.C.*, XXIII, 1968, pp. 9-30.
With George Rudé, *Captain Swing*, London, Lawrence & Wishart, 1969. 2nd edition, revised with a new Introduction, Harmondsworth, Penguin, 1973.
'Introduction' to J.L. and B. Hammond, *The Village Labourer 1760-1832*, New York, Harper Torchbooks, 1970, pp. vii-xiii.

GANGSTERS

'Political Theory and the "Mafia"', *Cambridge Journal*, VII, 1954, pp. 738-55. Incorporated into ch. 3 of *Primitive Rebels*.
'The Economics of the Gangster', *Quarterly Review*, 604, 1955, pp. 243-56.
'Thomas Greene' (pseud.), rev. of Billy Hill, *Boss of Britain's Underworld*, *Book & Bookmen*, February 1956.
Rev. of F. Sondern jun., *Brotherhood of Evil: The Mafia*, *TLS*, 12 June 1959.
'The Criminal as Hero and Myth', *TLS*, 23 June 1961. (signed.)
Rev. of Michele Pantaleone, *Mafia e Politica, 1943-1962*, *TLS*, 21 September 1962.
Rev. of Gus Tyler, *Organized Crime in America*, *NS*, 19 October 1962.
Rev. of Andrew Sinclair, *Prohibition*, *NS*, 16 November 1962.
'Mafia in Sicily', *N.Soc.*, 30 April 1964.
Rev. of Norman Lewis, *The Honoured Society*, *NS*, 12 June 1964.
Rev. of *Antologia della Mafia*, ed. N. Russo, S.F. Romano, *Storia della Mafia* and F. Chilanti and M. Farinella, *Rapporto sulla Mafia*, *TLS*, 5 November 1964.
'The American Mafia', *Listener*, 20 November 1969.
'The Age of the Mobsters', *TLS*, 27 June 1980. Rev. of Alan Block, *East Side - West Side. Organizing Crime in New York, 1930-1950*.

MODERN CAPITALISM: ORIGINS, DEVELOPMENTS, RESULTS

Rev. of J.H. Clapham, *A Concise Economic History of Britain. From the Earliest Times to 1750, TLS*, 30 December 1949.
Rev. of P. Gregg, *A Social and Economic History of Britain, 1760–1950, TLS*, 24 November 1950.
Rev. of J.H. Gleason, *The Genesis of Russophobia in Great Britain, Anglo-Soviet Journal*, XII, 4, 1951-2, pp. 48-9.
Rev. of A. Weber, *Weltwirtschaft, Econ. J.*, LXIII, 1953, pp. 677-9.
'The Crisis of the Seventeenth Century', Part 1, *P & P*, 5, 1954, pp. 33-53; Part 2, *ibid.*, 6, 1954, pp. 44-65. Repr. with a Postscript in *Crisis in Europe 1560–1660. Essays from Past and Present*, ed. T. Aston, London, Routledge & Kegan Paul, 1965, pp. 5-58.
See also: contribution to discussion on 'Seventeenth Century Revolutions' (conference report), *P & P*, 13, 1958, pp. 63-72.
'Trevor-Roper's "General Crisis" - Contribution to Symposium', *ibid.*, 18, 1960, pp. 12-14.
Rev. of T.S. Ashton, *Economic History of England. The Eighteenth Century, Daily Worker*, 28 July 1955.
Rev. of J.H. Plumb (ed.), *Studies in Social History, Books & Bookmen*, February 1956.
Rev. of W.T.O'Dea, *The Social History of Lighting, Time and Tide*, 17 May 1958.
Rev. of N. McCord, *The Anti-Corn Law League, 1838–1846, NS*, 26 July 1958.
Rev. of G. Unwin, *Industrial Organization in the Sixteenth and Seventeenth Centuries, NS*, 22 November 1958.
Rev. of G.R. Elton (ed.), *The New Cambridge Modern History vol. II. The Reformation 1520–1559* and H.C. Porter, *Reformation and Reaction in Tudor Cambridge, NS*, 6 December 1958.
Rev. of Asa Briggs, *The Age of Improvement, NS*, 14 February 1959.
Rev. of W.K. Jordan, *Philanthropy in England 1480–1660, Observer*, 19 July 1959.
Rev. of R.G. Cowherd, *The Politics of English Dissent, NS*, 15 August 1959.
Rev. of M.S. Anderson, *Britain's Discovery of Russia 1553–1815, Anglo-Soviet Journal*, XX, 3/4, 1959, pp. 46-7.
Rev. of M. Lewis, *A Social History of the Navy 1793–1815, NS*, 30 January 1960.
Rev. of L.G. Johnson, *The Social Evolution of Industrial Britain, Econ. J.*, LXX, 1960, pp. 404-5.
'The Seventeenth Century in the Development of Capitalism', *S & S*, XXIV, 2, 1960, pp. 97-112.
Rev. of E. Halévy, *A History of the English People in the Nineteenth Century, NS*, 7 April 1961 (under the title 'The British Secret').
'Le origini della rivoluzione industriale britannica', *Studi*

Storici, II, 3-4, 1961, pp. 496-516.
With Paul Baran, 'The Stages of Economic Growth', *Kyklos*, XIV, 1961, pp. 234-42.
Rev. of W.H.G. Armytage, *A Social History of Engineering*, *TLS*, 26 May 1961.
The Age of Revolution. Europe 1789-1848, London, Weidenfeld & Nicolson, 1962.
Rev. of H.J. Habakkuk, *American and British Technology in the Nineteenth Century*, *TLS*, 27 July 1962.
'From Feudalism to Capitalism' (contribution to discussion on 'Stages of Social Development'), *MT*, VI, 8, 1962, pp. 253-6. Repr. in Rodney Hilton *et al.*, *The Transition from Feudalism to Capitalism*, London, New Left Books 1976, pp. 159-64.
Rev. of Werner Conze (ed.), *Staat und Gesellschaft im deutschen Vormärz, 1815-1848*, *TLS*, 21 September 1962.
Rev. of G. Kitson Clark, *The Making of Victorian England*, *Victorian Studies*, VI, 2, 1962, pp. 178-80.
Rev. of R. Cameron, *France and the Economic Development of Europe, 1800-1914*, *S & S*, XXVII, 1, 1963, pp. 84-6.
Rev. of Asa Briggs, *Victorian Cities*, *NS*, 20 September 1963.
Rev. of J.D. Mackie, *A History of Scotland* and Ian Grimble, *Chief of Mackay*, *NS*, 12 February 1965.
Rev. of John Nef, *The Conquest of the Material Word*, *NYRB*, 11 March 1965.
'"First Comers" e "Second Comers"', *Problemi Storici della Industrializzazione e dello Sviluppo*, Pubblicazione dell' Università degli studi di Urbino. Serie di Economia, vol. VI, Urbino, Argalia editore, 1965, pp. 71-101.
'Recenti Studi Sull'Industrializzazione in Gran Bretagna', *ibid.*, pp. 185-201.
Rev. of *The Cambridge Economic History of Europe*, vol. VI, *Parts I and II, The Industrial Revolutions and After*, ed. H.J. Habakkuk and M. Postan, *NS*, 17 September 1965.
Rev. of A.J.P. Taylor, *English History 1914-1945*, *NS*, 22 October 1965.
Rev. of S.G. Checkland, *The Rise of Industrial Society in England, 1815-1885*, *Ec.H.R.*, XVIII, 1965, pp. 650-1.
'Capitalist Development: Some Historical Problems', *MT*, XI, 8, 1967, pp. 239-43.
Rev. of A. Marwick, *Britain in the Century of Total War*, *Observer*, 26 May 1968.
Rev. of Fernand Braudel, *La Mediterranée et le Monde Mediterranéen à l'époque de Philippe II* (new edition), *P & P*, 39, 1968, pp. 173-4.
Rev. of *The Cambridge Economic History of Europe, vol. IV, The Economy of Expanding Europe in the Sixteenth and Seventeenth Centuries*, ed. E.E. Rich and C.H. Wilson, *Econ. J.* LXXVIII, 1968, pp. 127-8.
Industry and Empire. An economic history of Britain since 1750, London, Weidenfeld & Nicolson, 1968. *The Pelican Economic History of Britain*, vol. 3. Published as such, Harmondsworth,

Penguin, 1969.

'Poverty', *International Encyclopedia of the Social Sciences*, 17 vols, New York, Macmillan and The Free Press, 1968, 12, pp. 398-404.

En Torno a los origenes de la revolucion industrial, Buenos Aires, Siglo Veintiuno Argentina, 1971. Contains translations of (1) 'The General Crisis . . .'; (2) 'The Seventeenth Century in the Development of Capitalism'; (3) 'Le origini della rivoluzione industriale britannica'.

Rev. of Peter Laslett (ed.), *Household and Family in Past Time*, *N.Soc.*, 21 December 1972.

Rev. of H.J. Dyos and M. Wolff (eds), *The Victorian City*, *Guardian*, 30 August 1973.

The Age of Capital 1848-1875, London, Weidenfeld & Nicolson, 1975.

Rev. of John Roberts, *Revolution and Improvement*, *Observer*, 14 March 1976.

Comment on Sidney Pollard, 'Industrialization and Integration of the European Economy', *Industrialisierung und 'Europäische Wirtschaft' im 19. Jahrhundert. Ein Tagunsbericht*, ed. Otto Busch *et al.*, Veröffentlichungen der Historischen Kommission zu Berlin Band 46. Publikationen zur Geschichte der Industrialisierung, Band 5; Berlin & New York, Walter de Gruyter, 1976, pp. 29-32.

Feudalism, Capitalism and the Absolutist State. Reviews of Perry Anderson by Eric Hobsbawm and Douglas Bourn, London, History Group of the Communist Party, 1976; Our History pamphlet no. 66. (E.J.H. on pp. 3-13.) See also, rev. of Perry Anderson, *Passages from Antiquity to Feudalism* and *Lineages of the Absolutist State*, *NS*, 7 February 1975.

'Gesellschaftskrise 1789-1848', *Wien und Europa Zwischen den Revolutionen (1789-1848)*, ed. R. Urbach, Wien-München, Jugend & Volk, 1977.

Rev. of A. Milward & S.B. Saul, *The Development of the Economies of Continental Europe, 1850-1940*, *Ec.H.R.*, XXXI, 4, 1978, pp. 692-3.

'The Development of the World Economy' (rev. of W.W. Rostow, *The World Economy: History and Prospect*), *Cambridge Journal of Economics*, III, 3, 1979, pp. 305-18.

'Publick Benefits and Private Vices', *NYRB*, 3 April 1980. (Rev. of various books on nineteenth-century England, including Norman Gash, *Aristocracy and People, 1815-1865.*)

IMPERIALISM

Rev. of Basil Davidson, *Black Mother*, *NS*, 17 November 1961.

Rev. of R. Robinson, J. Gallagher, A. Denny, *Africa and the Victorians*, *Labour Monthly*, XLIV, 5, 1962, pp. 237-8.

Rev. of B. Semmel, *Imperialism and Social Reform*, *S &S*, XXVI, 2, 1962, pp. 240-3.

'The End of European World Domination', *Afro-Asian and World Affairs*, 2, 1964, pp. 93-9.
'Eastern poverty, western theories', rev. of Gunnar Myrdal, *Asian Drama*, *NS*, 19 July 1968.
'Revolution east of Suez', *N.Soc.*, 30 January 1969.
Rev. of V.G. Kiernan, *The Lords of Human Kind, Guardian*, 20 February 1969.
'White Man's Burden', *N.Soc.*, 6 March 1969.
'Die Imperialismusdebatte in der Geschichtsschreibung', *Sozialistische Politik*, I, 1, 1969, pp. 16-25.
'Foreword' to Panchanan Saha, *Emigration of Indian Labour (1834-1900)*, Delhi, People's Publishing House, 1970, pp. vii-x.
Rev. of Hugh Tinker, *A New System of Slavery. The Export of Indian Labour, 1830-1920, Guardian*, 28 February 1974.

NATIONALISM

Contribution to 'Colonialism and Nationalism in Africa and Europe' (Conference Report), *P & P*, 24, 1963, pp. 65-74. (E.J.H. gave a paper on 'Nationalism and mass opinion in the nineteenth century'.)
'The limits of nationalism', *N. Soc.*, 2 October 1969.
'Tower of Babel', *N. Soc.*, 19 February 1970.
'The attitude of popular classes towards national movements for independence: Great Britain: The Celtic Fringe', *Mouvements Nationaux d'Indépendance et Classes Populaires aux XIXe et XXe Siècles en Occident et en Orient*, 2 vols, Commission Internationale d'Histoire des Mouvements Sociaux et des Structures Sociales; Paris: Armand Colin, 1971, I, pp. 34-44.
'Some Reflections on Nationalism', *Imagination and Precision in the Social Sciences. Essays in memory of Peter Nettl*, ed. T.J. Nossiter, A.H. Hanson and S. Rokkan, London, Faber & Faber, 1972, pp. 385-406.
'Lynn and nationalism', *N. Soc.*, 8 July 1976. Critique of Richard Lynn, 'The sociobiology of nationalism', *ibid.*, 1 July 1976. See also correspondence from Lynn, *ibid.*, 22 July 1976 and E.J.H., 5 August 1976.
'Some reflections on "The Break-up of Britain"', *NLR*, 105, 1977, pp. 3-23.
Rev. of H. Seton-Watson, *Nations and States, N. Soc.*, 2 February 1978.
'Los Movimientos Nacionales', *Anales del Centro de Alzira de la Universidad Nacional de Educación a Distancia*, I, 1980, pp. 7-27.

THE INDUSTRIAL WORKING CLASS AND LABOUR MOVEMENTS

Labour's Turning Point 1880-1900. Extracts from contemporary sources edited by E.J. Hobsbawm, London, Lawrence & Wishart,

1948; vol. 3 of the series 'History in the Making' under the general editorship of Dona Torr. 2nd edition, with a new Preface, Hassocks, Harvester Press, 1974.

Contribution to *London's Struggle for Socialism 1848–1948*, ed. George Armstrong, London, Thames Publications, 1948. Note: in his copy E.J.H. notes that 'probably cap. 6 is by E.J.H.'; the chapter is 'The Dock Strike and Unskilled Labour in London'.

'Peter Hill' (pseud.), 'Keir Hardie', *Communist Review*, June 1948, pp. 172-8.

Rev. of R. Goetz-Girey, *La Pensée Syndicale Française*, *TLS*, 13 November 1948.

'General Labour Unions in Britain, 1889-1914', *Ec.H.R.*, I, 1949, pp. 123-42. Repr. in *LM*, ch. 10.

Rev. of G.E. Fussell, *From Tolpuddle to TUC*, *Ec.H.R.*, I, 1949, pp. 167-8.

Rev. of H.W. Laidler, *Socio-Economic Movements*, *TLS*, 15 July 1949.

'Trends in the British Labour Movement Since 1850', *S & S*, XIII, 1949, 289-312. Revised and repr. in *LM*, ch. 16.

Rev. of A. Aspinall (ed.), *The Early English Trade Unions*, *Econ. J.*, LIX, 1949, pp. 407-9.

'The Tramping Artisan', *Ec.H.R.*, III, 1950-1, pp. 299-320, repr. in *LM*, ch. 4.

Rev. of J.W. Follows, *Antecedents of the International Labour Organization*, *Ec.H.R.*, IV, 1951-2, pp. 418-9.

'The Machine Breakers', *P & P*, 1, 1952, pp. 57-70. Repr. in *LM*, ch. 2.

'Economic Fluctuations and Some Social Movements Since 1800', *Ec.H.R.*, V, 1952-3, pp. 1-25. Repr. in *LM*, ch. 8.

'The History of Wages', *World News*, 16 January 1954.

'The Labour Aristocracy in 19th Century Britain', *Democracy and the Labour Movement, Essays in honour of Dona Torr*, ed. John Saville, London, Lawrence & Wishart, 1954, pp. 201-39. Repr. in *LM*, ch. 15.

Rev. of S.C. Gillespie, *A Hundred Years of Progress. The Record of the Scottish Typographical Association 1853–1952*, *Econ. J.*, LXIV, 1954, pp. 599-600.

Rev. of G.D.H. Cole, *Attempts at General Union 1818–1834*, *Ec.H.R.*, VII, 1954-5, pp. 118-19.

Rev. of E. Howe and J. Child, *The London Society of Bookbinders*, *Ec.H.R.*, VII, 1954-5, p. 120.

Rev. of *Untersuchungen über Berufsprobleme der niederösterreichischen Arbeiterschaft in Gegenwart und Vergangenheit*, vol. 4, parts 1 and 2, *Ec.H.R.*, VII, 1954-5, pp. 272-3.

Rev. of J. Kuczynski, *Die Geschichte der Lage der Arbeiter in Deutschland, 1789–1870; . . . in England, 1640–1760; . . . in England, 1760–1832*, *S & S*, XX, 2, 1956, pp. 157-160.

'Methodism and the threat of revolution in Britain', *History Today*, VII, 1957, pp. 115-24. Repr., with additional 'Note',

in *LM*, ch. 3.
'The British Standard of Living 1790-1850', *Ec.H.R.*, X, 1957-8, pp. 46-68. Revised and repr. in *LM*, ch. 5.
See also:
The Standard of Living in Britain in the Industrial Revolution, ed. A.J. Taylor, London, Methuen, 1975, in which the article was repr. This volume also contains an important 'Postscript' to the 'standard of living debate' by E.J.H. on pp. 179-88.
With R.M. Hartwell, 'The Standard of Living During the Industrial Revolution: A Discussion', *Ec.H.R.*, XVI, 1963-4, pp. 119-46. E.J.H. is on pp. 119-34. This followed an article by Hartwell in *ibid.*, XIII, 1961, pp. 397-416. 'History and the "Dark Satanic Mills"', *MT*, II 5, 1958, pp. 132-9. Repr. in *LM*, ch. 6.
'En Angleterre: Révolution industrielle et vie matérielle des classes populaires', *Annales E.S.C.*, XVII, 1962, pp. 1047-61.
'The Standard of Living Debate: A Postscript', *LM*, ch. 7.
Comment on David Landes, 'The Standard of Living During the Industrial Revolution', *Industrialisierung und 'Europäische Wirtschaft' im 19. Jahrhundert. Ein Tagunsbericht*, ed. Otto Busch *et al.*, Veröffentlichungen der Historischen Kommission zu Berlin, vol. 46. Publikationen zur Geschichte der Industrialisierung, Band 5; Berlin and New York, Walter de Gruyter, 1976, pp. 103-6.
Rev. of Tom Paine Exhibition at the Marx Memorial Library, *NS*, 6 June 1959.
Rev. of A.O. Aldridge, *Man of Reason. The Life of Thomas Paine*, *NS*, 10 February 1961. Repr. in *LM*, ch. 1, as 'Tom Paine'.
Rev. of B. Pribicevic, *The Shop Stewards' Movement and Workers' Control, 1910-1922*, *NS*, 20 June 1959.
Rev. of Asa Briggs (ed.), *Chartist Studies*, *NS*, 31 October 1959.
Rev. of M. Tylecote, *The Mechanics' Institutes of Lancashire and Yorkshire Before 1851*, *History*, XLIV, 151, 1959, p. 171.
Rev. of L.Dal Pane, *Storia del Lavoro in Italia, vol. IV . . .*, *Ec.H.R.*, XII, 1959-60, pp. 338-9.
'Custom, Wages, and Work-load in Nineteenth Century Industry', *Essays in Labour History*, ed. A. Briggs and J. Saville, London, Macmillan, 1960, pp. 113-39. Repr. in *LM*, ch. 17.
Rev. of S. Pollard, *A History of Labour in Sheffield*, *Ec.H.R.*, XIII, 1960-1, pp. 127-8.
'Hyndman and the S.D.F.', *NLR*, 10, 1961, pp. 69-72. Repr. in *LM*, ch. 12.
Rev. of John Stanhope, *The Cato Street Conspiracy*, *NS*, 4 January 1963.
Rev. of D.L. Horowitz, *The Italian Labour Movement*, *BSSLH*, 7, 1963, 38-43.
'Co-operative Work Groups', *P & P*, 26, 1963, p. 5.
A brief note on I. Katona, 'Types of work groups and temporary

associations of seasonal labour in the age of capitalism', *Acta Ethnographica Academiae Scientiarum Hungaricae*, XI, 1-2, 1962, pp. 31-85.

Rev. of K.S. Inglis, *Churches and the Working Classes in Victorian England* and N.C. Masterman, *John Malcolm Ludlow*, *NS*, 13 September 1963.

Rev. of E.P. Thompson, *The Making of the English Working Class*, *NS*, 29 November 1963.

Rev. of P.S. Bagwell, *The Railwaymen. The History of the National Union of Railwaymen*, *History*, XLIX, 165, 1964, p. 105.

Labouring Men. Studies in the History of Labour, London, Weidenfeld & Nicolson, 1964. Repr. with minor corrections 1968.

'The Nineteenth Century London Labour Market', Centre for Urban Studies, *London: Aspects of Change*, London, Macgibbon & Kee, 1964, pp. 3-28.

'Labour Traditions'. 1st published in *LM*, ch. 18.

Rev. of R. Harrison, *Before the Socialists* and H. Collins and C. Abramsky, *Karl Marx and the British Labour Movement*, *NS*, 5 March 1965.

'The formation of the industrial working classes: some problems', *Third International Conference of Economic History, Munich 1965*, 5 vols; Paris, École Pratique des Hautes Études/Mouton, 1968, I, pp. 175-180.

Rev. of Brian Simon, *Education and the Labour Movement 1870-1920* and Harold Silver, *The Concept of Popular Education*, *NS*, 31 December 1965.

'Thoughts on the "New Trades Unionism"', (abstract of paper), *BSSLH*, 13, 1966, pp. 14-15.

'Les classes ouvrières et la culture depuis les débuts de la révolution industrielle', *Niveaux de culture et groupes sociaux*, (Actes du colloque réuni du 7 au 9 mai 1966 à l'École Normale Supérieure). (École Pratique des Hautes Études-Sorbonne. Sixième Section: Sciences Économiques et Sociales. Congrès et Colloques, XI.) Paris/The Hague, Mouton, 1967, pp. 189-99, with discussion on pp.201-10.

'Trade Union History', *Ec.H.R.*, XX, 1967, 358-64. (Rev. essay of H.A. Clegg *et al.*, *A History of British Trade Unions Since 1889, vol. I: 1889-1910.)*

Rev. of E. Frow and M. Katanka, *1868: Year of the Unions*, *N. Soc.*, 16 May 1968.

Rev. of J. Kuczynski, *Die Geschichte der Lage der Arbeiter*, *Jahrbuch für Wirtschaftgeschichte*, 1968, iv, p. 225.

Rev. of D. Bythell, *The Handloom Weavers*, *N. Soc.*, 6 February 1969.

Rev. of Henry Pelling, *Popular Politics and Society in Late Victorian Britain*, *BSSLH*, 18, 1969, pp. 49-54.

'La marginalidad social en la historia de la industrialización europea', *Revista Latinoamerica de Sociología*, 2, 1969, pp. 237-48.

'Introduction' to F. Engels, *The Condition of the Working Class in England*, London, Panther Books, 1969, pp. 7-17. First published as the introduction to the French edition - *La Situation de la Classe Laborieuse en Angleterre*, Paris, Éditions Sociales, 1960, pp. 7-23.

Rev. of B. Inglis, *Poverty and the Industrial Revolution* and F.M. Leventhal, *Respectable Radical*, *NS*, 12 February 1971.

Rev. of A. Briggs and J. Saville (eds), *Essays in Labour History 1886-1923*, *BSSLH*, 24, 1972, pp. 66-9.

Rev. of Z. Bauman, *Between Class and Elite*, *Guardian*, 28 December 1972.

Rev. of J.M. Bellamy and J. Saville (eds), *Dictionary of Labour Biography*, vol. I, *Labour Monthly*, LV, 5, 1973, pp. 237-238. See also: 'Ordinary Lives', *N. Soc.*, 2 December 1976, for review of vol. 3.

Rev. of J.T. Murphy, *Preparing for Power*, *BSSLH*, 26, 1973, p. 78.

'Religion and the Rise of Socialism', *History and Humanism, Essays in honour of V.G. Kiernan*, *New Edinburgh Review* (special issue), 38-9, 1977, pp. 9-16. Revised version in *Marxist Perspectives*, I, 1, 1978, pp. 14-33.

'The Aristocracy of Labour Reconsidered'. Paper to the International Economic History Conference, Edinburgh, August 1978, mimeo; the papers have not as yet been published. See also: 'The Labour Aristocracy: Twenty Five Years After' (abstract of paper), *BSSLH*, 40, 1980, p. 6.

Rev. of Barrington Moore jun., *Injustice*, *Guardian*, 12 October 1978. See also: *Le Débat*, 1, 1980, p. 128: The journal asked for recommendations of foreign books which particularly deserved attention in France. E.J.H. recommended *Injustice*.

'Soziale Ungleichheit und Klassenstrukturen in England: Die Arbeiterklasse', *Klassen in der europäischen Sozialgeschichte*, ed. H.-U. Wehler, Göttingen, Vandenhoeck & Ruprecht, 1979, pp. 53-65.

'La culture ouvrière en Angleterre', *L'Histoire*, 17, 1979, pp. 25-33.

'Pact with the Devil', *NYRB*, 18 December 1980 (rev. of M. Taussig, *The Devil and Commodity Fetishism in South America*).

With Joan Wallach Scott, 'Political Shoemakers', *P & P*, 89, 1980, pp. 86-114.

Labour Movement Historiography

'Friendly Societies', *Amateur Historian*, III, 3, 1957, pp. 95-101.

'Commitment and Working Class History. A review of recent Labour Movement History', *Universities and Left Review*, 6, 1959, pp. 71-2.

'Records of the Trade Union Movement', *Archives*, IV, 1960, pp. 129-37.

'Trade Union Historiography', *BSSLH*, 8, 1964, pp. 31-6.

'Introduction' to *The Luddites and Other Essays*, ed. L.M. Munby, London, Michael Katanka (Books) Ltd, 1971, pp. 7-8.

'Foreword' to John Foster, *Class Struggle and the Industrial Revolution. Early industrial capitalism in three English towns*,

London, Weidenfeld & Nicolson, 1974, pp. xi-xiii.
'Ideology and labour history' (abstract of paper), *BSSLH*, 27, 1973, pp. 32-3. Printed in full as 'Labor History and Ideology', *Journal of Social History*, VII, 1974, pp. 371-81.

PRE-MARXIST SOCIALISM

Rev. of R.K.P. Pankhurst, *William Thompson, 1775-1833, Econ. J.*, LXVI, 1956, pp. 525-7.
'Capitalist who saw the gleam' (Robert Owen), *Daily Worker*, 17 November 1958.
'Noveishie Rabotý po istorii utopicheskogo sotsialisma v Anglii', *Istoriya Sotsialisticheskikh Uchenii (Sbornik Statei)*, Akad.-Nauk, Moscow, 1962 ('New works on the history of socialism in England').
Rev. of Thomas Hodgskin, *Labour Defended* and William Thompson, *An Inquiry into the Principles of the Distribution of Wealth*, *NS*, 8 May 1964.
Rev. of George Lichtheim, *The Origins of Socialism*, *Book World* (USA), 19 January 1969.
'Victims of History', *NS*, 4 April 1969. Rev. of J.F.C. Harrison, *Robert Owen and the Owenites in Britain and America.*

MARXISM

(a) Marx and Engels
'Marx on Poland', *Tribune*, 20 July 1945.
Rev. of Cyr van Overbergh, *Karl Marx*, *TLS*, 14 July 1950.
'Dr. Marx and the Victorian Critics', *New Reasoner*, 1, 1957, pp. 29-38. Repr. in *LM*, ch. 13.
Rev. of Siegfried Bünger, *Friedrich Engels und die britische sozialistische Bewegung, 1881-1895*, *Zeitschrift für Geschichtswissenschaft*, XI, 1963, pp. 614-17.
'Introduction' to Karl Marx, *Pre-Capitalist Economic Formations*, trans. Jack Cohen and ed. E.J. Hobsbawm, London, Lawrence & Wishart, 1964, pp. 9-65.
'Marx in Print', *TLS*, 9 May 1968 (leader).
'Commentary': On the UNESCO Conference on 'The Influence of Karl Marx on the Development of Contemporary Scientific Thought', Paris, May, 1968, *TLS*, 16 May 1968.
'Karl Marx's Contribution to Historiography', *Diogenes*, 64, 1968, pp. 37-56. Also available in *Marx and Contemporary Scientific Thought*, Publications of the International Social Science Council, 13, The Hague/Paris, Mouton, 1969, pp. 197-211. (Papers from the UNESCO Symposium of May 1968.)
'Karl Marx's Contribution to Historiography' is also in *Ideology in Social Science. Readings in critical social theory*, ed. Robin Blackburn, London, Fontana/Collins, 1972, pp. 265-83.
'Karl Marx and the British Labour Movement', *Marxism Today*,

XII, 1968, pp. 166-72. Repr. in *Revs.*, ch. 10.
'Un inédit du Marx d'avant le "Capital"', *La Quinzaine Littéraire*, 1-15 avril 1970 (on the *Grundrisse*).
Rev. of D. McLellan (ed.), *Marx's Grundrisse*, *N. Soc.*, 25 February 1971.
Rev. of Yvonne Kapp, *Eleanor Marx, vol. 1*, *Listener*, 7 September 1972. For rev. of vol. II, see *NS*, 7 January 1977.
Rev. of Steven Marcus, *Engels, Manchester and the Working Class*, *Observer*, 6 October 1974.
Rev. of W.O. Henderson, *Life of Friedrich Engels*, *N. Soc.*, 3 June 1976.
Contributions to *Storia del marxismo*, ed. E.J. Hobsbawm, G. Haupt, F. Maret, E. Ragionieri, V. Strada, C. Vivanti, Turin, Giulio Einaudi, 1978- (to be completed in 5 vols). Note: this history is also in Spanish and English (forthcoming).
Contributions to vol. I, *Il Marxismo ai tempi di Marx:*
'Prefazione', pp. xi-xxix.
'Marx, Engels e il socialismo premarxiano', pp. 5-34.
'Gli aspetti politici della transizione dal capitalismo al socialismo', pp. 247-87.
'La fortuna delle edizioni di Marx ed Engels', pp. 357-74. Note: volume I has been published in English as *The History of Marxism, vol. I: Marxism in Marx's Day*, Hassocks, Harvester 1982.
Contributions to vol. II, *Il Marxismo nell' età della Seconda Internazionale*. 'La cultura europea e il marxismo fra Otto e Novecento', pp. 61-106.
Contributions to vol. III, *Il Marxismo nell' età della Terza Internazionale*, parts 1 and 2: in part 1, 'Presentazione', pp. xv-xxii; in part 2, 'Gli intellettuali e l'antifascismo', pp. 443-90.
Rev. of G.A. Cohen, *Karl Marx's Theory of History*, *NS*, 2 February 1979.

(b) The Marxism of the Second and Third Internationals

Rev. of A.J. Berlau, *The German Social-Democratic Party, 1914-1921*, *New Central European Observer*, 16 September 1950.
'La Diffusione del Marxismo (1890-1905)', *Studi Storici*, XV, 2, 1974, pp. 241-69.
'Lenin and the "Aristocracy of Labor"', *Monthly Review*, XXI, 11, 1970, pp. 47-56. Also in *MT*, XIV, 7, 1970, pp. 207-10. Repr. in *Lenin Today. Eight Essays on the Hundredth Anniversary of Lenin's Birth*, ed. Paul Sweezy & Harry Magdoff, New York and London, Monthly Review Press, 1970, pp. 47-56. Repr. in *Revs.*, ch. 12.
Rev. of J.P. Nettl, *Rosa Luxemburg*, *Ec.H.R.*, XX, 1967, pp. 412-13.
Contribution to discussion in *Studi Gramsciani. Atti del convegno tenuto a Roma nei giorni 11-13 gennaio 1958*, Istituto Antonio Gramsci/Editori Reuniti, 1958, pp. 535-6.

Rev. of John M. Cammett, *Antonio Gramsci and the Origins of Italian Communism, The Nation,* New York, 18 September 1967.

'The Great Gramsci', *NYRB*, 4 April 1974. Rev. of *Selections from the Prison Notebooks*, and *Letters from Prison*, ed. Lynne Lawner.

'Il teorico del nuovo "principe"', *Libri Nuovi (Periodico Einaudi di informazione libraria e culturale)*, VII, 2, 1975, pp. 1-2.

'Gramsci and Political Theory', *MT*, XXI, 7, 1977, pp. 205-13.

'La scienza politica', *Rinascita,* 50-1, 23 December 1977.

Rev. of N. Bukharin and E. Preobrazhensky, *The ABC of Communism,* with an introduction by E.H. Carr, *TLS,* 24 July 1969.

Rev. of Cathy Porter, *Alexandra Kollontai, Guardian,* 6 June 1980.

'The Lukács Debate', *New Central European Observer,* 26 November 1949.

'The Mirror of Reality', *TLS,* 22 September 1950. Rev. of Georg Lukács, *Studies in European Realism.*

'Introduction' to Jozsef Revai, *Lukács and Socialist Realism. A Hungarian Literary Controversy,* London, Fore Publications, 1950. (The intro. is unpaginated but is 5 pp.)

'Marxism Re-opened', *TLS,* 28 March 1968.
Rev. of Karl Korsch, *Marxismus und Philosophie* and *Karl Marx.* Repr. in *Revs.,* ch. 16, as 'Karl Korsch'.

(c) Contemporary Marxism

Rev. of Paul Sweezy, *Socialism, S & S,* XIV, 1949-50, pp. 77-9.

Rev. of Leo Huberman, *The Truth About Socialism, S & S,* XIV, 1950, pp. 351-3.

Rev. of R. Guihéneuf, *Le Problème de la Théorie Marxiste de la Valeur* and J. Bénard, *La Conception Marxiste du Capital, Econ. J.,* LXIV, 1954, pp. 168-70.

'The Future of Marxism in the Social Sciences', *Universities and Left Review,* I, 1, 1957, pp. 27-30.

'To the Right of Left', *TLS,* 25 May 1962. Rev. of *Revisionism,* ed. L. Labedz. Repr. in *Revs.,* ch. 13, as 'Revisionism'. (The original review had a para. on N. Berdayev, *The Russian Revolution,* R. Luxemburg, *The Russian Revolution and Leninism or Marxism?.* and L. Trotsky, *Terrorism and Communism,* which was cut out of the repr. version.)

Rev. of R. Palme Dutt, *Problems of Contemporary History, Labour Monthly,* XLV, 5, 1963, pp. 238-240.

Rev. of Robert Havemann, *Dialektik ohne Dogma? Naturwissenschaft und Weltanschauung, TLS,* 3 September 1964.

'You Can't Go Home Again', *NYRB,* 30 September 1965. Rev. of Bertram D. Wolfe, *Marxism: 100 Years in the Life of a Doctrine* and *Strange Communists I Have Known.*

'The Dialogue on Marxism', *MT,* X, 2, 1966, pp. 43-8. Repr. in *Revs.,* ch. 11.

'Alive and Kicking', *NYRB,* 20 October 1966. Rev. of George Lichtheim, *Marxism in Modern France.*

'The Structure of Capital', *TLS*, 15 December 1966. Rev. of Louis Althusser, *Pour Marx*, L. Althusser *et al.*, *Lire le Capital* and M. Godelier, *Rationalité et irrationalité en économie*. See also correspondence from G. Lichtheim, J.P. Mayer and reply by E.J.H. in *TLS*, 29 December 1966. Rev. repr. in *Revs.*, ch. 15.

'Marxism without Marx', *TLS*, 3 December 1971. Rev. of Louis Althusser, *Lenin and Philosophy and Other Essays*.

Rev. of Roger Garaudy, *Marxism in the Twentieth Century* and *Le Grand Tournant du Socialisme*, *TLS*, 19 February 1970.

'Passionate Witness', *NYRB*, 22 February 1973. Rev. of I.L. Gendzier, *Frantz Fanon: A Critical Study*.

'Look Left', *NS*, 24 September 1976. Rev. of Perry Anderson, *Considerations on Western Marxism*.

Rev. of Lawrence Krader, *The Asiatic Mode of Production*, *Comment*, 2 October 1976.

COMMUNISM

'Problems of Communist History', *NLR*, 54, 1969, pp. 85-91. Repr. in *Revs.*, ch. 1.

Rev. of A. Rossi, *Physiologie du Parti Communiste Français*, *TLS*, 9 April 1949.

'Intellectuals and Communism', *TLS*, 22 October 1964. Rev. of David Caute, *Communism and the French Intellectuals*. Repr. in *Revs.*, ch. 4.

'French Communism', *NLR*, 31, 1965, pp. 95-101. Repr. in *Revs.*, ch. 3 - in a slightly shortened version.

Rev. of Paolo Spriano, *Storia del Partito Communista Italiano, vol. II: Gli anni della clandestina*, *TLS*, 11 December 1969. Incorporated into ch. 5 of *Revs.*, 'The Dark Years of Italian Communism'. See also: 'Storia del PCI e storia d'Italia', *Libri Nuovi (Einaudi)* December 1969.

'Confronting defeat: the German Communist Party', *NLR*, 61, 1970, pp. 83-92.

'Introduction' to Rosa Leviné-Meyer, *Leviné. The Life of a Revolutionary*, Farnborough, Saxon House/London, Pluto Press, 1973, pp. vii-x.

'Introduction' to Ilona Duczynska, *Workers in Arms. The Austrian Schutzbund and the Civil War of 1934*, New York and London, Monthly Review Press, 1978, pp. 15-26.

'The British Communist Party', *Political Quarterly*, XXV, 1954, pp. 30-43.

'Radicalism and Revolution', *NS*, 14 March 1969. Rev. of K. Newton, *The Sociology of British Communism* and W. Kendall, *The Revolutionary Movement in Britain*. Repr. in *Revs.*, ch. 2.

'The Historians' Group of the Communist Party', *Rebels and Their Causes. Essays in Honour of A.L. Morton*, ed. Maurice Cornforth, London, Lawrence & Wishart, 1978, pp. 21-47.

ANARCHISM

'The Spanish Background', *NLR*, 40 1966, pp. 85-90. Rev. of Raymond Carr, *Spain 1808-1939.* Repr. in *Revs.*, ch. 8.
'Bolshevism and Anarchism', *Anarchi e Anarchia nel mondo contemporaneo. Atti del convegno promosso dalla Fondazione Luigi Einaudi, (Torino, 5-7 dicembre 1969)*, Turin, Fondazione Luigi Einaudi, 1971, pp. 473-85. Repr. in *Revs.*, ch. 7 as 'Bolshevism and the Anarchists'.
'Was kann man noch vom Anarchismus lernen?', *Kursbuch*, 19, 1969, pp. 47-57. First appeared in English in *Spokesman.* Repr. in *Revs.*, ch. 9 as 'Reflections on Anarchism'.

REVOLUTIONS AND INSURRECTIONS

'1848: The Opening of a New Era', *New Central European Observer*, 22 January 1949. Rev. of *1848: The Opening of an Era*, ed. F. Fejtö. See below, '1848 and all that', 1967.
'A Fight Which Inspired All Europe', *New Central European Observer*, 18 March 1950 (on the Hungarian Revolution of 1848).
Rev. of George Rude, *The Crowd in the French Revolution* and R. Herr, *The Eighteenth Century Revolution in Spain, NS*, 28 March 1959.
'The Revolutionary Situation in Colombia', *World Today*, XIX, 6, 1963, pp. 248-58.
Rev. of Hannah Arendt, *On Revolution, History and Theory*, IV, 1965, pp. 252-8. Repr. in *Revs.*, ch. 20, as 'Hannah Arendt on Revolution'.
Rev. of Georges Lefebvre, *The Thermidorians and The Directory* and M.J. Sydenham, *The French Revolution, NS*, 18 March 1966.
'1848 and all that', *NYRB*, 1 June 1967. Rev. of *1848: The Opening of an Era*, ed. F. Fejtö and G. Duveau, *1848: The Making of a Revolution.*
'A Hard Man', *N. Soc.*, 4 April 1968. Rev. of Che Guevara, *Reminiscences of the Cuban Revolutionary War.*
'Theory turned sidways', *Black Dwarf*, May 1968 (on the events in Paris).
'Cities and Insurrections', *Architectural Design*, XXXVIII, 1968, pp. 579-88. Repr. in *Revs.* ch. 23.
'Birthday Party', *NYRB*, 22 May 1969. Rev. of: Daniel Cohn-Bendit, *Obsolete Communism: The Left-Wing Alternative;* Daniel Cohn-Bendit, Jean-Pierre Duteuil, Alain Geismar and Jacques Sauvageot, *The French Student Revolt: The Leaders Speak;* Henri Lefebvre, *The Explosion: Marxism and the French Upheaval;* Patrick Seale and Maureen McConville, *Red Flag/Black Flag: French Revolution 1968;* J.J. Servan-Schreiber, *The Spirit of May;* Alain Touraine, *Le mouvement de mai ou le communisme utopique.* Repr., with some passages

cut, in *Revs.*, ch. 24 as 'May 1968'.
'Revolution is Puritan', *N. Soc.*, 22 May 1969. Repr. in *Revs.*, ch. 22, as 'Revolution and Sex'.
'The Rules of Violence', *N. Soc.*, 24 July 1969. Repr. in *Revs.*, ch. 21.
Rev. of R. Atkin, *Revolution! Mexico 1910-1920, N. Soc.*, 29 January 1970.
Rev. of Richard Cobb, *The Police and the People. French Popular Protest 1789-1820, Listener,* 20 August 1970.
'Peru: The Peculiar Revolution', *NYRB*, 16 December 1971.
Rev. of John Dunn, *Modern Revolutions*, *Guardian,* 16 March 1972.
'Terrorism', *Listener,* 22 June 1972.
Rev. of Edward Malefakis, *Agrarian Reform and Peasant Revolution in Spain, Political Science Quarterly,* LXXXVII, 1972, pp. 298-9.
Rev. of Georges Lefebvre, *The Great Fear of 1789, Ec.H.R.*, XXVII, 1974, p. 507.
Rev. of Paul Wilkinson, *Political Terrorism, Comment,* 13 May 1975.
'Revolution'. Paper to the XIV International Congress of Historical Sciences, San Francisco, 22-29 August 1975. Issued as a pamphlet, reproduced from typescript, at the Conference. Published in Italian as 'La rivoluzione', *Studi Storici,* XVII, 1, 1976, pp. 5-39.
'How the media aid terrorists', *Journalism Studies Review,* I, 1, 1976, p. 11.
Contribution to 'The Bombings: Four Views', *The New Review,* II, 24, 1976, pp. 7-9. (Responses to a Granada TV programme, 'Does a political cause ever give us the right to kill?').
'Non ha radici popolari la nuova violenza', *Corriere della Sera,* 30 December 1977. Interview.
'Tecnica e anonimato', *Rinascita,* 12 May 1978. Interview on terrorism.
'1968 - A Retrospect', *MT*, XXII, 5, 1978, pp. 130-6.
Rev. of J.M. Merriman, *The Agony of the Republic. The Repression of the Left in Revolutionary France, 1848-1851, Ec. H.R.*, XXXII, 1979, pp. 621-2.

GUERRILLAS

'Goliath and the guerrilla', *The Nation* (New York), 19 July 1965. Revised version as 'Vietnam and the dynamics of guerrilla war', *NLR*, 33, 1965, pp. 59-68. Repr. in *Revs.*, ch. 17.
'Guerrillas in Latin America', *The Socialist Register 1970,* ed. R. Miliband and J. Saville, London, The Merlin Press, 1970, pp. 51-61.
'Why America lost the Vietnam War', *Listener,* 18 May 1972.
'Latin American Guerrillas: a survey', *Latin American Review*

of Books, I, 1973, pp. 79-85.

ON IDEOLOGIES AND IDEOLOGISTS

'John Harris' (pseud.), 'He shaped the face of modern Britain' (Jeremy Bentham), *Daily Worker*, 16 February 1948.
Rev. of H.N. Brailsford, *The Life-Work of J.A. Hobson*, *Ec. H.R.*, II, 1949-50, pp. 107-8.
'Who is for democracy?', *Modern Quarterly* (new series), VIII, 2, 1953, pp. 96-103. Rev. essay of J.L. Talmon, *Origins of Totalitarian Democracy*.
Rev. of I.L. Horowitz, *Claude Helvetius*, *Labour Monthly*, XXXVI, 7, 1954, p. 336.
Rev. of S. Maccoby, *English Radicalism, 1886-1914*, *English Historical Review*, LXIX, 272, 1954, pp. 462-5.
Rev. of *Schumpeter: Social Scientist*, ed. S.E. Harris and J.A. Schumpeter, *A History of Economic Analysis*, *S & S*, XIX, 1955, pp. 71-5.
'Science and Injustice', *Granta*, 14 May 1955.
Rev. of Samuel Bernstein, *Essays in Political and Intellectual History*, *S & S*, XX, 1956, pp. 254-7.
Rev. of C.N. Parkinson, *The Evolution of Political Thought*, *NS*, 14 June 1958.
Rev. of H. Stuart Hughes, *Consciousness and Society*, *NS*, 10 October 1959.
'Whatever happened to equality? Equality in the past'. Text of discussion with Robert Blake, chaired by John Vaizey, broadcast in Radio 3. Repr. in John Vaizey (ed.), *Whatever happened to equality?* London, BBC, 1975, pp. 31-46.
'Fraternity', *N. Soc.*, 27 November 1975.

FABIANS

Rev. of Margaret Cole, *Beatrice Webb*, *S & S*, X, 1946, pp. 321-3.
'Die Jungen Fabier', *Blick in die Welt*, 5, 1946.
'Bernard Shaw', *Zeitspiegel*, 3 August 1946.
'Bernard Shaw's Socialism', *S & S*, XI, 1947, pp. 305-26.
Rev. of Beatrice Webb, *Our Partnership*, *English Historical Review*, LXIV, 251, 1949, pp. 257-60.
'Fabianism and the Fabians, 1884-1914', unpublished PhD, University of Cambridge, 1950.
Rev. of *Beatrice Webb: Diaries 1912-1924*, ed. M.I. Cole, *English Historical Review*, LXVIII, 267, 1953, pp. 293-5.
Rev. of J.B. Kaye, *Bernard Shaw and the Nineteenth Century Tradition*, *S & S*, XXV, 1961, pp. 92-5.
The Lesser Fabians, London, History Group of the Communist Party, 1962; Our History Pamphlet, no. 28. Repr. in *The Luddites and Other Essays*, ed. L.M. Munby, London,

Michael Katanka (Books) Ltd, 1971, pp. 231-44.
Rev. of M.I. Cole, *The Story of Fabian Socialism, BSSLH,* 4, 1962, pp. 60-1.
'The Fabians Reconsidered', *LM,* ch. 14 (First publication).
Rev. of *The Letters of Sidney and Beatrice Webb,* ed. N. Mackenzie, *NS,* 19 May 1978.

POWER, POLITICS AND THE STATE

Rev. of E. Kogon, *Der SS-Staat, New Central European Observer,* 29 May 1948. Also reviewed in *TLS,* 28 August 1948.
Rev. of A.J.P. Taylor, *From Napoleon to Stalin, New Central European Observer,* 22 July 1950.
Rev. of A.B. Levy, *Private Corporations and Their Control, TLS,* 13 October 1950.
'The Taming of Parliamentary Democracy in Britain', *The Modern Quarterly* (new series), VI, 1951, pp. 319-39.
'The Political Theory of Auschwitz', *The Cambridge Journal,* V, 1952, pp. 455-67.
Rev. of A.J.P. Taylor, *The Struggle for Mastery in Europe 1848-1918, Daily Worker,* 11 November 1954.
'Thomas Greene' (pseud.), rev. of Robert Blake, *The Unknown Prime Minister, Books and Bookmen,* December 1955.
'Thomas Greene' (pseud.), rev. of J.E. Wrench, *Geoffrey Dawson and Our Times* and James Pope-Hennessy, *Lord Crewe, Books and Bookmen,* February 1956.
'Twentieth-Century British Politics', *P & P,* 11, 1957, pp. 100-8. (Review essay.)
Rev. of Richard Barkeley, *The Road to Mayerling, Time and Tide,* 31 May 1958.
Rev. of M. Djilas, *The New Class, Cambridge Review,* 7 June 1958.
Rev. of W.W. Gottlieb, *Studies in Secret Diplomacy During the First World War, The Contemporary Review,* October 1958, pp. 220-1.
Rev. of *Britain: An Official Handbook,* NS, 6 June 1959.
Rev. of C.N. Parkinson, *The Law and the Profits, NS,* 21 May 1960.
Rev. of T.A.B. Corley, *Democratic Despot* and Joanna Richardson, *My Dearest Uncle, NS,* 22 September 1961.
Rev. of Douglas Johnson, *Guizot, NS,* 24 May 1963.
Rev. of Harold Kurtz, *The Empress Eugénie* and Ernest Knapton, *Empress Josephine, NS,* 22 May 1964.
Rev. of E.E. Barry, *Nationalisation in British Politics, NS,* 9 July 1965.
Rev. of Barrington Moore, *Social Origins of Dictatorship and Democracy, American Sociological Review,* XXXII, 1967, pp. 821-2.
'The Fulton Report: a further view', *Listener,* 18 July 1968.
'How to plot your takeover', *NYRB,* 21 August 1969. Rev.

of Edward Luttwack, *Coup d'État, a Practical Handbook*. Repr. in *Revs.*, ch. 19 as 'Coup d'État'.
'Generals as revolutionaries', *N. Soc.*, 20 November 1969.
'Is Science Evil?' *NYRB*, 19 November 1970. Rev. of Lewis Mumford, *The Myth of the Machine: The Pentagon of Power*.
'Military "revolutionaries"', *N. Soc.*, 22 May 1975.
'Dictatorship with charm', *NYRB*, 2 October 1975.
'The West German Witch Hunt', *N. Soc.*, 22 July 1976.
Rev. of E.P. Thompson, *Writing by Candlelight*, *Sunday Times*, 1 June 1980.

ASSESSING CENTRAL EUROPE

'Bismarck and Oesterreich', *Zeitspiegel*, 7 April 1945.
'Die oesterreichisch - deutsche Grenze', *Zeitspiegel*, 2 June 1945.
'Der Fall Friedjung', *Zeitspiegel*, 28 July 1945.
'Austria and her non-German neighbours', *Austrian News*, August 1945.
'The Habsburgs', *Austrian News*, November 1945.
'Koeniggraetz: Die Liberale Zeit', *Zeitspiegel*, 15 December 1945.
'National Oppression in the Habsburg Empire', *Austrian News*, January 1946.
'12th March 1938', *Austrian News*, February-March 1946.
Three articles in the series, 'Englische Stimmen zur Geschichte Österreichs': 'Die Unabhaengigkeit Oesterreichs', *Zeitspiegel*, 9 February 1946; 'Die Habsburger', *Zeitspiegel*, 16 February 1946, 'Das Grossdeutschtum', *Zeitspiegel*, 23 February 1946.
'One Year of the Second Republic', *Austrian News*, May-April 1946.
Rev. of *Der Weg zum Wohlstand. Economic Plan of the Austrian Communist Party*, *New Central European Observer*, 7 August 1948.
Rev. of K. Renner, *An Der Wende Zweier Zeiten*, *New Central European Observer*, 21 August 1948.
'Berlin: The West in Trouble', *New Central European Observer*, 13 November 1948. Note: This was written by 'Our German Correspondent' but attributed to E.J.H. in the *NCEO* Index. A piece in the same issue, in the 'Comment' section, was also attributed to him, though the piece was not specified. Probably, 'The German Officer Corps'.
'Socialists in Eastern Europe', *New Central European Observer*, 24 December 1948 (unsigned).
'The Case of Guido Schmidt', *New Central European Observer*, 19 February 1949. Rev. of *Der Hochverratsprozess gegen Dr. Guido Schmidt*.
Rev. of A.J.P. Taylor, *The Hapsburg Monarchy*, *New Central European Observer*, 19 March 1949.
Rev. of Gustav Stolper, *German Realities*, *New Central European Observer*, 16 April 1949.

'Drang Nach Osten. Some Notes on German Revisionism', *New Central European Observer*, 14 May 1949. The author given as 'Our German Correspondent'.
Rev. of E. Buschbeck, *Austria*, *New Central European Observer*, 24 December 1949.
Rev. of H. Schacht, *Account Settled*, *New Central European Observer*, 4 February 1950.
Rev. of *The Cambridge History of Poland to 1696*, ed. W.F. Reddaway, J.H. Penson, O. Halecki, R. Dyboski, *New Central European Observer*, 13 October 1951.

ASSESSING THE PRESENT

Rev. of *Modern France: Problems of the Third and Fourth Republics*, ed. E.M. Earle, *Ec.H.R.* IV, 1951-2, pp. 258-60.
'Le view anglais', *Granta*, 2 May 1953.
Rev. of A.M. Carr-Saunders, D. Caradog-Jones and C.A. Moser, *A Survey of Social Conditions in England and Wales*, *NS*, 20 September 1958.
'Cuban Prospects', *NS*, 22 October 1960.
'La società: il nuovo e il vecchio', *Il Contemporaneo*, 63-4, 1963, pp. 91-104.
'The most critical area in the world', *Listener*, 2 May 1963.
'Social Developments in Latin America', *Listener*, 9 May 1963.

Articles on British politics for Rinascita, 1963-5.
Between September 1963 and August 1965 E.J.H. wrote twenty-one articles for the paper, in the form of a 'Letter from London', which surveyed the political scene, though this included one (on 23 May 1964), on the General Strike of 1926. He also wrote one, occasioned by the General Election, on 26 June 1970.
'Koestler's England', *NYRB*, 2 April 1964. Rev. of *Suicide of a Nation? An Inquiry into the State of Britain Today*, ed. Arthur Koestler.
Rev. of P.M. Holt, *Colombia Today - and Tomorrow*, *N. Soc.*, 22 April 1965.
Rev. of *Obstacles to Change in Latin America*, ed. C. Veliz, *N. Soc.*, 28 October 1965.
'The Cultural Congress of Havana', *TLS*, 25 January 1968.
'Little Englanders', *N. Soc.*, 10 April 1969.
'What's New in Peru', *NYRB*, 21 May 1970.
'Latin America as US Empire Cracks', *NYRB*, 25 March 1971.
'Twenty Latin Americas?', *Cambridge Review*, 5 May 1972. Rev. of Marcel Niedergang, *The Twenty Latin Americas*.
'Vulnerable Japan', *NYRB*, 17 July 1975.
'The Crisis of Capitalism in Historical Perspective', *MT*, XIX, 10, 1975, pp. 300-8.
'E'nella politica la debolezza del sistema', *Rinascita*, 10 November 1978.
'Veranno giorni duri, durissimi, e non solo nella vecchia

Inghilterra', *Il Manifesto*, 7 March 1981. Interview.
'Des voisins admirés mais peu populaires', *Le Monde Dimanche (Supplement)*, 29 mars 1981, pp. XVIII-XIX. (Contribution to 'Les Français vus de Grand-Bretagne'.)

PROSPECTS AND STRATEGIES FOR THE LEFT

(1) The record of the Labour Party

Rev. of R.A. Brady, *Crisis in Britain* and D.C. Somervell, *British Politics Since 1900*, *S & S*, XV, 1951, pp. 375-8. See also rev. of Brady in *The Modern Quarterly* (new series), VII, 1952, pp. 247-9.
Rev. of B. Sacks, *J. Ramsay MacDonald in Thought and Action*, *English Historical Review*, LXVIII, 269, 1953, p. 661.
Rev. of E. Windrich, *British Labor's Foreign Policy*, *S & S*, XVIII, 1954, pp. 88-9.
Rev. of S.R. Graubard, *British Labour and the Russian Revolution 1917-1924* and A.A. Rogow, *The Labour Government and British Industry 1945-1951*, *S & S*, XXIII, 1959, pp. 168-71.
'Parliamentary Cretinism?', *NLR*, 12, 1961, pp. 64-6. Rev. of R. Miliband, *Parliamentary Socialism*.
'Royaume-Uni: le conflit entre la droite et la gauche du parti travailliste tend à s'aggraver', *Le Monde Diplomatique*, October 1966. (One of a number of articles in a feature on 'L'évolution du socialisme européen depuis la fin de la IIe guerre mondiale'.)
'Ramsay MacDonald - a lesson for today', *Comment*, 15 October 1966.
'What Labour has done', *N. Soc.*, 15 January 1970.
'No entry for socialism', *N. Soc.*, 11 December 1975. Rev. of Richard Crossman, *The Diaries of a Cabinet Minister, vol. 1: Minister of Housing, 1964-1966*. See also 'I grandi errori di Wilson e dei laboristi', *Paese Sera*, 7 January 1976.

(2) The poor, the working class and socialist strategies

'Das Problem der revolutionären Praxis heute', *Notizen (Tübinger Studentenzeitung)*, 63, 1965, pp. 12-13.
'Revoluční praxe v dnešní době', *Student* (Prague), 4, 1966. Interview.
'Crisis in the ghetto', *Labour Monthly*, XLVIX, 9, 1967, pp. 399-402.
'Les racines de l'utopie', *Démocratie Nouvelle*, XXI, 1968, pp. 12-14.
'Chile: Year One', *NYRB*, 23 September 1971.
'Shop-stewards', *Listener*, 27 July 1972.
'The Murder of Chile', *N. Soc.*, 20 September 1973. See also: correspondence in *ibid.*, 27 September 1973.
'A Difficult Hope', *NS*, 1 March 1974. Rev. of *The Socialist Register 1973* and David Caute, *Collisions*.
'The Labour Movement and Military Coups', *MT*, XVIII, 10,

1974, pp. 302-8.
Revolutionary Perspectives. A discussion of alternative strategies, London, Central Students Branch of the Communist Party/ Birkbeck College Socialist Society, 1974 (Mimeo.)
The Crisis and the Outlook, London, Birkbeck College Socialist Society/London Central Students Branch of the Communist Party, n.d. 1975. (Pamphlet)
Revolutionary Advances, Swansea, Swansea Broad Left, 1976. (Pamphlet). (Text of an 'opening letter' delivered to a week-end conference organised by the Welsh Committee of the Communist Party of Great Britain.)
'Forty Years of Popular Front Government', *MT*, XX, 7, 1976, pp. 221-8.
'L'eurocomunismo e la transizione lunga dell'Europa capitalistica', *Rinascita*, 25 March 1977. Interview.
Giorgio Napolitano. Intervista sul PCI a cura di Eric J. Hobsbawm, Bari, Laterza, 1975. Translated into English by John Cammett and Victoria DeGrazia as *The Italian Road to Socialism. An Interview by Eric Hobsbawm with Giorgio Napolitano of the Italian Communist Party*, Westport, Conn.: Lawrence Hill; London, The Journeyman Press, 1977. Note: Prior to the English translation the book also appeared in French (Paris, 1976), Dutch (Amsterdam, 1976) and German (Frankfurt, 1977).
'Should the Poor Organize?', *NYRB*, 23 March 1978. rev. of F.F. Piven and R.A. Cloward, *Poor People's Movements: Why They Succeed, How They Fail.* A shortened version of this appeared as 'The left and the crisis of organisation', *N. Soc.*, 13 April 1978.
'Inside every worker there is a syndicalist trying to get out', *N. Soc.*, 5 April 1979.
Contributions to *The Forward March of Labour Halted?*, ed. Martin Jacques and Francis Mulhern, London, Verso/New Left Books with *Marxism Today*, 1981:
(i) 'The Forward March of Labour Halted?', repr. from *MT*, XXII, 9, 1978, pp. 279-86.
(ii) 'Response' to the original debate in *MT*, repr. from *MT*, XXIII, 9, 1979.
(iii) 'Eric Hobsbawm interviews Tony Benn', repr. from *MT*, XXIV, 10, 1980, pp. 5-13.
(iv) 'Observations on the debate', written for this volume.

INTELLECTUALS AND THE LEFT

'The Campus Rebellion', *NS*, 17 September 1960.
'Intellectuals and the Class Struggle', *Revs*. ch. 25 (1st publication).
'The new dissent: intellectuals, society and the left', *N. Soc.*, 23 November 1978.
'Intellectuals and the Labour Movement', *MT*, XXIII, 7, 1979, pp. 212-20.

INTERVENING IN THE PRESENT

'What Democracy Means For Us. A Report by E.J. Hobsbawm, Student Committee, British Youth Peace Assembly' (pamphlet, mimeo., no publisher). Written for the Third International Conference of the World Student Association, Paris, 15-19 August 1939.

In 1940 E.J.H. and Raymond Williams wrote a pamphlet on the Russo-Finnish War for the Communist Party. It was issued unsigned. (See Raymond Williams, *Politics and Letters. Interviews with New Left Review*, London, New Left Books, 1979, pp. 42-3. I have been unable to locate a copy of this.)

'John Harris' (pseud.), 'The Struggle For Equal Pay', *Daily Worker*, 9 April 1947.

'John Pearson' (pseud.), 'Peace Petition Has Great History', *Daily Worker*, 15 May 1950.

'F.H. Ramsbury' (pseud.), 'Franco's Police See The Writing On The Wall', *Daily Worker*, 1 May 1951. See also 'Franco in retreat', *NS*, 14 April 1951 (written anonymously).

'The Fight Against War In Britain's History', *Communist Review*, October 1952, pp. 297-303.

'Teruel is a hole', *NS*, 9 October 1954 (on Spain.)

'Opinions d'Outre-Manche', *Trygée*, December 1953, 38-40, published by Mouvement Université pour la Paix, Paris (on GB public opinion on a European army).

Member of the University Group on Defence Policy, chaired by David Glass, who wrote *The Role of the Peace Movements in the 1930s*, University Group on Defence Policy, Pamphlet no. 1, January 1959.

'Candid Friend', *N. Soc.*, 28 August 1969.

'Too late to be shocked', *N. Soc.*, 11 December 1969.

'Are we entering a new era of anti-semitism?', *N. Soc.*, 11 December 1980.

JAZZ AND POPULAR CULTURE

'The Evolution of Flamenco', *TLS*, 9 January 1953. Rev. of F.el de Triana, *Arte y Artistas Flamencos; Cancionero Flamenco*.

'A propos du Jazz', *Les Mains Ouvertes*, Paris, 5, 1953, pp. 8-10.

'The Viennese Popular Theatre', *TLS*, 11 February 1955. Rev. of Otto Rommel, *Die Alt-Wiener Volkskomödie*.

Writings as 'Francis Newton':-

1 For the *New Statesman*
The first article which F.N. wrote for the paper was on 30 June 1956. Thereafter he wrote regularly - e.g., fourteen articles in 1957 - until 1962. The articles then became less

frequent but continued until 25 March 1966, which seems to have been the last.

Some of these ranged more widely than jazz. See, e.g.:

'The Wild Side', 6 April 1962.

'Rumba Patriotica', 26 January 1962 (on Cuban popular music).

'Pop goes the artist', 6 July 1962 (considerations on 'star' quality, commercialism and the criteria for judging pop culture).

'Bob Dylan', 22 May 1964.

2 For the *Times Literary Supplement*

Between 29 November 1957 and 4 May 1962 F.N. wrote about ten articles.

3 *Others*

'"Trouble is a man". (The classic blues singer)', *The Decca Book of Jazz*, ed. Peter Gammond, London, Frederick Muller, 1958, pp. 62-74.

The Jazz Scene, London, Macgibbon & Kee, 1959. Revised edn, Harmondsworth, Penguin, 1961. The Czech edn, (1961), had a new 'Introduction'.

'Jazz Concerts', *This is Jazz*, ed. Ken Williamson, London, Newnes, 1960, pp. 11-16.

'Is American jazz on the decline?' *Melody Maker*, 29 October 1960.

'Lester Young', *The Jazz Scene*, I, 6, 1962, pp. 3-4.

'Eight of the Best' (British jazz musicians) and 'The jazz business', *Sunday Times* (colour section), 10 June 1962.

'Here today the throw-away art of pop', *Town*, May 1963.

'Goodbye to the Duke' (Ellington), *The Observer*, 26 May 1974.

'Airing their grievances', *TLS*, 21 December 1962. Rev. of P. Barbier and F. Vernillal, *Histoire de France par les Chansons*.

'Pop Goes the Artist', *TLS*, 17 December 1964. Rev. U.Eco, *Apocalittici e Integrati* and S. Hall and P. Whannel, *The Popular Arts*.

ART AND LITERATURE

'Johannes Nestroy', *Die Zeitung*, 18 February 1944.

'William Hazlitt', *Die Zeitung*, 9 June 1944.

'Sean O'Casey', *Die Zeitung*, 15 September 1944.

'William Morris', *Die Zeitung*, 10 November 1944.

'Albert Fuchs: Ein Sohn ans gutern hans', *Austrian Student*, July 1944. In English.

'Der Künstler William Morris', *Blick in die Welt*, 6, 1946.

'Is pamphleteering a lost art?', *Listener*, 3 July 1947.

'Morris on Art and Socialism', *Our Time*, April 1948.

Rev. of Egon Erwin Kisch, *Tales Of Seven Ghettoes*, *New Central*

European Observer, 11 December 1948.
Rev. of Ernest Kreuder, *The Attic Pretenders*, *New Central European Observer*, 5 February 1949.
'Dr. Faustus: Legend For Our Time', *New Central European Observer*, 11 June 1949. Rev. of Thomas Mann, *Dr. Faustus*.
'Little Man on Guard', *TLS*, 27 April 1951. Rev. of J. Hasek, *The Good Soldier Schweik*.
'"Of Poor Bert Brecht"', *Encounter*, September 1956. Comment on Herbert Luthy, '"Of Poor Bert Brecht"', *ibid.*, July 1956.
'The Principle of Hope', *TLS*, 31 March 1961. Rev. of Ernst Bloch, *Das Prinzip Hoffnung*. Repr. in *Revs.*, ch. 14.
Rev. of Karl Kraus, *Unsterblicher Witz* and Peter Altenberg, *Das Glück der Verlorenen Stuuden*, *TLS*, 12 January 1962.
'Art Appreciation', *Listener*, 13 July 1972.
Rev. of T.J. Clark, *The Absolute Bourgeois*, *Guardian*, 8 March 1973.
'Man and Woman in Socialist Iconography', *History Workshop*, 6, 1978, pp. 121-38. Also published as 'Sexe, symboles vêtements et socialisme', *Actes de la recherche en sciences sociales*, 23, 1978, pp. 2-18.
'Socialism and the avantgarde in the period of the Second International', *Le Mouvement Social*, 111, 1980, pp. 189-99. Special issue, 'Georges Haupt parmi nous'.

End-piece

ERIC HOBSBAWM: A CAMBRIDGE PROFILE 1939*

Pieter Keuneman

The 8 of June 1917, was a very hot day in Alexandria, Egypt. The sun shone, the earth steamed, and the sky was blue. In the street were two Armenians and an Assyrian policeman. The policeman had short, straight eyelashes and eight fingers and two thumbs. One of the Armenians was going bald. Apart from this there was only the heat. Waves after waves crowded on to the street displacing one another and then mingling into a harmony of hotness. Just like when Fletcher Henderson and the boys went to town in a jam session, before Fletcher ran to bits. Occasionally one special wave would break through and the heat would be on as when Krupa slays the drums. At the end of the street was a house. It had doors, windows and a roof in red tile. In it little Eric was being accurately and efficiently born into a milieu which suited his prose style down to the ground.

Little bits of all the world were to be found in Eric. His grandfather had lit out of Russia way back in the 1870's to become a cabinet maker in the East End of London. Assorted uncles had gone to America and Switzerland. The legend goes that some of them had been exiled to Siberia. His mother was Austrian. The family had held the local record for being most consistently unsuccessful in business, but Eric was their best investment with no premiums or odds on.

From the first he was a wise and observant little boy, often clouted over the head by his chums for knowing too much. For him the facts of life were only data in a higher cause, and he was aware without emotion of the rebus which is the human heart. At the age of two he had to be removed to Vienna, as Alexandria had grown too hot to hold him. Here he stayed till 1931, developing an interest in ornithology and the cruder forms of animal life, and it is whispered around the clubs that this is the only thing that he and Mr Chamberlain have in common. This interest in natural phenomena led him to the violent life of action and sensation, and he joined the Boy Scouts and rose to great eminence in this organisation. Eric speaks wistfully of these days when he combined the brutality of the established code with the advanced morality of one who handed out leaflets at street corners. Those were the days, and the nights weren't bad either. Eric had a large and vulgar patriotism for England, which he considered in weak moments as his spiritual home. To conclude these formative years he went to Berlin in 1931 where he stayed till Hitler came to power. Then he came to England.

All the while he had been steadily amassing knowledge, and

*From *Granta*, 7 June 1939.

had at his finger-tips the strangest details about the obscurest subjects and the names of all the authorities which he could bandy around with an easy familiarity. He went to St. Marylebone Grammar School and was chiefly bored. Then he came up to King's on a Scholarship three years ago. The usual rumours started. 'There's a freshman in King's who knows about everything,' were the words that got around. There was considerable difficulty about discovering what he was reading. He was at the English club asking puzzling questions about Wordsworth's parent symbolism; at the French and German societies he would let drop dicta of such profundity as might properly come only from God. To historians he was one adroitly persuading them that they were men hungry for an adventure in the cultural arts. In C.U.S.C. he was putting over the line with enough *savoir faire* to be marked out as a coming man. Later it leaked out that he read History, and when he landed a starred first on Part I nobody was very surprised. It was part of his character, they said.

It was in his first term that he walked into the *Granta* office, his raincoat buttoned to the neck, and asked to be given a job. He started like most of the old brigade under the bosomy protection of Elizabeth Schonberg, and handed in miscellaneous film reviews which showed considerable knowledge of the names of the technicians and minor feature players. Next he became a roving reporter, producing two famous features: 'Cambridge Cameos' and 'E.J.H. Observes'. Shop assistants and lecturers dreaded the grey figure which would slink in conspicuously and note down their foibles in a firm round hand. Next he became Film Editor, and has been editor during the last two terms, going off on hitch-hikes to France or jaunts to Algeria and Tunis in his spare time.

Those are all the facts that can be got out of Eric in his moments of greatest expansion. For he is extremely modest and self-critical, debunking himself with considerable thoroughness, even when there is no occasion for such self-effacement. There is not a nasty thing you can say about him with which he will not agree. Of his virtues he says never a word; never mentions his outstanding intelligence, his uncomplaining industry, his strong sense of humour, and his complete lack of personal malice even for those who have done him wrong. He is not easy to get to know. Despite his friendliness, one is awed by the legend and the erudition. It is like a bishop being matey with the choir boys. One is not surprised to hear that he played the *Demon King* in the school play, or that his friends call him the Buddha. As he sits cross-legged in his great chair, there is something of the condescension of the oracle gyrating on its tripod. But under the surface is the person whose friendship is intimate and valuable, and whose honesty in personal relationships one respects.

He is enthusiastic about jazz, and often brings it in by analogy into his articles. It is the golden age with which he is most concerned, and he can go lyrical on the respective merits of 'Pine-tops' Smith, 'Half-Pint' Jaxon, and 'Pee-Wee' Russell. He himself plays the mouth-organ. Rather mournfully, though with occasional touches of 'Pops' Bechet lifting the gobstick. He also likes the flicks in quantity and quality. He conceals the fact that he has been published by *Punch*. Admits a love for literature, English, French and German, but only specifies Thurber. Otherwise sticks to Lenin and Stalin. He is proud of the fact that he is the only man of his acquaintance who has not read Norman Haire, and he is only just getting used to living in the same college that produced Sir Thomas Inskip. He says it still gives him a thrill.

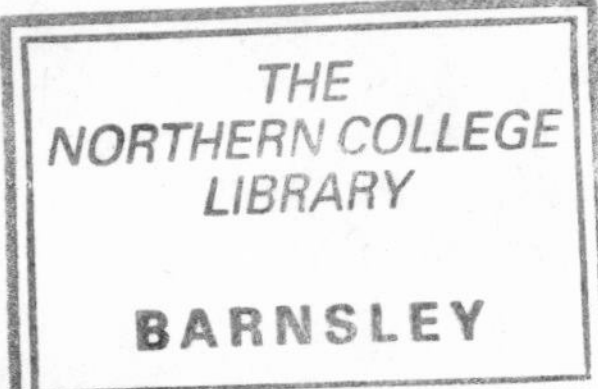